Quiet Success

The Introvert's Guide to a Successful Career

TOMAS KUCERA

This book is not meant to replace therapy, medical help, or professional counseling.
Whenever a gender-specific term is used, it is included solely for the purpose of
readability and should in no way be understood as an attempt at sexism
or any other form of prejudice.

There are examples and stories in this book based on real-life situations and people,
but they were anonymized, and fictitious names were used to ensure confidentiality.
Neither the author nor the publisher can be held responsible for the use
of the information provided in this book.

The author took the utmost effort to ensure the concepts described in the book
are either original or properly referenced. If the reader finds that some thoughts
appear to be plagiarized or no reference to the original material is provided,
he or she is urged to get in contact with the author to point it out.

Quiet Success: The Introvert's Guide to a Successful Career
Tomas Kucera
First edition 2022.

Published by Tomas Kucera
Otavska 15, Ceske Budejovice
37011 Czech Republic
www.kuceratomas.com

Edited by Bethany Davis.
Cover and book design by Vanessa Mendozzi.

ISBN 978-80-908399-0-8 (Paperback)
ISBN 978-80-908399-1-5 (E-book)

This book is dedicated to my parents,
Josef and Marie, who worked hard all their lives
and helped me to become the person I am today.
It is because of their sacrifices and love that I have
the opportunity to live a great and fulfilling life.

CONTENTS

Introduction

Iwas an anxious child who always kept to myself. I lived in my imaginary world and didn't particularly look forward to adulthood. It felt scary. When asked about what I wanted to be when I grew up, I would usually say, "a pensioner." I liked the life my grandpa had. Retired, living in a small village, surrounded by nature, quiet, no hassle. So I entered adulthood as a somewhat depressed youngster. Even though I had had a good education and a fine starting position in life, I still worried about everything. I got stressed easily and was overwhelmed by the noisy world outside all the time. I would regularly take the easy road and had a hard time springing into action. I was on my way to becoming a disillusioned hermit, hiding from the world. But I didn't.

What happened? It took a very deliberate approach over a long period of time, and only during the journey did I discover some of the best practices for success as an introvert and the science behind those practices that makes that success possible. I only wish I had known all of those things when I was eighteen so I could have implemented them sooner. Let me now share them with you in this book.

I grew up in a small city in the Czech Republic in a family of bookworms. I loved to read books. I enjoyed math, chemistry, technical stuff. I spent a lot of time on my own, playing and being in my imaginary world. I enjoyed the company of other kids, but I didn't need it. During my school years, I had a reputation as someone who is always there with the rest of the collective but who doesn't say much. But if I did say something, it was gold. I have a rather peculiar sense of humor, and I was lucky enough to attend an elementary school for "gifted" kids with a heavy focus on sciences. Luckily, most of the kids had the same weird sense of humor that I did. It was one of the best collectives I've ever been part of, and I had a heavy heart when we had to split up at the end to pursue college and, ultimately, university.

It was at the university that I started to realize who I was. Not surprisingly, I decided to study at a technical university, focusing on technical cybernetics, informatics, and even economics. I had my circle of friends but didn't feel the need to mingle too much with everyone in the class. I also realized that if I care about something, I'm much more likely to go out and seek other people with similar interests or to reach out and share what I know. I was completely willing to step out of my comfort zone to preach about topics I was passionate about. Once done, I would go back to being my quiet self.

I worked hard during my studies to make some money, and after I graduated, I moved to Australia to study English. Technical universities in the Czech Republic are great at teaching you science, but not particularly good at teaching you how to communicate in your language or others. The time in Australia changed my life. I realized that one of the skills you desperately need in today's world is the ability to communicate, and you need to speak a more widespread language than Czech. Being able to interact with students from more than thirty countries, hearing their views on the world, and talking about their countries and cultures had a significant impact on shaping my worldview. I realized that people are people, regardless of their cultural background, religion, or the color of their skin. I became obsessed with equality, treating everyone well, and finding the best in people. I also realized something else. I became much more confident about communicating and reaching out to people I didn't know. People say that wild animals are more scared of you than you are of them. I figured that the same applies to other people too.

When I came back to the Czech Republic, I worked for a small Czech government agency and an American start-up. Eventually, I ended up in a local subsidiary of a big international company. I started as a software developer but very quickly moved to project management and leadership roles. Working for a vast multinational corporation had its benefits. I got a lot of leadership and communication training. A transformation happened. I realized that, even though I love technology and enjoy software development, I enjoy working with people even more. Here I was, an introvert who hates the spotlight and big stages, who likes to work alone, and I was passionate about working with other people. And what's more, I was pretty good at it.

Since then, I have built, led, coached, and mentored teams in the Czech Republic, Austria, Germany, Romania, Poland, Belarus, the Philippines, India, Ukraine, and the USA. The passion for meeting people from other cultures and helping them grow and succeed never left me. I'm sure I made my share of mistakes, and I would like to apologize to all the people who suffered because of my inexperience as a manager and a leader. I also had a positive impact on the lives of hundreds of other people. Tapping into my strengths as an introvert, listening, guiding others, approaching things in a calm and non-threatening manner, and continually thinking about how to do things better made me who I am today: an introverted engineering and operations leader passionate about setting up offices, building teams, helping people grow, solving challenging problems, and sharing the experience with others.

There are many books on the market dealing with success and careers, but very few deal specifically with what introverts need to do to succeed. *Quiet Success* is here to fix that. Regardless of what type of introvert you are—more on this later—I made an effort to highlight specifics relevant to you.

The approach I took in this book is more holistic than just looking at a career. The goal is to let you think about your life as a whole and to help you realize how what you do at work impacts the rest of your life. I will be talking about your life's mission, which is not necessarily connected only to what career you chose, but reflects how you behave during your life in and out of the work environment.

I won't tell you that you need to become an extrovert if you want to be successful. I'm not going to tell you that the road to happiness is through becoming a manager. I will definitely ask you to get out of your comfort zone and learn new things, but at its heart, this book is about showing you how you can utilize your existing strengths as an introvert to turn this perceived weakness into an advantage, as well as how to find the right job and have a satisfying career that will support you in living a life you can enjoy.

I hope to give you the confidence and the tools to pursue a career that you will be satisfied with. You will learn to get out of your comfort zone to get what you need and want while still being your authentic self. No need to pretend to be extroverted. No need to behave like someone you would despise. If things get tough, you will have a shell of habits and tools that you can rely on to keep you safe.

Who Is This Book For?

Are you someone who just finished school and is trying to figure out the right career? Are you someone who realized that you are an introvert and wonders how that impacts your career options? Are you someone who wants to coach others and help them find the right career? Are you someone who wants to learn more about career development and introversion? Are you someone who wants to understand how to take ownership of your career and be successful? Are you an introvert who wants to influence others? If you answered yes to at least one of these questions, then you can find some answers here.

Half of the population are introverts, even though we may not be the most visible. We make great employees and leaders. We are all good at something and deserve a chance for a good life. And if you are an introvert who believes that only extroverts can make it in today's noisy world, you are wrong. This book aims to change your mind and give you the tools to have a successful career, in spite of your introversion.

As you will learn in the following chapters, not all introverts are the same. I'm sure you will strongly identify with some parts of the book regardless of what type of introvert you are. There are also parts of the book you will question. The one thing I would ask is that you keep an open mind. There are seven billion people on this planet, and everyone is different. We are all individuals, and what works for one person may not necessarily work for someone else.

The thesis of this book is that it is never the job, the position, the boss, or the company that is the problem when you're feeling dissatisfied with your work or worrying that your workplace isn't compatible with your introverted nature. I won't list a bunch of introvert-friendly jobs and claim that you need to take one of them to be successful and happy. In fact, I believe you can be successful and enjoy any job in the world as long as you care about it. Some jobs will be more challenging than others, some will come more naturally to you, but when you adopt the right attitude and work hard enough, you can succeed at anything.

I will start with a claim coming from the world of coaching that everyone has the resources they need to succeed at the things they care about. At its core, finding the right job and being satisfied with your job is easy, even though a large percentage of people struggle to find meaning in their work. It is all in your head. Only you can decide whether you want to be happy, a decision that is not as easy as it sounds. In this book, I will help you make that decision, make that agreement with yourself, and allow yourself to have a career that will help you be satisfied with your work life.

What Will You Find Here?

To organize the thoughts I present here and make it easier for you to get a better handle on the topics I discuss, I decided to split the book into several parts. I suggest you go through them in the order they are presented, as they build on each other.

In the first part, I talk about introversion and introduce the subject of a successful career in general. I will talk about introverts' strengths, how they can help us, and how not to overuse them.

You can't reach your life goals and fulfill your dreams if you don't know what those goals and dreams are. Therefore, I will show you how to analyze yourself and your life and find out who you are and what you expect from your life. This part of the book is about self-discovery.

Since you picked up this book, I assume you want to have a successful career. However, success looks different for different people. I will discuss how to find out what a successful career looks like for you and introduce you to the Successful Career Wheel framework, which summarizes the critical aspects any successful career needs to have.

In the second part, I will talk about where you fit in when it comes to your career options. I will introduce you to the Quiet Success Sweet Spot concept to help you figure out what work will lead to your life satisfaction and a fulfilling career. You will discover, not surprisingly, that not all jobs are created equal. However, it is not the job title that differentiates them. Instead, it is your approach that makes the difference. It is about understanding what the world needs, who you are surrounded by, what skills you have, and what you love to do. The learnings from the first part of the book will really come in handy here.

I will follow this up by showing you how to get to your Sweet Spot. You will learn about professional and personal development, networking, marketing, and selling your skills, as well as how to reframe your view of the world and build the right habits and attitudes. This wouldn't be a career book without some suggestions about the recruitment process and interviewing, so I will offer you suggestions on how to use your introversion to your advantage during the job search process and how to overcome any anxieties you may have.

Since the book's whole premise is that you don't need to rely on others and you have the power to take ownership of your own career, the last part of the book will help you do just that. I will help you understand and adopt the principles, habits, and practices that will make it easier for you to not only get to your Sweet Spot but also stay there. I will introduce you to a comprehensive concept I call Quiet Success Principles. I will walk you through this set of ten principles that should be close to the hearts of most introverts and that, if followed, will increase your chances for a successful career and satisfying life. This section aims to help you look at the world from a new perspective and gradually adopt the introduced practices to become better and more successful at anything you decide to do.

At the end of each chapter, I will summarize the chapter's Key Takeaways to remind you what to, well, take away. I will also offer some food for thought in the form of Questions and Next Steps. I highly recommend that you give these sections serious thought. Deep reflection and overthinking are allowed in these instances. I may offer you an exercise or two, and, again, to get the most out of this book, I suggest you give them a go.

Why Did I Write This Book?

I started writing this book in 2013. In fact, at that time I started writing a completely different book. My original plan had been to focus on leadership and the way introverts can succeed in management roles.

As I was collecting materials, writing my blog,[1] and talking to people, I realized that there is a much bigger need to talk about a successful career in the first place. That is when I shifted my focus and decided to first write a guide for introverts on how to have a successful career before I follow up with a book about leadership.

In *Quiet Success*, I summarized the years of my own experience in the corporate world, and I collected stories and experiences of other people. I have done a decent amount of research in libraries and on the internet. I read tons of books on introversion, success, and leadership. I kept my eyes and ears open for years to get a better understanding of what makes successful people successful. I even ran a survey among the readers of my blog and interviewed numerous people, most of them introverted leaders, to understand how they ended up with successful careers, what things worked for them, and what challenges they faced.

I'm building on the works of those who came before me. Authors like Susan Cain and Jennifer B. Kahnweiler helped me to wrap my mind around introversion. Dale Carnegie and Stephen R. Covey showed me the importance of a holistic approach to life and career and that even introverts can benefit from relationships with other people. Angela Duckworth, Daniel Gilbert, K. Anders Ericsson, and Viktor E. Frankl formed my approach to personal development, grit, deliberate practice, and the meaning of life. Adam M. Grant, Daniel Goleman, Marshall Goldsmith, Daniel Kahneman, Patrick M. Lencioni, John C. Maxwell, Cal Newport, Daniel H. Pink, Phil Rosenzweig, Kim Scott, Joe De Sena, Jocko Willink, and many others supplied me with an endless inspiration about work-life integration, what success looks like, and the idea that with the right type of approach you can become whoever you want.

The combination of all of this led to the book you hold in your hands. It is by no means the ultimate guide to success and eternal happiness. Still, it is something that can get you started on the path to a successful career and a satisfying and happy life as an introvert.

PART I

Who You Are and What You Want

1

Are You An Introvert?

Let's start with answering some fundamental questions: Who is an introvert and who is an extrovert, and why should you care? I'm not too fond of generalizations, but since introversion and extroversion are terms described by psychologists, let's refer to them. Carl Jung originally coined the terms, and the definitions below are taken from Merriam-Webster Dictionary:

> "Extroversion is the state of or tendency toward being predominantly concerned with and obtaining gratification from what is outside the self: a personality trait or style characterized by a preference for or orientation to engaging socially with others."

> "Introversion is the state of or tendency toward being predominantly concerned with and obtaining gratification from one's own mental life: a personality trait or style characterized by a preference for or orientation to one's own thoughts and feelings."[2]

I consider myself a very introverted person. Even with that "handicap," I built and led global teams in several companies and countries. And it is not just me. Look around and you will see that there are many successful introverts and introverted leaders in the business world. A couple of years back, I read *Quiet* by Susan Cain. She introduced the idea that society misunderstands and undervalues introverts and brought a lot of hope that nothing is lost, even for those on the quiet side.[3] This book resonated strongly with me. It influenced the way I started to look at the potential introverts have and even the way I looked at my career. For starters, let me list a couple of famous introverts:

Abraham Lincoln (former US president), Al Gore (politician and environmentalist),

Albert Einstein (physicist), Alfred Hitchcock (film director), Angela Merkel (German chancellor), Barack Obama (former US president), Bill Gates (founder), Bob Dylan (musician), Calvin Coolidge (former US president), Charles Darwin (scientist), Charles Schulz (cartoonist), Clint Eastwood (actor), Eddie Murphy (actor), Franz Kafka (writer), George Orwell (writer), George Washington (former US president), Gwyneth Paltrow (actress), Harrison Ford (actor), Hillary Clinton (politician), J. K. Rowling (writer), Jerry Seinfeld (comedian), Johnny Depp (actor), Larry Page (founder), Mahatma Gandhi (humanitarian), Marcel Proust (novelist), Marie Curie (scientist), Marissa Mayer (CEO), Mark Zuckerberg (founder), Martin Luther King Jr. (civil rights leader), Michael Jackson (singer), Michael Jordan (basketball player), Mother Teresa (humanitarian), Neil Armstrong (astronaut), Reid Hoffman (founder), Rosa Parks (civil rights activist), Sir Isaac Newton (physicist), Socrates (philosopher), Steve Martin (comedian), Steven Spielberg (film director), Thomas Edison (inventor), Tony Hsieh (founder), Warren Buffett (investor). And the list goes on.

These traits are not so black-and-white. Introversion and extroversion are a continuum, and many people sit close to the middle, so-called ambiverts. In fact, if someone were 100 percent introverted or 100 percent extroverted, they would probably end up in an insane asylum. This book will help you even if you are an ambivert leaning toward introversion.

Many other traits are often confused with introversion. The most common is shyness. It is true that some introverts are also shy, but that is not the rule. According to an article in *Psychology Today*, shyness is defined as "the awkwardness or apprehension some people feel when approaching or being approached by other people. Unlike introverts, who feel energized by time alone, shy people often desperately want to connect with others but don't know how or can't tolerate the anxiety that comes with human interaction."[4] Shy people are often extroverts who have trouble connecting with others. The critical difference between introversion and shyness is that shy people are scared of social interaction, while introverts are just not interested in it all the time.

Psychologist Elaine Aron coined the term "highly sensitive person" (HSP). She claims that about 20 percent of the population can be classified as HSPs.[5] Not surprisingly, there is a significant overlap between HSPs and introverts. Highly sensitive people are more attuned to their environment and are better and getting cues from it. They are more receptive and more sensitive to others' emotions. The research done by Aron and her team gives us some clues on why introverts are sometimes seen as too sensitive. But just as with shyness, there is not a complete overlap. Introversion doesn't necessarily equal shyness, and every highly sensitive person isn't necessarily introverted and vice versa. In fact, according to Aron, about 30 percent of HSPs are extroverts.

To make things even more complicated, not all introverts exhibit the same traits. Psychologist Jonathan Cheek and his colleagues postulated that there are four types of introversion: social, thinking, anxious, and restrained.[6] This provides an easy-to-remember acronym, STAR. When you look in the imaginary mirror, you will discover that you are a mix of several introversion types, and that makes you unique with a unique blend of strengths, needs, and anxieties. This is an important realization, as it means that later in the book you will identify to various degrees with the suggestions I'm making. Some may work better for you than others.

Social introversion is described as the preference to socialize with a smaller group of people you know, sometimes even with a group of zero people—alone time. People fitting this type of introversion prefer to stay at home with a book rather than going to a party. I guess this is the most common view of introversion.

People falling into the thinking type of introversion are thoughtful and reflective. They are likely to daydream and get lost in their imaginations, though they have no problem socializing with others.

Those fitting the anxious introversion criteria also prefer solitude to bigger crowds of people, but for different reasons than the social introverts. They are driven to be alone because they feel awkward in the presence of other people, especially if they don't know them. They are not confident enough in their people skills, so they would rather avoid people.

Finally, restrained introversion applies to people you would consider reserved or restrained, who think carefully before speaking, don't get excited easily, and possibly run their lives at a slower pace.

It is tough to put people into narrow boxes. Each of us is a unique individual, and so the many faces of introversion help explain why some introverts are a bit more introspective, some are more social, some are confident but prefer alone time, and some are more anxious when dealing with crowds. It also makes sense that being an introvert has a relatively broad meaning. You can change and evolve however you desire as long as you accept your introversion, recognize your strengths, and use them to your advantage when dealing with the world.

Introversion is about the intensity of experiences and the way we recover from those experiences. For many introverts, the intensity of a given experience feels more significant than the same experience feels to an extrovert. For example, you may join a group of friends for dinner and have a great time. However, once the dinner is over and your extroverted friend suggests that the night is still young and that the group should move to a club, you may decide that you have had enough for one evening. The noisy restaurant and the several hours of chatting with your friends was enough intensive experience for you. Your extroverted friend needs a more crowded and noisier environment with more action to get the same level of satisfaction.

This then means you need sufficient time for recovery and recharging your internal energy. By recharging, I don't mean relaxing. There is a difference. Relaxing doesn't necessarily help with recharging your energy. You can spend the whole day relaxing in front of the TV and be more tired in the evening than you were before you started the day. Recharging, by its definition, is about activities that fill you with energy. At the end of your recharging, you are in a better place than when you started. Being able to recharge is not a choice. You have to learn to do it. If you don't renew your energy, you won't keep up the pace and achieve your goals and your life's mission. Being constantly without energy will influence your ability to get things done, your mood, and your happiness. Therefore, finding the right way to recharge and recover from high-intensity experiences is essential for having a successful, meaningful, and happy life. Recharging is then best done in solitude. For many introverts, it includes reading, writing, playing a musical instrument, painting, getting out in nature, meditating, or going for a run. Anything active or creative where you can disconnect from the world usually works just great.

Take the Quiz

If you are unsure whether you are an introvert or not, take the following quiz. Even though it is an informal quiz and not a scientifically validated test, it is based on characteristics of introversion generally accepted by modern researchers. Ideally, take the quiz when you are relaxed and in good spirits so it is not influenced by short-term anxieties and stresses. Get a cup of your favorite beverage, sit down comfortably in a quiet place, and consider each question in terms of what usually applies to you and answer either "True" or "False."

1. ____ After spending time surrounded by a lot of people, I need to get away and be by myself.
2. ____ I believe others may consider me dull or shy.
3. ____ I don't need to be around other people, and I enjoy alone time.
4. ____ I feel anxious and uncomfortable in new settings and when I'm around strangers.
5. ____ I feel drained after social situations, even when I enjoyed myself.
6. ____ I frequently analyze my thoughts and actions.
7. ____ I hate idle chitchat, and I feel awkward when doing it.
8. ____ I like to celebrate with only one person or a few close friends, rather than having a big event.
9. ____ I often daydream and fantasize about things that might happen to me.
10. ____ I often don't pick up a phone without taking time to prepare for the conversation in advance.

11.____ I overanalyze everything and have a hard time making decisions.

12.____ I prefer lectures when I can listen and learn over workshops and seminars that require interaction.

13.____ I prefer one-on-one conversations over a group chat.

14.____ I prefer prudence over risk-taking.

15.____ I prefer quiet environments and get overwhelmed when being surrounded by too much action.

16.____ I prefer texts over phone calls, and I dread calling other people.

17.____ I prefer vacations in places with few people and a quiet atmosphere.

18.____ I sometimes promise to join others for an activity and then find an excuse not to show up at the last minute.

19.____ I usually prefer to do things alone.

20.____ I typically think carefully before saying anything.

21.____ I'm attentive and tend to notice things that others miss.

22.____ I'm not comfortable talking about my work or showing it before it is finished and perfect.

23.____ I'm not particularly impulsive, and I prefer to watch an activity before joining in.

24.____ I'm uncomfortable introducing myself and prefer to be introduced by others.

25.____ I'm uncomfortable with conflict, and when others argue, I prefer to be elsewhere.

26.____ It takes me a long time to build relationships, but when I do, they last.

27.____ Unexpected changes and disturbances to my routine make me anxious.

28.____ When being presented with lots of information, I take my time to sort it all out before I make conclusions.

29.____ When I enter a room full of people, I often become self-conscious and feel that everyone is watching me.

30.____ When in a group of friends, I'm comfortable sitting in the corner and just listening.

Now add up the number of times you answered "True." All these statements are more accurate for introverts than for extroverts. Therefore, the higher the number of "Trues," the more likely you are an introvert. A lower number would indicate you are somewhere in the middle on the introvert-extrovert scale. You might be an ambivert, someone who acts as an introvert in some situations and an extrovert in others. If you answered "False" to most of the statements, then you might be a full-fledged extrovert.

It's All in the Brain

It is all about our brains. Each of us is unique, but at the same time, there are similarities in how our brains work. In her book *Quiet Impact*, Sylvia Loehken summarizes the mounting scientific evidence when it comes to introversion.[7]

Introverted people have greater electrical activity in their frontal cortices than extroverts do. These cortices deal with our inner processes, learning, remembering, and problem-solving. This greater level of electrical activity ultimately leads to introverts generally being good problem solvers.

Blood flows in different pathways in the brains of introverts and extroverts. For introverts, the stimuli need to travel deeper into the brain along the neural pathways. That is why introverts have slower reactions and take longer to reflect. This indirectly leads to introverts not speaking up without careful deliberation.

Different neurotransmitters dominate the brains of introverts and extroverts. Introverts have more acetylcholine, while extroverts have more dopamine. Dopamine impacts curiosity, drive, the expectation of reward, or the search for variety. Acetylcholine is essential for concentration, memory, and learning.[8] This feeds introverts' ability to focus and stay on a given topic longer than an extrovert would and be less prone to addictions and relying on external rewards.

In a study about the link between extroversion and dopamine, researchers concluded that the reward system in the brains of extroverts responded differently than that in the brains of introverts. By using MRI scans, the researchers examined the responses of participants involved in gambling. The findings were that when gambling brought positive results, the extroverts exhibited a stronger response in the amygdala. It makes sense that if extroverts respond more strongly to gambling winnings, they will react more strongly to adventures and taking risks in general.[9] This reflects even in career aspirations, where extroverts tend to be more motivated by titles and positional power than introverts, as we will discuss further later on. Extroverts might take on lofty sales quotas, chase high-level promotions and deals, or frequently seek to move between projects, while introverts might be more content to stay where they are and avoid rocking the boat.

Everyone has a sympathetic and parasympathetic autonomic nervous system. The first one prepares the body for attack, flight, or a major effort in the external world. The second system deals with the opposite. It works to ensure calm, relaxation, and conservation of energy. It lowers the heart rate by using the neurotransmitter acetylcholine. As it happens, introverts tend to use the parasympathetic nervous system more than extroverts do, and this allows them to stay more level-headed under pressure. You can observe this in work settings in times of crisis, when extroverts are in fight-or-flight mode and may distract their teams from solving the problems in front of them. Because of their assertive and dominant approach, extroverts may push their solutions to problems, even when those solutions don't necessarily have buy-in from the rest of the group. This can create discord within the team. Introverts may look at situations with a more thoughtful and collaborative approach and plan their way out of the mess.

In one study, scientists found that introverts have higher volumes of gray matter in areas that allow them to control their behavior and excel at social-emotional processing.[10] In contrast, another study found that extroverts have more gray matter in the amygdala, which helps to regulate the response to fear. And yet another group of scientists found that introverts have more activity in the brain regions needed for solving problems, making plans, and recalling events, while extroverts have more activity in the part of the brain responsible for interpreting messages from senses.[11]

Neuroscientist and psychologist Randy Buckner and colleagues discovered that introverts tended to have thicker gray matter in their prefrontal cortex than extroverts have.[12] The prefrontal cortex is a region of the brain that is linked to abstract thinking and decision-making. This may account for introverts' need to think things through thoroughly before making a decision, and on the other hand, extroverts' ability to take action and risks without hesitation.

When you search through available literature, you will find many studies and personality testing systems that touch on introversion in one way or another—be it research done by Carl G. Jung or Isabel Briggs Myers and Katharine Cook Briggs (who developed the popular MBTI system), or what you can see in the Big Five personality system. Some of the literature mentions that introverts are still in the minority, with around one-third of us being introverted. Still, some research, such as the third edition of the *MBTI Manual* published by Consulting Psychologists Press, which collected data on personality dimensions for more than half a century, shows that introverts and extroverts are represented at the same levels. Based on this study, 48.3% of people are extroverted, which means introverts may comprise 51.7% of the population.[13]

Modern humans evolved over millions of years. If, even after all that time, half of the population is introverted, there must be a reason. The process of natural selection would have wiped us out a long time ago if we were not critical to the survival of humankind. If you ever doubted whether you are of any use or hated yourself for not being more extroverted, remember that you do have an important role to play. You need to embrace who you are, tap into your strengths, and put them into use as nature intended.

Myths About Introversion

There are many false and even harmful myths about introversion. Many of us heard throughout our lives that there is something wrong with us and that we need to behave in a more extroverted way. If we don't, we just look weird in the eyes of extroverts.

I like weird. Being a little weird gives you character, a unique quality. But it must be a weirdness you are proud of, not weirdness imposed upon you by those who want to hurt you or who have the need to show their superiority. Introversion is not weird. Remember that half of the population are introverts. And if you still experience situations when you feel like your introversion makes you weird, then embrace it and be proud of your uniqueness.

So how do you respond to questions and myths about introversion? Here are some common ones.

Introverts Need to Be Fixed: There is nothing to fix. Introversion is not a disease that needs to be cured. After millions of years of evolution, nature made half of the human race introverts. It is by design. It means that the process of natural selection led to us being here. Introverts are needed.

Introverts Are Shy: Some of us can be shy. However, we are mixing apples and oranges here. Introversion and shyness are different things. An introverted person doesn't feel the need to talk to others and be the life of the party. A shy person would love that but doesn't know how. Shy people who genuinely struggle with their shyness are shy extroverts.

Introverts Don't Like to Talk: Many introverts do like to talk. We just don't feel like talking all the time. Someone just needs to bring up the right subject, something we are passionate about, and we can talk for hours. It is during a small talk and generally any shallow conversations without deep meaning that we stay quiet.

Introverts Are Slow to Speak, so They Must Be Dumb: Introverts take their time to come up with answers. We like to make sure that what we say means something. Introverts think first, then speak. There is no correlation between introversion/extroversion and intelligence. In fact, because of our ability to listen, focus, dive deep, and persevere, introverts often attain a better education than extroverts.

Introverts Lack Social Skills: This one depends on what you mean by social skills. I know many introverts who have excellent social skills. They can listen, empathize, are witty, prefer social harmony over drama, and are great to be around. They may not be the hilarious, outgoing life of the party, but that doesn't mean they don't have social skills.

Introverts Don't Care About Other People: This is just wrong. Not only do introverts care about others, but we can also be fiercely loyal. It may not always be easy for introverts to make new friends, so when we do, we do our best to keep them. In fact, according to various studies, introverts tend to be more externally oriented than extroverts. Extroverts are more individualistic than introverts. Introverts are more willing to put the good of others ahead of their own to preserve harmony.

Introverts Are Loners: Just because we prefer to renew our energy in a quiet environment doesn't mean we want to avoid others at any cost. Introverts like to be alone regularly, but just like extroverts, we don't want to be lonely. Even introverts need to feel that we belong and that we are loved. We may enjoy spending our free time in nature, yet we are comfortable bringing a friend.

Introverts Can't Be Good Leaders: A couple of researchers, including Adam Grant, already debunked this myth.[14] Introverts make great leaders, especially in a knowledge-based economy. Grant's research showed that extroverts are better at leading passive people who need to be told what to do. Introverts are better at leading proactive, creative, knowledgeable people who need someone to help them remove roadblocks.

Introverts Hate Public Speaking and Are No Good at It: Guess what? Extroverts hate public speaking too. Many introverts are great public speakers because they are passionate about the topics on which they are speaking. Public speaking is a performance, it is an art, and it has nothing to do with extroversion. It requires proper preparation and lots of practice. And introverts are great at these things.

Introverts Are Not Good at Selling: Adam Grant proved that introverts are as good at selling as extroverts.[15] We are then both beaten by ambiverts, who sit in the middle of the extrovert-introvert spectrum and outsell us all. Selling is not about talking. It is about listening, asking the right types of questions, having strong arguments, and telling the right stories while keeping things calm and professional. These are the strengths of many introverts.

Next time you hear someone describing you or other introverts in these terms, don't take it personally. They don't know what they are talking about. If you feel like it, you may try to educate them a bit. If you think doing so would sound defensive, then just smile knowingly and let it pass. You know in your heart that you might be a little weird in their eyes, and that is fine. Consider the words of Sue Fitzmaurice: "Being a little weird is just a natural side effect of being awesome."

Summary and Key Takeaways

Introversion is not a disease or something to be worried about and try to cure. It is simply a trait you and I were born with that makes us who we are. It is about the intensity of experiences and the way we resupply our internal energy. We often find pleasure in solitary activities but are also great leaders of people. To make things more complicated, there are different types of introversion, and no two introverts are alike. Due to differences in introverts' and extroverts' brains, we react differently to external rewards, have a different predisposition toward risk-taking, and have different ways to handle pressure. Introverts and extroverts are not better or worse than one another. We are simply different. Half of the population are introverts, and we are here for a reason.

- According to the latest research, half of the population are introverts.
- There are four types of introversion: social, thinking, anxious, and restrained.
- The brains of introverts and extroverts differ. The neurological differences cause introverts to have slower reactions, be more thoughtful, concentrate better, and be less dependent on external rewards.
- There are many myths about introversion. Don't believe them. Introversion is nothing to be ashamed of or to be cured. There is nothing wrong with you. You are just fine the way you are.
- Introverts make great leaders and can be witty and fiercely loyal friends who care about others.
- We are all unique.

Questions and Next Steps

- Take the quiz from this chapter as the first step in self-discovery. When thinking about the questions, what more did you learn about yourself? Is there anything that surprised you?
- Think about your life and career so far. When did your introversion feel like a burden and liability? When did it feel helpful?
- Are you proud of being an introvert? If not, why not? What would you need to learn to become more comfortable with who you are?

2

What Are Your Hidden Superpowers?

One thing that many introverts have in common is the fact that we have been told so many times that we are shy or too quiet so we start believing it. We sit quietly in the corner, even in situations when we know we should be out there. We use the introvert label as an excuse to stay in our comfort zones. Sometimes we even begin blaming our introversion for our failure to get ahead in life to achieve our dreams. We feel like victims. And, as any self-fulfilling prophecy goes, we then *become* victims. We become the label that we give ourselves.

But it is all in the head. Yes, you were born with some specific traits, and introversion might be one of them, but who says you can't live your dreams? You have so many strengths and tools at your disposal that have the potential to help you to achieve so much. You need to do only one thing: you need to allow yourself to be successful.

If you feel the need to use labels, then use the introvert label with pride and focus on the strengths that come with it. And there are quite a few.

Let's start with the definition of what strengths are. A strength is something you are naturally good at and enjoy doing. Strengths are patterns of thinking, feeling, or behaving that engage and energize you and allow you to perform at your optimal level. Even though they are natural, you can still improve them through practice.

According to the VIA Institute, your signature strengths have three fundamental properties. They are essential, meaning they feel like they are part of you, like they make you who you are. They are effortless, meaning they are natural to you, and you don't need to exert an effort to exhibit them. They flow. They are energizing, meaning using these strengths energizes you and leaves you feeling happy and in balance.[16]

As Michelle McQuaid and Erin Lawn point out, there are obvious advantages to using your strengths. People who use their strengths are happier, experience less stress, feel healthier, have more energy, and feel more satisfied with their lives. They are also more confident, experience faster growth and development, are more creative and agile, and experience more meaning in their work.[17]

When using your strengths, it is essential to find your golden mean. This is a level where you don't overuse or underuse your strength. You are using it at an optimal level. For example, if your strength is honesty, you can misuse it by being too blunt and therefore hurt others. If your strength is humor, you may misuse it by using it all the time, even when not appropriate. Prudence can make you too hesitant and not willing to take any risks. Humility can make you a doormat.

In the following pages, I will propose a model of introvert strengths that I believe covers most of us. If you feel you have additional strengths not listed here, good for you. If you think that you lack in some of the areas described as strengths, don't despair. You may have different strengths not mentioned here, or, quite possibly, you may have these strengths and not realize it.

As part of the research for this book, I ran a survey to identify what people believe are introverts' strengths. As a starting point, I based my questions on the work of other authors and on my experience when working with and coaching other introverts. I then sorted through the answers to better understand whether there is a significant difference in how introverts and extroverts identify with particular characteristics.

Do you consider this to be a strength of introverts or extroverts?	Neither	Extroverts	Introverts	Both
Introspection	0%	5%	85%	10%
Ability to listen	0%	3%	82%	15%
Thoughtfulness	2%	0%	73%	25%
Self-awareness	5%	8%	70%	17%
Humility	0%	3%	64%	32%
Focus	0%	2%	63%	35%
Attentiveness to feedback	2%	5%	63%	30%
Preparation	2%	3%	62%	33%
Empathy	2%	10%	55%	33%
Prudence	4%	4%	49%	44%
Loyalty	7%	3%	40%	50%

Independence	2%	10%	38%	50%
Perseverance	5%	7%	32%	56%
Ability to multitask	10%	20%	20%	49%
Ability to work as part of a team	3%	12%	18%	67%
Creativity	2%	12%	17%	69%
Ability to lead	3%	19%	14%	64%
Resistance to stress	9%	33%	9%	50%
Ability to present a vision	3%	50%	8%	38%
Public speaking skills	3%	69%	3%	24%

Table 1: Results of Survey on Introverts' Strengths

When comparing the responses of introverts and extroverts, there was a difference in some of the perceived characteristics. Introverts believe that listening, humility, thoughtfulness, empathy, self-awareness, prudence, and introspection are introverts' strengths. Independence and public speaking skills are seen by introverts as strengths not directly correlated with extroversion or introversion.

When looking at this data, focus on the last two columns, the strengths specific to introverts and strengths of both introverts and extroverts. The goal of the table is not to say who is better but to show you what strengths you have regardless of whether extroverts have them too. For each row, you can add the values from the last two columns and see the overall percentage of people who indicated that introverts have that particular strength. In fact, I have used these particular numbers as a guiding principle for developing the Introvert Strengths introduced later in the chapter. The top strengths that participants mentioned when given a chance to list anything they wanted while answering the question, "List the three most important skills or characteristics of successful introverts," are summarized in Table 2.

Skill/Characteristic	% of Respondents
Ability to listen	53.2%
Empathy	21.3%
Thoughtfulness	19.1%
Self-awareness	19.1%
Focus	17.0%
Introspection	14.9%
Perseverance	12.8%
Analytical approach	12.8%
Independence	10.6%
Creativity	8.5%

Table 2: Top 10 Skills of Successful Introverts

There was also a wide array of other strengths mentioned by the participants of the study, such as (in alphabetical order): ability to be alone, ability to observe, calmness, communication, competitiveness, consideration, critical thinking, curiosity, decision-making, deep thinking, detail-orientation, humility, imagination, influence, integrity, intelligence, loyalty, organization, originality, ownership, passion, patience, planning, preparedness, process orientation, resourcefulness, respectfulness, result-orientation, self-composure, servant leadership, strategic planning, supportiveness, and team focus.

You can see that ability to listen was mentioned most often by a wide margin, coming up 53.2 percent of the time, while the second most frequently mentioned trait, empathy, was only brought up 21.3 percent of the time. I suggest that while the ability to listen certainly is a strength of most introverts, its overall lead is also caused by the fact that introverts are labeled by society as good listeners, so we are more aware of this particular strength. In contrast, we may not be aware of the other ones we've got.

The one area that is often mentioned by other authors and generally associated with introverts is creativity. The association between introversion and creativity comes from the idea that for creativity, you need to think deeply and spend some alone time to produce great work. However, my own survey doesn't really support this notion—only 8.5 percent of participants quoted creativity as a top strength of introverts, and when specifically asked about it, 69 percent of participants said it applies equally to introverts and extroverts. I also haven't seen any convincing research indicating that introverts are any more creative than extroverts. Both extroverts and introverts can be equally creative. Both need some time alone, interlaced with conversations with others, to get the creative juices flowing. The best creative people are complex individuals who can find inspiration both in solitude and with people. It is only the way they process their thoughts that is different for introverts and extroverts, but that doesn't make one group stronger and more creative than the other.

The aspects that make introverts appear more creative are the ability to focus and dive deep into a given topic, perseverance and thoughtfulness, and the ability to work independently. These traits ensure that what may have been just a passing thought evolves into a creative idea that gets ironed out and implemented. Donald W. MacKinnon found out in his research that creative people are often self-centered, egoistic, and have no desire to listen to others.[18] That makes them free of the need for social approval and thus able to come up with unorthodox ideas.[19] Does that sound like your typical introvert?

By analyzing all the data from the survey and verifying it with external research, I created the Introvert Strengths, as depicted in Figure 1, as an overview of the strengths most introverts possess.

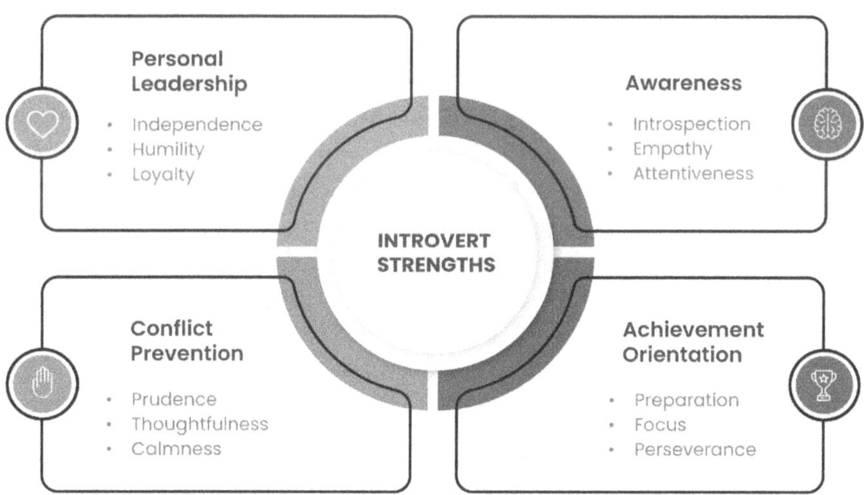

Figure 1: Introvert Strengths

To create some order out of all the strengths, I decided to split them into four thematic categories:

• Awareness, which deals with our senses and creates our view of ourselves and the world, includes Introspection, Empathy, and Attentiveness. Awareness is a key overarching theme. It allows us to see the world as realistically as possible and to tune in to how others see it.

- Achievement orientation, which focuses on getting things done, includes Preparation, Focus, and Perseverance. A successful career can't happen without delivering stellar work. Lean into these strengths to drive toward your goals. Prioritize good preparation, focus on the top priorities, and persevere in the face of adversity and you will get there.
- Conflict prevention, which helps us prevent misunderstandings, avoid disasters, and keeps us safe, includes Prudence, Thoughtfulness, and Calmness. Introverts are not big risk-takers, so let's use this trait to our advantage. Prudence and thoughtful analysis combined with calmness in case things go wrong will keep you out of trouble.
- Personal leadership, which helps us own our lives while relating well with others, includes Independence, Humility, and Loyalty. We are responsible for our own fortunes, but that doesn't mean we have to do things alone. Our strengths of independence and humility will help us to avoid relying on others and to take care of our own needs while not becoming arrogant about it. Personal leadership makes us great team members and friends.

In the following pages, I will talk about what each strength is, how to build them, how to use them, and how not to abuse them. When people identify that they have a particular superpower, they tend to overuse it. As the saying goes, if all you have is a hammer, everything looks like a nail. It is very tempting to use a specific strength even when it is not appropriate. The misuse or overuse of particular strength can lead to adverse effects, and with overuse, a strength can become a weakness. For each of the strengths mentioned below, I will also highlight the dangers of overusing it.

Attentiveness

Attentiveness and excellent listening skills help you in numerous obvious and not-so-obvious ways. It starts with increasing your understanding of the other person and the situation. Listening enables you to ask the right questions, thus getting more clarity. It helps you show that the other person matters to you, giving you a bigger chance of getting their attention and increasing your influence. It enables you to build a rapport and attune to their emotions, thus building empathy and helping you find the right words to get them on your side. It allows you to be seen as credible.

Introverts are naturally good listeners. Because we don't need to talk, listening is what is left. We don't have the need to push our ego into the conversation. We just absorb what the other person says without being judgmental or without the need to have the last word in every conversation.

However, attentiveness is much more than just listening. It is about being present and trying to understand. It is about curiosity. Being attentive means that you are genuinely listening. The fact that you don't talk and you nod in agreement doesn't mean that you are listening. You need to hear not only the words but also the meaning. Listening without understanding is useless. Only true attentive listening counts. When you listen, hear, and understand what is being said, you can list listening as your strength.

As an introvert, you already have a big head start, and you are a natural listener. However, the environment may diminish your listening skills. Media—both social media and mass media—are not particularly good at forcing you to listen. In fact, the exact opposite! The thirty-second news clips or 140-character tweets that you are constantly bombarded with are killing your listening skills. We are used to getting a first impression, often wrong, and moving on to the next piece of information.

To improve your listening skills, start digging into details. Don't read just the headline of the article. Read its entire contents and think about it. When talking to people, don't be satisfied with one-word answers to your questions. Ask follow-up questions that will show that you heard what was said and you want more. When listening, do just that. Be in the moment, listen with the intent to understand, and then paraphrase in your own words. Learn a simple mantra: first listen, then think, then speak. Listening and thinking about the answer at the same time is the biggest killer of genuine listening. You don't listen. You just nod, thinking about what you are going to say.

Attentiveness or attentive listening is a superweapon in the corporate setting. We all want to feel that we belong and that other people care. By listening to others, you are showing them respect, and they feel that they matter. They matter to you. Therefore they are more likely to want to work with you and help you succeed. This is doubly important when you are in a leadership position. Listening will help you to make better decisions and to build buy-in from the team. Just imagine how different it feels when your boss comes to you with a task and instructions on how to do it, versus when they first ask your opinion and only then decide. You will feel much more cooperative with those who listen to your opinion.

The ultimate test of your listening skills comes when you work in a multinational environment. There, listening is genuinely a critical skill. When you work with people similar to you, people from your culture with an educational background similar to your own, you can make many assumptions about what they mean. You don't need to listen too much—you can guess. However, once you work with someone very different from you, there is no way you can afford to guess. You can't make any assumptions. You need to listen.

Every strength has the potential to turn against you if you rely on it too much. Overuse of attentive listening can annoy people. Asking questions is a great way to get others talking, but if it feels like interrogation or coaching when none is appreciated, it will put people off. It can also lead to lost credibility if you ask too many questions and don't have answers on your own, especially if the questions you ask were already answered.

If you spend too much time listening without a clear outcome, it can stifle action, and you may end up being the sounding board for all sorts of complaints and issues that will eventually lead to you being depressed.

Lastly, listening too much without ever stating your opinion will leave you without a voice in decision-making and ultimately without any influence at all. People will just ignore you.

Empathy

Raw intellectual power doesn't cut it anymore. Even if you are the smartest person in the room or the loudest, that doesn't mean that others will listen to you. On the other hand, you may be so self-absorbed and living in your own world that you have trouble getting on the same wavelength with others. Luckily for you, many introverts exhibit a great deal of empathy.

But what exactly is empathy? And what are the different ways it manifests? There are three types of empathy you can recognize.

Cognitive empathy is an ability to put yourself into someone else's shoes, to take their perspective. At first glance, it may not look like empathy at all, since you are using your reasoning skills rather than your emotions. Cognitive empathy is more about your ability to understand human psychology. Interrogators and torturers need to have excellent cognitive empathy to get what they want, get information, or hurt people without any emotional attachment.[20]

Emotional or affective empathy is an ability to feel what others feel. If someone feels sad, you can understand it not on a logical level but on an emotional one. It is not your brain that tells you to pretend to feel sad. You can genuinely feel the sadness, and the other person feels the connection. This is most obvious with small babies. If you smile at a baby, it feels happiness and smiles back. If it hears other babies cry or sees its mother in distress, it starts crying too. The problem with this type of empathy is that it can lead to empathy overload. Instead of dealing with a potentially tricky situation, you add to it.

According to Sara D. Hodges and Michael W. Myers, this type of empathy consists of several components.[21] First is feeling the same emotions as others, second is feeling distressed in response to the emotions of others, and third is feeling compassion for another person. Emotional empathy is often an autonomous reaction that happens unconsciously. Cognitive empathy is a more conscious and deliberate process.

Compassionate empathy is when you feel that something is not right and jump in and help. It is a combination of the two previous types. This type of empathy has the best balance of genuinely connecting with another human being while not being sucked in to the same state and getting overwhelmed. You understand the other person's feelings on a logical level. This allows you to take action to help the other person resolve the situation. From a usefulness perspective, this is where you want to be.

If you look at empathy from the perspective of emotional intelligence, you discover that cognitive empathy is all about self-awareness and social awareness, as it helps you to understand why something is happening. Emotional empathy relates more to relationship management, as it automatically tells you how to behave. Even though it is automatic, you can still influence it by understanding yourself and being more deliberate in managing your emotions and reactions to the outside world. Cognitive and compassionate empathy are the two most flexible and easy to improve.

To increase your empathy, work on your self-awareness. In fact, "Know Yourself" is the first in the Quiet Success Principles I will talk about in later chapters. When you understand yourself and why you feel a certain way about others, you can mitigate any bias those feelings may bring. By understanding your feelings, you are also more likely to get them under control and not let them cloud your judgment. You are then more likely to empathize with others and understand where they are coming from. Empathy as a strength makes you easy to work with. It helps you to build rapport with other people without the need for annoying idle chitchat. Introverts tend to show respect and avoid acting or speaking in ways that would lead to others losing face. We think before we speak. We can put ourselves in another person's shoes. We are ready to compromise and often communicate in a politically correct way. We try to remove friction from our communication and avoid conflicts as much as possible.

Most introverts are sensitive to other people's needs and feelings, which creates a significant advantage when you find yourself in leadership roles. Empathy can help you navigate complex situations and influence others in a way that is just right for them. Empathy is essential. It helps us show compassion and connect with others while taking appropriate actions to help resolve emotionally charged situations.

Lack of empathy often leads to people getting into arguments and not understanding. They form opinions and are unwilling to back off, even when evidence shows they are wrong. It leads to seeing other people as weak or too sensitive, being reluctant to listen to different points of view, blaming others, holding grudges, not hearing when others speak, or being generally unwilling or unable to work in teams.

Overuse of empathy manifests in being too bogged down by the problems and feelings of others. You may try to do the right thing for the good of the world, but because you tune to the needs of a particular individual, you may miss the big picture. You may get unnecessarily stressed by other people's emotional states, and it may derail your performance. Yes, you should connect with others and try to understand where they are coming from, but it doesn't require you to follow them to a potentially self-destructive place.

Introspection

Introspection can be defined as an act of self-awareness that involves analyzing your thoughts, behaviors, and actions. There are two types of introspection: self-reflection and rumination. Self-reflection is a positive trait that helps you learn from your mistakes and increase your self-awareness.

Introverts tend to spend lots of time in their heads analyzing the world around them and reflecting on their actions. If we keep it positive, this can be a considerable strength. We learn from our mistakes. We plan strategies for the future. We get better prepared for the next time something comes up. Introspection helps us be the best human beings we can be, and it also helps us when leading others. If you understand your own actions and emotions, you can approach others the right way.

We often have a very clear idea of what is important to us and why. We are not satisfied with a high-level answer but dig deep into our unconsciousness to truly understand ourselves. We may never be satisfied with what we find and may keep on soul-searching throughout our lives. Introspection is the first step in understanding who you are. Being self-aware, being able to receive feedback, knowing what your core values are, and being able to transfer them to your daily routine is then a second step to understanding who you are.

If you overuse your strengths of self-awareness and introspection, you may forget about the rest of the world. You may spend too much time in your head and ignore your impact on your surroundings. Ruminating is a negative spin on introspection. It is what happens when you obsess over your shortcomings. It leads to low confidence levels, doubts, and the inability to use your energy in a constructive matter. You fixate on your faults, exaggerate your weaknesses, and paint a negative picture of yourself. And all of this in your head. You do a lot of self-inflicted damage.

Ruminating is rooted in need to think deeply about what is essential and the tendency to delve too much into the past. Focusing too much on the past is a sure path toward not having a future. Ruminating often leads to self-incrimination, loss of confidence, and increased risk-aversion. Nothing good can ever come from repeatedly reliving past mistakes, regardless of whether there were yours or others'. Ruminating makes you feel bad and prevents you from acting. Learn to analyze past mistakes, learn from them, and move on.

Perseverance

Perseverance, tenacity, patience, and being able to pursue things methodically and calmly. These all describe yet another strength of most introverts: we don't give up easily. This is not necessarily because of the pressure of the outside world, but there is this inner drive that forces us to figure things out. When we do, we feel a level of satisfaction greater than any external praise—at least, we do when we work on things we care about.

You probably saw this picture on many occasions in your life. People work on a problem, they are trying to get something done, but the solution eludes them. At some point, they get angry about the problem and with themselves and just walk away. We don't let our emotions push us away from the problem. We may still get frustrated a bit, but that often leads to increased focus and a change of approach. When something doesn't work, we analyze why and try something else.

Perseverance also feeds on three other strengths we have—focus, thoughtfulness, and preparation—and I will talk about all of them later in the chapter. Because we can focus and don't split our attention in many different directions, it is easier for us to get into the flow and use all our potential on the problem at hand. This single-minded focus helps marshal all our internal forces to get things done and pushes us to spend more time on the problem. When you are in the flow, you ignore the passage of time and keep working on the issue until resolution.

Not jumping to conclusions and thoughtfully and systematically analyzing the situation to come up with the best approach helps us stick with a task longer than an extrovert would. We prepare, and if you prepare, have a plan, and can split your plan into smaller chunks, you are more likely to see progress, feel the small wins, and persevere.

Aside from preparation, what is the recipe for how to get your strength of perseverance to the next level? Purpose and hope are the two ingredients that will help you. Purpose means that you develop a genuine interest in an activity, and you see the big picture. You understand what is at stake and how the activity helps you to achieve your bigger goal. Hope is rooted in optimism that when you try hard enough, you will succeed. You know that you don't have the necessary skills today and that there is a long journey in front of you, but you approach the activity with a can-do attitude and hope that you will prevail.

Not giving up is a great strength that helps you in pretty much any type of work and any aspect of life. Being able to stick with a problem and get it resolved regardless of obstacles is a hallmark of a successful person. And then there is learning. Just consider the last time you had to learn something complex and challenging, maybe a foreign language, a software development language if you are in IT, or international accounting principles. Most of the things that will help you move forward in your career require perseverance.

Overuse of perseverance manifests as stubbornness. You shouldn't give up easily, but you also need to understand when your insistence on something is foolish and is not helping you move forward. It is this critical balance, knowing when to push forward and when to walk away, that makes all the difference.

Stubborn people will often tell you that you could have gotten the work done if you kept going as they did. What they forget is that in the time they spent accomplishing that one thing, you were able to do five different ones with higher value. Not giving up is a great trait, but always analyze what the opportunity cost of not doing something else instead is.

Focus

Multitasking is often portrayed as a great skill to have and is even used as a requirement in job postings. The trouble is, multitasking is a myth. People are terrible at multitasking, and if you believe that you are an exception and you can multitask well, it most likely means that you are deluding yourself and don't even realize it. The majority of significant work gets done by people who focus on what they are doing and limit distractions.

I spent several years as a software developer. The best code I produced was when I was "in the flow," focusing on the problem, ignoring the environment around me, ignoring what time it was, whether I was hungry or tired, and getting things done. Yes, you can do many things in parallel, and we all often do, but in retrospect, the quality of our work and the total time we spend on tasks is heavily in favor of serial execution and not parallel. And, at the end of the day, having five tasks finished feels much better than having ten tasks started and none finished.

If you have ever worked with a computer, you may believe that these machines are the ultimate multitaskers. You can run numerous applications in parallel, do complex computations, and have a video chat with your friends, all at the same time. Well, not really. That's not how computers work. Assuming single processor computers, what looks like multitasking is a technique you may call time-sharing, with individual tasks waiting their turn to perform a simple operation and then letting the other process have their turn. The human brain works pretty much the same way. It switches from one context to another, and it does so really fast, so it creates an illusion of multitasking. Unfortunately, this context-switching has a price in terms of energy and time spent on it.

The context-switching is happening in the prefrontal cortex, part of the frontal lobe. This part of our brain allows us to shelve a task we are working on and switch to something else. After completing the other activities, we can get back to the original task at the stage where we had left it. Curiously enough, the prefrontal cortex is one of the last parts of the brain to mature and the first one to go, so our perceived ability to multitask will be smaller when we are kids or when we get older.

Some tasks, like breathing or highly automated tasks like walking, can be done very well in parallel with other tasks, as they are managed by different parts of the brain. But the moment you need to use the same part of the brain, context-switching comes into play.

David E. Meyer, a professor of psychology in the cognition and perception program at the University of Michigan,[22] says that "when you perform multiple tasks that each require some of the same channels of processing, conflicts will arise between the tasks, and you're going to have to pick and choose which task you're going to focus on and devote a channel of processing to it. The bottom line is that you can't simultaneously be thinking about your tax return and reading an essay, just as you can't talk to yourself about two things at once."[23]

In a study performed by Cliff Nass from Stanford University, focused on our ability to consume multiple streams of media content at the same time, researchers compared two groups of people, ones who were used to routinely multitasking, absorbing various media content at the same time, and those who weren't. The results showed that multitaskers are "lousy at everything necessary for multitasking." The funny thing is that because the same parts of the brain responsible for cognitive thought are also responsible for evaluating our performance, we don't realize that we are bad at multitasking.[24]

All this is excellent news for introverts. We prefer to focus on one thing at a time. That is our strength. You need to protect this ability with your life. Don't get dragged into multitasking hype just because others are doing it. Let others boast about their ability to multitask. They are lying to themselves. Just focus on one thing at a time, and not only will it make you feel better, but you will also get more done.

The focus is a critical skill when it comes to living in the moment, not getting distracted by social media, building strong relationships by focusing on the person you are talking to, listening, thinking deeply, and pretty much every aspect of life.

To build even better focus, you need to get rid of distractions. You can't really will yourself to focus, as your thoughts about focusing are distractions by themselves. A good way to start is to create an environment where focus comes naturally. For example, when I needed to focus on writing this book, I would isolate myself from others, switch off my phone, and even disconnect from the internet to remove the temptation of social media. I set up the environment to make it easy for me to focus.

The second approach you may consider is mindfulness. There are various other definitions of what mindfulness means, but in the end, it all comes back to paying attention to what is going on with you and in your surroundings at any given moment—being in the moment. It helps to focus attention and reduce distracting information. It allows you to disengage from emotionally disturbing reality and enables you to focus, even under stressful conditions. It reduces rumination, negative thoughts, and depressive symptoms that, again, prevent you from concentrating. By practicing mindfulness, you learn to focus on the here and now. You learn to remove any anxieties about the future by fully embracing the present, and you get better at not distracting yourself with stray destructive thoughts.

Overuse of focus can come into play when you are unable to prioritize correctly. You may focus on the wrong thing, and then the important things don't get done. Real high performance comes only at the point of focusing on the right stuff.

Another time when focus can become a liability is when you get thrown into a noisy environment where you still need to keep up with many things happening simultaneously. Focusing on one particular aspect may lead you to miss something important in another area. Introverts can be easily overwhelmed in such environments and freeze. The best way to deal with these situations is prevention. Don't get pushed into environments like that. If there is no way around it, know that it is not just you—everyone will struggle in such situations. The difference between you and others is that you are aware of human limitations.

Preparation

If there is one strength that defines most introverts, it would be the ability and willingness to prepare. Whether it's a speech in front of an audience, meetings with our teams, or even one-on-ones with our bosses, we like to be ready. I sometimes joke that I write notes from the meeting before the meeting even starts. And I actually do!

How do you increase your strength of preparation? Well, there's no easy way around it: with hard work. Preparation is closely linked to your ability to focus and to another of your strengths: thoughtfulness. By thinking things through ahead of time, considering risks and challenges, you create a list of things to prepare for and brainstorm mitigation strategies and options, so you are ready for the most likely scenarios.

When it comes to your career, preparation helps you in a couple of ways. First, you should become a subject-matter expert or at least knowledgeable enough to have your facts straight. Whatever your role, you need to communicate with other people, sell your ideas, and persuade those around you to listen to what you are saying. Preparing your arguments ahead of time will make you more coherent and persuasive—definitely good for your career.

Preparation also helps you think of alternative options and have them ready as a backup plan, available to pull out of your sleeve when needed. When I was at school, I had a reputation for being someone who can think fast on his feet and improvise quickly. The fact is, I don't improvise quickly, I'm just really well prepared. What may look like intelligent improvisation is just good preparation. Use your strength of preparation to help you think fast, as that will make you seem more competent. Preparation will also make you feel more confident and more likely to speak up and have your voice heard.

Preparation helps with rapport and building alliances. Before you talk to someone, don't just prepare what you want to say and achieve, but also try to learn something about the person you are about to talk to. Finding out that the two of you have the same hobby can be a great way to build rapport and make the whole conversation smoother.

Overuse of this skill can lead to paralysis and can slow you down. There is no formula for figuring out how much preparation is needed for a particular activity. Still, common sense dictates that low-priority low-risk initiatives require less preparation than something that is critical and has a high risk of failure.

The need to be prepared is inversely proportional to your confidence levels and worry about what others will think about you. If you are confident or you are entering familiar situations, you will be less likely to over-prepare than if you are faced with the unknown. The questions I would always ask when making preparations are, "How much do I care about the outcome of this activity? What are the risks associated and their likelihood of happening? What is the worst thing that can happen if I fail?" The chances are that, often, you are over-preparing and thus taking up time that you could be spending doing other work instead.

This perfection trap comes from the need to be perfect for everyone and to not disappoint. It also means that you want to make sure anything you or your team does is pitch-perfect. And it often leads to being worried about delegating work, both at work and home. You know that your team or spouse may not do as good a job as you would do, so you instead do the work yourself. That means you are constantly overworked and frustrated. Learn to delegate effectively and get comfortable with the fact that others may not do as perfect a job as you would do, and that it is just fine.

Calmness

Years back, during a somewhat slow period when not much was happening in the company, I realized how much I thrive in crises and that I need a certain level of pressure to be at my best. I also discovered that I don't panic easily. Due to the time I spend preparing and thinking about possible issues, it doesn't often happen that something will genuinely surprise me.

I'm good at my job, and not many things stress me out anymore. I spend most of my time during the week in the office in a familiar environment with people I know and feel comfortable around. I still get anxious when confronted by unknowns. When I get a dose of cortisol in times of crisis, it forces me into full-throttle action—unless it is too much, in which case I get paralyzed by fear or the inability to pick the right priority and get moving.

Regardless of the situation, I may panic internally, but I won't look that way to the outside world. I have worked with many introverts over the years who seemed very calm in times of crisis. While others may panic and make bad decisions, these introverted individuals thought about things before spurring into action. They didn't react. They responded.

Emotions come from within and not from outside. It is you who decides how to feel about external stimuli. The great news is that introverts don't get easily influenced by either panic or excitement from the outside world. Most of our anxieties and wounds are self-inflicted.

Calmness is a natural strength, but like any other, it can be improved by utilizing your other strengths, particularly preparation and thoughtfulness. When you are prepared, when you consider various risks and come up with mitigation strategies, you can handle issues when they materialize. Similarly, when there is a problem, you don't jump into thoughtless action but consider the implications of what is happening and thoughtfully come up with an appropriate response.

Aside from using your other strengths to increase your calmness, you can look again at mindfulness. I mentioned it already when talking about focus, and it is relevant here too. Training yourself to focus your attention and awareness to have your mental processes under your control leads to better concentration, clarity, and calmness. When you get your cognitive processes under control, you can also get your emotional states under control. According to Daphne M. Davis and Jeffrey A. Hayes, mindfulness brings several benefits.[25] Aside from the improved focus and reduced rumination mentioned before, it also reduces stress and decreases anxiety. You become less reactive and have more cognitive flexibility. This manifests itself in faster recovery times after dealing with stressful situations and increased calmness in times of adversity.

When it comes to the corporate setting and your career, who do you want to have around in times of crisis and when conflict within the team erupts? Introverts. The researchers Kristin L. Cullen-Lester from the Center for Creative Leadership, Hannes Leroy from Erasmus University, Alexandra Gerbasi from Grenoble Ecole de Management, and Lisa Nishii from Cornell University observed twenty-seven teams comprised of 162 business students and found an interesting phenomenon. Generally, extroverts seemed to have the advantage when it came to building relationships. They were seen as more enthusiastic, sociable, and assertive. However, their advantage had its limits. It is great to have lots of extroverts on a team when things are going well since they bring energy and good vibes. When things aren't going well and conflicts emerge, however, the domineering extrovert can make matters worse and create even bigger tensions within the group.

"Extroverts are able to develop energizing relationships with their teammates; this is a valuable quality that organizations may want to consider when staffing teams," researchers said. "However, this advantage appears to be lost, and to even become a disadvantage when task conflict exists within a team."[26] When the conflict in the team emerged, the energy that extroverts initially brought in that made them great contributors suddenly started to play a different role. The extroverted team members took energy out of solving the problem. Because of their assertive and dominant approach, they pushed their solutions, which didn't necessarily have buy-in from the rest of the group, and so the internal team struggle persisted. Herein lies the answer to why you should care: Being calm in times of adversity can have a tremendous impact on your career, as it helps you to be seen as someone who takes charge when times get tough. It makes you a natural leader. It makes you someone people will listen to when they are panicking.

Overuse of calmness can manifest in an inability to show emotions and a tendency to let them eat you from within. You are probably still stressed internally, and you need to find ways to deal with that. If you don't let the outside world know that you're stressed so you don't add to the panic, you need to have other mechanisms in place to get your anxieties under control. Too much calmness can also lead to prolonged inactivity. While a bit of stress and a light panic could spur you into action, unnatural calm can prevent you from taking necessary action or contributing to the resolution of a problem. Others may shout over you.

Thoughtfulness

Thoughtfulness is defined as an ability to be absorbed in thought or think things through. You can see it manifested in a combination of critical thinking and deep conversations.

Critical thinking brings out another one of introverts' advantages. With the overwhelming amount of information available, it is critically important to distinguish facts from falsehoods, understand what is essential and what isn't, and make the right choices.

Thoughtful thinkers find creative solutions to situations where others see only problems. They spot flaws in decisions and arguments others accept without the slightest protest. They make well-informed decisions based on data and not just feelings. They can sift through lots of data and find what's relevant. All this gives them an enormous advantage over others. It is very difficult to walk over or manipulate a thoughtful person.

Introverts are usually rather good critical thinkers. Because of our tendency not to rush into action but instead first analyze a situation and carefully think it through, we can tap this strength to our advantage. Not rushing into action and instead thinking things through can slow you down initially but will pay a dividend in the long run. Thoughtfulness is not only about the way we think about the world, but also about what we say. We don't talk much, but when we do, we mean what we say.

This has obvious implications for your career. By being thoughtful, you are more likely to find solutions to problems where others fail. You don't jump to conclusions, and you exhibit better judgment. Therefore, you are seen as someone who should be listened to. Your boss may learn to rely on your analysis of problems and actively ask your opinion, increasing your chances of more autonomy, bigger responsibilities, and a faster career progression.

I'm a man of very few words, but when my curiosity or passion for a topic is engaged, you won't be able to shut me up. I have met many managers and leaders who have gotten positive feedback and love from their followers for this particular strength—the ability to listen and then have a deep conversation about the topic in question. Introverts are often able to focus, sometimes even with a single-minded purpose, on a single activity. And the same applies to conversations.

This thoughtfulness and focus then translates to interest in getting to the root cause of a problem or a key topic in the discussion. The fact that you don't just glide over the matter and move on but truly dig deep is a considerable advantage when leading others and solving problems. It taps two main areas. It creates a feeling in the other person that you are interested and that you care. More trust is built, leading to more information shared and deeper and more honest conversation.

Together with empathy, the thoughtfulness and focus help you connect on a more personal, emotional level, leading to better relationships. When you are on a path toward a career in management, keep this in mind. Leaders should be fast and decisive, but more importantly, they shouldn't be reckless and chaotic. Thoughtful leaders are more likely to develop successful strategies and rally people to execute them. Thoughtfulness will make you a better leader.

Sometimes you are not given the opportunity to think. The person you are talking to is talking fast, pushing for answers, and needs them now. Don't let them pressure you into doing or saying something you are not comfortable with. You have the right to think. If someone wants an answer right away, then tell them no. It is always easier to change no to yes than the other way around. If someone pressures you to do something because they need it, keep in mind that it is their pressure, not yours, unless you make it yours. You have the right to get more information before making decisions. You have the right to remain silent.

However, it is also our tendency not to speak up that often makes this worthless. What's the point of coming up with a solution when you won't share it with others? Doing so only guarantees it won't get implemented.

To improve thoughtfulness and critical thinking, focus on three things. First, don't make assumptions. Every time you make assumptions or hear others making them, stop and think about it. What data support the assumptions? What other explanations are there? Where is the information coming from, and how reliable is the source? Second, use logic to avoid simplistic explanations. We like to simplify the complex world around us, but there is a difference between finding a *simple* explanation and finding a *simplistic* one. Learn to question cause and effect situations and don't force correlation when there is none to be found. Just because birds start singing at sunrise doesn't mean they woke up the sun and caused it to rise. Third, learn to recognize cognitive biases. We are all prone to unconsciously select information and points of view that support our own beliefs. A wide variety of cognitive biases are at play here. Learn about them so you can identify when you are a victim of your own beliefs. Learn to listen to people with diverse opinions and try to understand their points of view. All this will help you be more thoughtful in your deliberations.

The overuse of thoughtfulness manifests itself as overthinking. Introverts tend to analyze how we interact with others and find meaning in things that have none. We tend to overthink and overanalyze. And it holds us back.

Overanalyzing can lead to indecisiveness, to continuing to gather data instead of just making a decision and moving on. Just consider this example: Your washing machine just broke down, and you need to buy a new one. There are two approaches you can take. The first one is to jump into a car and drive to a nearby store with five washing machines. You look at them, check the prices, talk to the store attendant about their features, and quickly mentally compare whether they satisfy the criteria of how you want to use your washing machine. In the end, you pick the one you like and drive home with it. The second approach is to do detailed research into all the washing machines on the market and all their features. You end up with a list of fifty different models and compare twenty features, even though you know you will be using only two or three of the features. After a couple of days of research, you shortlist ten that are more or less the same. Each of them is a bit better in different areas, but they are very comparable and a similar price. And you are in a deadlock. You have so much data that you can't make up your mind. You worry that you will make the wrong choice. You are suffering from decision fatigue, so over-prepared that you can't get it done. And the pile of dirty clothes is growing.

Overanalyzing also leads to finding meaning where none exists. You make assumptions based on something other people did or said and construct a whole world around that assumption. And you even worry about what they said and why, while in reality, the person who made the comment didn't mean anything and already forgot about it. Because of overthinking, introverts are hardwired to worry much more than extroverts. It keeps us grounded with all its advantages and disadvantages.

Prudence

This is one of the characteristics that has its advantages as well as disadvantages. Prudence, or aversion to risk-taking, is a valuable strength to have, but it can also backfire when you are not willing to take any risks at all.

Extroverts often seek more thrill than introverts do and are more sensitive to external rewards. This then leads them to take unnecessary risks and make unsound business decisions. Introverts tend to be more measured, "think twice before cutting once" types of people, and are seen as more level-headed when it comes to leadership. A typical introvert will think about all the data before making a conclusion and taking action. A typical extrovert will just get going. Both approaches have their merits.

Prudence is a significant advantage when dealing with limited resources—be it finances, people, or time—and when the consequences of bad decisions can be disastrous. Every now and then, you hear about someone who made it big because they bet all their fortunes on one card and it paid off, but that is not a solid business strategy, that is a gamble. Yes, they may have been lucky, but that doesn't mean that they did the smart thing. It could as easily have turned the other way. They could have been bankrupted, and you would have never heard their name.

In the majority of business situations, gambling is not a smart strategy and can hurt your career. Use prudence as your strength and be very deliberate in your actions and decisions. Prudence and thoughtfulness will help you avoid costly mistakes. Whether you are in finance, project management, sales, IT, or any other field, prudent decisions have a much higher chance of leading to success, reflecting positively on you, and improving your career prospects. Use prudence to underpromise and overdeliver rather than the other way around. Don't promise more than you can realistically do. That's just gambling.

In most business decisions, prudence is preferred to risk-taking. That doesn't mean you never take any risks. You do, but you should be very deliberate on what risks to take. You take calculated risks. This is very similar to how you deal with your own money and what investments you make. A well-thought-out investment strategy will result in a portfolio of investment products that range from stable low yield investments to riskier ones with a potentially bigger windfall.

To become more prudent, focus on what you already know for sure. Use critical thinking and don't make assumptions. This requires a level of introspection and self-awareness. Before saying or doing anything, consider the people you talk to, the context, the actual content of what you are about to say or do, and the likely consequences. Consider asking yourself some of these questions. Is it appropriate in this context? Am I allowed to do this? Is it moral, ethical, and legal? Has this person asked for my opinion, advice, or help? Do I have all the facts? Do I know the other side of the argument? What might happen if I say or do this? To build prudence, start with the way you think about the world and what you say. You will then naturally act with prudence.

Overuse of prudence can lead to missed opportunities and to not taking actions when one should. If you are too careful, waiting to get yet another piece of data, talk to one more person, or get one more confirmation that you made the right decision, someone else may just jump in and take your opportunity from you.

If this happens, then your reaction will likely then come in the form of anger at the other person or regret that you should have moved faster. Regret is a powerful emotion. It is more likely you will regret action not taken than something you have done. You need to learn to find the right balance between risk-taking and playing it safe. Alternately, you can identify the type of opportunities and events that may require a risk-taker and put someone else in charge of these while you focus on those where prudence will be advantageous.

How do you measure the amount of risk? It is always a bit of an art, but you can look at it from two perspectives. What will happen when you fail? And how likely is it that you fail? If the potential consequence is small and it's not very likely, then just go for it. If the likelihood of failure increases or the negative consequences have a more meaningful impact on your business, then a bit of prudence is of considerable benefit.

Loyalty

Loyalty is an underappreciated strength. Managers often invoke it in a negative context when they feel betrayed by someone who does something they don't like, regardless of whether it was a sound decision by the culprit or whether it was a true betrayal and backstabbing. There are also those managers who reward loyalty, meaning blind obedience, with more money, better tasks, or promotions, regardless of whether the person in question has the qualifications and deserves it or not. That is not what I'm talking about.

What does true loyalty mean in a broader context, and why is it a significant strength? Why do introverts tend to be more loyal to their bosses, teams, and companies? *Collins English Dictionary* defines loyalty as "the quality of staying firm in your friendship or support for someone or something."[27]

If translated and expanded to the corporate world, this means that if you are loyal to your company, team, or boss, you will stick with them through both good and bad times. You will stay with them even when things don't go as planned. You will support them through highs and lows until the team finds ultimate success.

People with low levels of loyalty will jump ship the moment the going gets tough. They will care about themselves first and foremost and not about the greater good of the team. Disloyal people may not necessarily be bad. They are just not as reliable as loyal ones.

The same goes for leadership. Who would you prefer to work with? A loyal leader is someone who cares for their team. They will always have the team's back. They will fight for what is right and for the good of the team. A disloyal leader will first take care of their needs before considering the team. They will be the first to quit when things go wrong and will leave the team behind to fix the mess.

Being loyal is an essential trait for building lasting relationships, in turn, is vital for influencing the world around you. Loyal people are more trustworthy and worthy of following.

Even though you may often hear that employees are loyal to their companies, this is not entirely true. Human beings are, above all else, loyal to other human beings. They are loyal to their teams, to their colleagues. There are situations in which someone would be loyal to a brand, but in work settings, loyalty is most often about other people.

That is when the introvert's advantage kicks in. Because introverts generally don't need to have tons of friends around them, we tend to treasure those we have. It is a lot of work to connect with another individual, communicate at a deeper level, and let them know us. That means that once we go through this process, we will do our best to preserve the relationships we've formed. Because our circles of friends are smaller, we are more loyal to them. The same goes for our relationships in the corporate world. Once we get comfortable with the people around us, we do our best to maintain those circles. We care about the other people on our teams and are willing to go above and beyond our job descriptions to make our teams successful. We are often the invisible glue that helps to smooth friction within our groups and keep everyone focused in times of crisis.

To learn how to cultivate loyalty in yourself, start with your values. By understanding what your values are and what is important to you, you can start being loyal to yourself. You know what behavior is okay with you and what you would never tolerate. Then look outside. Mapping your own values to the values of your boss, your team, or your company makes it easy to find commonalities. Then their values become shared values. You are more likely to stay loyal in this case, as you will feel like part of the tribe. For example, if treating people with respect is important to you, if that's who you are, you can look at whether that is also true for the company you work for and for your boss. If you discover that that it is indeed the case and you see it in practice daily, you will feel more at home and will be more loyal to your organization due to this awareness.

I already talked about humility. Loyalty builds on that. Loyalty requires a certain degree of humility and willingness to put others in front of our own needs in difficult times. To increase your loyalty, you need to trust others, recognize the value they bring to your life, and make working on your relationships with them one of your priorities.

As with other strengths, there are dangers associated with an excess of loyalty. What does the overuse of loyalty look like? There are two most common situations when loyalty backfires.

Loyalty sometimes leads to putting your job before your career. You need to take care of the job that needs to get done in the moment before you can start thinking about the future. With too much loyalty, you often stay in your job for too long even when you aren't learning anything new, your impact is diminishing, and your career is plateauing. It is often risk-aversion and loyalty to a company, manager, or team that keeps you on the job. And your career suffers. Being a team player, caring about your company, and being loyal is undoubtedly good, but a bit of healthy self-interest is important too. If you find that you are essentially being taken advantage of for being loyal, it is time to move.

Another problem is when you are loyal and closely connected to someone who abuses that loyalty. Fool me once, shame on you; fool me twice, shame on me. It might be a cliché, but there is something to it. Loyal doesn't mean being gullible or being a pushover. If people repeatedly abuse your loyalty, they don't deserve it. That abuse may take different shapes, and some of them are not very apparent. Just consider working consistently above what can be reasonably expected and not getting a single thank you. That is an abuse of loyalty. Or, even worse, so is offering help and then being exploited by being given more and more work while the person you are helping slacks. They don't deserve your loyalty, and you shouldn't extend it. Don't forget to be loyal to yourself as well as to others.

It is acceptable to be selfish every now and then to make sure you are fine and are not being dragged down by others. This also means being loyal to who you are. You may feel the need to act like an extrovert from time to time, but constantly living a fake persona because you think the world around you expects that and you want to be loyal to them means you are not being loyal to yourself and your needs.

Humility

Another strength of introverts is being able to put your ego aside. Because we live in our own worlds and are not as dependent on acceptance and praise from others, we also don't need to push our way on others and make everything about ourselves. We may sometimes hurt a bit inside when our work is not recognized; ultimately, though, we do the right thing and won't let the need to take credit compromise the way we interact with others.

Humility comes from self-reflection and realizing that we are not perfect. By knowing our strengths and weaknesses, we are more grounded, and we know there is always something we can learn.

When you think about it, you can easily see the advantages introverts gain by being more humble. If you push your ego aside, you are more open to the opinions of others. You don't need to be the smartest person in the room. That generates engagement from others on the team, promoting sharing opinions and creativity. When you are humble, you are better equipped to listen to and digest feedback. That means you are removing any blind spots you might have and building a more realistic view of your abilities. Because you aren't worrying about your ego, you are more likely to admit a mistake and learn from it. And because you don't need to feed your ego by taking credit for everything, you are more likely to allow others to shine. You share the credit and the rewards for a job well done. All these things help you be successful at your job and become a great leader.

You should always see humility as a strength and not an excuse for poor self-image. You are humble because you want to be. It is the right thing to do. You are not humble because you don't know how to ask for what you need. Humility works well only when paired with healthy self-confidence and assertiveness, which help you to be humble while asking for what you need at the same time.

Humility has a positive impact on your career as it makes you easy to work with. People don't like working with arrogant jerks. We all want to work with selfless and humble colleagues who are willing to help us succeed. And then we are eager to reciprocate. When you are humble, you may not be the most visible person on the planet, but everyone will want to have you on their team. In *The Ideal Team Player*, Patrick Lencioni notes that when building a culture that values teamwork, you want people who work hard, are good with people, and don't put their egos above everything else. Lencioni suggests that you hire hungry, humble, and people-smart employees.[28] Humility is critical for any organization trying to build a team where people care for and help each other. Therefore, humility is an excellent trait for any employee to have and is critical to your long-term career success.

Of course, being too humble has its problems. Overuse of humility manifests itself in various negative ways. The most frequent ones are lack of confidence, reluctance to claim your achievements, becoming invisible, becoming a doormat, and being completely ignored.

Reluctance to claim your achievements is based on humility and willingness to give credit to others. It is okay to give credit to others, but you shouldn't overdo it. Learn to promote your achievements effectively. Otherwise, you may never get the opportunity to achieve your full potential.

Becoming invisible by staying in the shadows and never speaking up is a classic problem introverts tackle. Your teammates may like you when you are sitting in the corner throwing out ideas, working hard, and never asking for anything. The problem is that you may never be recognized for your achievements. You are being too humble, hoping that your boss will recognize you and reward you appropriately. Unfortunately, the world doesn't always work that way. It is your responsibility to raise your hand and ask for what is due to you.

Becoming a doormat is closely related to the previous item. It is the next stage. Not only are you not being recognized, but others are abusing you. They exploit your talent and your humility to their advantage. Ultimately, you will feel drained, disillusioned, and angry with the world.

All these come together into being ignored. If you are too humble, you can end up with no credibility and with people simply ignoring your input or you personally. It doesn't matter what you know or can do. By overplaying humility, you make yourself obsolete and irrelevant.

To fight your invisibility problem so your career doesn't suffer, you have several options. You can simply claim credit for the work you did by clearly stating it. "I did this" is very straightforward but also very unnatural to introverts. I personally never do this, as it makes me feel petty and not in line with my sense of humility. A better approach is to strongly hint that it was you who came up with the idea. "I agree with Peter's suggestion. That's why I originally proposed we move in this direction." Even better is to take ownership of the activity. "I agree with Peter. Let me take the lead on the initiative." Lastly, you can find a third party to talk you up. This is where building alliances is vital, and I will talk about this in later chapters. There is no better way to claim credit for your work than to have someone with higher status remind everyone that it was you who did the work. This might often be your boss or a vocal colleague who knows that you did the work and mentions it to others. This may feel a bit awkward, but don't be afraid to give them a hint that getting credit would be appreciated. In my time in various leadership roles, I would often ask those on my team to talk to me if they felt they were not getting the credit they deserved and if they wanted me to speak on their behalf and provide them with recognition. It may sound sad, but the reality is that the bigger a team the manager has, the less likely it is that they see all the great work done by every member of that team. There is nothing wrong with bringing that work to their attention. You are not asking for something you don't deserve. You are asking for recognition for a job well done. Do this with humility, and your career will thank you.

Independence

One of the biggest strengths introverts have is the ability to work alone. This may sound a bit counterintuitive in today's world obsessed with teamwork, but the actual work is done by individuals. It is, of course, beneficial to be able to ask for help or share ideas, but ultimately the ability to focus, work on your own, deal with roadblocks, and just get things done without relying on constant input from others is a huge advantage that separates the best from the mediocre.

This then comes into the spotlight when you get to a leadership role. You need to be able to make decisions with limited information. You need to be able to make tough decisions. You need to be able to stand by your decisions and be accountable for the results. This creates a lot of pressure on any individual. Being comfortable with taking the stand and often being alone is a must.

Being clear on our core values and living by our principles makes us more independent. It may sometimes leave us standing alone against the world, and that is fine. We can find the strength to do that in our inner worlds and don't need a big support group to gather courage and do what is right. This is critically important when leading others. As a leader, you need to have a strong moral compass and always be willing to do what is right and not what others want or what would make you popular.

Independence doesn't mean individualism. Individualism is about doing your own thing without regard for others. Individualists promote pursuing one's goals and desires. They believe that the interests of the individual should take precedence over the state or a social group. They achieve their goals through independence and self-reliance. Independence means you are self-sufficient but doesn't automatically mean that you value your needs more than those of people within your social circles, like your family and friends. Independence puts you in a position to help others who may rely on you. For introverts, it is important not to stand out but rather to blend in, to ensure a harmonious interdependence in one's group even at one's own expense.

Overuse of independence can sometimes go against the need to collaborate with others. It is great to work alone and figure out problems on your own, but there is a clear line when it goes against efficiency and effectiveness. Why should you waste hours trying to solve a problem that your teammate on another project already solved? Wouldn't it make greater sense just to ask for guidance? Even worse is not communicating about what you are doing, so people find themselves working in parallel on the same problems. Independence is a strength that only works when combined with transparency and a culture of sharing and helping each other.

Independence holds you back when you believe that you should first work hard to get a job done on your own and ask for help only when you can't manage. Learn to reach out to others as quickly as possible. Knowing the people in your organization who can help you succeed in your job and asking for their help early on can significantly accelerate your career.

The rule of thumb is to reach out when you know that the problem you are working on will take you a long time to solve, while someone else can do it in the nick of time without much effort. The important thing is to use this as a learning opportunity. When asking for help in these situations, make sure you do the work under the guidance of the person you are asking, rather than letting them do the work while you get a cup of coffee. That would be a lost opportunity to learn, and it would make the person helping you feel used.

Connecting with others will lead to more visibility, more support, better results, less work, and a feeling of belonging. Try to find a mentor and build a strong network of allies. That, in turn, will attract potential sponsors who will act as your fans and advocates within your organization.

Summary and Key Takeaways

Using your strengths is the easiest path to career success. You are not starting from scratch. You are not trying to be someone you are not. You are simply using your introverted nature to your advantage. Using your strengths is inherently motivating and energizing. It comes naturally, and it feels good. It feels like you are good at something. It flows. Learn to use your strengths as much as possible without over-relying on any one in particular. Your strengths are your superpowers. But as Uncle Ben of the Spider-Man franchise would tell you, "With great power comes great responsibility."

- When leading proactive and creative people, introverts are more effective than extroverts.
- The ultimate twelve strengths many introverts have can be split into four categories:

  » Awareness: Introspection, Empathy, Attentiveness
  » Achievement Orientation: Preparation, Focus, Perseverance
  » Conflict Prevention: Prudence, Thoughtfulness, Calm
  » Personal Leadership: Independence, Humility, Loyalty

- People who use their strengths are happier, experience less stress, feel healthier, have more energy, and feel more satisfied with their lives than people who don't. They are also more confident, experience faster growth and development, are more creative and agile, and experience more meaning in their work.
- Overuse of your strengths can make you dependent on a very narrow set of tools. It can make you obnoxious and unlikable and can derail your career. Learn to use the appropriate strength at the appropriate time.

Questions and Next Steps

- I would encourage you to think deeply about each of the strengths I presented in this chapter. For each, consider to what extent it is also your strength. Since we are all different, not all of them might be your superpowers, but the chances are that many of them are.
- For those strengths I listed that you don't think apply to you, consider why not. Could it be that they are simply neglected? Could it be that you never really

thought about them as your strengths but you are still pretty good at them? If yes, consider using some of the strategies I suggested to build those potential strengths up so you can use them to your advantage when building your career.

- Do you have other strengths I haven't mentioned? What are they? How can they help you to have a successful career? How can you build them up even more? What do you need to be careful about so you don't overuse them?

● **3**

What Is Important to You?

Before we dive into figuring out what your career should look like, it is essential to understand who you are and what is important to you. We talked about you being an introvert and what that means. But what about you being a daughter or a son, husband or wife, friend, relative, neighbor, teacher, worker, manager, or whatever else your role at work and in society can be? You have various roles, and you need to understand which of them are important to you. You can't ignore them just for the sake of your career, and it is not advisable to fixate on just one of them, to put all your eggs into one basket, so to speak.

Then you have a personality that is a combination of characteristics, qualities, and traits. It shows in patterns of thinking and behaving. It is what makes you unique. However, your personality shouldn't be a driving force when you are looking for a job. For example, just because someone says that introverts are not suited to a particular job or career doesn't make it true.

Who you are is not only defined by your roles and personality but also by your core values. Your core values are so deeply ingrained in your psyche that they drive your behavior, even at the subconscious level. You may not be aware of what your core values are, but they guide your decisions anyway. When you make a decision that clashes with these values, you feel that something is not right. You are not happy with your life even if, at first glance, you should be.

Passions are the things and activities you are enthusiastic about and that fill you with excitement. They often involve strong feelings and a desire to spend as much time as possible working on them. They are the things you live for. They might be your hobbies, but ideally, they should be what you do for a living, as that will increase your chances for a successful career. Understanding what your passions are is therefore pretty important. Equally important is finding out that maybe you don't have any passions, which is still fine as it leaves the door wide open to build some.

Understanding your roles, personality, core values, passions, and simply knowing who you are is important for living a satisfying life and having a successful career. You need to have a holistic view of your life and make sure that all the parts of your life work together, as they influence each other. If you have a family, consider your reactions when you come home after a particularly unsuccessful day full of bad interactions with your boss. You will be irritated and no fun. Your family will be impacted. You will be failing in your role as a parent and spouse. Or consider how satisfied you would be working for a gun producer while being a passionate anti-gun activist and having "do no harm" as one of your core values.

We introverts like to think about and overanalyze everything in our lives. This chapter will help you to do that in an organized manner so you can get something useful out of it. The work you do here will be helpful in later chapters when we talk about your career options and your "Sweet Spot."

Roles

Who are you? It's a simple question with a very complicated answer. You are a human. You are a son or a daughter, a husband or a wife, a father or a mother, a student, a teacher, a neighbor, a customer, an accountant, a manager. You may have several different roles that you play in your life, several different personas. Each of them contributes to who you are. Some of them are applicable only for some phases of your life. Some of them are more lasting. To be completely satisfied with your life, you need to be satisfied with what you do in each of your roles.

If you ignore one of the roles, it doesn't go away. It is still there, and it may unconsciously prevent you from being happy in your other roles. If you, for example, define yourself only as a manager and ignore that you are also a spouse, you are creating an imbalance. If you put all your energy and effort into one of your roles, it may bring you more success and satisfaction in the moment, but the other parts of your life will suffer.

I'm a believer in work-life integration rather than work-life balance. Work-life integration means that you stop looking at your work as a necessary evil to support the rest of your life. You only have one life, and work is part of it, so get the most out of it. You spend most of your waking hours at work, so it is nonsensical not to consider it part of your life. The phrase "work-life balance" feels too much like it implies that work is not part of life. It is. It is one aspect tightly integrated with all the other elements. Identifying the individual roles you play is not about trying to say that each of them needs to be allocated an equal amount of hours in each day. It is about making sure that they are integrated and support each other.

Let's imagine that you are a parent who wants to raise healthy kids. You are also a manager at a tobacco company. You are making money by creating a product that causes health issues. You are using this money to raise healthy kids—kids who one day start buying the products your company is making. You can try to balance these things, but there is dissonance. Isn't it better to try to integrate these two roles? What about being a manager in a company that promotes a healthy lifestyle? This persona blends nicely with the persona responsible for raising healthy kids. I understand that this is a bit oversimplified, and I don't want to vilify anyone, but it is a point worth making. All your roles, all your personas, all your goals need to be in balance. There needs to be ecology. Your roles, personas, and goals need to support each other, and they need to be aligned with your core values.

Personality

We talked about your introversion, but you have many other personality traits that define who you are. Even your introversion shouldn't be the defining factor when you try to find a job that will fit you. The moment you select a job only based on your personality or what you believe your personality is, you are drastically decreasing the available job pool.

What's worse is that you might have a self-limiting belief that some jobs are not for you. The typical example would be an introvert who decides not to apply for a managerial position because "I don't have the right personality to be a manager." Says who? There are all sorts of managers with a wide range of personalities, and many introverts make great managers and leaders. Just because you've read somewhere that a particular personality is not a good fit for a job doesn't mean you should give up on it if you feel that you would genuinely enjoy the work and be good at it.

Introverts are, by nature, less likely to crave leadership positions and top spots in their companies. We get swept into these roles because of our passion and commitment to what we are doing. We become leaders in spite of ourselves. However, this doesn't mean we don't make great leaders. The opposite is true.

Adam M. Grant, Francesca Gino, and David A. Hofmann found somewhat surprising results in a study about introversion and leadership. While extroverts are more successful when leading passive employees, when it comes to leading proactive ones, they struggle. When leading proactive and creative people, introverts are much more effective. Based on the study, extroverted leaders failed to listen to ideas, and there was more in-team fighting for power and recognition on extrovert-led teams than on the teams led by introverts. Studies like this show that extroverts don't always have the advantage. The universe is in balance, and introverts have traits that give us a considerable advantage when leading others.[29]

For modern leaders in a knowledge-based economy, the old dictatorial approach doesn't cut it anymore. Leadership is about rallying the forces by tapping their intrinsic motivation, giving them autonomy and purpose, and letting them be the best they can be. You do this through listening, empathy, thoughtfulness, and humility. As it turns out, these are all strengths most introverts have. In fact, I would imagine you have many strengths that can help you have a successful career. But why talk about strengths in the first place?

Based on the data analyzed by Marcus Buckingham and Ashley Goodall in their book *Nine Lies About Work*, there is one particular condition that high-performing teams have in common: members of these teams can say that they have a chance to use their strengths every day at work. Regardless of what your team is doing, it will be at its most productive when most of the team members can say the same.[30] Using your strengths at work will not only feel good, allowing you to be authentic, but it will also help you be good at your job and therefore give you a higher chance for a successful career. In this chapter, I will walk you through some of the strengths most introverts have and help you identify how to use them in your job. You are a complex and unique individual, and boxing your identity into a narrow category and then using it to pick a job significantly limits your career options—and without good reason. There is very little scientific evidence that personality and personality tests are predictive of actual job performance, both for individual contributors and for management roles. I've been asked several times throughout my life to take various personality tests, and I've gone through assessment centers. Sometimes I even got something out of it, some insight that helped me focus on a particular area I needed to improve, but none of them ever gave me the answer to the question of who I am and what job is best suited for me. Life is too complicated to be analyzed with a couple of questions. In fact, over the years, there have been a number of works done on how to influence personality tests to get the results you want. Some even suggest that you cheat when an organization asks you to take a test so that you can get the results that you expect the organization wants you to. In *The Organization Man*'s appendix, "How to Cheat on Personality Tests," William H. Whyte notes that these tests are often loyalty tests that value if you conform and you come out the same as the rest of the organization.[31]

The fiction of personality tests is a convenient way to sort people and slot them into appropriate jobs so that people believe it is their destiny to be where they are; therefore the tests help to retain a high-functioning and productive social order. Don't let personality tests drive your future!

Core Values

But if not personality tests, what should drive your decisions? What about your core values?

What are core values, you ask? Core values are a set of fundamental beliefs held by a person or an organization. They define the person and answer the question, "Who am I, and what is important to me?"

Core values are the North Star that will guide you in times of change. Your life circumstances may change, the environment around you may evolve, but your core values are more or less stable. They help guide you about what is right and what is wrong, they help influence your day-to-day decisions, and they set basic rules about how you work and interact with others.

How do you find your core values? You need to dive deep into yourself to find out. The best way would be with the help of a life coach, but alternatively, you can use one of these simple approaches to get started. Find yourself a quiet and relaxing place where you can think. Answer these questions, and don't let the first obvious answer stop you. Always dig deeper and try to understand "why."

The Animal Exercise

Let's imagine you could transform into any animal. Which one would it be? Now, close your eyes and imagine that you are that animal. Why? What does it bring you? How do you feel? Why is it important to you? What environment are you in? What actions do you take? What skills do you use? What values govern your life?

I was once asked this question in an interview: "If you were an animal, what would you be?"

I didn't even give it a second thought and answered, "A turtle."

As expected, follow-up questions came. "Why?"

"Well, I would love to have the freedom of the turtle swimming in the ocean, exploring places, not rushing anywhere while having a shell that protects me from predators." Later, when I came home, I thought about my answer a bit more, and, like a good introvert, I overanalyzed it to death. I realized that even though it was an honest answer, it wasn't complete. I have liked turtles since childhood, but I have only genuinely loved them since I got into the corporate world and started to identify myself as an introverted person. In my mind, turtles have the freedom to majestically glide through oceans while being safe in their shells. What impresses me the most is that they appear to think carefully before deciding to do something. They are in no rush. They are very deliberate in everything. They don't flock or herd but spend lots of alone time swimming in the ocean, exploring the world. They have a safe place to stay with them all the time. If a turtle has had enough of the world, it can hide in its shell, but it also dares to explore the world! All in all, it is an imposing animal, for an introvert. This exercise helped me understand what some of my priorities are and who I am inside.

The key is to keep asking the why questions and consider various aspects of the animal's life to see which one attracted you to them. For example, I heard one introvert strongly identify with giraffes. When I asked why, she said that it was because she is very tall, like a giraffe. However, when we talked about it more and asked more why questions, she realized that it is the majestic way these animals move that she was attracted to. She was very self-conscious about her height and deep inside envied giraffes for how well they manage it. This exercise is all about metaphors. Therefore, you need to peel off several layers to get to the real reason for your choice.

This exercise can give you all the answers you need about your core values. However, on its own, it didn't help me personally to discover everything important to me, either due to the limitations of the animal kingdom or of my own imagination. Some of my core values are to being useful, helping others, and living a meaningful life. These were uncovered through the Peak Moments Exercise.

The Peak Moments Exercise

Pick a couple of moments from your life where you felt great and happy. Get back to each moment and feel it. Why was it so special? Where were you? What did you do? Why did you do it? Who were you with? Consider all these moments and ask yourself: What were the common values in all these peak moments of your life? Why do you consider them the best?

I did this exercise with one coaching client who we'll call Jeff. Jeff was a financial manager for a nonprofit organization and was struggling with getting satisfaction in his life. He felt that even though he worked for a nonprofit that helps other people, his own life was meaningless and empty. When he listed some of his peak moments when he felt happy and satisfied with his work, we realized that all of them had one thing in common: they had nothing to do with finance but instead involved him interacting with people and negotiating complex agreements. The satisfaction he felt when closing a deal was something that he never felt in his finance role. The next steps were to find out how he could get more involved with business development and even sales.

Similar to the previous exercise, it is all about asking the why questions and not being satisfied with just the first answer that pops up. I would also suggest that you think of at least three peak moments to consider, if not more, to be able to search for commonalities.

The Remote Island Exercise

Let me introduce one more exercise to help you discover your core values. Imagine you get stranded on a remote tropical island. What three friends would you take with you? And why these three in particular? What qualities do they have? Why are they so special to you? What values should the best friend have? What three things would you take? What three books or movies? And always ask why these books, why these movies. What do they have in common that makes you like them? What values do they represent?

These three approaches should be enough to get you on the right path of self-discovery. Select the exercise that you feel would work for you. Don't rush it. Try to find the values behind the values. Don't let the first obvious answer stop you.

For example, when you look at the last exercise, you may be tempted to say that you would take physical, material things with you. If you say you would take a credit card loaded with money and the answer to "Why?" is "So I can buy stuff," don't stop there. Dig deeper and examine what kind of stuff you would buy and why you would want to buy it. What would buying it bring you? Maybe you discover that your wish to bring a credit card is not about buying stuff, but that some more profound value manifests this way. Most of us pursue the acquisition of material possessions not so we have them, but so we feel important and secure. We want to be respected, want freedom, and want to provide for our kids. Many potential reasons point directly to your core values, so don't get satisfied with the first answers. Keep asking, "Why?" until there is nothing more to dig out. If the answer to your last "Why?" is, "I don't know, it just feels that way," you know you have found one of your core values.

Passions

Your core values are often reflected in your passions. "Follow your dreams." "Do what you are passionate about." Have you ever heard advice like this? Have you ever tried to follow that advice? And have you ever seen someone who followed that advice fail miserably?

Do you have friends who are happy at their jobs? If you are one of the lucky ones and *you* are happy, have you ever analyzed why you are happy at your job while others around you, doing the same work, complain? Let me give you some answers and some more questions to think about.

Cal Newport provides a somewhat controversial view of what makes people happy at work. He proposes a rather useful way to look at your career choices. He says it's not about passion. It is about mastery.[32]

Being passionate about something sounds like the best place to start when you are looking for a job. But frankly, what are the things you are passionate about, and how many of them have any relation to a potential job at all? You might be passionate about collecting stamps, fishing, walking in a forest, and observing nature. All these things sound great, but you might be hard-pressed to find a job where someone would be willing to pay for those passions. If no one is willing to reward your enthusiasm, you don't really have a job that can cover your basic needs—you have a hobby.

Another thing to consider is that, based on research mentioned in Daniel Pink's work, you will find that when you start rewarding people for something that used to be a hobby for them, they may lose the passion for it. Their intrinsic motivation goes away as the external motivation—in this case, someone paying them to do what they once did for fun—increases.[33]

So if no one is willing to pay for your passion, then what do you do? Well, you need to start doing something that people are willing to pay for. You do what you are good at. And the chances are that the better you are, the more value you bring, the more others are willing to pay in return. Passion comes later.

This is, of course, rather tricky. Not only do you need to figure out what you are good at, but you also need some competitive advantage. Understanding the broader field you selected for your career is the essential first step. For example, there are different ways to become a great manager. Depending on your personality and your skills, you can have a style more focused on numbers and metrics, you can be more focused on hard skills to get things done, or you can be more on the empathetic side, mentoring and coaching others. Numerous strategies can help you to become a genuinely great manager, and you don't need to pursue all of them. Just pick the one for which you have a competitive advantage and relentlessly work on it to hone it to a level of ultimate mastery.

In the end, it is all about mastery. When you examine the causality relationship between passion and skill, you will discover that skill comes first. I urge you to consider some hobby you are passionate about. Take running, for instance. I have seen this time and time again with people who decided to do something for their health. Running seemed like a good idea to these people. Were they passionate about it? Not really. It was a dreary, painful, and not at all enjoyable experience. They ran a quarter-mile and felt tired, sore, miserable, out of breath. I wouldn't describe passion this way. But they persevered. With enough focus, energy, and routine, they were able to train their bodies to run longer and longer distances. They could see the improvements in their performance and their health, and that led to more enjoyment. That fueled even more effort and dedication. They became truly passionate about running. Why? Because they became good at it. It wasn't a tedious activity anymore—it became a gratifying experience, and they started to love it. It became a passion.

All humans have unlimited potential. At least, that is what I chose to believe when I decided to use coaching as my primary management style. However, most humans also have limits to what they are willing to sacrifice and how they measure greatness. We tend to do only as much as is needed, and very few of us are willing to go above and beyond. Maybe that is why so few people become genuinely great at what they do. Most of us will be only "okay." Once we get to a certain level of performance that is acceptable to others—and, more importantly, that satisfies us—we stop improving. We level off because we feel we are good enough. It is good enough to be good enough. This mindset has one big pitfall: good enough today may not be good enough tomorrow. Today's satisfaction with your performance and your job will turn to dissatisfaction, complaints about lack of advancement, and feeling that others are getting more opportunities than you are and that life is not fair.

So instead of endlessly jumping from job to job, from career to career, trying to find your passion, I would suggest that you focus on doing whatever work you do exceptionally well. By doing a great job, you will gain the respect of others, get more autonomy, and find more satisfaction from a job well done. All of this will feed back into the loop of excellence. In the end, people are passionate about things they are good at.

Life Balance Wheel

I talked about work-life integration earlier, so now let's dive deeper. To do that, let's use, embarrassingly, a tool that has "life balance" in its name. The Life Balance Wheel is a great way to sort out priorities in your life and realize what you don't pay attention to. The concept of the Life Balance Wheel or Wheel of Life was created by Paul J. Meyer, founder of Success Motivation Institute, Inc., and it is a widely used tool in the coaching community. The Life Balance Wheel provides a helicopter view of the most critical aspects of your life. It is not meant to solve all your problems but rather to help you ask the right questions and articulate what in your life is out of whack and needs to be fixed.

When I work with a new client in my coaching sessions, figuring out where to start is often a challenge. Sometimes the clients come with a clear idea about what they want to work on, but sometimes the problem is defined in more general terms, like, "I just want to feel happy," or "Something is missing from my life, and I'm not sure what."

This is the same reason why I want you to do a quick exercise. Before you spend too much time figuring out what is wrong with your job, let's make sure that your job is the problem you need to solve. The goal of this exercise is to identify areas of your life where you feel low levels of satisfaction. Your satisfaction level has nothing to do with how much time and effort you put into a specific area of your life. It is about whether you are happy with the outcome. You may have no money but still be pretty satisfied with the "money" area because you have your needs covered.

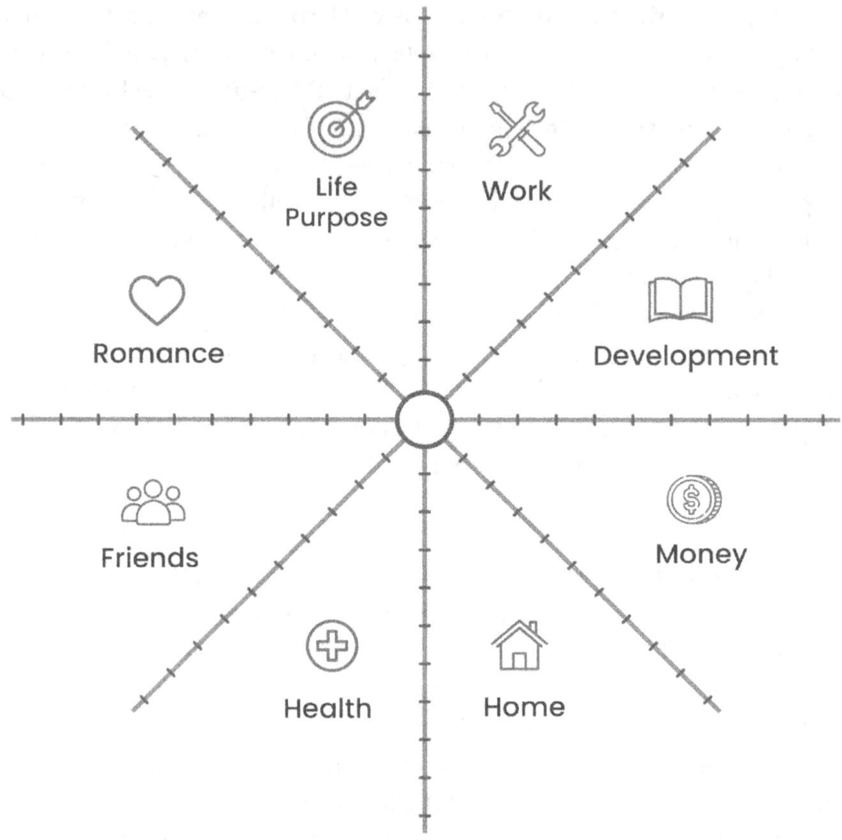

Figure 2: Life Balance Wheel

Steps to follow:

- Identify significant areas of your life—the most common are:

  » Work: anything related to your work, career, colleagues, boss
  » Development: professional and personal growth
  » Money: your income and your expenditures
  » Home: your family, parents, kids, free time, hobbies

» Health: your physical and mental condition
» Friends: your friends (past and present), social life
» Romance: your love, spouse, matters of the heart
» Life Purpose: your mission in life

- Draw a wheel. The most often used design is a simple pie chart with eight pieces as in Figure 2, but you can be more creative and add more sectors as needed depending on the number of areas you identified.
- Go through individual areas and ask yourself, "How satisfied am I with this part of my life?"
- Evaluate individual areas on a scale from one to ten, where one means "Unsatisfied" and ten means "Completely satisfied." Keep in mind that we don't talk about how much that particular activity is present in your life, but how satisfied you are with it.
- Connect the dots in the pie chart to show the areas of high and low satisfaction more visually.
- Take a moment to reflect on the picture and ask yourself:

  » What does this mean for me?
  » Does this bring up any realizations that I need to address?
  » What is most important for you?

Next, pick one area to work on. It is important to realize that this is a complex system. Change in one area will most likely affect the other areas too. For example, if you are low on "money" satisfaction and you decide to focus on increasing your income, it will most likely have a positive effect, and eventually, you will get more money and, hopefully, more satisfaction with that part of your life. However, your satisfaction with "home," "friends," "romance," or "health" may suffer as a result. So always consider all the aspects and work on things that have a synergetic effect on the others. Ideally, find something that, when increased, will also increase satisfaction in several other areas.

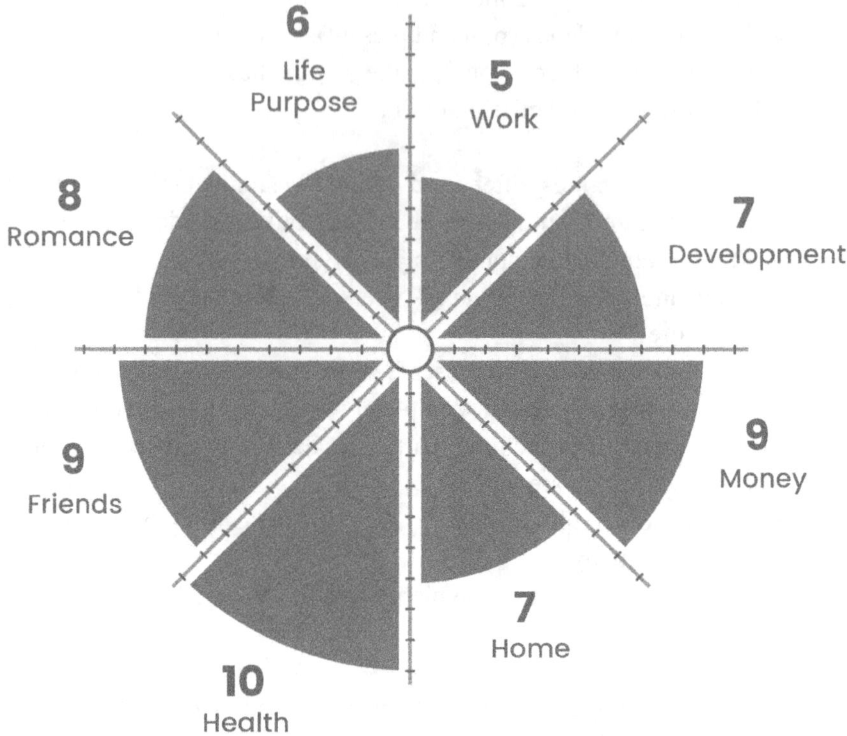

Figure 3: Example of Completed Life Balance Wheel

Once you identify the area to work on, you need to start asking more questions to figure out what specifically you can do to move the needle. Consider some of these questions:

- How satisfied are you with this part of your life?
- Are the activities you do in this area fulfilling?
- Think about this part of your life. How much energy are you prepared to put in (1–10)? If you are not willing to put much energy into this area, consider whether this is truly the area you really care about and should focus on.
- What could you do to have more satisfaction and fulfillment in this area?
- What could stop you from making it work? How would you recognize/ mitigate that?
- Who could help you to make it work?
- Who could remind you/help to keep you on track?

As you can see, once you start digging deeper and deeper, you may come up with realizations that things are not as bad as you thought. When done regularly and followed up with a couple of actions, this exercise can have an impact on how you see your life. Every time you do this exercise, draw a new wheel. It creates a new unbiased picture of your life as it is today. I would often use the Life Balance Wheel with clients I coach to create a before (at the beginning of our coaching relationship) and after picture (after several sessions working together) so they see the positive change they achieved and stay motivated going forward.

Logical Levels

If you don't like the Life Balance Wheel, you can try a tool called Logical Levels. It is a tool to help you structure your thinking about who you are, where you are in life, and what is important to you. The concept of logical levels of learning and change was initially formulated by anthropologist Gregory Bateson and later adopted by psychologist Robert B. Dilts as a way to think about personal transformation.[34]

The Logical Levels Exercise takes a holistic view of your life or, in this particular case, of your career. While the Life Balance Wheel focuses on various external roles you play and the different areas of your life, logical levels focus on how your external circumstances influence who you are and vice versa. It can be particularly powerful to realize ways out of being stuck in a job that doesn't work for you. You go up and down the logical levels pyramid and analyze how each step influences and builds upon the previous one.

You can use this model to define your purpose in life and what you need to change to focus on the right career to bring you the most satisfaction. This model is frequently used in Neuro-Linguistic Programming to explain how our thoughts and words shape everything around and inside us. I don't necessarily subscribe to the notion that logical levels are an all-powerful system. I consider logical levels to be a somewhat simplified way to look at a system as complex as human behavior. However, that doesn't change the fact that it is a helpful tool for analyzing where you are. I follow the Dilts model and add a level of "choices." Choices are a way we express our values and make them visible to the real world. This level helps to anchor the model in reality and helps with making the model more usable in everyday work.

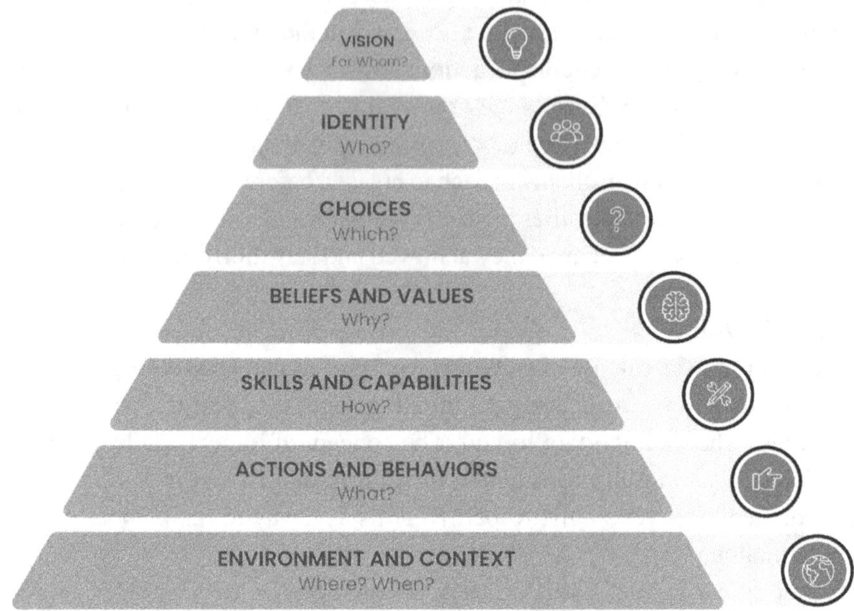

Figure 4: Logical Levels

The whole concept is depicted in Figure 4. I will first explain the individual steps of the logical levels pyramid and then follow up with a suggestion on how to use it. This exercise is a bit more tricky than the previous ones. It is often best done under the guidance of a professional coach, but you can give it a go on your own too.

Environment and Context: The bottom level of the pyramid describes your physical location. This is where you live, work, and spend most of your time. Where are you, and why? Why do you live in this city? Why do you work for this company? Why do you live in this particular house? What about the climate? Does it work for you? Why do you live in this country or this neighborhood? How does environment influence your life? How does the home you live in influence your work? How is the commute? What kind of environment works best for you at work? What kinds of people do you enjoy having around in the workplace? Where do you do your best work? Where do you gain support from? How does your working environment make you feel?

Understanding why you are in this particular environment is essential. It will tell you what the constraints related to the careers you can pick are. For example, if you need to live in a particular city because that is where your parents and friends are, they won't move, and they are important to you, you know that your job can't be an ocean liner captain.

The work you do is constrained by the environment that you want to live in. It can also be the other way around. You realize that you have no attachments to your environment, or even worse, that you don't want to be in your environment for various reasons. Well, if that is the case, you just significantly expanded the opportunities you may consider. Just be ready to move.

Actions and Behaviors: This level describes what steps you take to respond to the environment you live in. It is what you do day in and day out. What do you do? What profession have you chosen and why? What do you do in your free time and why? What made you do a particular thing? Do you get up every morning full of energy and ready to go to the office? Who are the people you spend your time with and why? Are you able to do the things that are important to you? How much time do you spend doing things that you don't want to do? What task do you perform that makes work fun and exciting? How does your behavior impact your goals?

The goal is to figure out how you spend your time, whether you do the things that are important to you with the people you want to be with. If not, identify the gaps and come up with a plan to address them.

Skills and Capabilities: This level is about the skills you possess and what made you develop them. Are you using the skills you have? What would you love to learn and why? Then look at the actions you want to take and identify the skills you are missing and why. How can you develop these skills? What do people who know you say you are good at? How do you know you are effective?

Consider also your attitude toward life. It is often not a lack of skills that holds you back, but rather the wrong attitude. As long as you are able to show passion and muster the energy, you can learn the skills and get the capabilities you need. If you have the will, you will get the skill.

Beliefs and Values: These are the things that give direction to your life. Often they work on the subconscious level. Surfacing them is helpful. They are the answer to your "why" questions. Why do you do what you do? Why is something important to you? Why do you behave or react to external stimuli in a certain way? What are the beliefs you have about your job? Are they helpful? What beliefs might help you get better results? What beliefs hold you back?

Once you know your values, then consider how they match the company you work for. Similarly, it is important to consider your values when applying for a new job. Beliefs and values are essential aspects of company culture. If a company's values are misaligned with your own, you will feel uneasy and won't easily fit in.

Just make sure you understand the real values of how the company operates and not just those they put on the website. In an ideal world, they should be the same; often, though, they are not. No one cares about proclaimed values. It is the real ones you experience every day that count. If you discover a misalignment, there are two ways to deal with it: Either you leave the company if the misalignment is so dramatic that in your heart, you know you can never be satisfied in a place with these values, or, going the less extreme way, you do your best to narrow the gap. This is the right thing to do when the proclaimed or aspirational values of the company are close to your own, but you see that the company doesn't live them. Well, guess what? The company is a group of people. If you can lead by example, live the values, and influence those around you, that example is going to spread, and the gap will get narrower and narrower. More importantly, you will be able to live your values. Even if the rest of the company may not be that diligent, you may still be able to do what you believe is right.

Choices: Choices are the way your beliefs and values manifest in the real world. It might be that your value is "helping others," but that by itself is not visible to the outside world. That is hidden in your inner self. Only by making choices like giving people a ride to the airport, sacrificing your afternoon to help your friend finish a presentation, and volunteering to help in the local community are you giving your beliefs a form that others will recognize. What choices do you make? Why have you decided to do a certain thing and not something else? What are you saying no to, and why? Are you happy with your choices?

The choices you make tell a lot about who you are and what you value. You may say a thousand times that you value being humble, but the fact that you chose to say it a thousand times clearly shows that you are not. Bragging that you are humble? That doesn't sound right! Go back to the drawing board and think again about what your actual values and beliefs are.

Identity: Your identity is not a summary of your actions and beliefs. You are much more than that. Your actions are often a reflection of your environment and not necessarily of your identity. What kind of person are you? What kind of person do you want to be? How do the people who know you describe you? What labels do you get? How do you want to be seen by the world? In what situations do you say, "This is me"? What does the way you live say about who you are? Are you happy with who you are, or do you want to be someone else?

Remember the beginning of this chapter? Remember the roles you play, your personality, core values, and passions? It all influences who you are, your identity; therefore it also means your identity is malleable and can change if you choose to change it.

Dissatisfaction with life is often not driven by the environment or by a particular job we hold right now but by our internal feeling of dissatisfaction with who we are. It is often a self-limiting belief that is the problem. If you can break it, you can quickly get to a much better place even though everything else in your life stays the same.

For example, let's assume you believe you are bad at sports but decide to take up tennis anyway. You are not particularly good at the beginning, but as you practice, you get better and better. You get a coach, join some competitions, and start feeling good about your game. It is becoming your lifestyle. You are a tennis player now. It is not what you do, it is who you are. You just created a new identity for yourself. Being able to say, "I'm doing this because that's who I am" is much more powerful than saying, "I do this because I have to," or even "I do this because I want to." The power of identity.

Purpose: This is your life's mission and your reason for being. Why are you here? What are the things you can do that will make the world a better place? And don't try to be too grandiose. You can have a big impact on the world even by helping a single individual. What do you contribute to the greater good of the universe, and how comfortable are you with it? Do you feel you need to do more? What is the mission of your life? Do you think that what you do matters? And if not, why is that? Is it because it genuinely doesn't matter or because you simply don't see it? What would you like other people to remember you for?

The logical levels model helps you analyze the real problem and then find a solution that addresses it. A great way to understand the model is to consider some of the statements you are making about yourself. For example, let's analyze a sentence like this: "I can't drive a car to a ski resort." There can be a range of reasons for this, from a lack of skill that is solved by training to a lack of self-confidence solved by coaching and continuous practice.

I can't drive a car to a ski resort. (Deals with *identity* and means that you consider yourself not to be the person for the job.)

I **can't** drive a car to a ski resort. (Deals with *beliefs* and can mean that you don't have the self-confidence even though you may have the skill.)

I can't **drive a car** to a ski resort. (Deals with *skills,* as you simply have no idea how to drive a car.)

I can't drive a car **to a ski resort**. (Deals with the *environment,* as you may be very comfortable driving around the city but worry about snowy roads in the mountains.)

The way to work with this model is to start at the bottom with the environment and work your way up, analyzing the situation. Once you get to the top, you review where you are, and you have a good understanding of why. You look at all the levels and your life and consider how satisfied you are with it.

If you discover that you are not happy with a particular aspect—let's say the apartment you live in is in a terrible neighborhood and far from work—you can move up a level on the pyramid and take action to change that. If you realize your action of getting your dream job is failing, move up a level and focus on the skills you need to build to get the job. It is often one of the higher levels that can help you solve a problem at a lower level.

Once you get on top of the pyramid, you can also use it in the reverse direction and start with a mission of your life and move downward. You know what you want, and you need to understand who you want to become, what choices you need to make, what values are behind your actions and what beliefs are holding you back, what skills you need to build, what actions you need to take, and in what environment you need to be to get where you want to be.

Logical levels provide a robust and structured way of thinking about your life and your career. They prevent you from making rash decisions based on an incomplete understanding of the real root cause of your dissatisfaction with your job and life.

Highly Valued Accomplishments

"Tomas, I feel frustrated and a bit lost. It seems that my work doesn't have any meaning, and I should change something. I'm not sure what to do that would bring me more happiness. It might be the boss, the job, the company, or my personal life. I don't really know what is important to me, but it must be different from what I have now. I'm lost."

A variation of this monologue comes up at the beginning of every conversation about careers that I have had with accomplished individuals who suddenly don't know where to go next. From the outside, they seem to be successful, achieving a high level of proficiency, respect, status, and high compensation. Yet something is wrong. They don't seem to be able to enjoy what they've got. They don't know what they want. In fact, they don't know who they are and why they should be proud of themselves.

How do you figure out who you are and what is important to you? We already talked about the personas you have in life, your personality, your core values and passions. So let's now talk about your highly valued accomplishments in each one of your roles, or at least in your professional roles. I will use an example from the workplace, but you can do the same for any other persona you have. Let me show what Highly Valued Accomplishments (HVAs) look like in my case. The example is from my early days in management. Back then, the accomplishment I share was a big deal for me, even though it may seem a bit more trivial today after years in the business. I will dissect it and show you a set of questions that will help you build your own HVAs.

Running Industry-Wide Project for GSM Association

[What Happened] The GSM Association (GSM-A) is a trade body of 800 mobile operators and an additional 300 companies in the broader mobile ecosystem. The GSM-A represents its members via industry programs, working groups, and industry advocacy initiatives. Between 2005 and 2007, I represented Siemens in GSM-A SIP/IMS Technical Expert Group & Trial Management Group. Due to my active participation, I was asked to act as a Campaign Manager of the GSM Association OMA PoC campaign. It was a six-month project that required me to coordinate activities of around twenty companies from the telecommunications industry. The focus was on testing interoperability between mobile phone vendors, network providers, server vendors, and telecom operators.

[How It Happened] The project required me to negotiate participation with several mobile phone operators and vendors, who provided the systems to be tested. Then I built a project plan and managed the setup and execution of the tests. I had backing from the GSM Association leader and strong support of several mobile network operators (essentially future customers of the IMS technology).

[Results] I gathered enough participants from the industry to have a meaningful interoperability trial. The team was able to get the project accomplished as planned even though we were constantly running into technical obstacles resulting from the fact that every vendor had a slightly different implementation of the tested protocols and technologies.

[Why Is It Notable?] I was a very junior manager back then, and this was a significant accomplishment that very few people in the industry could claim they had done. I was able to get cooperation from companies and people who had no direct incentive to cooperate—since all the vendors were also competitors on the market—and potential customers were watching. I was able to manage a project that involved people from across several continents and different cultures. The campaign was successful, and in October 2006, I held a presentation in front of the industry representatives at the 3GSM World Congress in Singapore.

[Why Is It Important to Me?] It was an opportunity to use people and project management skills. I found that I can have a considerable impact on the world without having a big team. The project was way out of my comfort zone. It required a massive amount of interaction with people from all around the world and the negotiation of tough agreements. It also made me realize that in order to be satisfied at work, I need to see other people be successful too. I need to learn something new myself and build something.

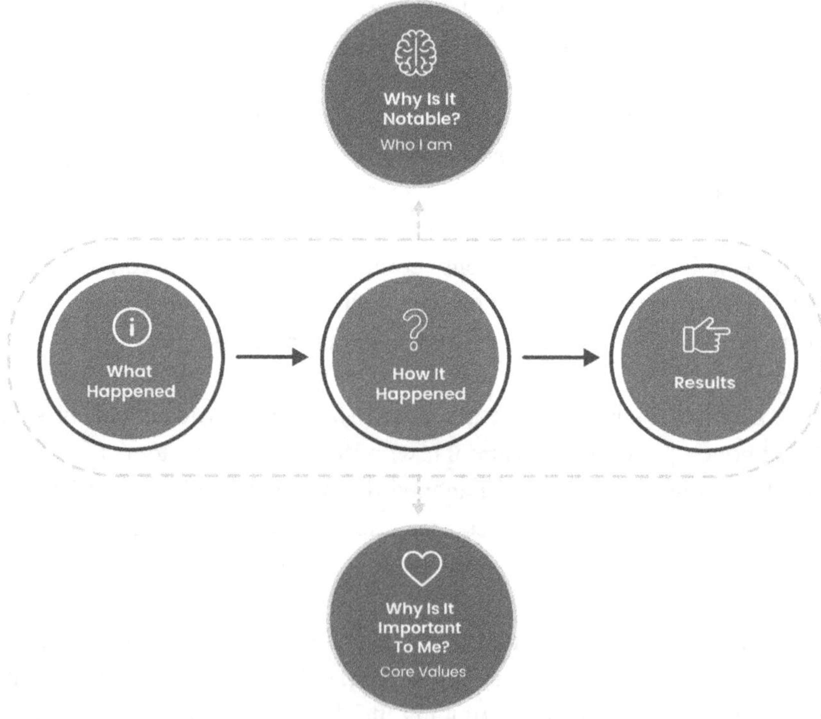

Figure 5: Highly Valued Accomplishments

Ignore all the technical mumbo jumbo and the irrelevant abbreviations. I'm sure you will have your own jargon when describing your HVAs. Let's analyze the core of the highly valued accomplishment you just read, focusing on structure rather than content, and pose the questions needed to build your list of HVA stories.

[What Happened] Any story needs a background and description of the main characters. If you want to use HVAs as a way to not only analyze your role but potentially use it in mentoring sessions or interviews, it is good to set the context. What is the context in which you accomplished the work? Can you share any data that will make it more authentic?

[How It Happened] Describe your role in the initiative, focusing on some of the critical aspects. The goal is to show what skills you had to use to get the work done or to identify some significant challenges you faced. Was there anything in particular worth mentioning? What were your main tasks?

[Results] Clearly articulate the outcome of the initiative with lessons learned. The results don't have to be positive. It is not that much about the actual result, but about what skills you learned and what you learned about yourself in general. Your HVA can be a failed project, but because it stretched your limits and it was a non-trivial project in the first place, you can still consider it an HVA. What happened in the end? Was it successful, and, if not, what did you learn?

[Why Is It Notable?] You need to connect your accomplishment to something important to others. If the positive effect is only on you, you are not getting the power of the HVA. Just connecting your accomplishment to some benefit for others will give your work meaning. It will also show that what you did was something others appreciated, either through emotional or monetary reward. How did others benefit? Why do you want others to know this about you? What benefits can this bring to your future work?

[Why Is It Important to Me?] This is the part where you learn about yourself. Consider why you picked this HVA. Why are you proud of it? Did you learn anything? Which of your core values did it satisfy? Is this the type of activity you would like to do more of? Or was the lesson learned that, even though this experience was a good learning opportunity, it was not your cup of tea?

The key is to think about any activities, projects, or even smaller tasks that you have done in your life that you are particularly proud of or that have had a life-changing impact on you. Once you have the list, then dig into the details of why. Why was it a notable accomplishment for you, and why should others see it as highly valuable? When you look at the set of these highly valued accomplishments, you start seeing who you really are. They shape your identity. They make you proud. They give meaning to your life; therefore you should do more of them. When you look closer, you will also find some common aspects that will point to your core values. It is these values that are important to you, so again, you should do your best to find ways to integrate them into everything you do.

As you go through your life, you will collect more and more of these accomplishments. Since we are all changing during our lives, these accomplishments, these things you are proud of, will evolve too. It is a good practice to regularly stop and think a bit about what you have recently achieved that you can add to your list. It helps you adjust your course, keep doing the things that have meaning for you, appreciate what you achieved, and feel good about yourself. This constant reminder that your life has meaning is what will fuel your continued growth and happiness.

Later on, I will talk about the Sweet Spot concept. Keep your HVAs in mind since they are a great way to find the type of activities that fit the Sweet Spot definition. If you go through several HVAs, you will see patterns that will all point to your Sweet Spot. Then it is only a question of finding a company and a role where you have the opportunity to pile up this type of highly valued accomplishment, for the benefit of the company and yourself.

Summary and Key Takeaways

You have many roles in your life. All these roles need to support each other. Then add in your personality, core values, and passions that drive your beliefs and actions and that have an outside impact on your success at work and satisfaction with your life in general.

You need to have a holistic view of your life and make sure that all the parts of your life work together because they influence each other. We introverts like to think about and overanalyze everything in our lives. This chapter helped you to do that in an organized manner. You are now ready to move to the next step and talk about careers and what a successful career looks like.

- We all play multiple roles in life. They are all important and necessary in supporting each other.
- Don't let personality tests and labels you give yourself guide your life.
- Find out what your core values are, then live according to them.
- Forget about following your passion and instead do what you are good at. Passion comes later.
- Find out what parts of your life you are dissatisfied with and fix them. Work-life integration is a thing.
- The Life Balance Wheel and Logical Levels Exercise are great tools to make sense of your life and admit hard truths to yourself that you might not want to hear.
- Highly Valued Accomplishments can help you to understand where you bring the most value and what you enjoy doing. They also make a great elevator pitch when presenting what you do for a living.

Questions and Next Steps

- Have you done the exercises in this chapter? If not, now is the right time to do so.
- Do you know what your core values are? If not, try at least one of these exercises: The Animal Exercise, The Peak Moments Exercise, or The Remote Island Exercise. What did you learn? What are your core values? How do they influence your decisions? How do they manifest in your life?
- If you are unhappy with your career, or anything else in your life, consider doing the Life Balance Wheel Exercise. What did you learn? Is your career really the problem? Remember that your life is a complex system where things influence

each other. Are there any areas of your life you are dissatisfied with? What are you going to do about it?

- Who are you? Why are you in your current job? What holds you there? Consider doing the Logical Levels Exercise to analyze how you ended up with the job you have and what you can do to get it to the next level.
- What are the things you most enjoy doing? What parts of your job fill you with pride and energy? Consider doing the Highly Valued Accomplishments Exercise to find aspects of your job that you are good at, passionate about, and proud of. What did you learn? What does this mean for you going forward?

● 4

What Does a Successful Career Look Like?

How do you define success? Traditionally, success is defined by gaining fancy titles, reaching a certain position in the hierarchy, or making a desired amount of money. However, that is the definition of success imposed on you by society, and that definition may be wildly different from what is important to you. You may achieve it and still not feel happy or successful. For many, success is not defined by the number of things they own, but by their feeling of purpose. Success may mean having a good quality of life, being useful, having an impact, and seeing one's contributions. Success may mean helping others and seeing their success, personal growth, recognition from others, and feeling of belonging.

According to Western standards, I can be considered pretty successful. I have an excellent education, a successful career, and enough money to satisfy my needs. However, for me, none of this defines success, as I never really strived for any of that. It is all a byproduct. For me, success is living a useful life. Seeing people around me grow and being successful in their own right while knowing I contributed to their success is what keeps me going.

In fact, this is directly related to one of my core values: usefulness. It is important to me to feel that I'm useful, which has direct implications on my definition of success. I hope that now you understand why, in the previous chapter, I pressured you to figure out your own core values. They are a great starting point for thinking about what success means to you.

Consider writing your manifesto. What is the purpose or mission of your life? What are the things you stand for, both publicly and privately? What are the things you are willing to fight for? The mission of your life and your definition of success should be big enough that you can work on it for years to come. It should be aligned with your values. It should be something you would be proud to talk about when asked.

Having a mission is not enough. You need to have a plan. You may say that having a plan in today's fast-paced world doesn't seem to make any sense, as things are changing too fast—and you would be right, if you have the wrong plan. A good plan should account for ever-changing conditions on the market and in your life.

Let me give you an example from my early career. When I graduated from university, I already had experience as a software developer. Since childhood, I have loved computers and programming, so it was only natural for me to get a career in IT and become a software developer. I was lucky enough to start focusing on developing dynamic websites, which was a new thing back then. Later on, I caught another trend, developing software for smartphones. I was a reasonably competent developer, and I had a clear career path in my mind: keep getting better and better at developing software, share my knowledge, and, when I reach the age of forty, move to management.

I made these plans when I was twenty-four. At the time, I worked for a small US-based start-up. Two months later, the start-up went under, and I joined a big multinational. Another three months went by, and I was promoted to team leader. Within the next two years, I moved to management completely and stopped writing software. All my career plans didn't survive even half a year. The good news is that my plans got significantly accelerated. The bad news is that I wasn't ready. I had spent all my time getting better at technical things, and I hadn't paid enough attention to other aspects necessary for a successful career in management.

Luckily, I didn't just have a plan. I also had a philosophy that later evolved into my life's mission. It was more important to me to learn new things and build something than to have a fancy title or a big paycheck. I figured that it was better to create my career on a solid ground of habits and principles that would survive whatever life threw at me.

If you asked me ten years ago what my career objectives were in terms of positions and titles, I would tell you the same thing I will say to you today. I feel that the role of COO in a mid-sized company would be a nice fit for the later stages of my career. It would fit my skill set, my aspirations, the things I love to do. However, I don't actively pursue that particular title. If I did, I would already have it. In the past, I have gotten job offers that included that specific title. However, for me, it is not about the title. It is about the joy and fulfillment I get from the work I do.

What do I expect from a successful career? I want to learn new things, build something, help other people grow, and have an impact by solving challenging problems. Then I'm happy with whatever title or role I have. As long as I like the environment, the culture, and the people I work with, I don't necessarily care whether I work for a small company or a big one, in management or as an individual contributor.

Who you are changes. There is no fixed "you." You are a set of the inborn traits, experience-based personality, and habitual patterns you happened to fall into. You will get more experience as you go through your life, and that will change you. You will build new habits and shed old ones, and that will change you. You will get older, your priorities will change, and that will change you. In ten years, you will be a completely different person with different preferences, dreams, and expectations. The world around you will also change. New types of jobs are popping up all the time, and some old ones are becoming less relevant. There might be great jobs on the market in ten years that don't even exist today. Planning a long-term career, hoping that you will eventually enjoy it when you get to your destination, is not wise. Plan a general direction, adapt frequently, and don't be afraid to pivot if you realize things are different than they were when you set off.

In their book *The Path*, Michael Puett and Christine Gross-Loh suggest that you are being abstract by making very specific plans. You are making plans for a future you, an imaginary version of you that will most likely never exist. By making detailed plans, you are assuming an ideal world, and you are ignoring the messy reality of the real world. You are eliminating options from your life based on specific interests your current "you" has. You are limiting your potential.[35]

Instead of making long-term plans, create conditions that will help you move in a general direction of learning and growing. That will allow you to adapt to the changes in the world. You will keep changing who you are. You will be evolving to survive in an evolving world.

There is a difference between success and achievement. Achievement refers to completing a specific goal. Success relates to satisfaction with one's life. Achievement is measurable. Success is not. It is a feeling. Success starts with a clarity of your life's mission and following it wherever it leads. You are successful when you wake up every day with clarity on what you need to do and why and a feeling that you are working toward something greater than yourself. Achievements are then the milestones on your journey that keep you on the right track.

A successful career is more about attitude and how you see life than about anything else. Having the right mindset is what will make you good at what you do. If you are good at what you do, you will get offers for promotions, more money, and other things you can't control directly.

In this chapter, I will show you what other introverts consider a successful career. This doesn't mean that you should define your career the same way, but it is a good inspiration. I will then guide you through an Employee Emotional Life Cycle at a company. It will help you identify where you are in your career and give you an idea of what your next move should look like. And I will then describe some of the standard career moves you can choose from. Finally, I will outline eight components of a successful career. My goal in this chapter is to help you diagnose your career, find out what doesn't work for you, and give you some ideas for a possible way forward.

How Introverts View a Successful Career

In 2018, I ran a survey to understand what introverts see as a successful career. The results of the key question of how important various aspects of a successful career are summarized in Table 3. This table is specifically filtered for answers given by introverts. As you can see, some things are consistently rated as important or extremely important, things like having autonomy, seeing personal and professional growth, having good relationships with the manager and the team, and understanding the impact on the lives of others. Curiously enough, job security or regular promotions were not rated as that important. Apparently, for most introverts, titles are not everything, and in the growing economy with low unemployment, job security is not a big thing.

	Not Important	A Bit Important	Important	Extremely Important
Autonomy in the Way You Get Work Done	0%	2%	**52%**	46%
Personal Growth (Learning Something New)	0%	4%	12%	**84%**
Professional Growth (Mastery)	0%	4%	24%	**72%**
Relationship with a Direct Manager	0%	6%	**46%**	**48%**
Relationships Within the Team	0%	8%	36%	**56%**
Getting Regular Feedback	0%	10%	**50%**	40%
Understanding Your Impact on the Lives of Others	0%	10%	32%	**58%**
Fair Opportunities for Everyone on the Team	0%	12%	42%	**46%**
Cultural Fit with the Company (Shared Values)	2%	12%	40%	**46%**
Compensation Aligned with Your Needs	0%	18%	**54%**	28%
Compensation Aligned with Your Contribution to the Company	2%	14%	**46%**	38%
Understanding the Mission of the Company	4%	12%	30%	**54%**
Being Appreciated by Your Manager	0%	20%	**56%**	24%
Regular Promotions (Career Progression)	0%	26%	**46%**	28%
Security (Knowing That Your Job Is Safe)	8%	18%	**42%**	32%
Getting Recognition Within the Whole Team/Company	4%	**40%**	**42%**	14%

Table 3: Results of Successful Career Survey—Introverts

When I looked at the respondents and their self-proclaimed introversion or extroversion, I could also see a couple of interesting trends worth mentioning. Introverts are less likely to select extreme values. Those who identified themselves as introverts were less likely to choose "extremely important" and "not important" than those who self-identified as extroverts or ambiverts.

Since the survey was designed explicitly for introverts, it didn't provide a big enough sample of extroverted participants to make a solid comparison on whether extroverts and introverts see careers differently. However, some extroverts answered, providing at least a partial glimpse into some of the differences.

Then there are a couple of aspects seen by introverts as less critical than by extroverts—specifically, these four.

Regular Promotions (Career Progression): The explanation here is that introverts are less motivated by external recognition. The status is not what we see as a measure of success—at least, not to the extent that extroverts do.

Getting Recognition Within the Company/Team: Being put into the spotlight is something many introverts are scared of. Even though we want recognition, we are not delighted when we are placed on a podium to receive praise in front of the whole company. An acknowledgment from our manager or colleagues is much more meaningful.

Compensation Aligned with Contribution: This is interesting, and based on some of the comments from participants, it feels like introverts are more willing to live within their imaginary worlds and less likely to compare themselves with others. That leads us to be less impacted by external factors and not to feel the need to see whether our pay reflects our contribution. However, introverts felt, more than extroverts, that the impact we have on the lives of others is rather important.

Relationship with the Team: While still important, this isn't as crucial for introverts as it is for extroverts. This is not a surprise. For introverts, it is essential to have a couple of close friends, but we are also more comfortable working alone, and that makes it less critical to have a bunch of buddies at work. That being said, it is still important to feel that there is a good atmosphere. Dysfunctional teams and stressful environments would overwhelm introverts quickly.

These four aspects deserve a pause and consideration of the implications. When you look at them, they are mostly related to external rewards. It seems that introverts consider intrinsic rewards, like mastery of their field, personal and professional growth opportunities, and the impact of their work on the lives of others, significantly more important than extrinsic ones. We seem to measure our success less by what others say about it and more by what we feel. Think about this when you are working toward your next promotion. Will it truly bring you the feeling of success? Or is it something you do because it is expected by others around you, and when you achieve it, you won't be as excited as you think? Keep this in mind when we talk about various career paths later in the chapter.

Employee Emotional Life Cycle

Before we dive into details of what makes a successful career, let's talk about the different stages of your life at a company and the various career moves at your disposal. Why do employees leave their employers? And more importantly, can you predict when you are more likely to leave and for what reasons? Over the last several years, there have been an eruption of studies and articles focused on happiness, employee engagement, the need for purpose, the ever-increasing mobility of the workforce, and generational differences. You can read about companies creating happiness officer roles, introducing new benefits, coming up with motivational mission statements, and investing in more luxurious facilities. When you talk to dissatisfied employees who are considering leaving a company, they will talk about the lack of meaningful work, lack of growth, bad managers, or inadequate compensation.

When you are planning your career, it is beneficial to understand what I call the Employee Emotional Life Cycle within a company. You can have two people with the same skills, doing the same job at the same company, reporting to the same manager. Yet their performance will be radically different. One of them is engaged, and one of them is disengaged. Let's start with what engagement means.

William Kahn first used the term "employee engagement" in 1990.[36] It was defined as how much an employee identifies with their job role or work persona. It has nothing to do with the actual content of their job or their job title. You can have an extremely engaged office cleaner and a disengaged CEO.

Engaged people are those who bring all their abilities and enthusiasm to their job. They see the reason why they are there, they want to do their best, and they want to help others. They will go above and beyond. They volunteer; they find ways to have an impact.

Disengaged employees view their job as just a way to get a paycheck. They find ways to do the minimum work, they never volunteer for anything, they have no energy and no enthusiasm for the work.

Disengaged employees were not born that way. At some point in their career— in fact, most likely at some point in their time with the company—they were engaged. But then something happened. Now they are not engaged anymore, and what is worse, they can become actively disengaged.

Actively disengaged employees not only try to get away with minimal work, but they will sabotage those around them. Not only will they not bring any added value, but they will take the value out. They are unhappy, and they show it. They will constantly complain, actively badmouth others, and blame everyone around them for their misery.

Then you have happiness and fulfillment. Happiness is a short-term reaction to specific stimuli. In the workplace, you can be happy when you get promoted, get a raise, finish a project, or laugh with coworkers. But it won't last. It is gone the moment you learn the project is delayed, you have a hundred emails to go through, or you need to have a tough conversation. Fulfillment is more long term. Your work can be mundane and yet fulfilling. Fulfillment comes when what you do is important for some larger mission. If you can see the impact of your work on the team's success or see that what you do helps a specific individual, you feel fulfillment. What you do matters to someone. You can get a promotion and yet not be fulfilled if the work you do doesn't align with your core values, with who you are. You can get a raise, but you won't feel fulfilled if you can't see sense in the work you do and you don't see the positive impact on others and on the world around you. You are fulfilled when you know that others need you and that if you disappear tomorrow, others will miss you. With this in mind, let's jump into the Employee Emotional Life Cycle.

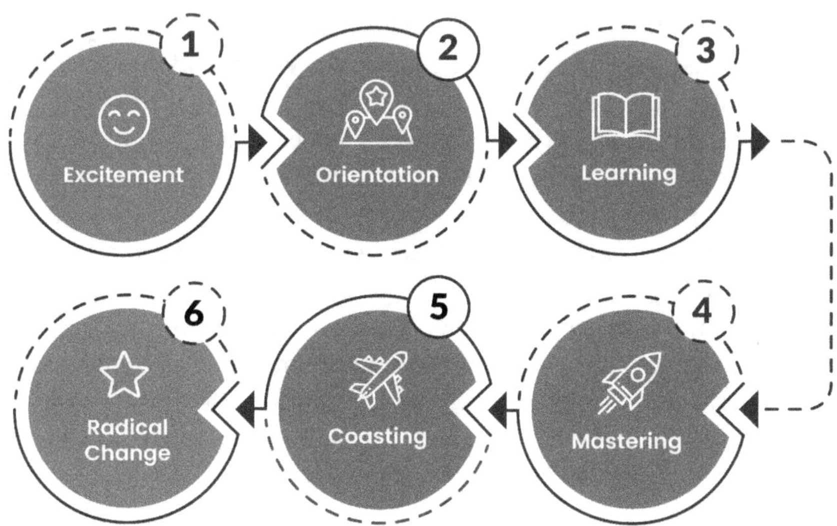

Figure 6: Stages of the Employee Emotional Life Cycle

Once you finish the interview process and join a company, you go through several stages. The Employee Emotional Life Cycle commences with getting started, finding out how things work, learning the ropes, and mastering the job. It ends by getting on autopilot and coasting.

Each of these phases has unique challenges for both the employee and the organization. Let's focus on what each means for you, an introverted employee who wants to have a successful career and is dissatisfied with how things are going right now.

Excitement—Getting Started: You are excited about the new opportunity. Whether you are new to the job market or changing jobs after years with your previous company, there is something new and shiny ahead of you. You are a bit nervous, as you are getting into unknown territory, but you also have ideas and aspirations about what things will look like.

You are coming in with some expectations and maybe a bit of naivete. You will face reality and may need to reset some of your expectations without immediately jumping into depression and disappointment. Setting a new, realistic bar is important for your long-term satisfaction. It is also helpful to have a conversation with your manager about what could be done to align your job more with what you expected.

Orientation—Finding Out How Things Work: In most cases, *this* phase will happen anywhere between one to six months on the job. You realize that not everything is as you thought. Maybe there is much more bureaucracy than you expected, or it is total chaos. Perhaps you don't have the work-life balance you wanted. Perhaps most of your colleagues are fine, but there is one person who is a total jerk. You wanted to build cool new products, but now you also have to support those products. You wanted to work with the latest technology, but you do so only 10 percent of the time, and the rest of the time you're working with the technology that the customers actually want to use. You are moving from your dream world to real life.

If you still feel like an outsider after six months on the job, you didn't make any friends, and you have no emotional connection to the team, something is wrong. You should think hard about your attitude and effort and get feedback from others to understand how you are being seen. There might be something you can do, or this may not be the right team for you.

Learning—Getting It: In this phase, you start to feel comfortable with how things are. You understand who is who and what processes are in place. You understand your role and the roles of others around you. You know your place. You know you belong. You finished your first projects, have some successes under your belt, and are being valued. And you are starting to be genuinely productive.

Frequent feedback is important. Keep asking for it. Setting clear goals, both job-related and developmental, will help you to understand where you are heading. You will start to see your future with the company.

The biggest danger here is that you get impatient, believing that you know everything there is to know about the job. You may get dissatisfied with a lack of career advancement or visible progress in how the company values you. Many people jump ship at this point and start the cycle all over again in another company. They never allow themselves the chance to be truly great at their jobs. Pity.

Mastering—Being Good At It: For most people, this phase happens after a couple of years on the job. You are at the top of your game. You might even be indispensable to the team. You are one of the "old hands" who knows the company inside and out. If there is a challenging problem to be solved, you are the one who gets approached to solve it. You are mentoring new colleagues, and you are having an influence on how things are done.

This is where most of the meaning and satisfaction come in. This is not superficial—it is deep and real. This is when you are in your sweet spot. You do what you are good at, hopefully you enjoy it, and you are in the position where the company needs you to be.

Coasting—Getting on Autopilot: Sooner or later, you will hit a wall and move to the last phase. More and more, you are starting to describe days as "business-as-usual." The challenges you face get lower and lower with your increased mastery. At some point, you may discover that there are no more challenges. You get too settled. If you never get out of your comfort zone, you stop growing, and you are going to get bored. Even if you get a new challenge or a new project, you are going to tell yourself, "Meh, another challenge, another project, what's new?" You are sort of on autopilot. You can do most parts of your job with your eyes closed, and you are starting to get tired. You are still valued, others still see your contributions, but you don't see them anymore. And in time, this shows in your performance. You are not as flexible as you used to be. You are not volunteering for anything new. Even if you get moved to another project, it quickly settles down to the same routine. You just go to the office to get a paycheck.

Once you reach the coasting phase, you are essentially too tired with the job and often with the company. A radical change within the company may work to get you engaged again. A job realignment or reassignment are great ways to skip the coasting phase, if done early enough. But often, it may be too late, as you probably don't care anymore. Once you reach the coasting phase, it might be the right time to leave, before your performance deteriorates to the point that you are being asked to leave.

Disengagement is a real career-killer. Everyone sees when people are disengaged, and it leaves a black mark on their performance. No manager is going to promote you, give you opportunities to do something interesting that can help you grow, or even increase your salary if they see that your heart is not in your work anymore. Analysis of where you are within your Employee Emotional Life Cycle can give you an understanding of what you should focus on to get your engagement back and what career moves are open to you.

Four Types of Careers, and Six Career Moves

Traditionally, a career involves climbing the corporate ladder and either becoming better in your field and gaining more senior titles or jumping over to the management track. For some people, this is the only thing they think of when they hear the word "career." This path might be especially daunting for introverts. As we have learned in the previous chapter, we introverts are not motivated by positional power and often don't seek it. Therefore, we could easily come to the conclusion that we are failures, as our careers don't seem to be as good as those of colleagues who just got managerial jobs.

Fortunately, this picture is far from complete. There are several other ways to move your career forward. In the following paragraphs, I will briefly outline the most common options in the hopes of opening your eyes to what is out there.

To figure out what career options are close to your heart, we can borrow from a career model proposed by Robert N. Llewellyn.[37] This model talks about four concepts and the motivations behind them. In the following four paragraphs, I will describe each of the concepts and their benefits or pitfalls for introverts. I will then talk in greater detail about career moves that you can use to build up your career within these concepts.

Linear: Power and achievement. For someone motivated by this concept, success comes from moving up the corporate ladder. For many introverts, this is not a particularly attractive proposition—though for full disclosure, this is the career move that worked quite well for me. Curiously enough, it happened to me by accident. I never sought managerial roles, but they were pushed on me by my bosses. That is what often happens to introverts who deeply care about a particular cause or project. They exhibit enough enthusiasm and dedication that they naturally end up running the whole thing. I would strongly discourage you from trying to use this career move just for your career's sake. You should never try to become a manager just for the sake of being a manager, just for the status and power. However, if the work you are passionate about requires you to step up and lead, then go for it. This is especially the case for those who fall into the social and thinking introversion types (Remember the STAR model by Jonathan Cheek from Chapter 1?). Linear career is most often represented as a vertical move.

Expert: Expertise and security. For someone motivated by this concept, success comes from being recognized among one's peers for one's expertise. Introverts thrive in this type of career. This is especially true for anxious and restrained introverts. We like the security that comes from the fact that we are really good at something, and this makes us feel needed. We are motivated by the fact that we know we are the experts. We feel the intrinsic reward of being able to do a good job. Then there is the feeling that what we do matters, that there is something we can provide to others. This gives us confidence. Look at all the lawyers, accountants, scientists, or software developers who are not interested in managerial jobs. All they want is to be as good as they can be at what they do. Expert career is often facilitated by job enrichment moves.

Spiral: Growth and creativity. Here the success comes from being able to move from one position to a related but broader position. From an outside perspective, success is not that apparent. You work for some time in one role and then move to an adjacent role. You are not becoming a bigger expert in your narrow field. You are not moving to management. You are broadening your field of expertise. You consider yourself successful when you can learn something new and see the big picture. Having a good understanding of various jobs or fields of expertise gives you a unique view of the world, and you bring value by coming up with creative solutions that experts in a given field would never think about. A great example would be an accountant who moves to the legal department or a software developer who moves to technical support. A spiral career can be achieved through lateral moves.

Roamer: Variety and independence. In this concept, success comes from being able to change jobs often and provide one's skills to a wide variety of businesses. This approach to a career can be useful early on when trying to find your place in the world. It affords you flexibility and lets you try various things. However, to be a successful roamer, you need to focus sooner or later. However, you don't need to commit to a specific company or a specific domain or industry. Consider management consultants. Their job is to be independent and have a vast database of knowledge that can be applied to various types of problems across different industries. Alternately, you may be one of those restless individuals who are motivated by novelty. It is not enough to learn something slightly new—it needs to be something completely new. I would suggest that few introverts would consider this career approach. There is little security or comfort. It is a constant stream of new people, new information, and new tasks, which can get overwhelming. The only exception would be a career realignment utilized by those who want to shift their careers entirely.

And now on to the various career moves that you can use to navigate the four types of careers. I will talk about vertical and lateral moves, job realignment, temporary assignment, reassignment, and job enrichment.

Vertical Move: This is the most obvious of career moves—promotion to a higher level. You move up the ladder within the same organization. This gets you more responsibility and a bigger title. This is what most people think of when you talk about building a career.

There is nothing wrong with this approach, but it has certain limitations, the most important being that it relies on the presence of a managerial opening, so either the business needs to grow fast, or, in a more stable business, someone needs to leave. This limitation means that you don't have your career under your control, and you are also limiting your mobility. You work hard on your promotion in your current company and don't want to leave and start from scratch somewhere else.

The more dangerous aspect of this particular career choice is motivation. When you have an "I want to be a manager/director/vice president" attitude toward your career, you are motivated by a position within the hierarchy, a fancy title, and the feeling of power. I say "feeling" because being the boss doesn't necessarily mean that you have any power at all!

I find this type of motivation hazardous since titles are a moving target. Once you get your manager title, you start looking at what you can do to get to a director level. You keep chasing more and more, and you are never satisfied with what you've got and are never really happy. What's worse, this is a terrible motivation for those in leadership positions, as they focus on their careers rather than on helping those around them. They surrender their responsibilities.

Lateral Move: A lateral career move is not a promotion or a complete change of direction. It is a move to another role at the same level. You would make a lateral move if you want to learn something new (maybe a new technology), improve a particular skill, or gain experience in an area that will benefit you long term. This is a good choice for roles where you need to broaden your skills rather than specializing in a particular field.

Lateral moves might also interest you if you are the type of person who just loves experiencing new things, learning new skills, and meeting new people without the bounds of a particular domain or organization. You may say that these people are unfocused or lack clear career paths, but this approach may work very well for them.

If you belong to this group, the goal of your career is not a specific position or being the best at one particular thing. You could say that there is no goal, or rather, that the goal is to gather new experiences. For someone who loves change, this is an excellent option—though keep in mind that there should be some logic behind the individual moves. The roles should be connected and complementary to each other, or your transitions will be too erratic and you will feel lost and dissatisfied with your career. Stay true to your life's mission.

When you have this type of career, you are challenged continuously, frequently experiencing a "back-to-school" feeling. You regularly find yourself outside of your comfort zone. You have to adapt continually. But you also get a broad range of skills and experiences, you meet tons of interesting people with varied backgrounds, you build strategic relationships, you are very often the person who brings new points of view to the organization, and you will always be a bit different. You will stand out in the crowd and be a leader.

Job Realignment: Realignment needs a bit of sacrifice, as it requires you to move down a career level to start on a new path and open new opportunities. It might be that your interests shifted, and now you love different things than you did in the past. It might be that you were in a managerial role and want to get back to being an individual contributor. It might be that you were in a highly stressful role and want to move to one that will allow you more peace of mind. Or it might be that you see a unique opportunity on the market, a new technology that came up, a new type of role that was created, and you want to use that opportunity.

With job realignment, you go in an entirely new direction and often start in a junior role. You may not have the skills to allow you to keep your seniority level and your compensation. For example, you may be working as a senior accountant but hating the job, and you know in your heart that the role is not your calling. You may decide to realign completely and start teaching small kids to play soccer, and there is an opening for a coach at a local school. You don't start as a senior coach but as an assistant.

This move, as well as the lateral move option, are great ways to get some energy back into your career. If you get to the coasting stage of your career, as described in the Employee Emotional Life Cycle, you can either quit the company and go somewhere else, hoping it will get better, or you can use the lateral move or job realignment to reinvent your career from the ground up.

Realignment is often the only way to get out of a dead-end job you hate. However, because it requires certain sacrifices and feels like a step back, few people are comfortable doing it. Keep this career move in mind when I introduce the Quiet Success Sweet Spot in the next chapter. It is this move that may often get you to your Sweet Spot.

Temporary Assignment: This is the obvious choice when you don't know what you want from your career and you want to explore some options. People sometimes use this option to try project management or similar fields. They take responsibility for a smaller project to understand what it all encompasses. Only after doing the job can they truly appreciate what it means.

Temporary assignment is also an excellent opportunity to develop skills or get the experiences you lack to progress vertically in your career. A typical example would be going on an expat assignment to another country. Having gone through this myself, I can attest that the way it broadens your horizons and the type of experiences you may get is invaluable and can boost your vertical climb of the career ladder significantly. The flip side, especially for introverts, is that it requires adjusting to a new situation, new environment, and new people. This may be very uncomfortable; therefore the only reason to do it would be that you feel you get something out of it. If you see the long-term benefit, it is easier to endure the short-term discomfort. I should acknowledge that my expat assignment was one of the most stressful times in my life, yet it was also incredibly rewarding and had a substantial positive impact on my career, not to mention my personal growth as a human being. I will mention this thought several times throughout the book. Success rarely comes without getting out of your comfort zone. Learn to find satisfaction in being uncomfortable.

Reassignment: Reassignment is a move to another organization without changing career and even without changing career level. This is an entirely appropriate move when your skills are not needed in your current organization and do not fit the work you are doing today. It may also be that the long-term goals you have are not aligned with the organization's long-term needs. It could also apply when your skills are not valued by the organization you work for but might be valued significantly more elsewhere.

Job Enrichment: This move is not a move at all. The focus is on growing in place, on mastery. In this case, you are already in your Sweet Spot, and you want to stay there. However, as the world is changing, you need to keep growing, to keep improving and polishing your skills, if you want to stay in your Sweet Spot. Job enrichment may include some minor enhancements of the role to keep it challenging. Just do more of what you love and are good at.

Job enrichment is a great way to prevent getting into the coasting phase of the Employee Emotional Life Cycle at the company. It will keep you in the mastering phase a bit longer.

As you can see, a successful career can mean many different things to different people. It is up to you to figure out what is important for you personally. Don't let others dictate what success should mean to you. If you succumb to the pressure of your environment and follow a path that doesn't align with your beliefs about what success is, you will never achieve it.

You Work in the Business of One

All the talk about Employee Emotional Life Cycle, various career types, and career moves is meaningless if you don't take charge of your own career. To have a successful career, you need to be in control. You understand that and you want to be in control; otherwise, you wouldn't have picked up this book. So let's talk about what being in control of your career means.

I like to coach people in their careers. This usually stems from a simple complaint about not getting the promotion they deserve or not seeing where their career is heading. They are stuck in their role for years and don't see a way out. Their bosses don't seem to care. The human resources department listens and doesn't do anything. Thus, the employees feel like the only way out is to jump ship and go to another company. So they jump. And it starts all over again. They are promised exciting work but end up with a routine job that doesn't excite them. They don't see how their work makes a difference in the world. They keep complaining about how life is unfair, how their boss doesn't do their job to help them to the next promotion. And they are right. Life is not fair, and their boss's job is not to promote them.

You Are Responsible for Your Career: It is not the job of your boss, the human resources department, or your coworkers to help you. Sometimes they do help, but you can't rely on it. It is you, and only you, who is responsible for your fortune, your career, and your impact on the world. Whether you freelance or work for a small start-up or a big corporation, in the end, when it comes to your career, you work only for yourself. You are in the business of one.

Ask for What You Want: A couple of years back, I coached a person born in Asia who moved to the USA. He came from a culture that didn't encourage asking for promotions, as doing so was seen as a bit disloyal. He was afraid to be seen as someone more interested in his own needs than the needs of the team and the company. He was worried that his boss would believe that he valued a fancy title more than doing a good job.

Suddenly, he worked in a culture where it was expected that you ask for what you want. You can do the best work in the world, but if you never ask for a promotion, you may never get it, as the boss assumes that you are happy where you are. And you start thinking that since you are not getting promoted, the boss probably doesn't believe that you are at a promotion-ready level or thinks that you have some other issues. So even though you may like the job, you eventually leave frustrated with the lack of career progress. All that was necessary was to have the conversation and remove the assumptions.

This episode taught me a valuable lesson. Yes, I still believe that it is the manager's job to recognize and reward great work. I also believe that it is your responsibility as an individual who owns their career to remind the boss what a great job you are doing and that you want to be rewarded accordingly. It is your responsibility to ask for what you need and want. You may not always get it, but you at least need to make it clear what you expect.

This applies to any culture. What differs is the way you go about it. In some cultures, you need to be very direct with your boss and clearly state what you want and what you expect to get. In other cultures, you may need to take a more indirect route.

I can hear the little introvert inside you freaking out. Asking for what we want is not one of our strengths. In fact, I would argue that if there is one thing holding introverts back, it would be our reluctance to ask for what we want and need. I will talk in greater detail about how to build confidence, assertiveness, and proactivity when I talk about the Quiet Success Principles. For now, let me offer you some suggestions.

Know Why You and Not Someone Else: When it comes to asking for what you want and need, the tricky part is to understand what value you bring to the company. If you are in the business of one and you want to manage your career as a business relationship between you and the company, you need to be able to sell your service. Have you ever thought about these questions?

- What value do you bring to the table?
- What problem can you solve for the company?

- Why should someone pay for your service?
- What is your competitive advantage over others?

Great news: you can use your strengths of introspection, preparation, and thoughtfulness to figure this out.

When you answer these questions, you get a better understanding of what role to apply for and what compensation you can realistically ask for. The problem, of course, is to find the correct answers to the questions. Sometimes it is difficult to answer them since you just can't figure out "why you?"

Learn How to Sell Your Services: Once you are clear on what you know and can do, and there is a need for that type of work on the market, you need to beat the competition: in this case, the other candidates who are applying for the same role.

The best strategy is to ask the right questions, find out what the pain points are, and then show the hiring manager how you can solve those problems and why you are uniquely qualified to do so. You can shift the interview's focus from what skills you have to a conversation about the problems the company is trying to solve.

During that conversation, you can show what you have done in the area and provide insights that demonstrate your knowledge and help you empathize and bond with the hiring manager. The feeling you want to elicit is, "Yep, this person knows what I'm talking about. They have been there and can help us solve it." Sold. It is utterly irrelevant that someone might have a fancier resume or better technical skills that might be mostly irrelevant, or that they speak ten languages they will never use on the job. The conversation is only about what matters, and all the fluff goes away. This is an excellent antidote to hiring managers having a list of twenty requirements, going through them one by one, checking boxes.

Next time you go to an interview, try to look at it from the perspective of two adults with equal rights and needs talking business. The past doesn't matter. What you did in your previous jobs is irrelevant by itself. What matters is whether you can take the lessons learned and use them to solve the problem the hiring manager has. If you keep the conversation focused on the needs of your potential employer, you are halfway there. And the added benefit is that you will learn a lot about the company and can then make an educated decision whether to join or not.

Be Grateful for What You've Got: This is an important aspect to consider when searching for a new job. It applies not only to a job but to your life as a whole. If you tend to complain about everything, just stop for a minute and think about how lucky you are. You are fortunate that you even have a job, that you have a regular income, that you have shelter, food, friends, and family. You may consider this normal, but it is not. The majority of the seven billion people on Earth don't have the kind of luxury that you take for granted.

The problem with ignoring what you have and just complaining is that you will bring this attitude to your next job. You may escape all the problems and issues you are facing today, but you will be faced with a load of problems and issues in the new place too. The only difference is that you know about your current problems and don't know about the future ones, so right now it feels like you are in a bad place. There will always be problems, if that is how you look at life. The way out of this cycle is to show more gratitude and look at life more positively. You can rely on your strengths of humility, attentiveness, and introspection to avoid this pitfall.

Understand What You Are Willing to Sacrifice: When you get into the mindset of owning your career, you also need to understand that nothing in life comes for free. If you do one thing, it means you can't do another thing at the same time.

When people talk about their careers and their dream jobs, they often forget to consider what they are willing to give up to achieve their dreams. You can see this especially in high-intensity, high-stress, high-responsibility jobs. People dream of becoming doctors, soldiers, or CEOs, but they forget to consider what doing so may cost them: The endless hours in the office or on a mission. No time for family. A continuous row of stressful decisions and damaged relationships.

You need to consider the opportunity cost of your aspirations. If you do one thing, that means you can't do anything else. If you spend all your time becoming the best manager there is, that means you can't spend that time on becoming the best accountant, writer, or engineer.

There Is No Satisfaction Without Suffering: There are no shortcuts to lasting success. If everything in your life goes smoothly, you are less satisfied with your achievements than if you have to work hard for them. It is the obstacles and difficulties that you need to overcome on your way to success that will eventually give you a feeling of satisfaction. If things go too easily or you don't need to work at all, you finally get bored with everything, life included. You won't feel the joy anymore. You won't feel the satisfaction of a job well done if you don't do any work.

Take Care of Your Health: The most significant sacrifice some professionals make without even thinking about it is their health. You need to be extra careful and mindful of your health. Damaging your body and soul is the one sacrifice you really shouldn't make. You have a limited number of internal resources. Not eating properly, not keeping your body in shape, and ignoring your health will eventually lead to limiting what you can do.

This is where your ability to focus and persevere can work against you. Think back about how not to overuse your strengths, as we talked about in Chapter 2. Make sure you have your priorities right and you don't mindlessly focus just on one aspect of your life without regard for the rest. This was the reason why we talked about the Life Balance Wheel.

When you look at some of the most successful people on the planet, you will quickly discover that most of them take care of their health. They have a routine of taking care of themselves, and they follow it religiously. That is one of the reasons why they have the energy, focus, and perseverance that helped them to get where they are.

Next time you have an urge to start complaining about how miserable your life is, take a breath and consider things in perspective. Maybe you will realize that, compared to the rest of the human race, you are doing really well, and things could be much worse.

Successful Career Wheel

In this chapter, we talked about how introverts view a successful career, various stages of the Employee Emotional Life Cycle, types of career and career moves, and the importance of owning your own career and not relying on anyone else.

With all the preliminaries done, it is time to analyze different aspects of a successful career. The more you have of each of them, the more satisfied you will be with the job you are doing. The more satisfied you are, the more likely you will give it the effort you need to. The more effort you put in, the higher the chance of a more significant success in the future. The bigger the success, the more motivated and engaged you will be.

Let's start with the model depicted in Figure 7. I have developed this model using the insights from the surveys mentioned earlier in the book in addition to building upon the work of the various psychologists and business writers I mention throughout the book. This model also has a loose relationship with Maslow's Hierarchy of Needs. It shows the critical aspects of a successful career and can be divided into four categories:

- *I Learn*: You need to feel you are growing as a person and getting better at your job.
- *I Matter*: You need to have autonomy and feel that you are relevant.
- *I Survive*: You need to be adequately compensated, and your work needs to be appreciated.
- *I Belong*: You need to feel you are being treated fairly and to enjoy working with people around you.

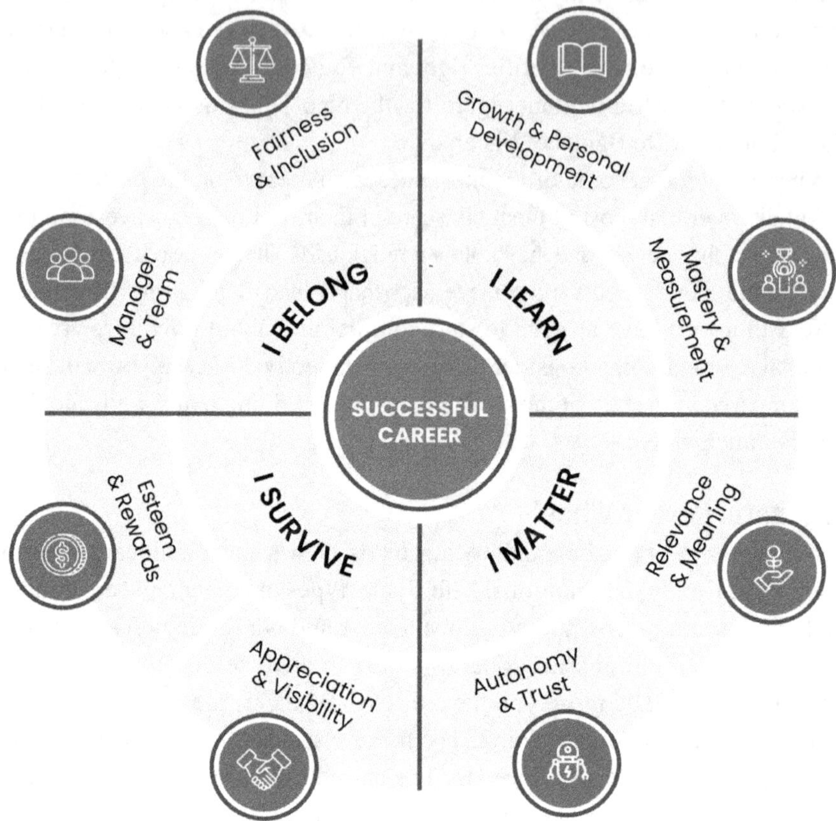

Figure 7: Successful Career Wheel

In the following paragraphs, I will talk about each component. I will show you what each component is, why it is important, how it is related to introverts, how it impacts your engagement and satisfaction with your job, and what you can do to get more of it. This section aims to provide you with a framework for an analysis of your current job. You may use it to find out why you might be dissatisfied and disengaged and use the knowledge, together with the Quiet Success Sweet Spot concept introduced in the next chapter, to plan your path toward a more satisfying and successful career. It is not only about money—believe me.

I Learn: Growth and Personal Development

Change is a part of life. The world is changing, and we are changing with it. Some of us are better at adjusting to change than others. Sometimes we resist change, hoping it somehow stops. It won't. The more you resist change, the more you will be left behind. Others will adjust and move on, while you will be stuck in your place by the resistance. You need to be able to adapt to change. You need to learn the right things and grow, not just as an employee, but as a human being.

Luckily, most of us understand this, and we want to grow. Introverts live rich inner lives, and we want to develop our skills. We want to become something more than what we are. Unfortunately, because that is what we want, we get dissatisfied when we see that we are not growing. We get even more disgruntled when we see other people around us growing, becoming better and better while we seem to stagnate.

To make things more complicated, we tend to equate personal and professional growth with climbing the corporate ladder. If we see that someone got promoted, we start asking questions about why it wasn't us. We start feeling that we are not growing. Learn to differentiate between vertical career moves, as I described earlier in the chapter, and professional and personal growth and development. They are not related. You don't need promotions to feel that you are growing and learning something new.

Personal and professional growth has a somewhat loose connection to job titles and promotions. You can be stuck in the same job for years and yet become a master at what you do. This means you developed as a professional. The fact that you have the same title is irrelevant.

The same also applies the other way around. You can get promoted to a senior job title without having the experience to back it up. You've got the title, you've got the official status, but you do not have the competence required to be good at the job. You may experience short-term happiness with the promotion, but ultimately it will cause you a lot of anxiety as you try to do a job you are ill-equipped for—that is, unless you focus on getting better.

Growing as an individual has numerous benefits. If you are learning new skills or improving your current ones, you are also becoming more confident. You know that you can now do things you couldn't do yesterday. You know that you are getting better at what you do. You see the potential and the opportunities. By developing yourself, you are getting hope for a better future.

Getting better at something creates future opportunities. Getting better at something tells you that you are not wasting your time. It brings you the satisfaction of successes and wins. That is why so many people believe that personal development is key to satisfaction at work. That is why most companies spend lots of money to develop their people. It is not only so they can do their jobs, but it is also to show that the company cares.

The good news is that, as an introvert, you are naturally equipped for learning. You can rely on your strengths of attentiveness, focus, and perseverance and learn anything you put your mind to. The bad news is that this requires time and effort.

You can't take shortcuts. First, you need to decide what type of career you want to pursue and then pick the right things to focus on learning. I will talk about learning strategies in greater detail later in the book.

I Learn: Mastery and Measurement

I have carved mastery out of growth and development for a reason. Mastery is so much more than just learning a new skill or improving an old one. As Daniel Pink says, "Mastery is a mindset, a pain, and an asymptote."[38] If you go for mastery, be aware that you are committing to a lifelong journey. You will never achieve absolute mastery. It doesn't exist. You can only get better and better, but there will always be something more you can learn, and you can always improve.

Mastery means constantly getting a bit out of your comfort zone. It can be painful. However, if you can get to the right mindset, you will be comfortable with being uncomfortable. You will get used to the pain. You won't mind that you will never achieve perfection. And you will apply it in many different areas of your life and in many different skills. The mindset is everything. Get the mindset that everything worth doing is worth doing well. Always do your best, always try to improve, and be better and more satisfied than others, regardless of the activity. Mastery is a way of life.

The reason mastery is so vital for a successful career isn't just about getting good at what you do, but also about the journey of getting there. To achieve mastery at anything, you need to consider several things.

Priorities: You understand what your priorities are and why something is important to you. Achieving mastery at something requires knowing what your reason for being is and giving it the focus it requires. You are working on the right things, and you know it. It feels good.

Feedback Loop: You won't get to a master level without frequent feedback. Getting regular feedback on the things you can improve helps you to do better and gives you a chance to see your progress. It is very motivating to know that you are improving. This, of course, means you need to measure how you are doing. It might be a bit counterintuitive, but measuring things at work is good and will make you happier. The more things you can measure in your job, the greater the chance that you will improve them. The more you improve them, the more confident and satisfied you will get with your work.

Perseverance: Getting to mastery also means you have grit. You persevere and get things done, even if they take lots of effort and require you to focus on them for a very long time. This is good news. If you can do it in one area of your life, you will be able to do it in other areas as well. You learn to deal with adversity. You stop complaining and just focus on getting better. You know that you can do anything you put your mind to. And others will see it too. Being able to drive things to a successful end is a huge benefit that will move your career in the right direction. And it feels good.

Motivation: Passion and motivation come from within. By achieving mastery or striving for it, you are becoming more passionate about the topic and more and more motivated to get things done. Don't believe that you first need to get motivated to accomplish anything. That is a myth. Truly great and accomplished individuals do it the other way around. They just grit it out until they are as good as they want to be and see great results. Only then does the passion and motivation kick in and help them get to the next level. Passion comes from being good at things. Motivation comes from small wins and first successes.

You may start to see a pattern here. As an introvert, you are in an excellent position to achieve mastery. You are able to focus on priorities, you can persevere, and you are capable of introspection to understand what you need to improve. Introverts tend to be intrinsically motivated, so we can usually deal pretty well with a lack of external motivation and just keep going. The only part that is challenging is the uncomfortable notion of feedback. You may need to ask for help and feedback from others. It might be a bit scary at first, but it is the right thing to do if you want to achieve true mastery. On the positive side, you are humble enough to be able to take the feedback and get the most out of it.

I Matter: Relevance and Meaning

Let's look at the work of another great contemporary author, Patrick Lencioni. In *The Truth About Employee Engagement*, he proposes that the keys to employee engagement come in the form of people understanding their relevance (how they impact the lives of others), measurement (so they know whether they have done a good job), and the opposite of anonymity—let's call it visibility (whether they feel that others know who they are).[39] We have already tackled the second item. Measurement is an integral part of mastery. You won't achieve truly great competence in any field without a proper feedback loop.

I will talk about visibility later. For now, let's focus on relevance. It is human nature that we need to feel useful. We need to feel there is a purpose in our lives. We need to feel relevant.

Companies often tackle relevancy by showing what the mission of the company is. What is the reason why are we here? Being aligned with company goals is an excellent way to feel that what you do is important, that *you* are important.

However, it is often too abstract to link the meaning of the work to the company's mission. We need to feel this more on an emotional level. If you see how your work affects the lives of other people, you will feel more relevant. The most satisfying moments come from being able to point to a specific person you helped. If you see that what you have done helped this one individual, if you see their happy face and their emotions, it has a more significant impact on your satisfaction with your work than listening to the CEO talking about the company helping thousands of anonymous businesses.

Think about any charitable organization. Are they telling you statistics about how many people could be saved from hunger if you donated fifty dollars? Or are they showing you a video of the one starving child that needs your help? The second approach works much better than the first one. Emotions will always trump statistics.

If you see the people your work is helping, if you can connect, you will feel significantly greater satisfaction than if you try to identify with some high-level mission. Not to mention that you don't need to wait for the CEO's presentation. You have this under your control.

Relevance is derived not only from you understanding your purpose but also from being acknowledged by those around you. That is why it is critical to work with people and managers who don't see you only as a small cog in the machine but who treat you as a human being. If your coworkers and boss show interest in you and care about you, you will feel more valued than if they just throw money at you.

It is all nice and good to be great at something, enjoy doing it, and see how it helps others. But is it enough? Shouldn't your work have some more significant meaning? In the new millennium, it seems that the search for meaning is more important than ever. Companies frequently target potential employees with promises of meaningful work and serving the greater good. You jump on such an opportunity, only to find out that you spend your days answering customer complaints in a call center. Where is the meaning in that? I would argue that it depends entirely on you! Just ask yourself, why do you work? Do you believe that what you do in your professional life has meaning? What do you tell your friends that you do? And more importantly, what are you telling yourself daily to get out of bed and to the office?

Since I keep talking about purpose and meaning, let me provide a brief definition to help you understand the difference between the two. Purpose is an intention. It drives certain outcomes and has an impact, and that in turn creates meaning. Purpose is the "what." Meaning is the "why."

Do you genuinely believe that you need to have a larger-than-life purpose to have a meaningful existence? I don't think so. Whatever your job is, as long as it fulfills someone's need, it has a purpose. The real question is, are you able to formulate the purpose and meaning in a way that will motivate you and that you can be proud of?

It all comes back to your life's mission. Let's say you are a software developer. Could your mission statement read, for example, like this? *"I'm an enthusiastic hacker and geek who enjoys solving hard business and technical problems by producing state-of-the-art software."* Or if you want to be more specific about a particular domain, *"I'm an experienced software engineer with a knack for building well-designed, scalable, and easy-to-use IT management software that allows other IT professionals to have an unparalleled view of their environment and helps them to easily solve complex IT problems."*

If I were a developer and self-talked to myself like this, I would undoubtedly be proud of what I was doing and see a real purpose in my professional life. The great thing is that this is entirely under your control! No more complaints or excuses that "There is no vision!" You don't rely on your company's CEO to show you a grand vision of the future and on your HR department to paint a company mission on the wall. Regardless of what the company does or what your role is, you can create a mission statement for yourself, a mission statement that will make you feel valuable.

And it doesn't end here. Having a one-line sentence with your mission statement is nice, but it is pretty much an advertisement that may not provide enough insight into details of what you do and why you should be proud of it. It is a good reminder for you to know the big picture, but having a story or two that documents your successes, career highlights, or things you are particularly proud of is important to show who you truly are. Don't be afraid to be flexible and change your mission as you grow professionally and as a human being, but be very careful not to mix the mission with a short-term promotion or monetary rewards. Ultimately, your mission needs to give you the intrinsic motivation that no external stimuli can.

And now the bad news for introverts. You may have observed that I keep referring to other people quite a bit in this section. It is extremely difficult to see the meaning of your work without seeing a positive impact on other people. You might be the best accountant, software engineer, or writer in the world, but if you never see how the results of your work help other people in some way, you will feel your existence is meaningless. You need someone, at least one person, to benefit from what you do, and you need to see their emotions to feel truly great and know that what you do matters. It matters to that one person.

So what will you tell your friends next time they ask you what you do? And what will you tell yourself tomorrow morning when your sleepy self asks you why you should get out of bed and to the office? Remember, your work does have a meaning. You just need to take the initiative and put it into words!

I Matter: Autonomy and Trust

In his book *Drive*, Daniel Pink talks about motivation in a modern economy where you are required to use creative thinking. He postulates that there are three components necessary for people to be motivated at their jobs: autonomy, mastery, and purpose.[40] Autonomy is a state where you have the freedom to do what you want in the way you want it to be done. Mastery is a mindset that keeps you learning and getting better at what you do. Purpose sets the context for the previous two and keeps you engaged and fulfilled by contributing to something larger than yourself. These are all intrinsic motivators that each of us must find on our own.

We've already talked about mastery and purpose, so let's talk about the last one. Autonomy is the component over which we have the least direct control. You could say that it is up to your boss to decide how much autonomy you will get. To some extent, you are right, but there is so much you can do to influence it.

Lack of autonomy, often represented by managers who micromanage their employees, provide constant supervision, and don't allow even a hint of independence, is one of the biggest engagement killers. We are adults and want to be treated as such. If your manager treats you like you are a five-year-old kid, your engagement will plummet.

I have seen many people quit their jobs with words like, "I'm done with corporate life. I want to be my own boss." Good for them if they can make it on their own. I'm sure they are much happier. However, I'm also sure that they could be equally happy in a big corporation if they only changed their attitude toward work.

Many other people, myself included, have always had a boss, but it never felt like we actually had one. I always had enough freedom and autonomy to do things the way I wanted to. Even if I occasionally had a manager who would tend to micromanage, I quickly figured out an arrangement that gave me the autonomy I sought. This is very important to introverts. Independence is one of our strengths; we value it, and we are proud of it. Lack of autonomy can clash with our independent nature and lead to dissatisfaction. So what can you do to get more autonomy at work? There are a couple of steps you need to take.

Set Realistic Expectations for Yourself: Think about which things can be changed, are flexible are negotiable, and which aren't. Processes exist not to torment you or take away your freedom but to ensure that success is repeatable or that legal requirements are being met. You should not confuse autonomy with anarchy. Sometimes you have autonomy even if it doesn't feel that way.

Build Trust: Trust is a must in any good relationship. You can hardly expect to gain autonomy if your boss doesn't trust you. So the question is, what can you do to make your boss trust you? There are two aspects of trust: you need to show competence, and you need to demonstrate integrity. You show competence by getting things done right and by getting better at what you do. You exhibit integrity by honoring your commitments and by standing for what you believe in.

Deliver What You Promised: This is part of the trust-building. You can't expect to get the autonomy and freedom you desire if you are unreliable in delivering results. If your boss knows that you frequently won't deliver what you promise, chances are that they will micromanage you. You can complain about them micromanaging you, but the only thing you can truly do to change that is to deliver as promised, so you remove the need to be micromanaged in the first place. If even that doesn't help, find a new boss.

Ask for Help When You Need It: The one way to increase the chances of getting more autonomy and remove the dangers of being micromanaged is to ask for help. It sounds counterintuitive, but if your manager knows that you can get things done and that if you get stuck you will ask for help, they are less likely to keep checking on you. By asking for help, you show that you are a mature adult, confident in your abilities, who wants to get things done as effectively as possible, and who uses all the resources at their disposal. And your boss is one of those resources. Showing that you can ask for help when you are stuck is an integral part of getting things done.

Make Tough Decisions: You need to show that you can make the right decisions for the company. People are often uncomfortable making tough decisions, decisions that will hurt, or decisions that may have a short-term negative impact but that are critically important for the long-term prosperity of the team and the company. If your boss sees that you can make these tough calls, your value in their eyes will increase. You are not just someone who is obeying orders and who only protects their own interests. You are willing to make sacrifices for the good of the whole.

Become a Partner: Become more than just a person who accomplishes the tasks you are given. If all you do is wait for an assignment and then get it done, you won't get genuine autonomy. Maybe you will get a little bit of freedom in the way that you execute a particular task, but you will still feel restricted. If you want more autonomy, you need to expand your job to include portions of your manager's job. You need to care about the same things they care about. You need to come up with ideas and suggestions for how to make your manager's life easier and how to help them accomplish their goals. You need to become a sounding board, a partner who works toward the same goal they do. Autonomy is then a byproduct of this collaborative approach.

It is often up to your manager to decide how much autonomy you get, but ultimately it is in their best interests to empower you, to make you independent, and to allow you to do things the way you want. You will get autonomy if you work for it.

I Survive: Appreciation and Visibility

Visibility and appreciation are closely related topics that have a considerable impact on the way we see our careers. This applies even to introverts who may not enjoy being put in the spotlight. You still want to be recognized. You want to see that your contributions are appreciated, that what you do makes sense, and that you are being treated fairly. There are different ways to make yourself visible and appreciated, even without receiving an employee of the month award in front of the whole company.

Visibility is mainly about the ability to get things done, with a flavor of marketing. Visibility may not be the most important thing for many introverts who don't need to interact with others. However, it is so much easier to achieve more significant success if you know you are not alone and that there are others you can tap if you need help. That also means that these others need to know who you are, what you are doing, and why it is in their best interests to help you.

If you present yourself as someone who is easy to work with, who is always there to help, whose achievements and successes are visible to others, it will be much easier to get their cooperation. Not to mention that it will be easier for your boss to give you a salary raise or to promote you to the next level! If your boss doesn't have visibility into what you are doing, it is unlikely they will expend any effort in helping you out. You may believe you are doing the best job in the world, but if no one knows about it, then no one is going to appreciate it and recognize your contribution. Visibility matters.

Appreciation is then a natural side effect of having enough visibility. It is about feeling that someone recognized what you have done and sincerely appreciated your effort. It is closely related to understanding your purpose and who benefits from the work you are doing.

I firmly believe that, for the majority of people, introverts in particular, a sincere, heartfelt thank-you is often more potent than big awards and money. I've been on the receiving end of both types of recognition in my life, and I always found the personal words of thanks much more meaningful. They connected not only on the logical level but on the emotional one. Much more powerful indeed.

You may still not know what to say when faced with words of appreciation. You may even feel pretty awkward, as you just don't know how to receive praise, but it feels good. It makes your day. It is clear that the person truly means what they said. It fills you with energy and pride that what you do matters.

I Survive: Esteem and Rewards

In 1943, an American psychologist, Abraham Maslow, came up with a concept of a hierarchy of needs. It is often depicted as a pyramid where, on the bottom, you have the more basic needs required for survival. As you progress higher, you get to more social and self-related needs. It starts with physiological needs (breathing, water, food, sleep, shelter, etc.), safety needs (personal security, emotional security, financial security, health, etc.), social belonging (family, friendship, intimacy), esteem (self-esteem, feeling of being respected by others), and finally self-actualization and self-transcendence (motivation to reach one's full potential and then to live for some higher outside goal).

With this concept in mind, a successful career helps address a couple of levels. The fact that you are making money enables you to satisfy the two bottom levels of having the basic needs of life in modern society (shelter, clothing, food). As your income grows, it helps you satisfy the need for personal and financial security and gives you additional means to focus on health and well-being.

Money is important—to some extent. Once you satisfy the needs mentioned above, you don't need more money. Money no longer acts as a motivator. Things act as motivators only when they help us deal with an unsatisfied need. From this perspective, pursuing the goal of having as much money as possible won't bring you happiness and satisfaction with your career. In several studies focused on happiness, researchers tried to find the critical amount of money above which there is no increased happiness.[41] These studies were done in the USA and found that having a yearly income of around $75k–$100k is the threshold. Making more money won't make you significantly happier.[42]

As we go higher on the hierarchy of needs, we get to social belonging and esteem. Esteem and self-esteem are relevant to confidence and are important for our relationships, decision-making, psychological health, and general well-being. They also help with our motivation, as they lead to a positive view of ourselves. Status, positional power, and job titles are all covered here. If you don't mix well with your coworkers, you will miss an essential aspect of satisfaction with life. You may still have your family and friends, but considering how much time you spend in the office, you need to feel that you are part of a team, you have your tribe, you belong.

Esteem is then created not only through your internal judgment of how good you are but also by those around you. There are many ways in which your self-esteem and the feeling of being respected can get a boost. The most obvious one is a promotion, getting a fancy job title, or getting some positional power. You are the boss. That should make you feel good about yourself and your achievements. You have gotten the "director" title. That tells the world you matter.

I'm not a big believer in fancy titles. They work reasonably well for extroverts, but they often don't work that well for introverts. Fancy titles are a way to prove to the world how good you are. They don't necessarily prove it to *you*. They help you build an image, which is important, but they don't bring you satisfaction with what you do. Introverts build self-esteem from the feeling of actual accomplishments. If we see the results of our work, if we see that what we did was helpful to another human being, if we get thanks, if we are recognized for our competence, it builds up our self-esteem much more than a promotion can.

I Belong: Fairness and Inclusion

Life is not fair! Who told you it is? It is not, and let's be grateful for that. Why? Because what is and isn't fair means different things to each of us. *Merriam-Webster* defines "fair" as "marked by impartiality and honesty: free from self-interest, prejudice, or favoritism; conforming with the established rules; consonant with merit or importance."[43] This means that fairness requires impartiality. Considering how full of unconscious biases we are, it is tough to be genuinely fair, especially when comparing ourselves to others.

We all want to be treated fairly. That means that we expect our bosses to remove any bias, injustice, or dishonesty from their decision-making process and from the way they treat others. It doesn't mean that we expect them to treat everyone the same way. As Jacob Morgan writes in *The Employee Experience Advantage*, treating everyone the same way is an excellent way to make employees feel like cogs. If managers treat everyone the same way, we inevitably end up with mediocre teams where no one will strive to get better and push the boundaries of what is possible.[44]

There is a blueprint for treating employees fairly. Just look at it the same way you would look at treating your kids. You love them, and you care about them. You want the best for them, and you want them to grow up and be successful. But you don't treat them all the same way. Depending on the age of your kids, you establish different rules they need to follow. They get a different amount of allowance, a different curfew, but you still treat them fairly. The same goes for employees. Don't push for being treated the same way as others are. Push for being treated the way you deserve to be treated.

Fairness has a little sibling called inclusion. We expect our managers to be inclusive, to give everyone an opportunity to excel, contribute, and be successful. However, sometimes we misinterpret what that means. Once again, we believe that inclusion means treating everyone the same way, giving them precisely the same opportunities. You were given a chance to spend six months working on a project in another country, away from home. Jim got the same chance and refused. What was he thinking? He was given the chance, and he blew it. He can't expect the promotion since he was given the same assignment as you and didn't step up. No matter that you are single and he has a family to take care of. You both got the same opportunity. You both got included the same way. Or did you?

We often claim that we support equality, inclusion, and meritocracy, while in reality we ignore all the hidden forces that push privileged groups up and put minority groups down. Before you use the words "meritocracy" or "equality" again, consider whether your definition of these words is inclusive or whether it ultimately applies only to people from the privileged group.

There is a crucial difference between equity and equality. Equity and equality are two ways you can achieve fairness, but equity is much more potent, as it removes biases and privileges from the equation. Equity is giving everyone what they need to be successful, while equality is treating everyone the same. Equality is truly fair only when everyone starts from the same starting position and requires the same help.

For the majority of employees, being treated fairly is vital to feeling valued. For those who belong to any sort of minority in a given environment, equity and the feeling of inclusion are much more critical. It is not only about feeling valued; it is more fundamental. It is about feeling that you belong. If you are excluded, if you don't feel like part of the family, part of the group, you won't be satisfied with the job.

The problem for introverts is that we don't like pushing our own interests. Unfortunately, you need to get out of your comfort zone, ask for what you need, and voice your concerns. Too often, managers are blind to the impact their actions or words can have on specific employees. They mean no harm but simply never think about it. If you have a decent relationship with your boss, then telling them how specific actions or words make you feel can be an eye-opener. Alternatively, you can approach it as a team and ask someone from the team who has the manager's ear to voice the concern. You would be surprised how often this works. Managers are human beings just like you and me, and unless they are toxic jerks, they will adapt. You may even hear a variation of, "I'm sorry, I didn't realize what I was doing. I didn't mean to make you feel disrespected, and I will do better in the future."

I Belong: Manager and Team

A good working relationship with your manager is one of the critical prerequisites for happiness at work. I'm sure you've heard the old cliché: "Employees don't leave companies, they leave managers." If you have a supportive, empowering manager who truly cares about you and gives you credit and praise in front of others, your work experience will be a very different situation than having a manager who is a micromanaging paranoid jerk who cares only about themself, takes all the credit for your work, and demeans you in front of others.

You may think it is a lottery. "There is nothing I can do about it. We don't pick our bosses," you may say. And you would be wrong. There is quite a bit you can do. Obviously, it is not entirely under your control. You can't change someone else's behavior. But you can still do several things to improve the odds of working for a manager who will help you and your career.

Interviews work both ways. When you are interviewing for a position with a company, it is not just the hiring manager who is trying to figure out whether you fit their team—you are also trying to find out whether you would enjoy working with this group of people and specifically with this manager.

When I was interviewing with one of my employers, I experienced this very directly. The director and the potential future boss I was talking to were new to the company. My potential boss seemed smart, full of energy, and, at first glance, it felt like she would be someone who would be able to get things done. So far, so good—until she asked me a question about my weaknesses. I gave her one of the standard non-answers, and we somehow got into a conversation about manipulating people and ethical behavior. I quickly realized that she was someone who would do whatever it takes to get the job done, even if it meant manipulating others and bending ethics. For me, this was a no-brainer. I liked the company a lot, but there was no way I would ever work for someone like that. It went against my core values, so after the interview, I had a very easy decision to make. I politely quit the interview process with clear feedback that things wouldn't work between this manager and me. And guess what? After a couple of weeks, I got a call from her boss telling me that she had gotten fired and asking whether I would be willing to talk to them again.

Your direct manager can have a significant positive or negative impact on your career. If they are supportive and helpful, your satisfaction with the job will be at a very high level, even though you may not like some of the tasks you are required to do. If the boss is a backstabbing, unhelpful individual who holds you down, you will likely quit even if you love the work itself.

The need to belong is one of the most basic human needs, even for introverts. We all need to feel that we belong and that we are loved. We may go to spend our free time in nature, but we are comfortable bringing a friend. You can satisfy the need to belong in many ways, but you can't exclude work. Having a family, loved ones, a couple of friends, or a romantic partner is important, and they will help to anchor your life. But consider how much time you spend with your friends and your family and compare it to the number of hours you spend at work. You spend forty or fifty hours a week at work. That is a lot of time to spend with people you don't like and are uncomfortable being around! If you don't feel like you belong, you will be miserable, and having a loving family won't fix it. You will still feel unhappy with your life, or at least with a significant portion of your life.

Having a job you love, being paid well, and having a fancy job title is great, but unless you enjoy working with the people around you, that is not enough. You need to feel as if you are a part of a team. Your workplace is your tribe, a group of people you belong to, a group of people that can rely on each other for help and support. You don't necessarily have to have your best friend forever working with you, but you must enjoy working with your team.

For many introverts, their time in the office is, to a large extent, also their social life. We don't need too many people in our lives, so building strong relationships with a couple of colleagues is enough to satisfy our need to belong. And then we get hurt when these people leave for another company or move to another team! This has a significant effect on our happiness, and it takes time for us to adjust.

If you fit in well within the team, if you like interacting with a couple of your closest coworkers, you will be happy. You will look forward to coming to the office every day, and you will be able to give the work your best.

If you don't like the people you work with, you will get anxious when interacting with them. It will hurt your ability to get things done. You won't be able to give it your all. You won't focus on the right things, you won't grow, you won't achieve mastery, you will question your purpose at work, and, in the end, you won't receive recognition. You shouldn't be there. If you don't click with the people you need to work with daily, you should be elsewhere. At the same time, you should always give some effort to making things work, especially if you like the work and see a significant opportunity for the future.

Don't rely on your employer to provide a social anchor for you. Things can change, and you have little control over who you work with once you join a company. Do your best to get comfortable working with the people around you. This often requires getting uncomfortable and being the one to reach out to others. Build an image of yourself as someone who is easy to work with and who is always helpful. When people see you in a positive way, they will act more positively toward you. You may enjoy interacting with them a bit more.

Summary and Key Takeaways

Success means different things to different people; therefore you can't expect others to give you success. You are responsible for your own career. Don't blame your boss or your company if you don't get anywhere. Instead, consider changing your mindset and make your approach a more proactive one that will help you get the career you want.

In the previous chapters, we talked about introversion, your strengths, and what is important to you in life. We have now added a way to define a successful career, as well as the Employee Emotional Life Cycle and the Successful Career Wheel, methods to analyze why you may not be satisfied. With that clarity, you can then consider the several career types and career moves at your disposal to plot your unique path toward a successful career.

- We all have our own definition of success. Don't let society impose a definition of success on you that is not yours. Otherwise, you will spend your life chasing something you don't care about.
- Introverts often see autonomy, personal growth, professional growth and mastery, relationships with their manager and team, and understanding their impact on others to be much more important than compensation. Don't let money drive your career choices.
- There are five phases of the Employee Emotional Life Cycle within an organization: excitement, orientation, learning, mastering, and coasting.
- There are more career moves available than just climbing the ladder to management. Ignore what others are saying and find a career path that will resonate with you.
- You work in the business of one. You and you alone are responsible for your career.

To feel good about your career, you need to check four boxes. You need to feel that you learn, you matter, you survive, and you belong, as defined by the Successful Career Wheel:

- "I Learn" requires growth, personal development, mastery, and measurement.
- "I Matter" requires relevance, meaning, autonomy, and trust.
- "I Survive" requires appreciation, visibility, esteem, and rewards.
- "I Belong" requires fairness, inclusion, and strong relationships with your manager and team.

Questions and Next Steps

- Consider what type of career resonates with you.

  - » *Linear*: Power and achievement. For someone motivated by this concept, success comes from moving up the corporate ladder. It is most often represented as a vertical move.
  - » *Expert*: Expertise and security. For someone motivated by this concept, success comes from being recognized among their peers for their expertise. It is often facilitated by job enrichment moves.
  - » *Spiral*: Growth and creativity. Here, the success comes from being able to move from one position to a related but broader position. It can be achieved through a lateral move.
  - » *Roamer*: Variety and independence. In this concept, success comes from being able to change jobs often and provide one's skills to a wide variety of businesses. It can take the form of a realignment and is often utilized by those who want to shift their careers completely.

- Look at the Employee Emotional Life Cycle and think about your situation. Where do you think you are? How long have you worked for your current company? How long have you been in your current position? How engaged are you? Do you still have things to learn? Do you feel that you're at the top of your game? Do you feel you are just coasting? What can you do about it?
- Look at the Successful Career Wheel, then go through it section by section and consider how your job fulfills each part. How satisfied are you in each of the areas? Is there a particular section that spoils your whole career? How could you address it?

Where You Fit and How to Get There

Quiet Success Sweet Spot

There is a place for each of us to do great work that is appreciated and has meaning, no matter how talented or smart we are. To this day, I remember one of my summer jobs when I was still in college. I spent two months working in a paper mill, standing next to a conveyor belt pushing paper cartons back and forth—the most boring job of my life. I was so bored that it showed in my attitude and my performance. Next to me worked Ellis, a mentally challenged woman who had worked in this job for years. She was always the first to start the shift, working with complete focus and incredible dedication. One day, she approached me with a frown and pushed me aside. Then she showed me how to do my job properly and with enthusiasm. She just couldn't watch how I didn't care, and she took it on herself to provide me with feedback and show me how the job was done. This job was her Sweet Spot. She could contribute, she was useful, she was really good at it, and she just couldn't stand the mediocre worker standing next to her. I remember feeling embarrassed that day. It changed my perspective on work and life. First, I realized I needed to study hard to make sure I didn't end up with a tedious job I would hate. Second, it showed me that everyone, regardless of their talent, knowledge, or IQ, can have a fulfilling career they love. It is all about finding your Sweet Spot.

The Four Dimensions

The goal of the Quiet Success Sweet Spot framework is to open your eyes to what opportunities you have in your life and what you can do to take advantage of those opportunities. The framework in Figure 8 is depicted as four circles or four dimensions: what you love, what you are good at, what someone needs and is willing to pay for, and who you work with. When I built the Quiet Success Sweet Spot, I wanted to make sure it mapped nicely with the Career

Success Wheel so you can see that "I Learn" maps into "What you love," "I Matter" into "What you are good at," "I Survive" into "What someone needs," and "I Belong" into "People you like."

Successful Career Wheel	Quiet Success Sweet Spot
I Learn	What you love
I Matter	What you are good at
I Survive	What someone needs
I Belong	People you like

Table 4: Successful Career Wheel and Quiet Success Sweet Spot Mapping

You can map any work you do on this diagram. To have a successful and satisfactory career, you want to get to the middle, to the Sweet Spot. It is an intersection of working with great people on what you love, what you are good at, and what someone needs and will, therefore, pay for. If only some of these criteria apply, you will end up in one of the other parts of the diagram. For example, you may be good at accounting ("What you are good at"). It is indeed a skill that people will pay for ("What someone needs"). Every company needs an accountant. But you may not enjoy it ("What you love"). It is tedious work for you, so you are unhappy about doing it. It is not your Sweet Spot unless you start loving it. Within this framework, it is either a "Job" that just pays the bills if you like the people who you work with, or it can be a "Toxic Job" if you don't.

Or you may love collecting pebbles—all the different colors and sizes ("What you love"). But you are not a geologist. You don't know much about rocks, so you are not that good at it ("What you are good at"). And no one needs your pebble collection ("What someone needs"). It falls into the "Hobby" slot within the framework, and it is a nice hobby. But that is all it is, unless you put serious effort into education and become a geologist, making rock collecting into something you are good at and something someone needs.

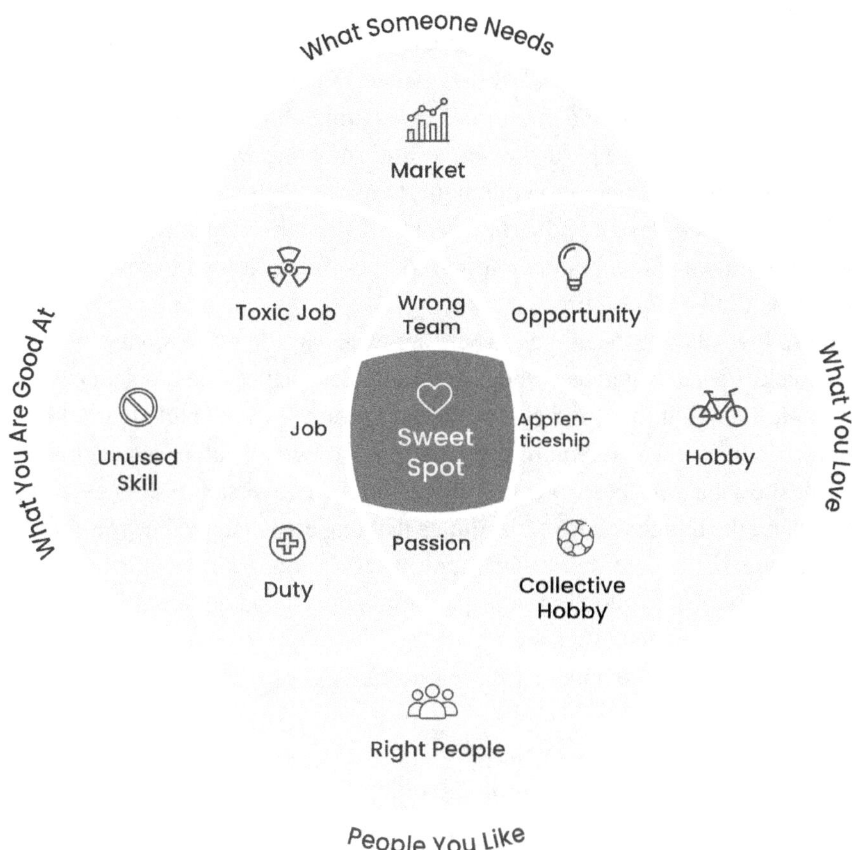

Figure 8: Quiet Success Sweet Spot

Before we talk about the individual parts of the framework, let's start by asking four crucial questions. As you can see, these four questions correspond to the four dimensions of the Quiet Success Sweet Spot: what you love, what you are good at, what someone needs and is willing to pay for, and the people you work with.

- What are the things you love?
- What are the things you are good at?
- What does someone need that they are willing to pay for?
- What people do you enjoy working with?

What Do You Love?

Think about the idea many lifestyle gurus like to push: "Follow your passion," or "You should do what you love." At first glance, this sounds like good advice, until you start thinking about it a bit more. I love eating chocolate. I'm pretty good at it. However, I would be hard-pressed to find someone who would be willing to pay me to do it. Not to mention that it might not fit well with the rest of my life's goals, as it would have an adverse effect on my health. This passion of mine is sweet, no pun intended, but not particularly helpful, as it won't provide me with the means to live a good life.

I also love playing the ukulele. There are even ways to make money by playing the ukulele. People would be willing to pay a ukulele player. The problem is, I really suck at it. I enjoy it, but I'm no good. What's worse, I'm not particularly keen on getting better, as it would require a lot of effort that I would rather spend elsewhere.

I'm showing you these examples to frame the conversation. It is essential to understand the things you love, the things that make you happy, but you shouldn't put all your hopes into them when looking for a job. As I will describe in the following chapters, following your passion is only good advice if it is the right passion and if you actually have one.

I would urge you to consider these questions:

- What is the mission of your life?
- Do you wake up every morning looking forward to going to work?
- What discussion topics are you passionate about?
- When was the last time you were "in the flow"?
- What do you need to feel you live a satisfactory life?

The answers to these questions should give you a better understanding of what the things in your professional life are that resonate strongly with who you are and have the potential to make you happy—the things you love.

If no answers come to mind, go back to Chapter 3 where we talked about your roles, core values, and passions. Have you done the exercises? Did anything come up? If you genuinely can't find anything at all that you love doing, then all is still not lost. As I mentioned before, passion comes from mastery. Simply pick something you are good at and, using your strengths of focus and perseverance, build it up. The better you get, the more passionate you become.

What Are You Good At?

Now let's move to another aspect of the framework. What are the things you are good at? What are your skills and talents? It is not necessarily vital to love a particular activity. The question is, are you good at it? You may say that you don't particularly enjoy driving a car, but you can do it very well.

Understanding what you are good at is essential when we start talking about mastery and how passion is created. Look at world-class piano players, chess masters, or runners. You will discover that they are passionate about what they are doing. However, they were not born with that passion. No one gets born with a passion for playing chess. You get it over time as you get better and better at it.

Passion grows out of mastery, and it doesn't apply only to world-class performers. I have a small niece. When she was three years old and tried to ride a bike for the first time, she wasn't particularly enthusiastic. She had fallen down a couple of times and then refused to sit on her bike for the rest of the summer. A year later, as she saw other kids riding their bikes, she gave it another try. And she didn't fall. She had better balance, and even though she was still a bit wobbly, she started to ride several times a day, every day. And she got better and better. She loves her bike now. You could say she is passionate about riding a bike. Why? It wasn't an inborn talent. It was the grit, the hard work, that got her to become good at it. She learned the skill, and that translated to passion.

This works the same way with any other activity in your life. That's why it is essential to think about what you are good at today and what you are actively working to learn and improve. So consider these questions:

- What skills do you have?
- What skills do/don't you utilize in your work?
- What unique expertise do you have?
- What things do you continually educate yourself on?
- What tasks challenge you and require you to use all your skills?
- What tasks do you find boring and a waste of your skill set?

Very few jobs require no skills at all, and you can't have a successful career without being good at what you do. Luckily, there are many skills you have that you can build upon. It is just a question of looking at all the things you can do and finding some use for them.

»Skill Inventory

Before we get into specific ways to get to your Sweet Spot, let's talk about a couple of ways you can analyze what you need to work on. One of the tools you can use is a skill inventory matrix. List essential skills you possess or skills you believe you may need in the future and analyze which of these are your strengths and which need to be developed. To help out with prioritization, you can then consider which of them are transferable across jobs and which are important for the future.

An example of the skill inventory matrix is shown in Table 5. When looking at this table, you can see that the person in the example considers their skills with MS PowerPoint to be at a master level, something they use right now in their job and that is transferable. However, if they decide that having an ice cream stand is their dream job, their PowerPoint skills may not be particularly useful in that context. Since they are planning to have their stand in a destination in Europe heavily visited by tourists, though, their German-language skills will be important. They also need to be able to negotiate with suppliers and various parties related to their business, something that they are not particularly good at today. If they picked a skill to focus on improving, negotiation would be a good choice.

Skill	Level [0–10]	Transferable to Next Job	Used Today	Needed for Future
German Language	8	X	X	X
Negotiating	4	X		X
MS PowerPoint	10	X	X	

Table 5: Skill Inventory Matrix

If you already have a clear idea of your dream job, then when you create your own skill inventory matrix you can populate the list with skills specifically required for that job. You can get this data from job postings and from CVs of people who currently hold these positions at various companies and use it for a gap analysis to find out what you need to focus on to be a serious candidate for the job in question. You can use this tool for long-term planning.

»Ask Others

You also need to consider that you might not be the best person to judge your strengths and skills. In 1955, psychologists Joseph Luft and Harrington Ingham came up with something they called the Johari Window model.[45] It is a technique that will help you understand your relationship with others and with yourself. You can split your strengths or skills into four quadrants: those that are known to you and others, those that are known to you but unknown to others, those that are unknown to you and others, and finally, those that are known to others but not to you. The last ones are important in this context. They are your blind spots.

Some biases make you overestimate your skills and underestimate the skills of others. The most relevant is a type of overconfidence called overplacement, a belief that we can perform much better than others: "If not the best, I'm definitely an above-average software engineer and should be treated as such."[46]

During a conversation with one of the best leaders and managers I've ever met, we turned to the topic of mentorship. I was recruiting her to become a mentor for some high-potential leaders. As we talked, I also started to describe how I mentor other people and on what topics. She asked me if I would be willing to become a mentor for someone on her team, and I was happy that I could help her and her team. "What should be the focus of that mentoring?" I asked, and her answer stopped me in my tracks. "Intercultural communication. I think you are uniquely qualified to help this person learn how to be better at leading teams across different cultures." It had never occurred to me that this could be something I could help others with. True, I had led international teams. I had lived in a couple of different countries, and I had significant experience interacting with various cultures. But because of that, I also feel that I don't know what I'm doing half of the time. There is so much more I can learn in that area. In fact, I spend a significant portion of my learning efforts working to become better at understanding different cultures and how to work with them. In my mind, I'm a beginner, while in the eyes of the people around me, I'm uniquely qualified to help others.

Don't rely on yourself to find out your strengths. I would strongly encourage you to consider approaching some people who know you well and asking them to help you out. What do they believe your strengths are? What are the things they think you are good at? What are the things they believe you could get better at? This type of feedback can be beneficial to make sure you make your career choices based on reality and not on some virtual world built inside your head.

What Do Others Need That They Are Willing to Pay For?

You might be the best bike rider in the world. You might even be passionate about it, but if no one in the world needs bike riders and if no one is willing to pay for their time, then you can't survive on that passion.

The third part of the Sweet Spot concept is to understand what the market looks like. What do other people need? And not just that. What are they willing to pay for?

This is a common problem in product management. You have a product manager who talks to many potential customers about whether they would love to have a certain new feature in a product. The response is overwhelmingly positive. All the potential customers are excited, and they want the feature. The product manager gets back to the engineering team, and they build the product. The first version is out there, and customers who tested the product praise it. The sales team starts selling it—and no one buys. It is one thing to like something and entirely another matter to be willing to pay for it.

When I talk about someone being willing to pay for your efforts, it doesn't necessarily mean you get a fat paycheck. You might be a monk who provides service to a local community, and that community donates food for you to survive. That still counts. You do work that someone needs and they are willing to give something back. People see that you bring value and they reward it.

What the world needs and what is a viable means of survival for you specifically are two different things. If you want to become an entrepreneur, you need to consider this distinction carefully. It is a bit more straightforward if you are looking for an existing job. The job exists, and that implicitly means that there is a need for someone to do the work, and there is a company that is willing to pay for it.

The last piece of the puzzle is what your image on the market is. There might be a significant need for airline pilots, but you need to ask yourself, is that truly a realistic market for you, who studied economics, now works as an accountant, and is afraid of flying?

And then there is the question of opportunities. In *Lean In*, Sheryl Sandberg talks about the advice she got from Google CEO Eric Schmidt when she was thinking about her next career move and whether to join Google. In his mind, only one criterion matters when you are picking a job: fast growth.[47] When companies grow quickly, it means a lot of change and new jobs and opportunities popping up all the time. There is more work than people, so it is easy to tweak or expand one's role. When a company stops growing, there are more people than there is work, so politics and infighting take hold of the organization. This means that sometimes it is worth taking a lower-level position in a fast-growing company rather than a big title in a dying one. It also means that sometimes it might be worth reinventing oneself and pursuing a new career if the growth opportunity is big enough.

So now consider some of these questions and do a bit of research to understand what the market looks like and how you fit in:

- What does the job market for your current skills and experience look like?
- What image do you have on the job market?
- What is your potential job market, and what skills might you need to improve?
- What area of the market is undersaturated, and could you be a strong candidate?
- How can you fit the mission of your life into the realities of the market?

You are a living being; therefore you need shelter and food. Whether or not money is important to you, in the society we live in, you need money to survive. That requires doing something that someone else is willing to pay you for. Luckily there is a ton of work to be done. It is just a question of mapping your skills and experiences to the job market and then building a personal brand so someone will be willing to hire you.

What People Do You Enjoy Working With?

You may think it a bit weird to have a people circle as part of the Sweet Spot concept. You are an introvert; therefore you don't need others, right? Wrong. No one can do everything on their own. We all need other people in our lives. What's more, we will have other people in our lives whether we want it or not. The question is not *whether* to work with others but *who* to work with.

The saying goes that you can't choose your family, but you can choose your friends. This is a bit of a bleak view of the family, since even though you can't choose it, you can learn to have a great life even in a family you haven't chosen. It just takes a bit more effort. However, you have more options with friends and coworkers.

Whether you realize it or not, those around you have a significant impact on your well-being. If you dread coming to work every day because you are scared of the drama your coworkers create, you have an obnoxious boss, or your customers treat you with disrespect, you can't expect to have a successful career. You will always feel that you don't belong. You will feel depressed, annoyed, even angry, and you will bring that mindset home with you. If you are surrounded by people who always put you down, you will feel down, and you will be down. No amount of money or status will make you feel great.

When you are surrounded by the right people, the situation is very different. You are part of a team that is welcoming and inclusive. You are being encouraged, appreciated, and you feel like you belong. You feel that those around you care about you and your well-being. You look forward to another day at the office. You feel like part of a team, and you are proud of the things you and your team do. You may be still introverting during the day, you may not say much, but you know that others are there to help you when you need them. And you are also there for others. You are delighted when you can help. You are part of a tribe, and it feels good.

For introverts, this is probably the touchiest area of the Quiet Success Sweet Spot—and also the most important. We don't tend to have too many friends, and the people we spend our time with at work are often our main social circle. If we are surrounded by the wrong people, we withdraw into ourselves, which is not a recipe for a successful career. You need to have the right people around you to fully enjoy your job and have a successful career. To find out whether you are in the right collective, one that allows you to thrive, consider these questions:

- Do you wake up every morning looking forward to the day with your colleagues?
- Do you have friends at work?
- Do you feel you need to constantly watch your back so someone doesn't stab you? Do you only worry about a specific person, or everyone?
- Are you nervous before every meeting with your boss?
- Do you socialize with your colleagues outside of work?
- If you could pick a manager, would you pick the one you've got? If not, why?

Being surrounded by the right people is critical for a successful career and for being in your Sweet Spot. You may have the best job in the world, one that you love and that fits your skills. However, if the environment is toxic, you will still dread it. Ultimately, you won't be able to do your best and enjoy it.

The Twelve Areas

The Quiet Success Sweet Spot has twelve areas split into several levels, defined by how the four circles overlap. At the zero-overlap level are Potential Market, Unused Skills, Hobby, and Right People. At the one-overlap level are Opportunity, Collective Hobby, Duty, and Toxic Job. At the two-overlap level are Apprenticeship, Passion, Wrong Team, and Job. When something falls in one of these categories, you have almost found your Sweet Spot, but you're missing one key component. And finally, where all the circles overlap sits the Sweet Spot.

Potential Market

The potential market can even be a job you hate and are not good at. Someone is paying you because they didn't realize that you are no good and that you don't like what you do, or because the job is the kind of job that no one wants to do, and they are desperate. In any case, you don't want to be in that situation. I call this part of the framework "potential market" to show that there are many opportunities out there if you only learn a new skill and push yourself to enjoy doing it.

At one point in my life, my dream job was to own a scuba diving facility. I imagined living on some lovely island somewhere in the Philippines or Indonesia at a facility with a boat or two and a couple of diving trainers (I envisioned myself to be one of them), enjoying life in the tropics, spending my time in the ocean while having a steady income. It was just a dream. I had neither a strong desire nor the skills to do it. But the market is there! I even made the first step and took PADI Open Diver training. I do enjoy diving, but I'm an amateur. I can't even call it a hobby, as I do it so rarely. All it would take is to give this activity some priority, spend more time training, get over to the Philippines, and start a business. I'm pretty sure I could make that happen. I could expand my Sweet Spot to contain managing a scuba diving school. I could do all these things. But I don't. It is a potential market, but I would have to change so many things in my life that my scuba diving facility dream is not a realistic option for me right now. I'm not willing to make all the sacrifices required. It is just a past dream.

It is good to understand the broader market and keep it in mind as you go through your life, especially when you get to the point at which you feel that everything you do is just wrong. Knowing that there are options out there that have nothing to do with your current circumstances can be comforting.

Unused Skill

You have many skills that don't translate easily into a steady job or that do have significant potential if you were only to give them a try. They are not your hobbies since you don't love doing them, you just have them. You might be a decent swimmer. You may be a good reader. You can drive a car proficiently. You may be skilled at explaining things in a way that helps others learn. There are many things like this that you can do—and you do nothing with them. This is where you might be overusing your strength of humility. You may have many skills that you don't even think about. If you have a good friend, ask them what they believe you are good at.

I would suggest you make an inventory of things you can do pretty well, the skills you have but are not using in your job. Then reflect on them. Is there something that sounds like a potential for a job you could enjoy? And why do you have this skill in the first place?

In most situations, building this skill took some effort and some motivation. What was it? Were you in love with the activity at one point in your life? What happened? Why don't you like it anymore? Is there an opportunity to light that fire again? Can you use some of these skills in your current job in some stretch tasks? Would your boss give you some exciting work if they knew that you have this skill?

To give you an example from real life, Jane, a sales representative, was hired to take care of some accounts in Australia. As the company expanded its reach, there was a need to negotiate occasional deals with Chinese customers. Many of them didn't speak decent English, and the company lost several sales deals because of that. Then, one day, one of these deals landed on Jane's desk. She picked up a phone, called the customer, and, to the surprise of her colleagues, started conversing in Mandarin. A sale! She had studied Mandarin Chinese for years, but no one at the company knew about it. She hadn't wanted to brag, and she had felt like she was no good at it anyway. But she was many times better at it than anyone else on the team. After that day, she became the go-to person for anything that required interaction with customers in China. Her job expanded, her value for the company skyrocketed, and she got a special commission when working on Chinese deals. She felt valued, recognized, and could practice and get better at her skill, even at work.

If you have skills you are not using today, make sure to uncover any hidden gems that can move your career to the next level.

Hobby

We all have hobbies. These are the activities that we do in our free time and that make us happy. This says nothing about whether we are any good at them. One of my hobbies is photography. I like to get into nature and take pictures. I generally like the pictures I take. I even put a bit of effort into becoming a half-decent photographer. However, I can't say that I'm good at nature photography. It is not my passion, so I don't give it the focus, time, and effort necessary to master it. It is just a hobby. Could I become a professional photographer? The market is there. However, the demand for someone with my skills is not there. To have photography as a genuinely marketable skill, I would have to give it focused effort and some deliberate practice. And I would have to build a portfolio and present an image as someone who knows how to take good pictures and is able to do it at a professional level.

There is nothing wrong with having hobbies. In fact, engaging in your hobbies is a great way to relax and get your creative juices flowing, and it is often a good way to socialize with similarly minded individuals. But be very careful about trying to take your hobby and make it a job. You could train yourself enough to get the skill and go professional, but by doing that, you risk losing the joy you had when it was just your hobby. You will make it a job that gets you paid, and the pleasure may evaporate. You will stop loving it. It is a well-documented phenomenon, described, for example, by Daniel Pink in *Drive*, that when we are starting to get an external reward for something we enjoy, our enjoyment goes down.[48] Initially, it was our intrinsic motivation that led us to practice the activity and to enjoy it. The moment we get paid for it, it is no longer a hobby. It is a chore. It is hard work. The external reward killed our enjoyment. This is especially true for introverts. There are ways to grit it out and get over the lack of enjoyment. In fact, by persevering, you may eventually get the passion back, as you may get extremely good at the task. You may become an expert. You may move to your Sweet Spot.

Right People

You not only need to learn, to matter, and to survive. You also need to feel that you belong. You need to work for the right company, or rather with the right people. Does that mean that you need to work for the company with the most daring mission out there, one that is going to change the world? Not really. Not even close. It might sound nice on national TV or on marketing materials if your company wants to put human beings on Jupiter by 2050, but that means very little to the accountants, software developers, customer support representatives, or janitors who are going through their daily work at your company right now. The company brand is important for attracting new talent, but the moment you join, other things start to matter much more.

Marcus Buckingham and Ashley Goodall have spent years researching leadership and management practices within large multinational companies. They used data from many sources, including the ADP Research Institute's Global Study of Engagement and several years-long studies at Cisco that focused on exploring the characteristics of the best teams. Buckingham and Goodall summarized some of their findings in the book *Nine Lies About Work*. And it all starts with why people work for a company.[49]

When someone asks you how it feels to work for your company, you won't talk about the Jupiter 2050 vision. You will talk about the endless meetings, the boss who yells at you, the coworkers who don't care and often don't show up. You will talk about not being clear about what is expected from you daily, the last-minute changes in direction, the fights between teams, and the politicking. These are the things that truly matter to you, as they directly impact how you feel every single day. That is why you often see significant differences in retention numbers across different groups in the same company. The employee experience varies more within the company than between different companies.

It is not the brand, the facility, the perks, or the vision that causes you to perform and be satisfied with the work you do for a company. It is the human part, the feeling that you are valued, that you are part of a tribe that cares about you and that you are surrounded by people you can care about. It is your relationship with the manager and the team. It is the small daily interactions you have with others in the company that matter. The team-level rituals and practices and the relationship you have with your closest coworkers matter much more than any company-wide events and processes. You may care a bit about which company you are joining, but you don't care at all about which company you work for in the long term. It is the people who are important, not the brand.

Even company culture doesn't apply to everyone equally. Teams have sub-cultures that can be significantly different from each other. That is why you are often confused when a person from another department or another location complains about the company and describes things that are very far from your own experience.

It is the emotional connection we build with our colleagues and teammates that often keeps us at the company. We are comfortable with the people around us. We like spending time with them. If we then see that they appreciate us for who we are, they value what we do, and they are willing to go out of their way to help us, we will be satisfied with the job. Creating teams that employees feel they truly belong to is the best retention strategy. No amount of perks and company slogans can replace that. This is especially true for introverts, as we are not that good at making new friends, and the thought of getting into a new collective and interacting with tons of new people can be frightening.

Opportunity

You've probably heard the phrase, "Fake it till you make it." It describes this part of the framework well. Opportunity is an activity that you love, that someone is even willing to pay you for, but that you are not good at yet. Either your pay-masters aren't aware that you are no good, in which case you are under stress to become better before someone discovers you are a fraud, or they are aware that you don't know what you are doing, but they are willing to give you a chance to learn. It happens all the time. The most typical example would be when you get to a management role. You love working with people. Your boss sees your potential and is willing to give you a chance, but you have never held a similar role before, and regardless of what you think about yourself, you have no clue what you are doing. This is a nice place to be in. You do what you love, and others are willing to pay you to give you a chance. The environment supports you. It is only up to you to provide the effort, to learn, and to practice.

Unfortunately, few people are willing to give learning the focus it requires. "I've already got the job, so that means I deserve it and I'm already good enough. Why should I learn?" is often the thought of many junior managers who don't realize that their journey is not finished when they get their title. They just finished their old career and started on a brand-new path, and they are often unaware that they have to learn a lot. It is a back-to-school situation.

That is why this part of the framework is called opportunity. If you give it the effort, learn, practice, and give it all you've got, you will obtain the skills, and you will make this new job your Sweet Spot.

If you don't give it the effort, you will stagnate and eventually slip back. What was an opportunity for greatness will become a chore. People around you will see that you have a job you are not enthusiastic about. They will see that you are stagnating or even losing your skill. They will respect you less and less and make it clear that they think you are useless. Eventually, this will spoil your love for the activity. You will start to despise it. You will have a job, but you won't enjoy it, and you won't be any good at it. At some point, even your boss will realize that, and you will get fired—a wasted opportunity.

Collective Hobby

Hobbies you can do on your own are great, and many introverts prefer them. Still, there is also the possibility of collective hobbies in which you not only do what you like, but you can use it as an easy way to socialize with others who have the same interests. With collective hobbies, it is much easier to connect with someone who is on the same wavelength as you.

Most often, collective hobbies are collective sports. Getting on the field regularly with others who love playing the same game you do makes you feel like a part of the tribe. You do what you enjoy doing, and you feel you belong. You may never even consider making this hobby a job. You may never even want to improve. For you, it is a way to get out there, socialize, and have fun.

The apparent danger is that, if the mood in the team deteriorates, the main reason for you to be there disappears. You may still like the activity, but not the people you are surrounded by. So you start finding excuses for not participating. Ultimately, you either find a different group of people or give up on your hobby completely.

A collective hobby can also transform into a passion when you put enough effort into it to get better. I know of several people who joined the Toastmasters International organization as a hobby. I was one of them. It started as an interesting way to improve my presentation skills and do it in a safe environment, surrounded by like-minded individuals. Over time, as some of us got better, we got more and more excited about the whole thing. Some started to take it more and more seriously and turned it into a real passion. One person in our group even got as far as to switch his job to use this newly acquired skill and passion. He got into his new Sweet Spot, training communication skills. And it all started with a collective hobby.

Duty

This is an area where you have the skill to do something, but you don't enjoy doing it. At the same time, you feel you have a duty to help others who need it. Even though there's no potential market, that doesn't necessarily mean the skill is not needed. It means that if you don't do it, then either nothing really happens, it won't get done, and no one will mind, or it will be done naturally without you. The most significant benefit of doing your duty is in strengthening your relationships.

For instance, you have a car, and you can drive, so you go shopping with your grandparents. Is that an exciting job you love? No. Will your grandpa or grandma pay you? Not really. They could do the shopping themselves. You still do it because you can, you like them, and it makes their lives easier. It is the right thing to do.

Volunteer activities in your community often fit this type of role. You get involved because you feel it would be helpful, you like the people involved, and you have the skill. With some effort, you can learn to love it. You can turn it into a passion.

Local nonprofit organizations can be the ones that profit from this dynamic. You want to help with something, and you enjoy working with like-minded individuals. You spend your free time volunteering. You may, for example, go with your colleagues from work to clean up plastic from a strip of a beach, or you might get together with a couple of friends to cut grass on a public picnic site. Duty often consists of activities that are helpful but are not important enough for anyone to be willing to pay for them. If you don't do these activities, they will most likely not be done at all.

Toxic Job

A toxic job is not only dull and unfulfilling work, but it is performed in an environment you dislike. It is often the coworkers or the boss who make a tedious job a living hell. You not only don't look forward to going to the office every day; you actively dread it. You suffer from anxiety because of the people you are forced to work with.

Having a boring job by itself is something that you can work with. You can find at least some meaning in it, or you can find satisfaction in other parts of your life. You never want to find that you're in a toxic job, and if you realize that you're in one, you should run away from it as fast as you can. Toxic jobs mean doing something you don't enjoy with people you dislike, and that means constant stress. You can try to change the environment. You can try to change your attitude. But you need to be willing to walk away, as the resistance to change might be significantly bigger than what you can overcome.

The main reason people endure toxic jobs is for the money. The knowledge that you are being overpaid and can't get similar money elsewhere often becomes the golden handcuffs that keep you in a toxic job. In a bad economy, it is often the knowledge that there are no jobs out there at all, and one has to be content with what they have. Having a toxic job will have a negative impact on your mental health. Your deteriorating mental health will then hurt other parts of your life and even your overall well-being. Since colleagues at work are a significant portion of an introvert's social circle, we suffer even more than extroverts, who can more easily find their sense of belonging outside of work. The question you need to ask yourself is whether the harm to your well-being is worth it.

Apprenticeship

Doing what you love with the right people and in an area that is attractive to the market is probably the best place to be when it comes to personal growth. You have an opportunity to learn from those around you and build up your skills.

It is often said that your first boss defines your whole career. If you finish school and can get a job in an area you like, and your boss is a true leader and a good manager, you are on your way to your Sweet Spot. All it takes is some effort from your side to purposefully work on getting better.

Apprenticeships or internships are a great way to get your foot in the door and start building some skills and credibility in the market. The key here is to be surrounded by people who will encourage you and help you to grow. This is not always the case.

Companies often use interns as a source of cheap labor without providing any meaningful support, guidance, or opportunities for growth. Interns are either left alone or, worse, abused. All this does to you is leave scars and a short paragraph in your CV. It may help you to get your next job, but it may also leave you dis-illusioned. Don't let such a negative experience weigh you down.

When you are in the right company, the opportunities are endless. You have your future in your own hands, and it is only your ability and your willingness to work hard and learn that will get you to your Sweet Spot. The great thing is that you can get to this spot at any time in your life. You can turn a hobby into your dream job by being willing to put your ego on the side and take on the role of an apprentice or junior associate. You may take a short-term financial hit, but this certainly is a path to an exciting new career.

Passion

If you focus on both values and passions, you will discover that they overlap. Examine what the things and activities you are passionate about are. There is a difference between a hobby and a passion. A hobby makes you happy, but you are not willing to make sacrifices to do it. Passion is different. It is something you love, and you are ready to sacrifice other things to do it. You give it the effort and the focus to master it. It is something that you love, and you can do it really well, better than most other people. You have a competitive advantage here.

I love seeing people around me grow and learn new things. When I look at a person on my team who accomplished something great that pushed them to the next level in a particular skill, it makes me genuinely happy and fills me with energy. When there is a discussion about developing people and growing the team, I'm the first to speak. When there is a need to work on developmental plans or performance improvements, I'm the first to raise my hand and get involved. I continuously study new management approaches. I love trying new things with my team, and I care about others. I prioritize helping others to grow over other things I could do, and I even make personal sacrifices to get better. All this indicates a real passion for working with people, growing, and leading teams. When I know this about myself, it is easy for me to get more of it into my life. I can steer my career in a direction that allows me to use this passion.

Passion is also easily recognized in others, especially in introverts, who often hold back until a topic of their passion comes up. Then they jump up and get engaged and even lead the effort. If you love something, you do it well, and you believe in it, you can make the sacrifice of extroverting a bit to make sure it gets done.

But what if you don't know what your passion is? You may feel that you don't care about anything. You may feel you don't have a Sweet Spot or passion at all. If you don't have a passion, then go and build it.

I said "build it," not "find it." Too many people feel they need to *find* their passion; therefore they endlessly jump from activity to activity, from job to job, and find nothing. Their heart is not in what they are doing, so they never find their passion. Passion is not something to be found. It has to be created. Only by giving an activity some serious effort, getting better at it, and getting into all the nitty-gritty details do you create passion.

Wrong Team

You do the work you love and are good at, and you are getting paid. Yet you are still not comfortable in your job, as you don't like the people you work with. You may work with people who don't care, or you may have an abusive boss. In short, you are in the right job but working in the wrong company.

The answer to this situation is very straightforward and, in most cases, also relatively easy to implement. Don't let those around you keep you down. Have an open conversation with your boss, the human resources department, or the coworker who creates the toxicity in the environment. Is it risky? Yes, but the alternative is worse.

You are good at what you do, and the market recognizes it, so the worst-case scenario is that you will have to leave. If you were no good at your job or didn't have market recognition, that could be a problem, but not in this case. You should be able to find the same opportunity at another company with relative ease.

Just make sure the problem is with those around you and not you personally. People often complain about how bad their boss is, that their boss is not giving them salary increases or promotions. Some people whine about negative feedback they've been given and say that they won't work with people who don't recognize their greatness. Double-check that you have realistic expectations, that you don't have an oversized sense of entitlement, and that you are not trying to save the whole world. Before you decide to switch teams and leave the organization, make sure you truly understand what makes the environment unacceptable and that you won't bring the problem with you.

Job

According to Gallup's State of the Global Workplace report from 2017, 85 percent of employees are not engaged or are actively disengaged at work. Of these, 18 percent are actively disengaged, and 67 percent are not engaged in their workplace.[50] That is just crazy! When you think about this a bit more, you will quickly realize that it can't be that such a massive percentage of the population would do things that are unnecessary and useless. The very fact that those jobs exist means that they are needed and that someone is willing to pay for them. No one is going to pay you for something that has no value to them. That means the purpose is there.

And you've got the job. You are probably reasonably good at it. Otherwise, you would get fired. But it is just a job, just a way to earn some income and nothing more. It is a chore, you don't like it much, but you feel that you don't have a choice. You need money, and this is the way to get it. Your job is also killing you. You have no satisfaction with it, and this dissatisfaction most likely also translates to your work outside of the office. You are not particularly happy with your life. You don't look to the future with any level of optimism.

This is a decent place to be short term. As we go through our lives, we have ups and downs, our priorities shift, and sometimes we end up in a job that we know is temporary. Those jobs are there just so we can pay our bills, but our focus is elsewhere. Maybe you need to take care of your sick family member, or perhaps you want to spend every waking moment with your kids. Maybe you are working on some pet projects at home. You have no desire to pursue a career, and you are willing to accept that your job sucks.

But it can't last forever. Sooner or later, you need to get your life in balance again. That means having a job that provides means for your survival and helps you have a satisfying life.

You can change your attitude. Realize the purpose of the job and understand that what you do has meaning for someone. With this realization, you can exert the effort to be good at what you do. You can achieve mastery. Your newly gained mastery and positive attitude will eventually become apparent even to your boss, who will rely on you more and more, and you will get the autonomy you're looking for. That will be the point where you will start loving what you do. You will be a respected professional who understands the purpose of their work and is appreciated by others. You will get to your Sweet Spot without even needing to change your job.

The alternative, of course, is to realize that what you do is simply not aligned with your values, needs, and wants and to make a change. The first step here is to determine whether you have transferable skills that could be used in other jobs and to identify what those jobs are. I like to use the ice cream stand example. If someone comes to me and says that they don't see a way to advance their career at their current company and therefore they want to change their job, I always guide them to consider what they want long term and whether they can use their current position to learn the skills necessary to get the job they want. Let's go back to an earlier example and imagine your dream job is to have an ice cream stand. You work as a junior accountant. Have you already learned everything you could in your current position that could get you a step closer to your dream job? Yes, you can count coins, but what about improving your communication skills, negotiation skills, or customer focus? Are there some aspects of your job that you can stretch to get the skills that would be transferable to the next job?

Before you jump ship, make sure you do it for the right reasons. Make sure that you know what you want and that you are leaving to get it. You are not leaving just to escape something, to get a job that will be pretty much the same. Before you make the ultimate decision, grit it out for a while to get the most out of the job you have today, learn everything that can be useful in the future, and leave with clarity about what you want and how you are going to get it.

The Sweet Spot

This is where it all comes together. You are in your Sweet Spot when you love what you do, you are good at it, you are surrounded by people you like, and they recognize your expertise and are willing to pay for it. This is when you get the most satisfaction with your job. This is when you create this self-growing perpetuum mobile that just keeps going.

It is all interconnected. You love what you do, so you make more effort to become good at it. Because you are getting better and better, you like what you do even more. Because you love what you do, you are good, and others see it, you get more opportunities to do it. Because you get more opportunities, you have more chances to practice achieving mastery, and you love it even more. And so on and so on.

It is important to point out that there is not a single Sweet Spot. There is no holy grail that you want to find. The biggest lie of modern society is the quest to find your dream job, as if there was one single unique job that would make you happy. In reality, any job can become your Sweet Spot if you work hard to make it so.

Since you have many different skills, love various activities, and the world is full of things to be done that someone is willing to pay you for, you can have several different Sweet Spots throughout your life. However, you should always focus on one at a time; otherwise, you will get distracted and will never actually reach your Sweet Spot.

If you choose to be a software developer, put all your focus and effort into being a great software developer. If you decide to be a manager and lead others, then focus on building your skills in that area. The worst thing to do is to do many different things half-heartedly. If you do, you won't become good at any one of them, you won't build an image of being good at anything, and you won't get into your Sweet Spot.

Once you are in your Sweet Spot, you can stretch it and expand. As long as the underlying core values that got you to the Sweet Spot are the same, you can do a wide range of activities and still be in your Sweet Spot.

Many people start their careers and their new jobs full of energy and even passion for what they are about to do. With time, routine sets in, and the enthusiasm evaporates. Instead of excitement and engagement comes boredom and even dread. The work is the same—what has changed is the person who does the work. They've gotten more skilled, they learned what needed to be learned, and they settled into a comfortable rut. Without realizing they were doing so, they stopped pushing forward and living to their full potential. They are not necessarily unhappy. The work is still okay. It is just not great, and they don't wake up looking forward to another day at work. The job is just a job. You still remember the Employee Emotional Life Cycle, right?

As people get into the routine in their lives, their curiosity about the world slowly disappears. You turn forty, and the idea of getting back to school to learn something new seems preposterous. Changing a field of work seems like a foolish proposition. You only have twenty-five years to go until retirement, so you will somehow muddle through. You have given up on life and on being all you could be.

When was the last time you were in the zone? When was the last time you experienced the flow, that sensation of being so focused on what you do that time disappears and you ignore everything around you? You are doing your best work. You are doing what you love. The world stands still. If you can't remember, then know that even though you are in your Sweet Spot, you are coasting, and you need a radical change. Go and find a new Sweet Spot, even if it means doing something as small as changing your team, and get to work with the new "Right People." Better still, start moving to a Sweet Spot that requires you to build new skills, as that will be much more exciting and will allow you to spend a longer time in the learning and mastering parts of the Employee Emotional Life Cycle.

Summary and Key Takeaways

The goal of the Quiet Success Sweet Spot framework is to open your eyes to what opportunities you have in your life and what you can do to get there. It is based on the ideas coming from the Career Success Wheel. Each area of the wheel can be mapped into a dimension of the framework. From this chapter, you can deduce that "I Learn" maps into "What you love," "I Matter" into "What you are good at," "I Survive" into "What someone needs," and "I Belong" into "People you like."

- The Quiet Success Sweet Spot has four main dimensions that need to align for you to have the job of your dreams. You need to:

  » Do what you love.
  » Do what you are good at.
  » Do what someone needs and will pay for.
  » Be with people you like.

- The Quiet Success Sweet Spot has twelve areas split into several levels, defined by how the four circles overlap. At the zero-overlap level are Potential Market, Unused Skills, Hobby, and Right People. At the one-overlap level are Opportunity, Collective Hobby, Duty, and Toxic Job. At the two-overlap level are Apprenticeship, Passion, Wrong Team, and Job. And finally, where all the circles overlap is the Sweet Spot.
- There is more than one dream job for each person. Most jobs can become your dream job if you put your mind to it.
- Once you are in your Sweet Spot, don't get comfortable. Keep stretching your Sweet Spot and expanding.

Questions and Next Steps

- Where does your current job fit in the Quiet Success Sweet Spot framework? Look at the framework, consider the four dimensions, and analyze where you are. Are you in your Sweet Spot? Then congratulations. Are you somewhere else? Then nothing is lost, as, in the next chapter, we will talk about how to get to your Sweet Spot. As a preparation, answer these four key questions:

  » What do you love? | What are you good at? | What do others need that they are willing to pay for? | What people do you enjoy working with?

6

How to Get to Your Sweet Spot

At this point, you have a good understanding of who you are, what your core values are, what is important to you, and why. You also understand the concept of the Sweet Spot, and you know what type of activities in your life fit into which category.

Now let's talk about strategies you can use to get to your Sweet Spot. Depending on what activity you want to focus on and where it lies within the framework, you can use one of these four strategies: training and practicing, reframing and coaching, marketing and selling, or interviewing and negotiating. Even though there are many different starting points, it is wise to consider the effort and likelihood required for success. The most common scenario will be that you start somewhere in the "what someone needs" circle. In rare cases, you may start with a hobby, passion, or simply utilizing an unused skill.

Take it one activity at a time, and don't try to do too much at the same time. If you decide to do everything, you won't be able to focus on anything. You will be busy but won't see the results you desire. You will be stuck where you are—only a bit more frustrated.

You don't need to do everything I describe in the following chapters. Each of us has a different way we learn. What I describe are guidelines and ideas to try. Following these will lead to success in most cases, but you are more than welcome to develop an approach that you feel will work best for you.

The second reason why you should focus on one thing at a time is that everything is connected. Once you start seeing improvement in one skill or one part of your life, chances are there will be a ripple effect that you will feel in other parts.

Let me give you an example that is close to the heart of most people: exercising. It takes a lot of effort and mental energy to get into the habit of exercising regularly. It requires time and energy, and it is painful. You need to push yourself. But with some perseverance, you start enjoying it. You feel better. You begin to see health benefits. With time, you can jog for miles and feel great. You start feeling better mentally as well. You have a more positive attitude toward life. You get more self-confidence. You start enjoying life itself. Something that started out as just simple exercise in your free time has impacted all aspects of your life in ways you may not have expected. It is all connected.

What do you do if you want to get from point A to point B? You look at a map. So what do you do when you want to get to a specific place in your career? You look at a map, plan a path, and then follow it. You need to understand where you are today and where you want to go. The important part is to be brutally honest about your starting point. If you are truly lost, you ask for directions or get a compass. If you don't have the stamina and can't walk long distances, you train. Similarly, for your career, don't overinflate your current knowledge, skills, and abilities. Ask for feedback from people you trust to ground you in reality. Return to the skill inventory matrix and consider once again what the things are that you are good at and why you think so.

Once you understand where you are and where you want to go, list all the skills and experiences required to reach the destination. Your learning and development efforts should then follow this list. Try to get work and assignments that will help you build the skills and get the experience to move you in your selected direction. The more focused you can be, the better. Every time you are faced with a decision on your career and you need to choose whether to go left or right, you have a good map. By asking, "How will this help me to get closer to my destination?" you will be able to make a decision.

There is no one size fits all. Each move to get closer to your Sweet Spot requires a different approach and different set of activities. In the rest of the chapter, I will guide you through some of the tools you can use on each of the four paths. The goal is to enable you to start on the right track toward your Quiet Success Sweet Spot.

Training and Practicing

Training and practicing are generally moves you use when you love what you do but are not particularly good at it. They are your way to mastery. Once you acquire the skills, you will instantly become more marketable and better able to get the career you want.

When you hear the word "training," you probably imagine a bunch of people sitting in a classroom being taught by a teacher. Of course, this is part of professional and personal development, but there are many other ways you can develop your skills. The framework I find extremely useful is the concept of 4Es. The growth comes from formal Education, on-the-job Experience, Exposure to other people, and Eminence coming from teaching others.

- *Education*: This is formal learning through classes, individual courses, and theoretical training.
- *Experience*: This is on-the-job learning and professional development, special projects, expanding your role, and volunteering.
- *Exposure*: This is the exposure you get from new experiences and people. It also covers relationships and the network of acquittances and people that shape you.
- *Eminence*: This is learning by teaching. It is about the thought leadership you exhibit, training and mentoring others, speaking at conferences, and knowledge-sharing in general.

To put the 4Es concept in a proper context, consider the 70-20-10 model. What are the most effective ways to learn and grow? In the 1980s, researchers from the Center for Creative Leadership, Morgan McCall, Michael M. Lombardo, and Robert A. Eichinger, came up with the 70-20-10 Model for Learning and Development. While looking into the developmental experiences of successful leaders, they concluded that the best way to develop your skills is by getting 70 percent of your knowledge from job-related experiences, 20 percent from interaction with others, and only 10 percent from formal education.[51]

The reason why the job-related experience far outweighs the knowledge you get by other means is simple. You get to a wider variety of situations that broaden your skills more quickly, and, more importantly, you get constant practice and immediate feedback. You immediately discover what works and what doesn't. Through continuous practice, you build not only your skill but also your confidence.

The 20 percent of interactions with others include coaching and mentoring, exchanging tips and tricks with colleagues, and seeing how others approach things. Again, the fast feedback and encouragement you receive as part of these interactions will propel you toward success faster.

Curiously enough, companies still spend significantly more focus, effort, and money on formal training even though the effectiveness is lower than the return on this investment is questionable. To be fair, the concept is not supported by much empirical data and should be used more as a guideline and a rule of thumb than as a guaranteed recipe for success. It also doesn't consider modern technologies and the vast amount of online resources and informal learning available to you today.

Let's start with education as the most obvious way to get the knowledge and experience necessary for getting practical skills. I will then move on to exposure and eminence as a way to hone your skills to the master level.

Education

Education encompasses all sorts of activities. It starts with the most obvious one that all of us went through: sitting in a classroom, listening to the teacher, and hopefully paying attention so we learn something that might have some value in our lives. I was never a big fan of that type of training, as I found it ineffective. I learn in different ways. Rather than listening to a teacher, I would pick up a book and read it at my own pace. I would research the topic on the internet, engage in a relevant internet forum, and ultimately tap some experts with questions.

There are many people out there who have academic titles, have papers saying that they are sort of experts in a given field, but don't actually know much. They went to school, they got those titles, but they didn't get an education. The moment they left school, they forgot everything they learned. For the purposes of this book, "education" has nothing to do with titles or what type of school you went to. It has everything to do with your ability and willingness to listen and learn.

When you start thinking about the need for additional education, don't stop in the classroom. Do your research and consider all the other options that might work even better for your introverted ways of learning. We live in the time of the internet. You can get valuable resources online without needing to leave your home. Your introverted heart should rejoice at this point. Getting an education is the most natural way for introverts to learn. We like to read. We like to think. We can use our strengths of focus, thoughtfulness, and perseverance.

Experience

Nothing can beat hands-on experience. You can read hundreds of books and listen to hundreds of teachers, but unless you roll up your sleeves and start doing the work, all your learning will be quickly forgotten. Of course, for many skills, especially in the knowledge economy, a solid theoretical background is necessary. But the ability to know things and talk about stuff is not enough. You need to be able to execute.

You might be the most skilled and knowledgeable person, but if you can't produce, if you don't deliver results, it is the same as if you didn't have the knowledge at all. That is why doing the work and learning by doing it is so important. It is also why, sometimes, hiring the smartest person may not be the best strategy. They might be smart, but unless they are willing to put in the effort to transfer the smarts to actual results, they are useless.

Especially for young professionals who are in their last years of university, getting real-world experience is vital. It will help you to learn proper work habits and reset your expectations and will allow you to observe others. Most importantly, it will give you the opportunity to do real work and learn things you would never learn in school.

This part of the 4E concept still works just fine for introverts. We don't mind getting our hands dirty and trying things on our own, as long as there is not too much pressure. Those with social or anxious introversion, as we discussed in Chapter 1, may enjoy the practice, especially if it can be done in solitude. We use our strengths of preparation, prudence, independence, and humility to try and try until we succeed.

Exposure

Since our birth, we learn by mimicking others. We observe the world around us and then copy what we see. Just look at any small kids you have in your life. Kids continuously copy what the adults around them are doing. That's how they learn.

When my niece was between two and three years old, this was very evident. She would see her mother eat something, and she would immediately want to taste it too. If her mother said she didn't like sweets, then this little girl would indicate that she didn't like sweets either. If her mother ate lunch with a fork, the little one demanded a fork too. That is how kids learn. That is how everyone learns.

The opportunity to observe others doing the work you are trying to learn can be invaluable. That is why, in many companies, shadowing others when doing new tasks is so popular. It helps us to understand what the best practices are in doing the work at hand.

Exposure is not only in observing other people doing the work but also in tapping the resources of more experienced individuals. There was a time when people, especially in bigger companies, felt that the way to move their careers ahead was to get an MBA. The idea was to get the formal education, and it would open the doors to a bright future. I must admit that I have an MBA myself. It was a good program, and I learned quite a bit. However, the most significant value I obtained was the opportunity to meet senior managers and leaders from other companies and industries and hear what problems they had to deal with, how they solved managerial issues I was facing, and how they viewed the world around them. This educational experience gave me some tools for strategic management, but most importantly, it opened my eyes to different ways to solve problems.

This is where things start to get a bit tricky for introverts. Exposure, by its definition, requires interaction with other people, and since you are the more junior and less skilled, it can feel awkward. One of the best ways to remove that awkwardness is to rely on a process and some sort of official relationship where everyone clearly understands what's going on and is comfortable with it. Get a mentor.

Mentoring

Mentoring is a great way to gain real-life knowledge from a more senior person. Homer, the legendary Ancient Greek author of two epic poems, the *Iliad* and the *Odyssey*, tells a story of the War of Troy.[52] When Odysseus, one of the Greek kings, set sail for Troy, he wanted to ensure that his young son Telemachus would get a solid education and that his palace would be in good hands. He asked a friend, whose name was Mentor, to get his son the education necessary for a long, fruitful life. Thus the first mentorship took place. It was based on a sympathetic relationship between two people of different levels of experience without any formal relationship or family and organizational structure.

Mentoring is a process of informal transmission of knowledge, psychological support, and even social capital that enables the recipient to increase their professional success in the realms of work-related tasks and personal development. The mentor is significantly more experienced in the area of interest and should be a level or two above the mentee. The mentee is someone who wants to receive professional mentoring to accelerate their growth.

The basis of mentoring is the professional, direct, and partnership-based relationship between a mentor and a mentee. At a high level, the main aim is to promote the professional and personal development of the mentee.

The mentee—you, in this case—is on the receiving end of this relationship. You are personally responsible for all your decisions, and the mentor is there in an advisory capacity only.

How do you find a mentor for yourself? In any bigger organization, you may need the help of the human resources department, which should have access to data to help you find the right mentor. If there is no formal mentorship process within your organization, then just working with your boss or even directly approaching someone senior who you see as a role model in the area you want to improve is an option.

Mentorship and potential sponsorship can help your career, so finding the right mentor can be gold. Studies indicate that mentors select mentees based on their potential and performance.[53] There needs to be chemistry, and more importantly, the mentor needs to see something in the mentee. They must see a potential that waits to be released. When asked about being a mentor, I always consider what I know about the potential mentee. I look for curiosity, energy, and grit. I need to see that the person wants to improve, cares, and is willing to put lots of energy and perseverance into making it happen. I keep investing my time if I see the mentee is open to feedback, and we use the time we interact with each other well. The better prepared the mentee, the more willing I am to help out. If you want to get a mentor, the best thing to do is exhibit the behaviors that will catch the mentor's interest. Only when you have created credibility as a potentially great mentee should you ask for a mentor.

Once you approach a mentor, you need to explain what you expect to get from the relationship and what the mentor can expect in return. The process is then rather straightforward:

- Upon meeting with the mentor for the first time, you should discuss the expectations of both sides in relation to a mentoring relationship. You may want to talk about some of the rules outlined below to make sure both sides are comfortable with them.
- You should agree on the frequency of meetings, duration, and high-level topics. I would suggest meeting monthly at first. Even though most of your conversations can be had over the phone or video conferencing, I would strongly encourage you to meet face-to-face at least twice a year to build a stronger relationship.
- It is your responsibility to organize the meetings and bring topics. The mentor can also bring topics that they see as crucial for the personal development of the mentee, but they are not the owner of the initiative, even though they are the senior partner in the relationship. You own it.

To have a successful and frictionless working relationship, both you and the mentor need to agree on some basic rules you will follow. These rules should cover at least these aspects:

- *Confidentiality*: Everything that is said between the mentor and the mentee remains confidential and shouldn't be shared—or, worse, used to gain some advantage over the other person.
- *Consistency*: To build a stable relationship, it is important to keep regular contact and ensure continuous free-flowing feedback in both directions.
- *Openness*: Keeping an open mind and understanding the other party's worldview is essential to ensure willingness to receive feedback and for growth in general.
- *Honesty*: Crucial for good quality feedback and the ability to have difficult conversations that enable both sides to learn.
- *Maturity*: Both sides need to be mature enough to provide and accept feedback, even when critical; they also need to be reliable enough to follow the agreed-upon rules.

When you put all this together, you can see that building a robust mentoring relationship can help you significantly in accelerating your personal growth and meeting your career aspirations. As an introverted person, you may feel that mentorship is overkill and that sharing your inner thoughts and weaknesses with other people is not particularly appealing. I would argue that it is worth the discomfort. Of course, as with all relationships, you need to build some level of trust. If you feel that there is no chemistry and the relationship doesn't work, it is better to end it professionally and spare yourself the anxiety and wasted time.

Eminence

Merriam-Webster defines "eminence" as "a position of prominence or superiority, a condition of being well-known and successful."[54] As the definition indicates, it is not something you can use when you are just starting. However, it is an excellent path toward mastery once you have a basic level of competence in whatever skill you are trying to build. In the knowledge-based economy, you can call it thought leadership. Thought leadership is an extremely powerful way to sharpen your skills and way of thinking. Only the true masters of a topic can explain it to others in a way that is easy to understand and digest.

It is not only about the actual delivery but also about the hours and hours of preparation that go into it. When you decide to teach something you know to others, and you are looking for ways to explain it in terms others will understand, you often realize that there are bits and pieces that you are not clear on yourself. This forces you to dig into details and learn more. And what about when people start asking questions? Or what if they have contrary opinions? All these things force you to become better and better on the topic. Thought leadership is not only about teaching others and sharing your wisdom with the world, but it is also about reflection and self-improvement.

Eminence also has another aspect that is more closely related to marketing. By sharing your wisdom with others, you are building a brand. You are telling the world who you are, what you stand for, what the things are that you care about, and what you are good at. Not only are you getting better in the process, but others see you as the expert. This is why it is so vitally important not to underestimate this aspect. What's the point of knowing something if no one knows that you know? It may feel good, but it won't make you successful.

When I decided to write a blog about leadership and introversion years back, I had several reasons for doing so, but two of them were prominent. First, I wanted to use the blog medium to share my experience with others. Originally it was meant just for a couple hundred former and current colleagues. Second, I felt I needed to make sense of all the things I have learned during my career.

I needed to get a better grip on my beliefs when it comes to managing people. I felt I needed to take a stand on some issues. Writing and sharing my thoughts with the world forced me to clarify some of my beliefs, abandon some practices that didn't fit the newly created image of how one should lead others, and double down on other things and practices that I felt I need to do more.

For introverts, getting the courage to share our views with the world in a written form can be a brilliant way to get a grip on who we are and to share who we are with others, even though doing so requires a bit of courage at the beginning. You are opening yourself to potential negative comments from those who will disagree with what you are writing. Get over it. Considering that I wrote this book, you can tell I believe so much in the concept of eminence that I was willing to spend an enormous amount of effort on it.

Perseverance and deliberate practice are your friends. It is only by sticking with the learning process for long enough and by practicing the right things the right way that you can achieve mastery.

Reframing and Coaching

Not everything is about building new skills. Sometimes what you need is to change who you are and change your behavior. Maybe you have a habit you would like to get rid of, or there are some behavioral problems that hold you back. It might be that you have the skills to do something and there is a market for it, but you don't see the meaning in it or you don't enjoy it.

Improving your skills doesn't solve the problem in this case. It is your attitude and behavior that need to change. A way to do this is through coaching and by reframing your view of the world. You can do a bit of self-coaching, but it requires some basic skills and self-discipline, so it is better to find a coach who will help you through the process.

Reframing and coaching are tools you use when you have the skills and can do something well but don't really enjoy doing it. These tools can help you learn to love your job and get closer to your Quiet Success Sweet Spot.

Reframing

I love the two sentences Dale Carnegie quotes in his book *How to Stop Worrying and Start Living* when he talks about the experience of a wife of a soldier who was posted near the Mohave Desert. She hated the place and felt she couldn't take it anymore. She wrote home about it and got this response from her father: "Two men looked out of prison bars. One saw the mud, the other saw the stars." She realized that experience is about point of view. She stopped obsessing about the hardship of the situation and started focusing on more positive aspects. The whole experience began to be bearable and even enjoyable. She made friends with locals and began to learn about the nature around her. She got interested in the history of the place and started enjoying being there. It is all about point of view.[55]

Reframing how you see the world and how you react to external events is often the best and most powerful way to get the happiness and satisfaction you seek. Reframing how you look at your job is often the best way to get to your Sweet Spot without even changing the position itself. Coaches can help you reframe things in your mind, while accountability buddies can help you build new habits and make sure that, once you enter a new frame of mind, you stay there. That's why coaching is the other aspect of this strategy.

People have different ways of looking at their professional lives. Some are just looking for a job, a necessary evil that they can endure to be able to pay their bills and survive. Others look at their profession as a career. In reality, this is saying that you see your job as a series of roles that lead to other roles. You are an accountant, and the reason you endure this current role and even excel in it is because you hope to eventually leave that job and become a senior accountant or a manager. The third way to look at professional life is as a calling. You have an overarching purpose in your life, and your work is deeply fulfilling for what it is. It is not about money or promotions. It is about the work itself and your impact on the lives of others.

I always frustrated all my bosses when asked about my career ambitions. I didn't answer in terms of roles or positions. My go-to answer was that "I want to build something, learn something, and help others to grow." What that "something" was just didn't matter. This answer shows the calling mindset—though for the record, it really is a frustrating answer, so you may not want to use it, as it leaves all the hard work of what to do with you to your boss! It is better to voice the sentiment with more specific ideas about what you can do.

What does it all mean? Whether you look at your employment as a job, career, or calling has nothing to do with the work itself. It is all about attitude. It is all in your head. Even a garbage collector can look at the work they do and say to themselves that their work has meaning. They provide a meaningful service to society. Without them, we would end up living in a heap of trash with our life satisfaction significantly diminished.

This is an important realization. It means that if you feel like your job doesn't have meaning, you don't necessarily need to change the job. You just need to find the meaning. You need to change your attitude and get satisfaction from the job you have.

Coaching

You have probably heard about sports coaches, but there are professional coaches who focus on areas of life, business, or career coaching. When you look at the research done by the International Coaching Federation, you'll learn that coaching is a worldwide movement, and you can find the presence of this profession in countries around the world. It is estimated that there are 71,000 professional coaches in business right now (26,700 in Europe, 23,300 in North America, 21,000 in the rest of the world). Coaching works everywhere and for everyone.[56]

Coaching is a way to find your answers from within. It is about exposing the things you know deep down but don't want to admit. It is about understanding your beliefs and working with them. A coach listens to you and encourages you to find your own solutions. A coach is just a sounding board and guide on your journey to figure out what to do. A coach will spend the majority of their time with you listening and only do minimal talking. At the heart of coaching is the idea that people have the resources to help themselves. A coach needs to trigger your hidden power. The best coaching session leaves you with a clear mind and objectives that you own because they came from your heart. To get you started, let me share a couple of coaching questions that are always a great first move. You can use them as a starter for self-coaching.

- *What do you want?* Before you start working on something, you need to understand what it is you want to get in the end. Coaching only works if the receiving side is willing to learn and give the necessary effort. A good coach will never waste time coaching someone who doesn't care. You shouldn't try to change something unless you believe that you want the result and you are willing to give it all it takes.

  » *What is it you want, and why do you want it?* People tend to have a good idea of what they want, but the "why" gets them confused. You may come to me and tell me that you want to figure out how to get more money. If I ask you why, you will probably say, "So I can buy stuff." So why do you need to buy stuff? "It feels good to have a new car." Why does it feel good? "I don't know. I just want a new car." Why a new car and not something else? Digging into the why can change the direction and lead to a different "what." Maybe instead of wanting more money, you really want to be valued by others. And perhaps there are better ways to achieve that, ways that will be more aligned with your abilities and values.

  » *Is it positive?* This one may not be so obvious, but it is important. If you want to motivate yourself, and especially if you want to see positive change, new behavior, and a positive outcome, the goal needs to be formulated positively. For example, "I don't want to feel miserable" wouldn't work. It is a nice sentiment, but it doesn't answer the question of what you want. It just states what you don't want. "I want to be happy" is much more positive, though you may still need to dig deeper to figure out what "being happy" actually means to you.

» *Is it under your control?* Make sure your goal is achievable and under your control. There is very little sense in coming up with a goal that sounds great but requires other people to do it for you. With a goal like that, you will feel helpless, things could go wrong, and you will have no way to influence the direction or quality of the execution. Whatever your goal is, it needs to be under your direct control. For example, "I don't want others to yell at me" is an admirable goal, but is your boss yelling at you under your control? Not really. So try instead, "I want to make it easy for others to treat me with respect." You still can't influence how others will behave, but you can exhibit behavior that will make it easy for others to treat you with respect and not yell at you.

» *Is it aligned with your other goals?* "I want to live alone on a tropical island" is a great goal and maybe even an introvert's dream, but how does it fit in with your other life goals of having a family, a couple of good friends, and a love of skiing? You should always do a sanity check to ensure that the goal you want to achieve won't have a disruptive effect on your other goals and on the goals of those around you who you hold dear.

• *How will you get it?* Since we know what you want, we can start talking about how you can get it. The goal of these questions is to identify what resources you need and how to get you started.

» *Who do you need to ask for help?* Is reaching your goal entirely under your control, or are there some areas where help would be welcomed? Would a chat with your spouse or your boss help you achieve your goal?

» *Do you need any resources you don't have today?* Do you need to buy something as a prerequisite to achieving your goal? Do you need to be in a specific time and place to achieve it?

» *What is your first step?* How do you get started? What is the first step you need to take, and when will you take it? Make sure you come up with a SMART (S—specific, M—measurable, A—achievable, R—relevant, T—time-based) goal.

- *How will you commit? N*ow comes the hard part. Especially for long-term goals, the challenge you will face is not about getting started but about how to keep going.

  » *Is there anything that may prevent you from reaching your goal?* There might be competing priorities. You might get bored. You may need the support of others.

  » *If yes, how will you mitigate this risk?* Have a plan for these eventualities, so when they occur, they don't stop you dead in your tracks, but you are ready to deal with them and push forward.

  » *What other ways of getting it could work?* Have you thought about different ways to achieve your goal that may not be as straightforward at the beginning? You want to learn a foreign language, so you decided to study every weekend for two hours and enroll in lessons at a local language school. What about living abroad for half a year? What about finding a friend who speaks the language? There are always many options, so make sure you consider what is out there before committing to a sub-optimal solution.

  » *How do you rely on others, and what are the consequences for them?* We talked about who you need to help you, and you have a plan to deal with drawbacks if they are not able or willing to help. Now comes the other side. You achieving your goal of living on a remote tropical island will, without a doubt, affect other people around you. Are you comfortable with that impact on your family and friends? How can you limit that impact? How will you feel about your decision in a couple of months?

- *How do you recognize when you've succeeded?* If you set a goal, you also need to be able to measure if you've reached the goal. Besides the fact that you might be curious, you also want to feel good when you finish your goal, and how can you feel good about finishing when you don't know that you finished?

  » *How will you track your progress?* You probably need some way to see that you are still on track to achieving your goal. Do you need a weekly follow-up? Do you need a measurable small step? Do you need feedback from others?

  » *How will you ensure you keep your momentum?* There will be bumps on the road, so how do you ensure you don't lose the momentum? When you check your progress and discover you are slowing down, how will you re-energize yourself to push forward?

> » *How will you recognize you succeeded and achieved your goal?* How will you know you are there? "I want to learn Spanish" is a great goal, but what exactly does it mean? Unless you set clear success criteria, you may never get there, as it is unlikely you will ever speak like a native speaker. "I will know that I have learned Spanish when I take week-long vacations in Barcelona and am able to get around, order dinner, go to the movies, and speak with locals without a need to have a translator." This is still a tall order, but at least it is something you can do to verify you succeeded.
>
> » *How will you celebrate your success?* Have a plan for the celebration. Why? It can act as an additional motivating factor if you can celebrate reaching your goal. "When I learn Spanish, I will go for a month-long vacation to South America, which has been my lifelong dream."

That's it. Pretty straightforward. Most of the difficulties will be at the very beginning, in trying to define what you really want. Introverts may struggle a bit with the idea of working with a professional coach. It requires us to be comfortable opening up to an unknown individual. Since I've been on both sides of the relationship, and in addition to being a coach, I've also been coached by professional coaches, I know how unsettling it can be at the beginning. The key is to pick the right coach. You need to feel some sort of chemistry and trust with the coach. Otherwise, it won't work, regardless of how great they might be. Good coaches are pretty good at building rapport, will spend enough time making sure you feel safe, and will make it clear that everything said during your sessions is confidential. Most importantly, the standard offer you will get from most professional coaches is to do a short test session. If you don't feel comfortable with their style or personality, simply walk away, no hard feelings.

Accountability Buddy

Sometimes coaching is an unnecessarily heavyweight solution to your problem. Other times, it is a good start but what you need is to build discipline to follow through. A great way to do that is to find an accountability buddy or an accountability partner.

In short, an accountability buddy is a person, a trusted confidant, with whom you are comfortable sharing your problem and who is comfortable giving you some tough love. It is someone who is there to help you along the way to build a habit or change an attitude. As the name suggests, they are there to help you hold yourself accountable. The concept is based on the premise that when you have someone watching over you and holding you accountable for your promises, you are more likely to stay on course and follow through. This obviously requires clarity of the goal you want to achieve. Your accountability buddy will help you reach the goal, but they won't help you define it. If you struggle with that, you need to go back to the coach.

Having an accountability buddy is a much more powerful concept than just sharing your goals with the general public. You may have decided to learn a foreign language, so you are not hopeless when traveling on your next vacation. If you start telling your friends that you just bought a bunch of audiobooks and a dictionary and that you are learning the language, you may do yourself a disservice. Chances are the friends will make statements like, "Oh, you are so good, I would never learn a new language," or "I admire your courage. Learning a new language takes a lot of effort that I would never put in." In short, you will get a lot of positive feedback that will mostly feel like you have already learned the language. People may admire your decision, but you will feel like you are halfway there and like now all you need to do is spend a bit of time learning the language. You already feel good. All that remains is hard work. And you will never do it.

The advantage of an accountability buddy is that, when you work with just one person, you don't shout out your goals to the world, but only to that one person, who you know will encourage you and put in the effort to help you follow your plans. They will keep you grounded and provide feedback so you don't get sidetracked.

What does working with an accountability buddy look like? It depends. It can be your good friend, or it can be a professional. If you decide to learn a language, your accountability buddy could be a good teacher, a teacher who will push you to work hard, will give you enough homework, will text you during the week to remind you to practice, and will provide both knowledge and encouragement.

In fact, if you want to learn anything new and the reason why you don't is a lack of self-discipline, then a professional is usually the best way to go, even though it is not a pure accountability buddy but is mixed with a teacher, a coach, and a mentor.

Accountability buddies won't sugarcoat anything. They will give you feedback as they see it. They give you that feedback for your own good. At the same time, they don't judge. They focus on what they see and don't interpret. If you set a goal to go to the gym every day and then don't show up two days in a row, they will call you and point out that you have set yourself a goal to go to the gym every day, and you didn't show up twice. They won't call you lazy. They will just state the facts and ask how you plan to fix the problem and how they can help you.

This concept is particularly powerful between friends if it is reciprocal. You are helping me achieve my goal, and at the same time, I'm helping you with a goal of your own. It builds more trust and can lead to a great relationship.

How Do You Get Started?

Find the Right Person: The key to a successful relationship is to find the right person, someone you will be comfortable with. It needs to be someone trustworthy who won't let you down, both because they have the ability to keep your struggles confidential and because they have the maturity and personality to hold you accountable. Your accountability buddy needs to be someone who will be willing to have a tough conversation with you when required to keep you on course. They also need to be someone who is willing to give the partnership the necessary time and effort and who can do it consistently. You may find a great person, but if they are not ready to commit or have a schedule that conflicts with yours, they are not the right person.

Discuss Your Overall Goal: Make it clear to your new accountability buddy what exactly you are trying to achieve and what your struggles are. It is essential for them to see the big picture and to understand how they can help.

Discuss the Details of How You Plan to Reach Your Goal: Obviously, there are many steps involved in reaching your high-level goal. If you already have an idea of what kind of help you need, then share it. If not, then brainstorm it together. Come up with a daily and weekly routine to follow, identify the weak spots where you need some help to keep going, and agree on what form of support fits. Also discuss any rewards for success and consequences of you breaking your routine and not following through. All this should come primarily from you. It is your goal and your approach. The accountability buddy is there to be your conscience and keep you honest. They shouldn't provide too much direction, as then you are even less likely to follow it. If you have trouble following your own plan, what are the chances you will follow someone else's plan?

Discuss How You Want to Work Together: Set clear rules of engagement. Make it clear how honest you expect the person to be and what form the feedback should take. Discuss how often you will meet or what the regular check-ins should look like. It may be necessary to meet in person, or it may be sufficient to text each other at agreed-upon times/intervals.

Build Weekly/Monthly PACT Agreements: What can be a potent exercise is building weekly or monthly plans. This will force you to break down the big goal into smaller goals and tasks. You can go with SMART (S—specific, M—measurable, A—achievable, R—relevant, T—time-based) goals or PACT (P—possible, A—actionable, C—clear, T—time-bound deadline) agreements. It will also help you to see progress and feel good regularly.

Review Progress and the Process Itself Regularly: Also agree on a frequency for a bigger review of the process and what should be tweaked to make it more valuable and fulfilling. You may say that you will do weekly reviews of goals and then once a month talk about the process itself.

Getting an accountability buddy is something that may feel awkward for many introverts. It requires you to get out of your comfort zone. However, the potential benefits are enormous and outweigh any discomfort you may initially experience. I would strongly suggest you try and, to make it less awkward, offer that you will reciprocate. This will balance the awkward discomfort. Keep in mind though that you will be required to provide direct feedback and will need to keep other people honest with themselves, which brings up a set of challenges and discomfort on its own.

Marketing and Networking

Having the skills and passion doesn't matter if no one knows you have them. The trickiest part of getting to your Sweet Spot is to market and sell what you can do. Marketing involves building visibility. It is all about telling the world, "Here I am, and this is what I can do." This may sound frightening to many introverts, but it is a necessary evil. You have your future in your hands, so get over the fear and dive right in. The marketing of your skills can be done in many different ways, and some of them may not even feel like marketing at all. In the following paragraphs, I will talk about social media, blogging, volunteering, or participating in various interest groups. All these things can be pretty fun, and you can get excited about them.

Conventional wisdom says that extroverts are much better at selling than introverts. This sort of makes sense, considering extroverts are much more comfortable around other people, enjoy interacting with others more, and are often fast talkers. However, an increasing amount of research says that things are not so black and white. Introverts often do very well on sales teams, and it's actually ambiverts who do the best.

Effective selling in today's world is not so much about a brute force of pushy salesmanship, but instead about researching the customer's problems, listening, and adapting to what the customer needs. These are the strengths of many introverts. As Matthew Pollard writes in *The Introvert's Edge*, extroverts' sales tend to be connected to their personality and their mood. If they feel great, they are on top of the world, and they do great. If they feel down, it reflects on their sales too. Introverts, on the other hand, tend to rely on a system. Have the right system, be well-prepared, and you will be able to sell your services just fine.[57]

From a career perspective, marketing your personal brand in today's world is done primarily online. I suggest you consider these everyday opportunities for a bit of marketing, and I'm sure you can come up with many more:

- *CV/Resume*: This is the primary marketing tool at your disposal. It is the very minimum you have to do to go out to the market and sell your services to companies.
- *Blogging*: Building an image of expertise through thought leadership is one of the best ways to get your name recognized and to show the world what you can help with. Keeping a blog or contributing to relevant industry blogs is lots of work, but it pays off.
- *Presence on LinkedIn and Other Social Media*: This combines aspects of the previous two opportunities. Having your resume, for example, on LinkedIn, directly linked with your participation in various conversations in interest groups, tells the reader not only what your opinion is but why they should listen to you, what your credentials are.
- *Volunteering*: Using your skills to help others doesn't just bringing value to the world and build your image, but also sharpens your skills and brings you a feeling of accomplishment.
- *Participation in Interest Groups and Professional Bodies*: There are many interest groups and nonprofit organizations where you can socialize with others with similar interests to your own. In these groups, you will not only be able to show off your skills and help others, but you will also learn from those better than you. And it will be fun!
- *Soliciting Feedback*: This may not sound like a selling and image-building opportunity, but it is. By seeking feedback from others, you can pique their interest and point their attention toward who you are trying to be. You show you own your future and have the desire to listen and become better. These are good traits for any employee.
- *Being Available and Consistent*: You may not realize it, but you are selling who you are every day. Acting with integrity, being consistent, trustworthy, and willing to help others will, step by step, build a powerful image of someone people want to work with.

It takes a long time and a lot of effort to build an image of a professional who can solve complex problems and help others. This is just a glimpse of the tools available to you to present your skills and interests to the world. I'm sure that if you consider your unique circumstances, you can come up with many more tools that might be relevant to your niche skills and market. The valuable lesson is that you need to get the courage and show who you are to the world. This is a very unnatural thing for introverts to do. Still, it is the necessary thing to do to be able to fulfill your dreams.

How to Network like An Introvert

I remember my first networking event. Well, I don't remember the details, like who organized it and even why I was there. But I remember how it made me feel: awkward. It was at the beginning of my career, back when I was getting into management, and networking with potential clients, partners, and even competitors became part of my job.

I knew only one person at the event, and more than a hundred people were participating. Most of them were much more experienced than I was, most had been in the industry circles a long time, and most knew each other. I remember spending most of the evening tagging along with the only person I knew, with frequent detours to the refreshment table for delicious food. It was exhausting, and it was awkward. I didn't get anything out of it except for the knowledge that it wasn't my thing. You see, as an introvert, schmoozing with a crowd of people I don't know is my ultimate representation of hell.

I dreaded coming to the event, I didn't enjoy it while I was there, and I was happy to escape. Yet, on my way home, while overanalyzing everything like any introvert would and having all the great things I should have said flooding my brain, I also had a good feeling. I was glad I had attended. I had gotten out of my comfort zone, and now that I knew how things worked, I also knew that I could do much better the next time with proper preparation.

Regardless of how much you may hate the idea of networking, you need to accept the reality of the world. And the world requires you to meet new people if you want to build relationships, sell your services, build a business, and be successful.

How Not to Do It

"Hi, I'm Tomas, how are you? Oh, you work for ThoseGuys? Cool. I work for TheseGuys. We sell some machines—maybe you could use some?" By this point, you are already exhausted, feeling silly, and you can see that both you and your first victim at the networking event want to be somewhere else.

This ad hoc, "let's just wing it" approach works only for charismatic smooth talkers who work the room with a ballet dancer's grace. It is the traveling salesman approach, where you don't bother building strong relationships before selling your services. You go for volume and try to shove your pitch down the throat of as many people as possible, as quickly as possible. It is not about them. This is not the introvert's way.

In *The Introvert's Edge to Networking*, Matthew Pollard talks in great detail about how even introverts can get the most out of networking events without feeling awkward or out of their depth. Forget about how extroverts do it; instead, focus on your strengths and make them work for you. Learn the art of strategic networking. Introverts excel at preparation. So, with proper preparation and by following a well-defined process, you can become pretty good even at something as seemingly anti-introvert as networking.[58]

Find the Reason: Before you even contemplate networking, you should figure out why you want to do it and who you are. What is so special about you? How do you want to present yourself to others? And who are the people you want to meet? It is never a good idea to try to please everyone. It will just stress you out and dilute your chances of becoming interesting. You need to identify your niche, and you need to tailor your life story so it grabs the attention of those you are targeting. Most introverts are very comfortable talking about things they are passionate about. It shows through our words. It grabs attention. And it removes stress and builds confidence. It makes us authentic. It makes us go-to people for specific needs. It also gives us the motivation to network. Set the right expectations. It should not be your goal to go to the networking event and collect as many business cards as possible. Change your goal to something more modest, like meeting one or two interesting people you can build a deeper relationship with.

Tell Stories: People don't like listening to you talking about your work, but they enjoy listening to stories. Come up with a couple of stories that will illustrate the value you provided to someone. Make them short and emotional and connect them with solving a problem that the people you talk to may have. You want to create an emotional connection that will make the potential clients say to themselves, "Yes, that is me in that story. Please, please, help me!" The story shouldn't be about you. It should be about the experience and the emotions of the person you helped. Just like in fables, make it very clear what the moral of the story is.

Create a Persona: How do you respond to the question, "What do you do?" Do you respond with the standard "I'm a lawyer, I'm an accountant, I'm a manager," or are you more intriguing? The standard answer doesn't mean much. It puts you into a standardized box but doesn't answer what you do, what your results are, and how you could be of service. Pollard has a better approach. He suggests you come up with an intriguing moniker that will invite further conversation. As an example, he answers this question with "I'm the Rapid Growth Guy." When you hear an answer like that, you don't have a choice but to ask, "What is that?" This allows him to tell a story and draw you in.

Research Participants: Your strength of preparation doesn't end here. Before you get out the door to attend a networking event, you should know who will be there. Ideally, you even want to know some of the people attending, at least a little bit. If you have already communicated with them and gotten conversations going before the event, it will be easier to fit in. Get online and do your homework. Often, you can find out who will be participating in an event, and you can identify those you want to approach. This makes your networking genuinely strategic.

Have a Script: Don't worry about coming up with new phrases and conversation topics for each person you meet at the event. Do the opposite. Prepare a story or two you can repeat to every person you meet and polish it to perfection. The people you talk to won't know you told the story to five other people already, and in the end, what's wrong with that? If improv is not your thing, why should you force it? When something you say works and helps you to build rapport with others, why change it? And if you feel that preparing and practicing the story will make you sound scripted, think again. Just consider any great actor or actress in your favorite movie. They certainly don't sound scripted, even though they repeat the lines someone wrote for them. Good preparation will make you more confident and will remove some of your anxiety. It will make you sound more natural.

Exit Gracefully: Pollard even suggests some scripts for you to consider if you don't know where to start. The thing to realize is that networking is not only about telling the story and explaining how you can help. You also want the person you are talking to to take positive action. You can end with something like, "I am enjoying this conversation, but I don't want to take up all your time. What if I reach out by email to schedule a coffee? Would that be something you are open to?" You might also offer to introduce some people, share some content. Regardless of future potential business, your goal now is to help keep the conversation going in the future.

Learn and Follow Up: After every networking event, consider the lessons learned. What went right? What could go better? Did you tell your stories right? What was the reaction? Did you follow your script? What derailed you? What were the unexpected responses that took you off balance? Which conversations led to action, and which didn't? Why didn't they? What will you do differently the next time? What do you need to do to prepare for it? When will you start? Not achieving what you wanted doesn't mean there is something wrong with you. It just means your system needs some tweaks and improvements. Remember, networking is all about the process. And don't forget to follow up. There is little point in having a great conversation at an event, making all sorts of promises, and then not following up. Great relationships require regular nurture, and it applies doubly when the relationship is just starting.

When You Build It, Use It: In *How Women Rise*, Sally Helgesen and Marshall Goldsmith talk about how not leveraging relationships is one of the habits that holds women back.[59] This applies to introverts too. It is rooted in the need to treat others for who they are rather than for what they could be useful for. Women are often good at building strong relationships but are very reluctant to use these relationships to their advantage. Being an introvert, I have a similar problem. Over my years in the business, I have built a vast network of acquaintances, yet I struggle to ask them for favors. Curiously enough, many of them don't have the same problem and ask me for favors all the time. And I oblige. You are building a professional network for a reason—don't be afraid to use it. The whole idea of a professional network is a mutual exchange of benefits. Learn to leverage the reciprocal quid pro quo. Help others, and be willing to ask for help in return.

The good news for introverts is that networking using a process like this is significantly less stressful than improvising. You are just following a scenario you prepared beforehand using your strengths of preparation, attentiveness, empathy, and humility.

If you still feel like you never want to stick your head into a room full of people at a networking event, consider that all this preparation and the whole process work online too. Figuring out who you are, finding the right persona, developing stories, and communicating your value will help you get to know people and bring in some business, not only in networking events but in online marketing too.

Interviewing and Negotiating

You may have the skills, you may love the work, but if you hate the job because you don't like the people you work with or there are no more career prospects at your current company as you are in the coasting phase of your Employee Emotional Life Cycle, then to get to your Sweet Spot, you need to change the organization you work for.

Life is too short to spend it with people you despise, who demean you, who abuse you, or who ignore you. You have the right to be respected. You have the right to feel like an equal and to belong. You have the right to work with people you can learn from and whose company you enjoy. The time comes when the best way forward is to quit and find a new job. And that requires interviewing and related negotiations.

Interviews rarely bring the best out of introverts. Since we don't get energized by social situations, we don't tend to exhume energy in interviews. The first step to being able to interview well is to get comfortable with self-promotion. It is part of the game, and regardless of how much you may detest it, it is important. An excellent attitude to adopt is that self-promotion is a skill like any other. It has nothing to do with your personality. It can be learned. And if it can be learned, you can learn it.

Interview Process

There are many books written about job searches, interviews, and general advice on how to get jobs. I'm not going to repeat what others have said, as the topic is rather complicated and not necessarily key to the message of this book.

However, I still feel that a book about careers wouldn't be complete without giving at least a glancing overview of the interview process and the means to land a job you want. In the following pages, I will provide some basic thoughts on what introverts should consider when interviewing for a job. For a much deeper dive into the topic, I suggest you look for a dedicated book, like the work of Gabriela Casineanu.[60]

What can you expect once you get on the phone with the hiring manager or to a face-to-face interview? You guessed it: it depends. Each company and each hiring manager have their style of performing interviews. Each of us has different values and ways of figuring out who the person sitting across from us is. In the following paragraphs are some of the interview types you can encounter. It is by no means a complete list, but it shows you the various approaches. The actual interview will most likely be an amalgam of a couple of these approaches.

A structured interview is when the hiring manager comes prepared with a list of questions and goes through them one by one. All the candidates get the same questions. Depending on the interviewer's experience, this may feel like a natural conversation, but more likely, it will feel a bit like an interrogation. To prepare for this type of interview, you can check the internet for the most common questions related to your chosen field of work. Sometimes the interviewer starts with some icebreakers to help you relax, but even those are often just an afterthought.

An unstructured interview (free-flow conversation) is often employed when interviewing for more senior positions. Your qualifications are not doubted and may not even be checked. Your past track record speaks for itself. It is the fit with the team and your attitude toward life and work that is being checked. The hiring manager wants to know you as an individual and understand what it would be like to work with you. This is also one interview where you can most easily turn the tables and ask lots of questions. You can end up asking more questions than are being asked of you. These interviews are a great way for both the interviewer and interviewee to get to know each other, and both sides will most likely leave the interview with a good sense of whether they are a good fit for each other. What I find essential in unstructured interviews is to be who you are. If you try to impress the interviewer by acting the way you believe is expected, you may end up with two bad outcomes. The first danger is that the hiring manager may see through you and recognize you as a phony, and you won't get the job. The second danger is that you will be convincing, and the hiring manager will feel you are the right person for the job. You get the offer, but it is bad news because it wasn't *you* who got the offer, it was your imaginary alter ego. The chances are that the real you will suffer on the job. You tricked yourself into taking a job you will hate.

A situational interview is when you are presented with hypothetical questions and scenarios and asked how you would behave or solve the problem. Sometimes they may be very specific to the company you are interviewing with, to check whether you would do things the way other people at the company would. Most often, there are obvious answers, and by using common sense, you can guess what the hiring manager wants to hear. If you have at least a decent experience in the field, you will likely go through these questions rather quickly. They weed out only those candidates who have no idea what they are talking about. That is why this type of question is often replaced by behavioral questions.

A behavioral interview is when the questions you are asked are about how you behaved in past situations. The intent is not to talk about hypothetical scenarios as in situational interviews, but for you to replay situations you have experienced in the past and talk about how you behaved at those times. The theory is that your past actions in similar situations are the best predictor of your future performance. Even though you can still come up with made-up situations, a skillful interviewer will see through them. They will keep digging into details, and you will be more and more hesitant unless you truly tell the truth. You will recognize this type of interview if you're asked questions starting with:

- Tell me about a time when you did XYZ.
- Share with me a situation in which you demonstrated XYZ.
- Describe a project when you were faced with problem XYZ
  and how you resolved it.

The way to prepare for behavioral interviews is to guess what the major pains of the company and the team are and to consider what projects or tasks you have done in the past that might be relevant. You may also talk about your past experience and what you learned from that experience. The lessons learned are an important aspect. They show that you already experienced a particular situation and also that you learned from it. To answer these questions, be brief and structured. It makes sense to follow approaches like STAR or SOAR.

The SOAR model of answering a question:

- *Situation*: Provide the context of the situation.
- *Obstacles*: Explain the problem you were facing.
- *Action*: Talk about the steps you took to solve the problem.
- *Results*: Describe the outcome of your efforts, and feel free to add lessons learned.

The STAR model is similar:

- *Situation*: Again, explain the background and the problem.
- *Task*: Talk about what you were trying to achieve.
- *Action*: Discuss specific steps you and the team took (make sure you are clear on what you did personally versus what the whole team did).
- *Results*: What was the outcome? (The more specific you can be, the better; if you can quantify the results to show the scope of the success, even better.)

I personally like the SOAR model for answering behavioral questions. It helps you to be pretty comprehensive while keeping things organized and easy to follow. The one point to be careful about is to talk about what you have done, not what the team was doing. If you don't want to use "I" too much and prefer to stay humble, this is not the right time. Nothing is more frustrating for interviewers than if you keep answering their questions with what "we have done," as it doesn't tell them what *your* personal involvement was. It may be good to start with, "it was a team effort," but then continue with what your role was specifically.

A case study interview is often employed in the consulting business. You get a case study, and your task is to show how you would solve the problem. It may be a rather complex task that can take up the whole interview as you walk the hiring manager step by step through how you would approach it. It is often less about what solution you can come up with and more about the process. It informs how you approach problem-solving, what questions you ask, what sort of experience you can tap into, your level of confidence, and many other traits.

A task-based interview is very similar to the case study but usually smaller in scope. You may get a couple of supposedly simple tasks to do during the interview to show you can do the job and how you approach it. Again, it is often expected that you walk the interviewer through your reasoning process by talking out loud about what's going on in your head. For some roles—for example, in software development—you may be required to write a piece of code and explain it afterward or even test on a computer whether it works. Alternately, you may be asked to do the same on a whiteboard and comment on it as you write it.

This can be extremely uncomfortable for introverts, and you may not even be able to give the task your best. If you know that you can't focus and think if you are asked to speak at the same time, it is probably better to say so and ask if you can first do the task and then explain how you went about it. If the interviewer is reasonable, they will grant the request to see the best you can do. If not, chances are you don't want to work for a company that will require you to work in an environment full of distractions and under tons of undue pressure anyway.

As you can see, there are many different approaches to interviews, and you never really know what the hiring manager expects when they ask you a question. Even though you can cheat your way through an interview by answering the way you believe the interviewer expects, I don't think you should. Unless you want to land the job at any cost, even at the expense of being unhappy the moment you start, I would strongly encourage you not to lie during interviews. Not only is it unethical, but it also sets you up for failure in your new job from the outset. It is one of the reasons why so many people are in jobs they don't like. Getting the job felt like a victory, but in reality, they shot themselves in the foot.

Introverts at Interviews

Interviews can be one of the most stressful situations in your professional life, regardless of whether you are an extrovert or an introvert. Your immediate circumstances can significantly improve or utterly destroy your chances of being successful and getting the job you want. So what are the things that work against you, and how do you mitigate them? And what are the strengths you, as an introvert, can use to your advantage? Let's start with the pitfalls. For an average introvert, there are a couple of obstacles coming from who you are.

Before the Interview

Unwillingness to Put Yourself on the Market: Most of us hate being uncomfortable. Human beings have a general tendency to find a state that is most comfortable for us and then stay there. During the decision-making process, we compare the alternatives against that status quo. If you already have a job, you will consider whether it is worth the pain of change and uncertainty to try to find a job that is more aligned with who you are or what you want to do. It often goes back to a simple formula. The amount of dissatisfaction multiplied by a vision of a better future must be bigger than the fear of change. If there is something to look forward to and you are dissatisfied with how things are, you are more likely to overcome the fear of change. If there is no vision of a bright future, or you don't mind being where you are, chances are you won't take the first step. Therefore, having a clear vision of where you want to be is important and something to work on.

Overthinking What May Happen: This goes back to fear of change. You spend so much time in your inner world, thinking, analyzing, and, unfortunately, over-analyzing that you come up with tons of reasons why not to make a change. So many things can go wrong. You may not be successful in your interviews, and it will diminish your confidence. You may not like the new boss and the team, and you may lose friends in your current company. You may end up without a job or make a wrong career move. All these things can happen. Don't let them stop you. Unless you bring the wrong mindset and negative attitude with you to your next job, the chances are that things will be fine. They will be different, but fine.

Getting Cold Feet: You already made the decision, sent out the resume, and got the interview, but at the last minute, you decided it was not worth the effort. Your boss just told you that you'd done a great job on the project, you just had a team dinner, and bonuses are coming in a couple of months. It is not the right time. All this may be true, but remember that there was a reason why you initially sent out the resume. When reevaluating the decisions you made, always ask yourself, "What circumstances changed? What new information do I have that I didn't have before?" If the answer is "Not much," then push on.

During the Interview

Interacting with People You Don't Know: You will be talking to people you don't know and who may have a potentially massive impact on your life from now on. You will speak with a recruiter, who will make recommendations, to your future teammates, who will form opinions of who you are, and to your potential future boss, who will decide your fate. This is a lot of pressure. How do you handle this?

Should you tell everyone what they want to hear? What about acting a bit more extroverted and outgoing to feel more like a team player? I personally always stuck with acting like who I am. Preparation is the key. Just being able to get the names of the people you will talk to, check them out on social networks, and get at least a bit of a feel for who they are goes a long way. The key is to treat them as equal human beings and not as some gods of whom you are not worthy. Just have a conversation like mature adults, and you will be fine.

Pressure and Need for Fast Responses: There is no need to feel rushed when responding. It is completely fine to take your time when answering questions. It always depends on circumstances, but one strategy that often works, and is even appreciated, is thinking out loud. People who interview you may enjoy it when they understand how you think about a problem. Saying something like, "Let me walk you through the way I would approach the problem" is a nice way to appear transparent while giving yourself time to think it through. If that is too bold a strategy, then something as simple as, "Please, give me a second to think this through" is also acceptable.

Fear of Failure: There is nothing wrong with failure, especially when it comes to interviews. Unless you are in a situation where there is only this one job you can do and nothing else, then the stakes are not that high. The one strategy I have always employed ever since school was to come to the interview with the mindset, "I like the job, but at the same time, if I don't get it, it is okay. The interview, at least, was a nice practice." This helps me to be relaxed and confident. I'm able to use humor and generally be the best professional I can be. In the end, you need to ask yourself, what is the worst thing that can happen? You don't get the job. So what?

Trying to Be Someone Else: Because you believe that acting a certain way increases your chances of success, you start extroverting. I would recommend you don't try to act like someone you are not. Not only will that make you behave in a weird, inauthentic way, but it will also serve you wrong when you finally get the job, only to find out that everyone on the team is an extrovert. They thought you were one, too, and you will suffer. Being the best professional is the right strategy to find the right job for you. Can it sometimes mean you won't get the offer? Yes, and that is good. If someone believes you are not a good fit for their team, there is no reason to push yourself into it. You will be the one who will suffer. Just remember the word "professional." Be the best professional yourself and behave the way adults are expected to behave.

How to Use Your Strengths

You Are Good at Preparation, so Use It: This is the go-to strategy for introverts in pretty much any situation. We are good at preparation, and that gives us an edge. Take the time to research the company you are applying to and make some notes, find out who is on the leadership team, find some information about your future boss on LinkedIn, see if there is someone you know at the company, and reach out for information about how things work over there. Browse the internet to see what sorts of questions are usually asked at interviews at this company or similar ones, then write those questions down. Have answers to the common questions around your strengths, weaknesses, what you want to do long term, what you enjoy at work and don't, what your willingness is to travel, and what your hobbies are. You can argue that many of the questions may not be relevant for the job, but they may be asked anyway, and it is good to be prepared. Write down a couple of questions you could ask the people who will interview you. Don't overdo it though. Preparing one or two questions is good enough for the first rounds of interviews, and a couple more are sufficient when getting the offer. What to ask depends on the role you are applying for. As a general rule, anything that shows interest in the company culture, goals, and priorities are good questions. They will give the interviewers the feel that you are interested in the company and the job, not only in money, and they will help you understand what sort of culture you are getting into.

You Are Good at Listening, so Listen: And feel free to take notes. Especially when you ask questions or when the job and the company are being introduced to you, it is time to employ your listening talent and attention to detail. Write down the critical information, highlight for yourself what you would be interested in exploring in greater detail, and either ask your questions immediately or, if not appropriate due to the interview format, return to them when the time for questions comes.

You Are Who You Are—Be Proud of It Since It Will Lead to Long-Term Satisfaction: I mentioned that before. Even though there is no inherent value in being yourself, there is value in not trying to be someone you are not for the sake of getting a job that will make you miserable. Being your best professional self is the strategy to go for. Be proud of your introversion. Focus on your strengths and show you can adapt. It will make the whole interview experience painless and much more fun for you. And when you act naturally, you appear more authentic, and that gives you an edge.

Negotiating a Salary

Negotiating fair compensation is often a stressful experience, and it can make you feel awkward. It is a tough conversation to have, where the stakes are pretty high and where both sides are not necessarily entirely aligned in terms of what they want. The chances are that both you and the future employer want you to work for the company. Chances are also that you want to maximize the reward you get for working there, while the employer may tend to offer as little as they can without losing you.

If you don't get comfortable negotiating a fair reward for your work, you will most likely still join the company, but from day one, you will feel resentful, and instead of giving all you've got to the job, you will have a lingering feeling that you sold yourself cheap. The more you learn what your friends make and the more you see opportunities from recruiters, the more resentful you will get. Eventually, you will jump ship and join another company.

You could spare yourself all this pain if you do a better job negotiating compensation that you consider fair in the first place. With this in mind, it is your duty to negotiate and accept only compensation that you find appropriate.

You and only you are responsible for your life, so if you believe that your employer doesn't compensate you adequately for your work, that is your fault. Either it is true, and that means you were not able to explain your value to the employer and negotiate a fair salary, or you don't have a realistic view of your value on the job market and, in fact, you are adequately compensated, but your ego doesn't want to admit that.

So how can you spare yourself all this grief, and what can you do to negotiate fair compensation that will leave both sides happy with the deal? You should follow a couple of basic principles using some of the strengths most introverts have:

Do Your Homework: It is all about preparation, and preparation is one thing that introverts often excel at. You should research a couple of different things to be well-prepared for the negotiations. First, do your best to understand why the employer even opened the position in the first place. What problem are they trying to solve? Understanding this will help you voice how you can solve their problem. And it doesn't need to be just a specialized role. Even if you applied for the role of receptionist, there is still a mission, a problem you will help solve. The company needs someone to meet and greet customers or candidates, file some paperwork, schedule stuff, work with suppliers, and do many other things to keep the operation running.

Listen Carefully: By listening well during the whole recruitment process and asking the right questions, you should have a good understanding of what the pains of the company are that your role will fix. Proactive and attentive listening is again one of your strengths, so make sure you use it. Asking the right questions will get you ammunition for the final negotiation and show your interest and acumen.

Articulate the Value You Bring: That leads to the second part of the preparation: You need to put together a short sales pitch that will clearly articulate the value you bring to the table. Not just, "I can do all these things," but more along the lines of, "This is how I will positively impact the lives of others." Not only will this approach help you make a more emotional connection with your counterpart at the negotiation table, but it will also help you visualize your mission at the company. You will feel more confident and in control. Let's look at the example of the receptionist role. You can start with something like, "I understand that the tasks this role should handle are managing calendars, greeting people, making travel arrangements, working with suppliers, and running the office. I have done all this before and know how to organize things to run an efficient operation. The way I see it, my mission at this company is to make your life and other people's lives easier. I can do this by handling tons of the small everyday details in the professional and personal lives of you and the other employees, by anticipating future needs, and by making sure others can focus on their key goals and don't get slowed down by bureaucracy." You showed the hiring manager that you understand what is in the job description and that you can take the role to a new level. This shows your passion for the job. It shows that you prepared. It shows that you are a level above everyone else they most likely interviewed.

Have a Story to Tell: Selling works best when you show that you genuinely understand the needs of the person you're selling to, and you can focus more on emotions than just on logic. You want to highlight the things you will bring to the table that are often unsaid yet extremely important. The best way to do that is to find an example in your life that you can present in the form of a short story. "Listen to this story," our hypothetical receptionist can say. "I understand that a big portion of the job is to book travel for the executive team. I know how busy executives are. They spend lots of time on the road and cherish every minute they can spend with their families. I see it as my mission to help others live happy lives. It reminds me of a recent situation when a CTO asked me to book him a trip that would make him miss his daughter's birthday. Since I knew the birthday was coming, I came up with an alternative to the usual flight he would take so he was able to get home just in time. It was a bit less comfortable than he was used to, but he was delighted that he managed to be there for his child." You are not only listing the tasks you have done before but the impact your work had on those around you. The chances are that the hiring manager, when listening to your story, can picture themselves in the role of your former boss and say to themselves, "Yes, this is the person who understands their job and will make my life easier." Sold.

Understand Your Value on the Job Market: When it comes to talking about money, I find the best approach is to try not to make a big deal out of it. The more you are focused on money, the more obsessed you are, the more you want to talk about it, the more the conversation will be about "how much you cost" and not about "what you bring." Don't push for a money conversation until you understand the role. It may sound like you will save everyone time if you first set expectations but realistically, you can't set the right expectations on how much "it" will cost before you discuss what "it" really is.

Before you say a number, do your homework. Research what someone with your experience in that particular industry, in that specific position, and in that particular country or city makes. You can find lots of information on the internet. You can even ask some of your friends, and you can ask some recruiters. This is helpful not only in giving you a feel for your value on the market but also in making the negotiation less personal and less stressful. It is not about "what you think." It is about "what is standard in the market." It will make you more comfortable with asking for a better compensation package.

You should apply critical thinking when going over the data. Not everything you read on the internet is true. Not everyone tells you what they make, and not every recruiter will give you a realistic number. Hopefully, you will come up with a range that will provide you with a good indication of your worth on the job market.

Don't Mind Going First: I have often heard that whatever you do, you shouldn't go first. Let the other side come up with a number. I find this to be very unfortunate advice. The moment you let the employer come up with an amount, you are being put in a position to push back and justify why you should be paid more. It puts you on the defensive. A better approach is doing your research, coming up with a range, and then asking for something at the upper end of that range—ideally a bit more than you hope for. You can start with something like, "Based on my research of the market and my experience, I believe that fair compensation for this role is in this range. Does it align with your expectation?" Now it is up to the employer to push back and justify why you are not worth that money.

Just make sure that the range is high enough that even the lower end is still a good outcome for you. By having a high range, you are creating what negotiators call an extreme anchor. If you feel you are worthy of $100,000 and ask for a range of $100,000 to $120,000, then the lower end of $100,000 doesn't look that bad compared to the high end. The other party may go for the lower end, and you will still feel okay.

If the employer is the one who comes up with a proposal first, and it doesn't align with your expectations, you can still get what you believe you are worth. Just take it as a first step in the negotiation, stay positive, and don't make ultimatums. You can react with something along these lines: "Thank you for the offer. I liked everything I heard during the interview process, and I would love to work for the company. I would just ask you to rethink the compensation package. I did extensive research and, considering my experience and the value I bring, I would expect something closer to $100,000."

During the negotiation cycle, you may ultimately decide to quote a non-rounded amount. If you say that you expect to get $100,000, it feels like a placeholder still open to negotiation. If you say that you thought about it carefully and can't accept anything lower than $101,500, it feels like a final number. It feels like you honestly thought about it and came up with the number after some careful calculations.

Focus on More Than Just Money: By going first, you are setting the range, you are setting the expectations, and you are framing the conversation. It can easily happen that the employer comes back and says it is too much for them, that the budget for the role is limited, and give you a lower number as a counterproposal. If that number is still within your expected range, you may take it but use the opportunity to get some non-monetary benefit.

For example, you may be willing to take that offer, but would it be possible for you to work from home? Whatever it is you care about and that is worth some money to you, ask for it. Just make sure you have realistic expectations. The bigger the company, the bigger the chance of a very rigid compensation system. That has to be the case. If every person in a company with a hundred thousand employees negotiated different benefits, it would be a mess and most likely also illegal. However, there can always be some level of flexibility, and it is good to explore it.

Be Willing to Walk Away: One of the most significant problems when negotiating a salary is that people don't want to lose. We are sometimes so desperate to make a deal that we make a deal that is no good, and we regret it later. You should have a precise number in your head that is the necessary minimum, and you should not compromise on it. If you did your research and know your value on the job market, then there is no need to sell yourself cheap.

Again, for this to work, make sure you think critically about the data you are getting. We all tend to think very highly about ourselves and often have unrealistic expectations. If you feel that what you are being offered is under your market value and there is no flexibility on the employer's side, just walk away. Of course, do so in a respectful, transparent way that will allow the employer to come back to you if the situation changes and they decide to offer more.

There are a couple of topics you probably shouldn't talk about when negotiating a salary.

Don't Talk About What You Make Today: I have often heard recruiters or hiring managers ask the question, "What do you make today?" It is no longer legal to ask this in some countries, but even if it were, it is an irrelevant question. What you make today has no relevance to what you should be making in your new position. I once even encountered a company that asked to see my pay slip to verify whether what I told them about my current compensation was true. That company must have been a charming culture to work in if they assumed from day one that a potential employee's word couldn't be trusted.

The reason for the question is often either that the company honestly doesn't know what to pay for the position, so by asking you, they are essentially doing market research, or that asking is merely a process, and no one ultimately cares. The more specialized the role, the more the first statement is true.

There are different ways to answer the question, so be prepared with an answer that will make you comfortable. You shouldn't lie. Whatever you say, don't make up untrue numbers. Building a future relationship on a lie is not good for anyone. Some companies have in their contracts that you are not allowed to talk about your salary, so if that is the case, you can use it as a way out. Or use a more direct approach and just state that you don't believe that your current compensation is relevant, as it is a different role and a different company. You can say that, based on your research and possibly the offers you have gotten in the past, you would expect a salary somewhere in this or that range, but you understand that different companies have different compensation strategies, so you are, of course, flexible in negotiating.

Don't Talk About Your Lifestyle Choices: Many times in my career, I have seen people coming to talk about salary and starting with, "I need a salary increase because I just got a big mortgage." Who cares? Not only does the employer not care about your mortgage, as it has no relation to the work you do for the company, but by framing the conversation in this way, you are actually saying that you can't plan your finances properly. Do you think the hiring manager wants to employ someone like that? Leave all your so-called needs aside. The whole conversation should be about what problem you will solve for the company and what your value on the market and for the employer is. Your lifestyle choices and expenses are irrelevant.

Most things in life are negotiable. If you don't ask for something, chances are you won't get it. This also applies to salary negotiation. Always negotiate. And always shoot for a win-win situation. If you accept lower compensation than what your value on the job market is, then you have lost. Eventually, you will resent the company and walk away, so *everyone* loses.

If you get more money than your value on the market, the company has lost. Eventually, because you are overpaid, you will be stuck in your job with golden handcuffs on your hands. You won't enjoy the job anymore, you will be dissatisfied, and you won't be able to leave because no one will pay you that much money. Again, everyone lost. The only way to have a good long-term working relationship between you and your employer is to go for a win-win. And that means negotiating fair pay—no more, no less.

Summary and Key Takeaways

Wherever you are in your career, you can use one of the four paths, or a combination, to get to your Sweet Spot. The Sweet Spot is the job that fulfills the four aspects of a successful career as noted in the Successful Career Wheel: I Learn, I Matter, I Survive, and I Belong. Being in your Sweet Spot means that you love what you do, you are good at it, someone needs it and is willing to pay for it, and you do it with people you like. The four paths toward your Sweet Spot are training and practicing, reframing and coaching, marketing and networking, and interviewing and negotiating.

- Depending on your Sweet Spot and the type of job you want, you have different strategies for reaching it.
    » Training and practicing—involves education, experience, exposure, and eminence.
    » Reframing and coaching—involves career coaching, accountability buddies, and reframing your world views.
    » Marketing and networking—involves publishing, volunteering, and networking.
    » Interviewing and negotiating—involves understanding and building job interviewing skills and being willing to negotiate fair compensation.

Questions and Next Steps

- In the previous chapter, I asked you to identify where you are in your current job on the Quiet Success Sweet Spot diagram. Now I will ask you to consider the four paths toward success to find a way to get to your Sweet Spot. Go back to Figure 8 to use it as a guide.
- What type of training and practicing would work best for you in your current situation? What educational experiences do you need to aquire? What experience do you need? Would it help for you to gain exposure to some people? If yes, who? Are you on your path to mastery, and would it help you to hone your skills if you provided thought leadership or trained others?
- Would reframing your view of your career help you? Would you consider a coach? What would you want to work on with them? Do you clarify what you need to do but don't think you have the will? Who could be your accountability buddy?
- Do you need to market yourself better? What is your online presence? Do you

need to get more active on social media? Would it make sense to start a blog? What about building a network of people who can help you out? Who are those people, and how can we reach them the best?

- Is it clear that you can't get to your Sweet Spot at your current company? What do you need to do to prepare for the job search and the interview process? Do you know what your value on the market is?
- Whatever you need to do to get to your Sweet Spot, now is the time to do it!

PART III

How to Succeed in Your Sweet Spot

7

Quiet Success Principles

At this point, you know what you want from your career and life and what success looks like to you. You understand what your Sweet Spot is, and you have a good grip on all the routes you can take to get there. What is missing is the bigger picture of what behaviors you need to adopt and to live by to get the success you desire.

I'm not going to talk about the traits of successful people. The basic premise of this book is that anyone can become successful regardless of their genes, background, or current skills and talents. All it takes is learning and internalizing the right attitude and set of behaviors, which can enhance your chance of success at any job you pick.

Whatever your definition of success is, the Quiet Success Principles will help you. Do you consider being successful as getting promoted? Getting more money? Having satisfaction from a job well done? Getting a better work-life integration? Working as part of a team of people who care about each other? The principles I present will help you in each of these cases. They are universally applicable.

I'm also aware of the fact that some of the behaviors and practices I will talk about may not come easily to introverts. There is an effort required. There is a change needed, and it may hurt. At least initially. Getting out of our comfort zone is how we learn and grow. And that applies to all of us, even introverts.

Nothing in the following chapters will work if you don't care and won't give it a serious try. I would also argue that, to get the most out of the ideas I share, you need to adopt the whole framework. I would also discourage you from trying to start practicing all the principles at the same time. Pick one principle, look at the practices it includes, and select one or two of them and get going. Gradually add more and more.

The Quiet Success Principles describe a set of behaviors and practices that can enhance your chances of success at any career you select. They are based on extensive research into what other authors, social scientists, psychologists, and fellow introverts suggest we do to reach our goals. They also align with the self-management practices that I personally favor and believe in.

I'm a big fan of Stoicism, and even though I would not describe myself as a practicing Stoic, I subscribe to most of the things Stoicism teaches. Stoicism, because of its basis in logic, can be a very attractive philosophy to introverts. Things like self-awareness, prudence, thoughtfulness, humility, preparation, and perseverance are valued by both Stoics and introverts. Some of the teachings of Stoicism are therefore reflected in the Quiet Success Principles. Some examples are things like focusing only on things you can control, using reason to work with your emotions, being content with the things you can't change, not placing undue value on external things, keeping calm and not getting angry with other people, always doing your best, and understanding that only you can make yourself happy and make yourself feel successful.

Being a white man with a good education who never experienced poverty or any real form of discrimination, I need to acknowledge that following these principles can be relatively easy for someone like me. It can be significantly more difficult for those who are not so privileged, and the impact of some of my suggestions won't be that great for those who aren't already in positions of privilege. However, the principles still apply. Whatever your background, you will still be better off following the Quiet Success Principles than ignoring them.

Figure 9: Quiet Success Principles

The Quiet Success Principles are depicted in Figure 9. You will see a decent amount of overlap, and the more practices you internalize, the easier it will be to do the rest. It is a complex system, and as such, each part has an impact on other parts. If you get better at one, it will have a positive ripple effect on the others.

Principle 1: Know Yourself ("I know myself. I'm confident and responsible for my feelings. I have the same rights as everyone else."): This principle includes everything related to self-discovery and self-control. It is essential to understand yourself and your emotions so you can use them.

Principle 2: Prioritize Well ("I focus on what is important. I let go of the past. I live a well-integrated life."): Before you can work on your success, you need to have your priorities straight so you can focus on what truly matters to you and let go of things that don't.

Principle 3: Own Everything ("I own everything in my life. I speak up and ask for what I want and need. I own my failures."): If you want to have a successful career, you need to take control of your life. You need to learn to own your future, be accountable for your actions, and proactively and assertively ask for what is yours.

Principle 4: Act with Integrity ("I'm dependable and trustworthy. I say what I mean. I do what I say, and I always do my best."): Success at any cost and on the backs of others is not success at all. It is just exploitation. Having true success requires you to act with integrity and always do what is right, not what is merely convenient. You need to be trustworthy, credible, and dependable. You need to show courage and be able to tell others, and yourself, not what they *want* to hear, but what they *need* to hear.

Principle 5: Keep Learning ("I want to learn. I'm curious about life. I listen to others. I keep getting better every single day."): Career success requires continuous growth, and that means constant, never-ending learning. You need to adopt a growth mindset and use your natural attentiveness and curiosity to build up your competence and become a bit better every single day.

Principle 6: Show Up ("I'm always prepared. I manage my energy. I'm disciplined. I show up even if I'm uncomfortable."): You can't build a successful career while hidden in your basement. You need to get out there to the real world, regardless of how scary it may look. Use your strengths of preparation and perseverance to challenge yourself constantly, adopt healthy routines, and become more resilient.

Principle 7: Work Hard ("I deliver results. I'm passionate about what I do. I don't give up easily. I do my best every single day."): No real success comes on its own. You need to work for it. You need to work *hard* for it. That doesn't necessarily mean working crazy hours, but it means working the right way on the right things, having passion and grit, and getting to the mastery level where things just flow and you genuinely enjoy what you are doing.

Principle 8: Respect Others ("I'm humble. I care about others and treat them with respect. I'm positive. I know that life is not only about me."): Whatever job you have, you need to interact with others. Having a positive attitude toward life, being humble and respectful, and working on your emotional intelligence will help you be more likable and more likely to succeed.

Principle 9: Build Alliances ("I need others, and I'm willing to admit it. I believe that people mean well. I extend trust and play nice with others."): You can't do everything alone. Accept that building alliances with others can increase your influence and give you a bigger chance at a successful career. You need to build trust and be a good team player.

Principle 10: Pay It Forward ("I add value by helping others. I'm fair, inclusive, and flexible. I keep giving without expecting returns."): Successful people rarely got successful only by caring about themselves and nothing else. Adopting an abundance mentality will allow you to work toward win-win scenarios, understand others who might be different from you, and help others succeed.

8

Know Yourself

*"I know myself. I'm confident and responsible for my feelings.
I have the same rights as everyone else."*

It all starts with you. If you don't know who you are and what you want, you can't achieve it. How can you reach something if you don't know what it is? Only by having enough clarity on what you want in your career can you succeed. What's more, you need to actively manage yourself to keep growing and becoming the best "you" you can be.

It starts with self-awareness. This is the ability and willingness to listen to others and confront harsh reality if you hear something you don't like. You need to understand the stories you tell yourself that are holding you back.

Building self-esteem, confidence, and self-control comes next. You need to learn to respond to whatever life and your boss throw at you on your own terms. This is key for all of the other nine principles I will discuss as well. Without a solid foundation in knowing yourself and being comfortable in your own skin, the rest won't work.

Once you have understood yourself and your emotions, you are better equipped to use that to your advantage. Utilize your strengths of calmness, thoughtfulness, and prudence to build strong self-control. There is nothing inherently wrong with showing emotions at work—it may even be good for you—but you can't allow them to take over. You need to be in control.

Next comes self-promotion. Many introverts will frown upon it, but as you already guessed, you need to adapt to the world you live in. And finally, knowing yourself is about being your authentic self and not letting the heat of the moment or the pressure of the environment force you to act out of character. This doesn't mean you shouldn't change—in fact, you have to change as you are growing—but you should remain true to your principles and core values.

Self-Awareness

Self-awareness is the ability to understand who you are, what is important to you, and what your strengths and weaknesses are. It also represents your higher awareness of how you are being perceived by those around you. And lastly, it allows you to analyze some of your behaviors that may hold you back.

Imagine that you are yet again late for a meeting, and when you finally arrive, you comment, "I know I'm always late. That's just me." It seems in that moment that you are self-aware, but not really. You need to take it to the next level. "Being you" is not an excuse. And if lateness really is part of who you are, why not change it and make the new you be on time? There is no inherent value in the extreme need to be "you" at all costs. You are just blaming your tardiness on some disassociated version of you. You are blaming this imaginary person for your own weaknesses, and that is holding you back.

Nothing prevents you from inventing a new you. All you need to do is catch yourself using those words, "that's just me," and say to yourself, "I want to be seen as someone who is always on time." And then stop using the "it is who I am" excuse.

Consider the advantages. You will be seen as more reliable, people will respect you more, and you will grow and become a better person. You will still be you— the new you.

Confront Reality

The best way to confront reality, discover your blind spots, and learn how others see you is to get feedback. How do you do that? There are tons of different ways, starting with anonymous surveys and ending with talking to people and asking them for their honest opinions.

The critical aspect is to pick the right people to ask. Why? You don't want to talk to people who don't know you or who you won't listen to. You don't want to talk to people who will just tell you what you want to hear. You want to talk to those who will tell you what you *need* to hear. These should be people who have at least a couple of the following qualities: you respect their opinion, they have been in your shoes, they genuinely want to help you, they know you, they know your work, they are very different from you, and they have nothing to lose by being honest with you.

It can be especially uncomfortable for an introverted person to ask for feedback directly. I believe that less is sometimes more. You don't need to get feedback from hundreds of people to get better at something. What you need is a couple of people you trust, who you know mean well and will provide honest and helpful feedback without hidden agendas. Even one such person is enough to expose your blind spots so you can start changing for the better. At any point in my professional life, I have about two or three people like that in my life who fulfill most of the above criteria. That's all it takes.

People often hint at what you should do differently without really telling you. It pays to keep your eyes open and to listen all the time for "weird" hints. Your strengths of attentiveness and subsequent introspection work for you here. Every once in a while it happens that someone makes an offhand comment about something you did that you find a bit strange. They may be trying to give you a clue. Use the opportunity to solicit some feedback. "Jack, you mentioned that there wasn't much communication on the project. Since I was responsible for the project, and I respect your opinion, I would love to hear your thoughts on what I could do better in the future."

I find that the best way to solicit feedback—even from people who worry that if they are too open with negative comments, it may destroy the relationship or that you will be angry with them—is not to talk about the past but about the future. As shown in the example above, don't ask what you should have done in the past. Instead, ask for suggestions of what you can do better in the future. This creates a significantly less threatening conversation for both sides, and not only will the person you ask be more open, but it will also be easier for you to listen and to take action. Instead of telling you, "Your communication with the stakeholders was bad," they can say, "It would be helpful if you would communicate more frequently with the stakeholders for future projects."

The key is to learn how to listen to feedback. If you get defensive and start arguing with the person giving you the feedback, you can be pretty much sure that that will be the last time they do it. Feedback is a gift. If you throw it back in someone's face, there is very little reason for them to try to present you with that gift again. There is only one correct answer in the face of constructive feedback: "Thank you." That's it. Don't try to come up with anything fancier. Just thank the person for their openness and willingness to help you.

Some of us—and I catch myself doing this from time to time—feel that a simple "thank you" is not enough. We want to elaborate a bit, so we say things like, "Thank you, this is extremely helpful." Don't do that. By doing this, you rate the feedback. What if the person gives you additional feedback tomorrow, and that time you say, "Thanks, I will think about it"? You just rated the first feedback as great and the second one as rubbish. Just stick with a simple, heartfelt "thank you," and you are safe. By keeping it simple, you also achieve another benefit: you make it easier for yourself to truly listen. The mistake many people make when listening to feedback is trying to concoct a response. Instead of listening and digesting what they hear, they spend the time coming up with some answer or defense. The result is that they don't truly listen—a wasted opportunity.

Stop Playing the Victim

In 1839, the playwright Edward Bulwer-Lytton wrote, "The pen is mightier than the sword." In one sentence, he summarized the fact that words have massive power over our lives, whether we realize it or not. The language you use when communicating your thoughts to the outside world impacts whether you will be taken seriously or not. Picking the right words can help you positively influence others. Selecting the wrong words can result in you being ignored or ridiculed.

An infamous German dictator allegedly said, "If you tell a big enough lie and tell it frequently enough, it will be believed." Unfortunately, that applies not only to persuading others but also to our inner voice convincing us. The words and the stories you tell not only impact those around you but also have a significant effect on your own well-being.

If you keep telling yourself that no one can be trusted and that everyone is trying to hurt you, that will impact how you act toward others. You will be unwilling to trust, will make sarcastic comments, and may even accuse others of lying and trying to harm you. Over time you will build a bubble around yourself. People will indeed stop trusting you. They will avoid you, will talk behind your back, and won't be willing to help you in times of need. And it all started with the victim story you repeatedly told yourself.

The stories you tell yourself create self-limiting beliefs. These are the beliefs ingrained in your brain that hold you back and don't allow you to realize your full potential. They are the basis for excuses you tell yourself that prevent you from facing reality and changing your behavior. It is so much easier to blame something or someone else for your misfortunes than it is to take a hard look at your life and make a change.

So what are the types of stories you tell yourself? And what can you do to reframe those stories so they are more helpful and give you a push in the right direction instead of holding you back?

Powerlessness Story: This is a story you tend to tell when you prefer passivity over action. Instead of admitting that you can do something to change the circumstances or outcome, you just say, "Well, what can I do?" You don't even try to do anything. You give up and say you are powerless to do anything about your situation. You quietly accept your fate. You are not even angry about it. You are just resigned. And often, there is a lot you could do if only you let yourself believe you could.

Victim Story: This is the type of story you tell when you expect others to react to your actions, and they don't. Let's say you offer to buy me lunch out of the kindness of your heart. I accept, and I'm thankful for that. But I don't reciprocate.

Why should I? But you had expectations that I would return the favor eventually. Now you feel like a victim who was cheated by the ungrateful person I am. You are making all this effort, even spent money on me, and I don't care. Poor little you. In this situation, you are making yourself feel like a victim of the situation you created. Instead of being happy that you gave me a gift that I appreciated, you turned it all around, and you feel bad. And I'm blissfully unaware. It is all in your head.

Villain Story: For you to feel like a real victim, it helps to find a villain. Sometimes there is even actual harm or potential harm done to you, but instead of shrugging it off, you start telling a villain story. It makes you feel better about your anger if you think that others are hurting you on purpose. You just assume that others have evil intentions and tell a story to yourself, and often to others as well, describing the individual as a nasty character who is there to harm you. Many of us do this all the time, even when we don't realize it. Imagine that you are driving a car, overtaking someone who is going slower than you, and they suddenly accelerate and prevent you from overtaking them. What do you tell yourself? "Oh, look at that idiot. He saw me overtaking him, but his ego wouldn't survive it, so he accelerated on purpose so I couldn't overtake him, even though he saw that there was a car coming in the other direction and there was a danger of an accident." That is a nice story to tell. Unfortunately, it has nothing to do with reality. The chances are that the other driver just didn't see you and accelerated since he saw a long stretch of beautiful road in front of him. He may not even be aware you exist. But in your mind, he is the villain who is trying to get you killed. So you get angry and want payback.

Cultural Story: In this type of story, you blame your parents, upbringing, and the environment for your misfortunes. To be fair, many self-limiting beliefs have real roots in your childhood. But that shouldn't be an excuse not to change. Even in your adulthood, you keep coming back to your childhood memories to explain why you can't do something. Let me use an example of one story I used to tell myself. I was brought up in an environment where it was customary to eat everything on your plate. It didn't matter whether you were hungry or not. It just wasn't polite to leave anything on the plate. It was this way through generations. I wouldn't be surprised if it started a hundred years ago during some war when there wasn't enough food and common sense was to eat as much as you could, while you could. The war ended; the practice survived. It was until I was well into my thirties that I lived by that rule. I would eat everything on my plate, regardless of whether I was hungry and even to the point of not feeling well. Why? Because "you don't leave food on your plate." That was the story I had learned from my parents and their parents, and that was the belief I held until the day I got sick and realized what a crazy story it was. I replaced it with another story: "It is okay to leave food on the plate if you have already had enough." Over a couple of months, the amount of food I ate started to go down. I only ate what my body needed, and I began to feel more energy and got healthier.

Genetics or That's-Just-Me Story: This is the kind of story most often used, generally as an excuse for inappropriate behavior. You do something that you know irritates others, but instead of trying to change your behavior, you just say, "Sorry, that's just me." A couple of years back, I was in a situation where, in an emotionally charged situation, one manager got angry and started yelling at a subordinate. Eventually, he calmed down and realized that it was unacceptable behavior. Still, instead of an apology and some plan for how to change, he just said, "I have a short fuse, and if I hear stuff like this, I get angry." That's it. Instead of changing the behavior that he knew was not okay, he just blamed it on his personality, as if there was nothing he could do about it.

Change the story. Being authentic is great. It is great to speak your mind. But you need to continually keep making sure that your honesty and authenticity don't hurt you and those around you. Changing the internal narrative, the story you are telling yourself, is the first step in a meaningful change in your attitude and life. Identify what your self-limiting beliefs are, and then, for each of them, create an alternative story that is healthier and that will lead you to success. Let me give you a couple of examples of how to revise a limiting story into an enhancing one.

	Limiting Story	**Enhancing Story**
Powerlessness Story	Someone cut in front of me in a queue. Well, what can I do?	It is not acceptable to cut in front of other people. I will address this calmly and assertively.
Victim Story	I was again skipped for a promotion. It is not fair.	Next time, I need to do a better job of showing my contributions.
Villain Story	He ate the whole cake. He's such a jerk who doesn't care about anyone except himself!	He may not have realized that I wanted some of the cake. I should calmly explain to him that it was meant for everyone.
Cultural Story	I can't help you. That's not how things are done around here.	Of course I can help you. I care about your success, regardless of what others say.
Genetics Story	I'm sorry for being late. That's just me.	I'm a professional who is always on time.

Table 6: Limiting and Enhancing Stories

Often, changing the narrative means learning not to assume anything. Making assumptions is the arch-enemy of good communication, especially between people with different cultural and educational backgrounds. Changing the narrative also means not being afraid to take action. When you tell a more effective story, it will make you take a stand and act more assertively. This will ultimately enhance the quality of your interactions and the satisfaction you feel with your life.

Stop Avoiding Hard Truths

Some of the most prominent stories we tell ourselves in the twenty-first century are so widely told that we don't even think about them. Yet they are the big lies we tell ourselves that keep us stuck in jobs we hate. To our detriment, we work really hard to avoid hard truths. Consider these most common lies, and if you recognize yourself in any of them, find a way to break the loop and stop lying to yourself.

I will be happy when I get my next promotion.
We are incapable of predicting the future. Our brains have a unique capacity to mislead us about what's to come. Why do you think that getting promoted from team lead to manager will ultimately make you happy? Sure, it will feel good for a couple of weeks, but then you will most likely figure out that you will only be satisfied when you get to the next level and become a director. And what about a vice president or CEO? If you are unhappy in your current role, the chances are that that promotion won't make you much happier. You should either rethink your field of work or learn to enjoy any job you have. Only then will you be pleased with your position in the company.

I just need to finish this project, and then I will have more time.
Good one. You have no idea how many times I told myself this lie until I realized that it is not my nature to get to a state of having nothing to do. As soon as one project comes to an end, two others are waiting and fighting for your attention. If you are unable to "make the time" today with your current workload, it is doubtful it will get better in the future unless you dramatically change how you approach your life and work on your priorities. What works is to dedicate specific timeslots every day for things that are important to you long term, and don't allow other people's urgent matters to trespass.

I cannot leave right now. I'm needed.
Whether it's a project, a company, a family, or any other area in your life, not being able to leave when the time comes is something that will hold you back. Everyone is replaceable. If you believe that things will go sour without you and that

darkness will descend on the world, you are most likely lying to yourself. I'm not advocating that you should leave when things are bad or run from responsibility. Perseverance and integrity are critical to success. I'm talking about situations when you did your duty, and it is time to move on toward new challenges and adventures with a feeling of a job well done.

I have to take care of my family or my team before myself.

This one sounds like the talk of someone you want to live with. Someone who will always consider your well-being before their own. Who wouldn't want to live with this person? The problem is that, if you are like this, then you don't live your life. You are just background noise in the lives of others who may or may not recognize your sacrifices. You focus so much on others that you forget to take care of yourself. You ignore your health, your desires, and your needs. Eventually, you may become the exact opposite of what you wanted to be. You become a dissatisfied and sick burden on others. Successful people will always find ways to give to others while taking care of themselves too. It is not an either/or situation. You need to take care of both yourself and others, and you need to start with yourself.

I can't leave the job I hate because it pays too well.

Too bad you got yourself into the position of being someone who is overpaid for the contributions you provide—the golden handcuffs we discussed earlier. Not many of us get to that position, but if you do, then you admit that you accepted a salary way above what you deserve, and the price you pay for that comes in the form of being stuck in a job that you may not even like. The knowledge that someone else on the job market is willing to pay a bit more than you are making today is the way to keep you happy. If you stop loving what you do, you won't be stuck in your current role just for the money. This gives you incredible freedom and peace of mind like nothing else. On the other hand, once you get the golden handcuffs, it isn't easy to let go.

When I move to another place/city/country, I will be happy.

I've been there. It didn't work. I'm originally from Europe, and I spent a year as an expat in the Philippines. Before I moved there, I had all sorts of plans for how things would be different. I planned how I would spend more time outside of work and be on the beach every weekend. After several months of spending virtually all my time in the office, I realized that I am who I am, regardless of the country I live in. Moving to another country or city will, of course, change some bits and pieces of your life, but your values, habits, and priorities will not change. For that, you need to work pretty hard, and you don't need to move to the other side of the world.

I'm self-sufficient, and I can do it alone.
Indeed, there are many things you can do on your own, but at the end of the day, you make it unnecessarily hard on yourself if you try to do everything yourself. If you are willing to ask for help, if you can surround yourself with good people, friends, and family, then everything in your life will get easier. Just having someone around to share your thoughts with, to talk to, to share a laugh or two will work miracles for your ability to get things done, renew your energy, and generally help you to live a happier life.

When you give these topics a bit of thought, you probably identify many other lies you tell yourself. My goal wasn't to have an exhaustive list since each of us is different. I just wanted to make you think. The stories I listed are those I most often encountered in professional circles, seeing them prevent people from truly exploring and utilizing their potential and reaching success and peace of mind.

Self-Esteem, Confidence, and Self-Efficacy

You don't need to be a super confident, egoistic human being to be successful. At the same time, if your self-doubt flourishes, it can paralyze you and impair your ability to get things done and be happy. You don't need super high confidence, but you need to be comfortable with who you are. You need to have self-esteem and some level of self-efficacy. Psychologist Albert Bandura originally defined self-efficacy as one's belief in their own ability to succeed or accomplish a task.[61]

People with strong self-efficacy believe that if they work hard enough and put all their focus on an activity, they will succeed. They are also likely to withstand pressure. They brush off physiological signs of stress as unrelated to their ability to perform tasks. Therefore, they show more resilience.[62]

On the other hand, people with weak self-efficacy interpret any signs of being under stress as their own inability to properly finish the task, thus lowering their ability to act. They are more likely to succumb to the pressure, quit, and fail.

If you have a weak sense of self-efficacy, you tend to avoid challenging tasks. You worry that you can't handle the project, and you have negative self-talk going on in your head. You focus only on the adverse outcomes, emphasize your lack of abilities, avoid risks, question your ability to succeed, set low personal goals, and have abysmal performance under pressure.

What can you do to build up your self-efficacy and ultimately be more resilient and increase your self-esteem? Work on your resilience. Resilient people share a couple of characteristics, beliefs, and habits.

- *They Own the World Around Them*: They don't feel like victims of external circumstances but rather believe that they can influence life events with their actions. They are in control.
- *They Try New Things*: The more varied experiences you have, the more likely it is that you won't get surprised when life throws you a curveball.
- *They Have an Ability to Adapt*: They are okay with change. They can quickly adapt to different environments or life situations.
- *They Learn and Ponder*: They accumulate life wisdom. They are able to learn from positive and negative experiences. They collect the lessons learned and, by doing so, realize that they can cope with lots of stuff.
- *They Are Optimistic*: The words "every cloud has a silver lining" ring true to them. They will find some takeaway from any situation and always look at the bright side of life.
- *They Understand That Stress Is Part of Life*: They are not bothered by external pressure. They know that external pressure is always there, and how to respond to it is their decision. They know they can't control the pressure, but they can control their reactions to it.

To start, consider taking these simple but not so easy steps.

Create Self-Awareness and Admit That You Have a Problem: This always begins with an understanding of who you are today. Getting feedback from other people surrounding you about how they see you is an excellent step to make sure you get the complete picture.

Discover How Your Thoughts, Self-Talk, and Actions Contribute to the Problem: It may be worth getting a coach and diving deep into some of the beliefs that hold you back. The way you see the world and the way you talk to yourself drive your actions. Understanding the root cause of your problem will help you focus on fixing the right things.

Adjust Your Communication Style to a Particular Situation and Individual: Understand that each situation requires something a bit different. Don't rely on preconceived notions and biases to guide your actions. Understanding some of the fundamental cognitive biases that you encounter when dealing with people is another step to self-awareness that will make you more comfortable with your ability to understand the world around you. You will get less surprised, you will be able to explain things to yourself better, and you will get less stressed out.

Accept That We Are All Only Human: Most important of all, don't try to be perfect—or rather, don't feel bad when you make a mistake and see that you are not perfect. No one is. We are all only human, and we all make mistakes. We all fail sometimes. And that is just fine. The confident people among us are usually those who are comfortable with failure. They know their strengths and weaknesses. They know their limitations, and they don't worry about them.

Stop Minimizing Yourself and Your Achievements to Boost the Confidence of Others: In *How Women Rise*, Sally Helgesen and Marshall Goldsmith talk about some of the habits that can hold women back, and minimizing is one of them.[63] And this applies to introverts too. Many introverts acknowledge the greatness of others by making themselves small. Unfortunately, by making yourself small, you become small. Others won't take you seriously. Learn to acknowledge the achievements of others with dignity and confidence on your own. Approach them as equals. Build an executive presence by being assertive, treating others as equals, and always fully focusing on the task at hand.

Stop Apologizing for Who You Are: If you look at Western culture, some things are not acceptable, and those are things that you should change. You should redefine who you are in situations like being late or yelling at people. These are disrespectful traits and hurt you and the relationships you have with other people. They are things you weren't born with. No one is born with a gene that says, "Always be late." Then there are some traits and personal characteristics that are entirely acceptable from your perspective, yet culture punishes them, so you tend to apologize for having them. I have often seen people with lower self-esteem start their sentences with, "I'm sorry, I have nothing to contribute," or, "I'm sorry, can I make a suggestion?" There is nothing to be sorry about. There is no need to apologize for having or not having an idea. In these situations, you apologize and feel guilty for who you are, which reinforces your low self-esteem. There is no need to apologize in these situations. It just makes you less credible. Always consider what sort of language you are using when talking to yourself and the people around you. By changing the words you use, you will eventually change how you feel about life.

With every small success, you build your self-confidence. Your level of serotonin rises, and it makes you bolder and more willing to try the next activity. You are more optimistic about the outcome, more willing to give it even more effort, and more likely to succeed again. It is a virtuous cycle. By adopting the signs of confidence, you can give yourself an edge. Stand tall, prepare well, act with confidence, ask for what you need, and persevere. Those around you will see you as competent and able to get things done. They will help you to succeed.

Stop Taking Things Personally

It's not you, it's me. If I yell at you, that doesn't mean that you have a problem—it means that I do. If I blame you for something, that doesn't mean you should feel bad—it is me who is weak. If I make sarcastic comments about you, it doesn't mean you should listen—it means I'm a jerk.

Because of introverts' capacity for listening, empathy, and overthinking, we read too much into the words of others, and what is worse, we take things personally and feel bad for the behaviors of others. When I talk to fellow introverts, I hear the same story over and over again. Lack of confidence is caused by listening too much to people who tend to put you down. Getting over this and learning to ignore those trying to make you feel bad can have an incredibly positive impact on your mental health.

I'm a worrier, but I used to be the *ultimate* worrier. I would worry about anything and everything in my life and create this constant pressure to make sure things would go well. It was totally self-inflicted stress. No one ever pushed me or held me to unrealistic standards. It was all in my head. I didn't want to disappoint. I didn't want to let people down. I didn't want to look bad.

Ultimately, I outgrew that mentality. With increased confidence and a more positive and optimistic outlook on life, I also learned not to stress myself more than necessary. I still do care about others. I do care about doing a great job. I do care about lots of things in my life. But I also understand that not everyone, including me, needs to be perfect all the time. I'm more comfortable with myself, and I stopped caring about what others think about me and about things I can't influence.

Decide not to take things personally. Don't overthink. Just briefly consider what the worst thing is that can happen. In the majority of situations, you will discover that nothing catastrophic is going to happen. Someone may scowl at you, someone may yell, someone may badmouth you, but in the end, nothing will happen. Things will blow over, and in a couple of days, no one is going to remember whether you did or didn't do something.

One of my former bosses used to repeat the adage, "Sticks and stones may break my bones, but words will never hurt me." I hadn't heard it before, and I worked hard to internalize it. I tend to ignore people raising their voices, and I don't get dragged into heated arguments or lands of self-pity. If someone yells at you, it means they have a problem. They are weak, disrespectful, selfish, and possibly scared. By caving in, you make their problem your problem. If you keep your cool in these situations and turn back to hard data and propose a more constructive way forward, you will defuse the situation. Eventually, people won't raise their voices in your presence if they know that it doesn't do them any good.

People often say things they don't mean. Even the best of us can sometimes slip and, in the heat of the moment, say something we don't mean and regret it later on. Don't overreact to people saying something hurtful. Chances are they regret it the moment it leaves their mouths but don't have the strength to apologize. Their egos won't allow it. Give them the benefit of the doubt and just brush it off. Of course, if what they say is regular abuse, you can't ignore it. But remember, no law mandates people to say hurtful things, so don't lower yourself to their level. It is they who have a problem, not you.

Sometimes people say things they don't mean, but sometimes they mean only what they say and nothing more. Don't read more into others' statements than is there. Many introverts tend to overthink and read between the lines, hearing things that just aren't there. If I tell you that I like your new shoes, it means just that. It doesn't mean that your old shoes were terrible or that I love you. If you strongly feel that there is a hidden meaning behind something, then ask. Clarify whether you understood the meaning well or whether there is something more you should understand. You are not a mind reader, so don't act like you are.

If you genuinely messed something up, that is still not a reason to yell at you, call you names, or belittle you in any way. Giving you feedback, having a constructive conversation about what to do better next time, and offering help is what adults would do.

Understand Your Own Successes

Life is complicated. Everything is connected to everything else. Cause and effect. There are so many variables. We can't accurately predict the weather or how much satisfaction we will get from a specific event in the future.

So what leads us to believe that we have things under control and that we can predictably repeat successes we had in the past? Many of us who reached some level of success often feel that we are entitled to it and that we are somehow better than everyone else, and thus that anything we do will always end up being successful. And then we are surprised and feel hurt when something doesn't go as we planned. But why? Mainly because we misunderstand what made us successful in the past.

Misunderstanding of Past Successes: Depending on your current frame of mind, you tend to either overestimate or underestimate your role in past achievements. Let's say you love running and just won a race. Why did you win? I already hear people saying things like, "I trained really hard, five hours a day, and gave it everything I had." And now imagine the same race but one that you lost. What would you say? "It just wasn't my day. I didn't feel on top of my game, and even during the preparation, I trained only five hours a day." You did precisely the same thing before the race you won and the race you lost. Maybe it wasn't just you. Maybe the environment was different, and the competitors were different. Perhaps it wasn't you that made the difference, but the people around you. As Phil Rosenzweig writes in *Left Brain, Right Stuff*, people have an imperfect understanding of how much control they can exert. When control is low, we tend to overestimate our impact, but when it's high, we tend to underestimate it.[64]

Correlation, Causality, and Single Explanations: In another of his books, *The Halo Effect*, Phil Rosenzweig talks about nine business delusions that cloud our judgment. Relevant to our discussion are those of correlation, causality, and single explanation.[65]

Why were you successful in the first place? Over my years in the business world, I have heard many times that "we are successful because of the way we work." But one has to wonder, is it really "because of" or "in spite of"? In a complex environment, it is often difficult to distinguish between what is cause and what is effect. It is challenging to understand whether something helped or hurt our chances, especially if you fall into the trap of a single explanation. We tend to blame one person when things go wrong or celebrate one hero when there is a success. We tend to forget all the other things and people that influenced the outcome. Keeping in mind that "everything is connected to everything" should help you keep an eye on these biases.

Overconfidence: One of the most dangerous reasons why you may easily fail in the future is overconfidence. Rosenzweig splits overconfidence into three categories. Overprecision is a tendency to be too sure that our judgment is the right one. "I'm an expert. I know what I'm doing. This and only this is the right way to do things to achieve success." Overestimation is a tendency to believe that we can perform at a much higher level than we are capable of. "Of course I can do it, even though I've never done anything comparable. With my track record of success, anything I touch changes into gold and can only end well." Overplacement is a belief that we can perform much better than others. "I'm a much better manager than the majority of others," or "I'm a much better driver than the others." This one is nicely demonstrated in a study performed by Ola Svenson asking students to compare their driving skills to those of other people. 93 percent of the US sample and 69 percent of the Swedish sample put themselves in the top 50 percent. This is a mathematical impossibility and shows what unrealistic views we have of ourselves.[66]

Because of the reasons mentioned above, most of us believe we are better than others; thus, we deserve more. We deserve better treatment, more money, better lives, bigger houses, and more frequent promotions, and we are unhappy when we are not getting those things. I can give you just one piece of advice on this: get a dose of reality, and switch your mindset to one that tells you that everyone is good at something. Everyone has the right to be happy, well paid, and treated with respect. You might have some strengths that others don't, but you also have weaknesses, and all in all, you are not much different from the other seven billion human beings on this planet.

Humility is your friend. Never assume that you are better than others just because you had some sort of success. The chances are that the victory wasn't yours alone. You should also reset your expectations of the future. Always strive for the best but expect the worst; thus, have a healthy, well-balanced level of confidence, a level that inspires you to do your best—but not too much, to take success for granted—or too little—to never even try.

Self-Control

Being able to stay calm under pressure is a critical skill for anyone and especially for leaders. In times of uncertainty, everyone looks for some anchor, someone who keeps calm, steps up, and knows what to do. Panic is good for spurring people into action, but it is terrible in terms of giving us the ability to make sound decisions. It is a calm person who can tap the energy of a panicking team and move them in the right direction.

Certain events occur regularly enough that you can train yourself for them and thus replace panic with process and discipline. In fact, some functions within every company operate that way. Look, for example, at a well-functioning customer service or technical support team. They are like firefighters. The moment they receive a call from an angry customer, they don't panic but instead follow a script, a process that they know will most likely lead to a professional resolution of the issue.

Communicate when you are ready and not sooner. Even during a crisis, you shouldn't succumb to the need to say something. Chances are, you could easily make the situation worse. If you see a fire, yes, you probably shout "fire" to make sure everyone knows what's going on and evacuates. But if you receive a strongly worded email from an angry customer, you don't shout back. You first calm yourself down, assess the situation, make sure you have your facts straight, and only then do you communicate back. It is the need for an immediate reply that creates so many misunderstandings in communication. Learn to be like a duck: stay calm above the water while paddling like crazy underneath to come up with a good response that will resolve the problem.

Find Out What Triggers You to Be Stressed

Many psychologists and social scientists describe the negative effects of stress. Numerous studies have shown that not only can stress reduce productivity but it can also lead to adverse health effects.[67] Stress comes in many forms for many reasons. The most common reasons for stress in a corporate environment are overwork and lack of recharging; being in the wrong role; high-demand, low-control jobs; people anxiety; lack of social support; and bad managers.

Overwork and Lack of Recharging: Meijman and Mulder proposed an effort-recovery model in 1998.[68] According to their model, the effort expended at work produces a negative physiological and psychological reaction. Even though it is short term, it can accumulate if there is no respite. If employees stop working and have an opportunity to relax, their systems return to their default levels.[69] The workload is a job stressor, as it reflects the demands placed on the employee in their jobs. It is no surprise that studies have shown the correlation and negative aspects the stress at work can have on family life and on the overall well-being of the person.[70]

Being in the Wrong Role: What leads to significant stress is when you are in a position you are ill-equipped to handle. You either don't have the skills or competence and know it, or you have some psychological problem that prevents you from enjoying that particular type of work. For example, if I ask you to get in front of an important audience and play a difficult piece on a piano, and you have never played the piano before, of course you will get stressed out. If I tell you that your career depends on it, you may try your best, but you will know that you just don't have the skills, and your stress level will skyrocket.

That is also why many of us feel slight apprehension when doing something for the first time, even things we want to do and we know we would ultimately enjoy. If the stakes are high enough and our skills and confidence level are low enough, we will get stressed. There's nothing wrong with it if it is a low level of stress that just helps us to focus and makes us prepare better. But the moment the pressure becomes too much, it becomes debilitating, we freeze, we can't make decisions, we can't get the job done. We are in the wrong role.

Having High Job Demand and Low Job Control: This happens even to the best of us. You love your job, you are good at it, you generally enjoy coming to work. But every now and then, you get a task that you don't have well under control. You may have the skills, know what needs to be done, and know that you can't or won't do it for some external reason outside of your control. This type of stress happens relatively often in bigger companies with significant bureaucracy or on projects with many parties. You are responsible for success, you have the skills, but you don't have the means to get things done. You see the failure coming, and you are helpless to prevent it.

If this happens irregularly, you can learn to live with it. But if you are in this high-demand job with low job control all the time, it will lead you to be stressed all the time, which is not healthy. Alternately, it may lead you to just stop caring about the work, which is not healthy and productive.

Having People Anxiety: Most of the work in today's world requires interactions with other people. Even for most introverts, that is fine. Over our lives, we learn that we have to interact with others. By itself, this can even be motivating and pleasurable. But everything needs to be done in moderation. If you prefer to work alone and you are required to spend every single minute of your time talking to others, you will not only get tired quickly, but you will gradually be more and more stressed. This happens especially when you need to deal with difficult conversations, difficult people, and people you simply don't like. It is often a combination of personal preferences, confidence, size of the audience, and topics that make you uncomfortable.

I know of many introverts who are very comfortable around people. They enjoy having conversations with others; they do very well in one-on-one interactions. But they get stressed when they have to operate as part of a larger group. They will still do it, they may still do a great job, but, similarly to the previous point, they feel that the stakes get higher with more people, and their own control gets lower.

Lack of Abundance of Social Support: Common sense would dictate that a lack of social support would be an additional stressor. If you have no one to talk to, no one to help you, no one who would care for you, you will get stressed out more easily. However, it is not that simple. A mounting amount of research shows that just receiving social support may not necessarily lead to less stress but may, in fact, increase it. Counterintuitively, what leads to lower levels of stress is actually to provide support to others. Researchers Inbal Nahum-Shani and Peter A. Bamberger found that when support given exceeds support received, an increase in support received is associated with a positive impact.[71]

Working for a Toxic Manager: Some managers still believe that increased pressure will yield increased performance. Unfortunately, that is not the case. Increased pressure may indeed result in a temporary increase in performance from people working with more focus and longer hours, but this will quickly backfire. Increased pressure increases stress. And more stress leads to loss of concentration and low motivation and impacts cognitive abilities. It leads to higher sickness rates and higher turnover.

I once interviewed a candidate for a director job. When asked about why he was leaving his current position, the answer was stunning. His boss had just left. She was someone he respected and liked working with. What was worse, according to him, he had been promoted to her role. One could argue that promotion is a good thing, but obviously not always. He had seen the incredible pressure his former boss had been under and couldn't imagine he would be able and willing to work in such an environment where he was constantly yelled at and held to unreasonable standards. His response to the promotion was simple: "If you promote me, I will quit." Since he was well-qualified for the job, he was promoted. And he did quit.

Accept That Sometimes Things Are What They Are: There are some things you can't control. That is the nature of the environment we live in. Some things are out of your control, and there is no point in brooding about them and overanalyzing what you would have done if you had the power. If you can't change something, just leave it or accept it. But don't obsess about it. As Dale Carnegie writes in *How to Stop Worrying and Start Living*, one way to manage stress is to stop obsessing about the future.[72] Learn to live your life in one-day compartments. Learn to live in the moment. Stop thinking continuously about the next thing you have to do or what might happen next year and just live in the now. You probably want to do a bit of strategic planning, but make sure you do it at specially appointed time slots and not continuously. You may take a bird's-eye view of where your life is going once a year, once a month, or once a week, but that's it. Don't worry about it every single minute of your life.

Self-control is an important ability that allows you to respond to external events on your own terms. You don't react based on your impulses. You respond based on your logical analysis of a situation. You are resilient and able to deal with stress. That is what makes you in control and what leads to confidence and success.

Self-Promotion

To a large extent, the corporate world is like a play in a theater. It is all about appearances. If you work hard and focus on your tasks and your tasks alone in the hopes your superior will recognize your achievements and help you to the next level, you are mistaken—at least most of the time. There are certainly great managers and leaders who recognize the potential in their subordinates and provide opportunities where the employee can prove they can do a job, but most of the time, you need to be a bit more proactive if you want to get to the next level on the career ladder. When you have a remote manager who doesn't see what you are doing every single day, then this applies even more. So what do you do to make sure your boss recognizes your contributions and helps you develop your career?

Image matters. Doing a great job is important, but it is not enough. You may be the best software developer in the world, but if no one knows about your work, then no one can recognize your achievements and appreciate what you are doing. A bit of self-promotion never hurts if done carefully.

At the same time, image without substance works only temporarily. If the only thing you do is pursue bigger visibility by taking credit for work you have not done, you may temporarily enhance your image with some people, but overall, your credit goes down. Ultimately, you may get your promotion, but the organization won't believe you deserve it. You will get in a vicious cycle of stress as you will be defending your title in front of others and, ultimately, you will fail and leave. I would argue that you will have a much happier life if you build your image on solid ground. This means that even your peers and subordinates believe that your promotion is well-deserved and that you have the skills to perform well without undue stress. It may take you longer to get to the next level, but it will be well-deserved when it happens, and you will feel good about it and not like a fraud.

Before you start complaining that you were once again skipped for promotion, be honest with yourself and look deep down into your inner self, whether the problem is outside of you or whether it is something internal you should work on. Ignore whether someone else around you was promoted even though they are no good in your eyes. Comparing yourself with others rarely leads to a happy life since there is always someone who will be better than you in something. Better is to compare your skills, behaviors, and achievements against a job profile required for the role you aspire to.

Consider some of these areas of image building and ask yourself how much you focus on them:

- Letting your boss know what you are doing.
- Reaching out, initiating meetings, scheduling one-on-ones with key people you interact with.
- Sharing who you are with your colleagues, talking about your hobbies, successes, and passions.
- Giving praise to others.
- Giving helpful and constructive feedback to others to show you care.
- Volunteering to help others, especially across departments and locations.

It may sound counterintuitive, but by giving and paying it forward, you can get much more recognition in the long run than you would by taking. You are building your image and good reputation step by step. You don't take shortcuts. You don't need to win every battle. You want to expand your influence and positive image by helping others around you to be successful without becoming a doormat yourself.

Stop Shying Away from Positive Feedback

Feedback is a gift. When you get feedback, you may ask clarifying questions to make sure you understand the message correctly, but don't judge. Don't argue. Just receive the message. Then when you have time to think it through, you may decide to either ignore the feedback or take action. It is up to you. That's how you deal with constructive criticism. But what if the feedback is positive?

Not much has been written about receiving positive feedback. This might be cultural since lots of the literature on feedback is written by American authors. In North America and some countries in Western Europe, people are conditioned from a young age to receive and, in fact, even expect positive encouragement and recognition. No big deal—how difficult can it be to accept words of praise?

Very difficult, at least when you are an introvert or when you come from cultures that emphasize humility and focus on helping others rather than getting into the spotlight yourself. I'm an introvert who comes from a culture that tends to criticize more than praise. I have no problems receiving negative feedback, and I always try to get the most from it and improve. What I struggle with is when someone tries to say something positive to me about the work I did.

Many introverts in these situations feel awkward. They don't know what to say and often believe that the praise is exaggerated. You can probably relate. You think you were just doing your job, and it should be a given that you did it correctly. What's the big fuss about?

Your Boss: "This was a great presentation. I was really impressed."

You: "Um, thanks. Just doing my job."

Your Colleague: "Thank you so much for helping me with this task. You are a lifesaver."

You: "Um, no problem."

Your Boss at a Big Meeting: "I want to thank you for leading the charge and making this happen."

You: "Yeah, it was a team effort."

By itself, the inability to accept praise wouldn't be a big problem if it wasn't for the side effects. If someone provides you well-meant praise, they deserve some sort of heartfelt response. More importantly, once you are in a leadership role, your job is to provide well-balanced feedback, which also means positive praise to your team.

If you don't like receiving praise, chances are you are not good at giving it either.

So what can you do to be more comfortable with getting words of encouragement and thanks? It is very simple: just say thank you and smile. This simple act will accomplish several things.

It Shows You Appreciate the Recognition: Let's face it: deep inside, we all like being appreciated, so you are not faking it. If you learn to react in this simple way, you may even start getting more comfortable with praise and begin enjoying it. By saying "thank you" and smiling, you make the person giving you positive feedback feel good as well. It is a win-win situation.

You Don't Marginalize the Praise: When you try to deflect a compliment by saying things like, "It was nothing," it may hurt the person giving the praise. The chances are that what you did meant "something" to that person, so if you marginalize the praise, you also cast a judgment on the person giving it.

It Gives You a Chance to Listen: As with negative feedback, there can be hidden gold in information surrounding a compliment. Listen to why the praise is given to you. You may unearth some future opportunities to repeat a good job or even discover some talents you didn't know you had. Outsiders may see things in you that you don't, so listening to feedback and not cutting it short or dismissing it is essential if you want to understand yourself.

You Embrace the Praise but Stay Humble: There is always a danger that you will overplay the response the other way and hype it to levels not intended. So when you embrace praise, make sure you stay grounded and humble. With a simple thank-you, that is what you accomplish.

You Learn to Enjoy the Small Things in Life: Happiness starts with little things. By accepting praise for little things and learning to enjoy it, you will feel better about yourself and the world. You need to realize that others probably don't compliment you without reason. You did something that caused the other person to offer praise, so there is no reason why you should feel awkward about it. Maybe it wasn't a big deal for you, but it might be for someone else. So feel happy for them.

It Reminds You to Praise Others: Once you realize how good receiving compliments feels and stop being uncomfortable about it, you will also remind yourself that others may enjoy positive feedback and praise too. That will make you a better colleague and a better leader.

Learning how to receive praise is important for your self-confidence as well as your image. You don't want to brag about yourself and self-promote too much, but you shouldn't fight someone who does it for you. So next time someone compliments you, stop fighting it and inventing ways to deflect, but smile and just say thank you.

Authenticity

As you get to know yourself, you will feel more comfortable with who you are, and you will be more inclined to be authentic. What does being authentic mean? It means that your words and actions align with your internal values. You have your set of values that you follow, and you walk the talk. That makes you authentic. This has nothing to do with whether you are introverted or extroverted.

In *Quiet Power*, Susan Cain talks about Free Trait Theory, postulated by Dr. Brian Little. According to this theory, we are all born with particular traits and talents, but during our lives, we can adopt additional characteristics that we need to achieve our life's mission. If you have a project you genuinely care about, one that resonates with your core values and that gives your life meaning, you will naturally step out of your comfort zone and adopt new traits to accomplish it. For introverts, this can even involve acting in more extroverted ways in the service of getting what we care about done.[73]

When you look at popular media, you see famous movie stars, musicians, politicians, and athletes who, by definition of their role, are very visible, performing in front of crowds, always talking, always in the middle of everything, beautiful and smiling all the time. In other words, they appear to be very extroverted personalities. However, many of them are, in fact, very introverted. They dread public performance and try to get out of the open as soon as they can. They play a role as required by their job and their life purpose. They are comfortable being uncomfortable.

I firmly believe that when you have a life's mission you are passionate about, your personality traits can and should be tweaked to help you accomplish that mission. If you want to see a real-life example, look again at Susan Cain, the author of *Quiet*. She is the best example of how an introverted person can step out of their comfort zone and take on the extroverted role. Just watch her fantastic TED talk *The Power of Introverts*.[74] At the same time, you should stay true to yourself and not succumb to social pressure.

Stop Insisting on Being "Me"

No matter who you are or what you do, "being yourself" has no value by itself. Being yourself is only valuable when it also brings value to others. It is not the goal.

What has value is to provide value to others, to fulfill your duty to the team, family, and company. Whether you are yourself while doing so is not particularly relevant.

Being yourself in terms of being aligned with your core values is something to strive for since it will lead to you being satisfied with your life, but you should never use it as an excuse. It all goes back to getting out of your comfort zone. You should occasionally do things that are "not you," that are out of your comfort zone, and that stretch you and allow you to grow and become someone new.

In *What Got You Here Won't Get You There*, Marshall Goldsmith talks about "an excessive need to be me."[75] This is a way people justify bad behavior. "It is just who I am," they will say to a critique or feedback. It is a self-limiting belief that makes you pretend that there is nothing you can do about it. You are comfortable with who you are, and this is a good excuse not to change. Once you realize that "being you" at any cost is not worth the damage you are causing, you are halfway to getting better.

This is particularly the case for many introverts who believe that they can't get to a leadership role because it is "not them." You should always carefully examine situations when you use an excuse either toward the outside world or toward yourself that something "wouldn't be you." Ask yourself a simple question: "Why not?" Why couldn't that be you?

I have a problem with giving positive praise. Not that I don't want to. I love giving positive praise, as I know it makes people happy and more productive, makes them feel appreciated, and improves relationships. I know all these things, and still, I don't do it as often as I should.

Why not? Because I forget. I forget because I don't have the need for praise myself. I'm a very internally referenced person. Even though I like it when someone appreciates my work, I don't need that appreciation to stay focused and motivated. Because I don't need it, I don't give praising others a high enough importance. I tell myself it just isn't me.

Once I realized that this was what I was doing, I decided that I wanted it to be me. I wanted to make other people feel appreciated. Now I'm giving it more focus and make sure that I praise someone every day. So, step by step, it is becoming part of me. Can I do better? Yes. I'm working on it and getting there. At least I stopped making the excuse that "it just isn't me."

Summary and Key Takeaways

Self-awareness is the key to personal and professional development. Without knowing yourself, your strengths, and your weaknesses, you can't work on them. Introverts have the strengths of attentiveness, introspection, and enough humility to help us be realistic about what we need to improve. However, we still have blind spots, so feedback from someone we value is always helpful, especially when we get into self-recrimination. Don't get into victim mode, where you blame yourself for all the pains of the world.

Realistic self-awareness helps with confidence and self-esteem. Introverts often struggle to point out their accomplishments, which may lead to minimizing ourselves, therefore lowering our self-confidence. We tend to apologize for everything, regardless of whether something was our fault or not, and irrespective of whether anyone even noticed. Don't be afraid to ask for what is due to you, and while you should always admit to and own your mistakes, there is no need to constantly apologize for who you are.

It is rare, but it is possible for introverts to become overconfident. For instance, this happens when you have a couple of successful projects, and you start believing in your own power—which is good!—but don't realize that a big part of the success was the environment and the people around you. You may get overconfident and then fail miserably at working on a project with different people. Self-awareness is crucial, and you should always use your strength of attentiveness to keep a realistic view of your own successes and failures.

Self-awareness then leads to better self-control. Better self-control leads to better relationships and being more at peace with yourself and your work environment, which directly impacts your ability to succeed. Some of the biggest stressors in the workplace are being in the wrong role, having a high-demand job with low job control, having a toxic manager, and not having enough emotional support from others around you. Yes, even introverts need to feel that others care about us.

With better self-awareness and self-control, we are more comfortable being authentic and promoting our strengths, abilities, and way of working.

- Build self-awareness to understand your values, what you want, who you are, and what you need to work on.
- Confront reality, identify your blind spots, and open your eyes to how others see you.
- Stop playing the victim, and stop telling yourself stories that hold you back.
- Work on your self-efficacy, resilience, and the belief that focus and hard work will lead to success.

- Stop taking things personally.
- Stay calm under pressure by slowing time down and thinking first before responding.
- Doing a great job is essential, but it is not enough—image and visibility matter as well.
- Learn to accept positive feedback, as it will give you an edge.
- Keep in mind that being authentic just for the sake of being authentic won't give you anything. "Being yourself" has no real value unless it serves your life's mission. Get comfortable reinventing yourself and becoming someone new.

Questions and Next Steps

- What did you learn in Chapter 3 that has a direct impact on your ability to succeed in your career? Do you worry too much? Do you take things personally?
- Consider what the victim stories you are telling yourself are. Can you reframe some of them to change them from limiting to enhancing your success?
- Are you stressed at work? What leads to that stress? Could it be that you are in the wrong role? Consider the Sweet Spot chart and look at what makes your life miserable. Could it be you don't have the necessary skills for your job and worry that you will mess up? Could it be that you are on a toxic team? What can you do to lower your stress?
- Do you know if you have any blind spots when it comes to your strengths, weaknesses, and career in general? Have you ever asked for feedback from those around you? No? Then do so. Find someone you feel you can trust and ask for their genuine assessment of your behavior at work. Don't argue with their feedback, and don't feel bad about it if it is negative. You want to understand how others see you so you can work on it. A genuine thank-you is all you need to offer, then sit down and dissect what you have learned and whether you can do things differently going forward to increase your chances of career success.

9

Prioritize Well

"I focus on what is important. I let go of the past.
I live a well-integrated life."

Be clear on your priorities, and don't lie to yourself about what is important. I mean it. Too often, we let cultural expectations blind us and make us lie to ourselves. Suppose I ask you to tell me what's most important to you. What comes to mind? Most people would say something like health or family. That is the right thing to say. But is it true? Your behavior may indicate that it is not necessarily the case. You spend all your time in the office trying hard to get promoted or spend endless hours working on your business to earn as much money as possible. You spend hundreds of hours a year in front of a TV, but how many hours a day do you spend with your family? When was the last time you exercised? Your actions suggest that family and health are not so important. "Family" or "health" are just the obvious things to say, as you don't want to look bad in the eyes of others or even your own.

If you genuinely want to achieve something, you need to be crystal clear with yourself about what is truly important to you and focus on that. This is the reason I asked you to figure out what is important to you in Chapter 3. It is okay to want different things than people around you do. You are a unique individual, so shed the guilt of not living up to the expectations of others. Make sure you live up to your expectations, and that means focusing on things that are important to you. Don't try to satisfy everyone. Don't try to have it all. The chances are that you will end up a rather unhappy person. Having a clear idea of your priorities and what a successful life looks like to you is the only way to reach it.

Priorities

Having a life's mission is a powerful way to stay focused on essentials and achieve your professional and life goals. It works the same way as a company mission. It helps you to prioritize. It helps you to focus. It helps you to make the right decisions.

In *Deep Work*, Cal Newport talks about priorities and two ways to decide what things to do or tools to use: the any-benefit approach and the craftsman approach. When you follow the any-benefit approach, you say yes to things and tools that may provide any benefit. Even if the benefit is negligible, you may still say yes for fear of missing out. The problem is that you completely ignore the negative aspects that come with the decision.[76]

For example, do you have at-work access to your favorite social media platform? How many times a day do you get distracted by it? Social media platforms are useful and have obvious benefits. They help you stay in touch with your friends and so-called friends. What you may not realize is that there is a negative side. You have a finite amount of time and attention. You just exchanged a bunch of instant messages with some acquaintances and read a couple of articles on vaguely interesting topics, but that time was taken from preparing for your next meeting and producing something on your own. You traded important, high-value tasks for unimportant, shallow entertainment. You lost. Your career suffers.

The craftsman approach to decision-making and prioritizing considers not only the benefits but also the negative aspects. You say yes to an activity only when the positives outweigh the negatives. This approach seems like a no-brainer, but many of us struggle with this concept and succumb to the any-benefit trap to justify to ourselves why we are wasting our lives.

Your Purpose Will Drive Your Priorities

You probably saw this coming, but the number-one challenge in prioritizing is understanding what you want and need. Of course, you may have a couple of important things in your life, but you don't prioritize them all equally. You may feel that raising your kids is essential. You may want to give back to the community and do volunteer work. You want to have a good career, and you may love playing the guitar or riding your bike. All these things are important to you. But there needs to be a priority list, and you need to be clear on the sacrifices you are willing to make.

Let's imagine it is Friday evening and you are at home with your kids, discussing what to do over the weekend. Everyone has some great ideas, and you are looking forward to spending your time with your family. Family is important to you. Then the phone rings. It is your boss. The request is simple: "I just got off a call with an important customer, and we have been asked to give a presentation to their CEO on Monday morning. Can you prepare something over the weekend? It shouldn't take more than a couple of hours, and you know you are the best person for the job."

Now, your family is important to you, but your career is equally important. What do you do? You will have to make a decision, and that decision will clearly show what your number-one priority is. If you go back to your kids and say that you will go with them for a trip on Sunday, but tomorrow you have to go to the office, your priorities are clear—and vice versa.

This example also illustrates how the introvert's strength of loyalty can be easily abused. We want to be loyal to the company and to our boss. And we often forget to be loyal to ourselves and to our family. The choice your boss gave you seems like a sucker's choice that will be followed by overanalysis the moment you put down the phone. If you are clear on your values, as we discussed in Chapter 3, and have your priorities straight, there is nothing to analyze. The decision makes itself.

This struggle is often demonstrated in how we approach urgent versus important needs. If you don't have a reliable compass and clarity on what you want from life, chances are that you focus on urgent things more than on important ones, and you justify why the urgent things are urgent and why you are the only one who can deal with them. However, often the urgent things are not as urgent as you make yourself believe. If you said no to your boss, mentioning that you have plans with your family, chances are that someone else could step in and do the work, someone for whom the career truly is more important and who is willing to pay the price. The work still gets done.

In workplace settings, you want to help others, you care about the company's success, but it has to be a win-win for you as well. If you help the organization while your own career suffers, something is wrong.

Every decision you make shows you clearly what your real priorities are, regardless of what you would like to think about yourself. Being crystal clear on your purpose in life, your career, and your priorities is a must. Otherwise, you will keep struggling with decisions, keep making excuses, and keep focusing on the wrong things. Once you understand your purpose in life and your priorities, most decisions are not decisions at all. Most other people's urgent matters are suddenly not that urgent for you. This gives you the freedom to focus on what is truly important—important for you.

Stop Saying "I Have To"

"I'm sorry, I have to finish this today, so I can't help you." "I have to go shopping on Saturday, so I can't make the trip." "I have to get a better-paying job so that I can pay back the mortgage." We often use the magical words "have to" as an excuse for not doing something we feel we should. You feel that you really *should* visit your parents more often, but because you "have to" do other things, you can't visit them. You feel you *should* take better care of yourself and exercise more, but because you "have to" go shopping, you can't exercise. And so on. You essentially claim that it is not you who doesn't want to do things; it is the environment that doesn't allow you to. You willingly give up your freedom by introducing artificial "have to" constraints.

And it gets worse. You use the "have to" language to trample all over your dreams. You really like your job, but it doesn't pay particularly well, and you really "have to" get more money to afford more stuff. So, you move to a job that is killing you but pays more. In your mind, you have no choice. You are willingly giving up your freedom and your dream job by introducing artificial constraints. You "have to" make more money, you "have to" get a new car, you "have to" watch your favorite TV show so you know how it ends. You are becoming a slave to your language. Either you are making excuses for not doing what you believe you should, or you are making excuses for not being satisfied with your life.

There is a better way. All you need to do is change the words you are using and stop lying to yourself. You really don't "have to" do anything. You should always use "want to" language. "I want to visit the art gallery . . . and it is more important to me than visiting my parents this weekend." "I want to get the new car I have dreamed about since childhood . . . and I'm willing to sacrifice a year of my life to make enough money to get it." "I want to travel around the world . . . and I'm willing to live without a family for the time being to do so."

"I want to" is a powerful phrase that will do two things for you. First, it creates clarity. You start being honest with yourself and the world around you. You don't need to make up excuses for why you don't want to do something. You clearly state what your priority is, and that is what you focus on. Second, "I want to" is much more positive language than "I have to." It helps you feel more in control of your life, and ultimately, if you feel more in control, you will be more satisfied. You are not a victim of your environment. You don't "have to" do things. You are your own master who "wants to" do what you are doing. You may still decide to work a dreadful job to make more money, but you will feel better about it.

"I have to do this miserable, high-paying job because I have kids I have to take care of" is a complaint about how miserable your life is, and if you could, you would change it.

"I want to do this miserable high-paying job so I can provide for my family" gives you purpose. You love your family, and this is a way you can care for them. You wouldn't change this for the world.

Focus

To survive and even thrive in the knowledge-based economy, you need two fundamental abilities. You need to be able to learn and quickly master new skills. And you need to be able to produce work at a high level in terms of quality and speed. With these two skills, you can beat the competition and get rewarded. This applies to both companies competing on the market with their products and individuals competing in the job market with their skills and experiences.

Knowledge itself is not enough. You may be the most knowledgeable person, but if you can't produce, if you don't deliver results, it is the same as if you didn't have the knowledge at all.

If you can't focus, you won't be able to learn as quickly as others. If you can't concentrate, you won't produce results at speed and with high quality. It is that simple. Focus is the road to success.

Focus has two aspects. The first aspect is doing what is important in your life. The second aspect of focus is being in the moment and not getting distracted by trivial matters not on your priority list. It sounds simple, but it is not easy, especially in today's world full of distractions and the need to multitask.

In Chapter 2, we talked about focus being introverts' strength and how multitasking is a myth. The human brain can't really multitask. It just very quickly switches context. And that has a price to pay. Several studies showed that when a person is interrupted while working on a complex task, it will take them up to 40 or 50 percent longer to finish it.[77] That means that two five-minute tasks, like writing an email and talking to your boss, will take you longer if done in parallel, and, most likely, the results will be a poorly written email and a crippled relationship with your boss. If you are constantly doing several things in parallel, you get the feeling of working quickly, but at the end of the day, you will find that you have produced less.

Psychologists Daniel T. Gilbert and Matthew Killingsworth ran a study to analyze what people feel and think during the day as they go through their lives. They discovered that 46.9 percent spend their days thinking about things other than what they are currently doing.[78] We spend half of our waking moments not being present, not focusing on the task at hand, not focusing on what is essential, not living our lives to the fullest. We let our minds wander, and that makes us unhappy since we are thinking about what is not happening instead of focusing on what is happening.

As Gloria Janet Mark of the University of California discovered, people are as likely to interrupt themselves as to be interrupted by external circumstances. Mark and her team found that people spend three minutes and five seconds on average on a single task before they get interrupted and switch. 82 percent of all interrupted work is then resumed on the same day. However, it takes on average twenty-three minutes and fifteen seconds to get back to the original task.[79]

Eyal Ophir, Clifford Nass, and Anthony D. Wagner published a paper discussing the results of their research into the impact of social media and multitasking on the human brain. It showed that the constant switching between tasks that addiction to social media causes has a profound and lasting effect on how your brain operates. Brain plasticity is a great thing that can help you grow, but it can also severely inhibit your abilities if you abuse it.[80] As Nass points out, those who multitask all the time can't easily distinguish what is relevant and what is not. The relevancy filter in their heads just doesn't work. They have trouble staying focused even if they want to. Their brains activate many areas that are not relevant to the task at hand, and they are just constantly distracted. The worst thing is that they don't realize it. This is very similar to addiction.

I believed that I was good at multitasking until several years ago, when in one day I had a couple of encounters that completely changed my perspective on the topic. I was running a fairly big organization back then, so people would come to me all the time with questions or problems. That particular day I was putting together a set of rules for a new initiative, preparing a presentation, and putting all my focus on getting the presentation done. It took me about three hours. During that time, several people from the team approached me, asking for help or just asking trivial questions. Every single time, I would say something like, "Hi, how can I help you?" without taking my eyes off the computer, and when the person started to talk, I would glance at them a couple of times to show that I was listening, but my attention was still on the work I had been doing. I promised all of them that I would deal with their issues, but forgot half of them and misunderstood the rest. The last person who came started to talk, then stopped in the middle of a sentence and said he would come back another time and left without waiting for my response. This woke me up! Up to that moment, I had believed I was doing two things in parallel, working on my presentation and helping my team with their problems. Now I realized that I had just been working on my presentation and ignoring my team while being disrespectful to them and lying to myself. Since then, I pay lots of attention to situations like that one, and if someone comes to talk to me, I either immediately tell them to come back at a different time, or I stop doing whatever I'm doing, take a deep breath, turn to the person, and give them my undivided attention.

Being in the moment is an incredibly powerful thing to do. If you lose interest in the conversation or in other people, your body will let them know, and they will lose interest in you. Not many people realize how damaging it is to their image if they don't pay attention.

Test this sometime. When someone talks to you, pay attention at the beginning, but in the middle of their monologue, shift your attention to your phone. You will see that their monologue will start to dwindle, and eventually, they will stop, sometimes even saying something along the lines of, "I seem to be boring you." You lost interest in them, so they lose interest in you. By paying attention, listening attentively, and asking questions, you not only show the other person that they are interesting, but you also become more interesting for them.

By being present, you are not only building better relationships with others and getting more things done, you are also feeling better. You get much more satisfaction from solving a problem or accomplishing a goal when you pay attention to what you are doing the whole time.

Just consider the last meal you had when you were eating and reading an article on your phone in parallel. Did you truly enjoy the meal? Were you able to savor all the flavors? Remember the pleasant smell of the food or coffee you had afterward? Or do you just know you ate something but can't even remember what it was? Being present and living every moment to its full potential allows you to enjoy the small things in life and is a great way to keep stress levels in check.

Stop Obsessing over Social Media

I said it before, and I'll say it again: social media is a distraction. Deprioritizing it will have a positive influence on both your career and your life in general, though you may experience some withdrawal symptoms.

Many introverts love social media. It allows us to communicate with the outside world, make friends, and keep in touch with like-minded individuals without the need to leave our homes. Social media sounds like a gift from heaven. Except it is not. Let's consider the impact the time you spend on your favorite social media has on the rest of your life.

Time and Attention: There is a finite amount of time and attention you can give to the activities in your life. The amount of time you have in a single day to use for your pursuits is constant. You may have more time if you sleep less, but on average, each of us can provide a number that says how many hours every day we have available. If you complain that you don't have enough time to manage everything you need to do, you are lying to yourself. You have the same amount of time as the rest of humankind—it is just a question of how you spend it. You can't manage time, but you can manage attention. It is only up to you to decide what you want to put your focus on. If you focus on the right things, you will quickly realize that you can do a lot with that time and be happier. Can you do everything in the world? No. Can you do the things that are the most important to you? Definitely.

Busyness and Productivity: In the good old days of mostly manual labor, it was straightforward to see how productive you were. Even today, some professions get immediate feedback on how well they are doing and what they produce. If you plant two hundred trees and your quota for the day was a hundred and fifty, you know you did a good job. You were productive, you achieved your goal, and now you feel great. You did something meaningful. If you are a knowledge worker who sits in the office all day long, it may not be that straightforward to figure out whether you are producing as you should. How do you measure whether you produced good work when you were reviewing documents all day long? How do you measure whether you produced enough good quality code when working as a software engineer? Since it may not be easy to measure output, we learn to measure effort. You may end your day with a bit of a vague idea of what exactly you achieved, but feel good because you were busy. We mistake busyness for productivity. Busyness is most easily achieved by being constantly involved in everything that's going on around you. If you go to every meeting, respond to every email, and always keep checking all your social networks and responding to the avalanche of small requests, you will be busy, it will feel good . . . and you won't achieve anything that truly matters!

Opportunity Cost: There is an opportunity cost to everything. If you choose to do one thing, you are also choosing *not* to do another thing. If you decide to spend an hour responding to instant messages on your favorite social media platform, that means you chose not to write a new blog post, go for a run, or have a meaningful conversation with your spouse. And yet you keep complaining about not having enough time to do those things. When you think about it a bit more, it was never about time; it was about your choice to prioritize interaction on social media above something else. We choose to get distracted by unimportant stuff and then have regrets that we can't do things that genuinely matter to us.

Life Priorities: In *Deep Work*, Cal Newport coined the term—wait for it—"deep work."[81] He talks about the importance of significant stretches of uninterrupted time to achieve your life goals and produce results. Social media, even though it does have some uses, often acts as a huge distraction. And not just social media! It is the constant electronic communication, including instant messaging applications and email, that makes it so hard to focus on what matters to us. We feel obligated to reply to others as soon as they ask us things, and we ignore our priorities. Imagine it is the end of the year, and you are looking back and analyzing whether it was a good year or not. In one case, you limited distractions from social media, television, emails, and the constant need for information. You managed to write a book that just went to press and started to sell. In the second case, you sent thousands of emails, tens of thousands of instant messages, and you read every single piece of news you could get your hands on. You were busy. In the first case, would you say you had a good year? And what about the second one?

Consuming and Producing: Most people are much more satisfied with their lives when they are producing rather than consuming. Most of us want to see that what we are doing makes sense, that what we do matters. We need to see the results of our work. We need to create things. We need to produce. Then we feel good about ourselves and our lives. Social media, for the most part, acts as a distraction in this effort. It forces you to consume. It gives you so much information to browse through, the information you never knew you needed. It allows you to have a shallow relationship with hundreds of people you wouldn't even talk to if you met them on the street. It gives you so many choices for how to spend your time. It abducts your attention so you don't focus on things that truly matter to you.

I'm an avid reader, and I spend quite a bit of time every weekend going through articles on various social media platforms. I start with one, then find another that is related, then another, and half an hour later I find myself reading about something I have no interest in. However, I also know that I'm not alone in this. The bright side of some of these platforms is that they encourage me to produce. If I write an excellent blog post, I can share my knowledge and thoughts with the world and hopefully make someone's life better.

Return on Investment: You should do an inventory of where you put your attention during the day. Do you have big uninterrupted chunks of time to produce your best work? Good. If not, what are the distractions? Can you limit them to specific times to free the rest of your day for deep work? Things like answering emails, going to meetings, and preparing reports are all tasks that don't require your complete, uninterrupted attention. They are what Newport calls "shallow work."

Organize your day, week, and month in such a way that you either eliminate the shallow work or bundle those activities together in a way that will allow you to spend enough time focused on what is truly important to you, whether that's deep work producing something great, building a healthy relationship with key people in your life, or recharging and taking care of your health.

Social media is very tempting to introverts, as it gives us a way to deal with the world on our terms. However, it attacks two of our key strengths: our abilities to focus and to think deep. If you let this happen, it will turn you into a disillusioned individual who will feel constantly busy and yet unable to create anything satisfying. You will feel envious of others and sorry for yourself. You will struggle more and more to achieve your life dreams, and your attention will be more and more turned to the negative aspects of life. Would I shut down all the social networks? No. Would I urge you to be very deliberate with how you use them? That would be a big yes.

Letting Go

Prioritizing well also means knowing when to stop doing what you are doing to focus on something new. How difficult is it to let go of something you created? One of the most challenging things for successful people is to leave a successful project, a great team they built, their pet project, or something they felt very proud of. And yet, letting go is often the best thing to do, both for you and others.

At some point, you have to admit that even though what you built is great, it is holding you back and preventing you from doing new cool stuff. There is an opportunity cost associated with everything we do, and sometimes, especially when we are doing something we enjoy, we don't realize that it costs us something even greater. At some stage, you feel that what you built is not providing you with a challenge anymore, and you are not as passionate about it as you used to be. The team is still great, and the project is still a good project, but you are different.

You are not your team. Is that a good thing or a bad thing? From my own experience with building several successful teams working on great projects, the most challenging aspect of letting go is that you feel like you are still crucial to the project's success, and you believe that if you leave, things will break down. This is evident if you are playing a critical role, if you are the founder or the leader of the team, or if you hold a wealth of technical knowledge that no one else has. You are afraid that, without your guidance, the team will not perform at its top level. Don't worry. People on your team are grown-ups, smart adults who will figure out how to make things work. And what if things don't work when you leave? Well, maybe that is not that bad either.

If you were the one who started the project, leaving it is like leaving a baby. Once you hire good people, you mentor them, and you build a great team, it becomes a sort of family. It is tough to disconnect and cut all ties completely. And that is not even the right thing to do. So what do you do if you feel the time is right and you need to move on? And how do you do it so you feel good about the whole experience? I would compare this to your family. You always have ties with your family, even if you move to work in a different city, marry, leave your parents and siblings behind, or move to another country. What do you do in such situations? You keep in touch! You don't tell them how to live their lives, you are not there daily to provide help, but you are available to talk, to offer a sympathetic ear.

The family analogy applies with one exception. Business is not a family, and it shouldn't be. Business is business. You don't need to sacrifice your whole life to make one particular business work. So what are the five steps to follow to be able to let go?

Understand the Opportunity Cost: Think about what things you are missing if you stay longer than needed. I suggest you read the *Who Moved My Cheese?* parable by Spencer Johnson. It is a short story discussing the need for change.[82]

Accept That You Are Replaceable: Realize that everyone is replaceable—even you. If you have done a good job building the team, you trust them, and they have the ownership of the business, your job is done anyway.

Keep in Touch with the Team: Not really to provide guidance, but to show that you still care about how they are doing—*them*, not the business. You are there to listen and provide mentoring or coaching so they continue to see you as the great person you are. Never try to give guidance on execution. You are not part of the team anymore; the dynamic has changed, you don't know what is going on, and the advice you would provide may do more harm than good.

Realize That Business Is Not a Family: And it shouldn't be treated that way if you want to maintain your sanity. Companies fail all the time, and you don't want to get too emotionally attached. Just keep a healthy relationship with the team. You don't want to burn any bridges behind you.

Focus on the Future: And never second-guess your decision. The human mind has an incredible power to misremember things, so don't try to live too much in the past, as you are likely to remember only the highlights and successes and not all the things that didn't go as planned. Don't keep saying to yourself, "This would never have happened in the good old days." Chances are, it would have, and it did.

And if you still struggle and are still not able to let go? Introverts tend to struggle a lot with letting go. Our strengths of loyalty and perseverance work against us in this scenario. Sometimes we need a kick to realize what is good for us and for our careers. Talk to someone you know who went through the same experience and get some coaching. Or hire a professional life coach to help you focus your mind on a positive future rather than living in the past. The experience is very similar to seeing your children, whom you dedicated years of your life to, growing up and going their separate ways. You spent years making sure they had the right values. They are self-sufficient, respect you, and love you. But you can't guide them forever, so at some point, you have to step aside and let them live their own lives.

Chasing Money

If you did the Life Balance Wheel Exercise, you discovered that money, while important, is not a solution to all your problems. And if you remember the Successful Career Wheel, you know that compensation is only a small part of what makes a successful career. Yet people tend to prioritize money and then are unhappy with their work, careers, and lives.

Let me tell you about Joe. Joe had the fortune (or misfortune) to get a super high-paying job fresh out of university. It was a job with a big prestigious company willing to wildly overpay to get the best talent. He was excited. Who wouldn't be? The problem didn't become apparent for several years. Joe got married, moved to a smaller city, and had to change jobs. He had several years more experience under his belt than he had had when he graduated. He joined a new company and was one of the best-paid people on the team. But the pay was nowhere near that of his previous job. Even though he was being appreciated and being paid well according to the local market, he was pretty miserable. He kept comparing his compensation to that with his previous employer. He often even mentioned that his former employer wasn't particularly good, and it hadn't been a pleasant working experience, but the money was out of this world. And he would keep bringing this up for years. The one overpaying job pretty much destroyed his happiness for years to come, and the culprit was having the wrong priorities. His single-minded focus on compensation made him blind to the other parts of the Successful Career Wheel and kept him unhappy.

Employees, especially in the knowledge economy, are free agents. You have the power to pack your things and leave tomorrow if you stop being satisfied with the employer you work for. Getting yourself handcuffed to a job you don't enjoy is a severe lapse in judgment.

Or is it? Only you can answer that. Just make sure you think it through. There are those among us who would be completely fine with golden handcuffs because they don't expect much from their jobs. For these people, a job is just a job. It is a way to earn money so they can realize their potential and dreams elsewhere. Having a job that pays as much as possible gives them the most freedom outside of work. They are willing to suffer eight hours a day for the rest of their lives just to get the chance to do what they enjoy for the rest of their day. I would argue that even though there are people like that, most of us wouldn't be satisfied with this scenario, as it violates the idea of work-life integration and living a complete life. Most people want to live satisfying lives, even when we're at work. We want to feel good about what we do, we want to wake up every morning looking forward to the day. We want to contribute. We want our work to have meaning. We want to learn and grow as people, we want to build careers, and golden handcuffs are a severe menace.

So what are the fundamental problems? How do you eliminate golden handcuffs and get out of their trap?

The Comfort of the Known: You are comfortable with where you are, you know that you are being paid well, and there is no reason to do anything about it. You may not be learning anything new, may not be growing, may not have big career prospects, may not particularly enjoy your work, but overall, things are fine. That is, until they are not. If you get stuck in this comfort zone for too long, you lose the joy coming from work and you become disengaged. With low engagement comes low productivity. With low productivity comes the danger of being fired. And with that comes stress. Think of the Employee Emotional Life Cycle.

Don't get too comfortable. If you start feeling that the work you do doesn't bring you any joy and the only reason you are doing it is the money, go and talk to your boss. Ask for something that will challenge you, that will bring something new into your life. Or go and start helping others around you, even with things that are not part of your job description.

Stress That You Might Lose the Job: The knowledge that you may lose your job is always stressful. It is doubly stressful when you know that it would be challenging to find a job that will allow you to keep your standard of living. The weirdest part is that you may be stressed out by losing a job you hate. That is a complete no-win scenario.

Just leave. If you get to the point where you genuinely hate your job, there is no better way to relieve stress than to leave and start fresh elsewhere. Of course, before you do that, make sure that you also reset your expectations. What are the actual costs of your lifestyle? Do you need to make the amount of money you're currently making to be happy? It may very well be that you keep asking for more, but you don't need it.

Knowledge That You Are Being Paid More Than You Are Worth: This is at the heart of the golden handcuffs. You know, deep down, that what you are being paid is higher than the level at which the market evaluates your skills and contributions. You might be smart and skillful, but you still don't want to get on the job market, as you feel that even if you get another job, you will still lose. What is worse, because of the standards you got used to, you may take a very long time to find a job. It's not necessarily that you won't get offers, but rather because you will keep looking for the one perfect job that you will love with a company willing to overpay you.

Never let the money, or lack of it, stand between you and a job you know would be perfect for you. You may take a pay cut, but your satisfaction with life will skyrocket. And ultimately, isn't the feeling of satisfaction and happiness one of the big reasons you work? Of course you want to be compensated fairly. Of course you need to cover your living needs. But make sure that you understand what these terms mean for you. Too often, people set a standard of living for themselves that they don't even enjoy. Do you need to go to a fancy restaurant for dinner when you could get a good meal you would enjoy elsewhere for a quarter of the cost? Do you need to drive a luxury car when you can't see a difference in driving experience with a car that costs half as much? Do you need a purse from a fancy brand when a generic one looks the same? Forget about what others are doing or saying. Forget about what others expect from someone of your status. Do what you believe makes sense and what makes you happy.

Feeling of Emptiness: Even if you don't get stressed, you may still lack satisfaction with your work life. You are willing to go through the dreary work day after day, just for the money. You feel that you are not contributing the way you could. You feel that you are wasting your life, day after day. Smart companies will not only give you golden handcuffs but will go out of their way to keep you engaged and will continually challenge you and give you more opportunities. It is those companies and managers who feel that, by throwing money at you, they have solved the problem. They have retained you. Your body didn't walk away, though your soul and mind might have.

I would suggest that you dive deep into your soul and find out which category of people you belong to. Do you take a job just as a way to earn money, and are you willing to suffer through it to get the biggest paycheck possible? Then you are good to get yourself locked into the golden handcuffs. However, if you want to live a more integrated life where you enjoy not only your free time but also the time you spend at work, you should be very careful and should frequently review why exactly you are still in your job. If you realize that the only reason you're in your job is money and that the rest gives you no pleasure, if you realize you don't enjoy the work, you are not engaged, and you are therefore not doing a particularly good job, start thinking about how to get out. And that means taking a closer look at your overall lifestyle and starting to make some changes, so you don't rely on being overpaid.

Summary and Key Takeaways

To have a successful career, you need to prioritize. You can't be all things to all people, and you can't say yes to every distraction. You need to keep your focus. This is good news for introverts, as focus is one of our strengths. But even we get distracted more and more easily with the onslaught coming from technology and social media.

One of the biggest enemies of our ability to focus on what's important is the feeling that we "have to" do something. Learn to remove those words from your vocabulary. Use "I want to" instead, as it will force clarity on the way you prioritize. This will also strengthen your ability to let go. It is easy to believe that we are indispensable and that we have to be involved even in things that no longer serve our careers. Learning to let go will allow you to pursue new opportunities and will ultimately enhance your career.

Prioritizing well also means being present to the fullest in anything you do. If you are at work, then be at work. Focus on the task at hand, and don't worry about anything else. If you are sitting in a meeting, then focus on the topics discussed and ignore your email. If you are at home with your kids, give your complete attention to them and don't check your phone every five minutes. It might be tempting to do many things in parallel in an attempt to achieve more, but the only thing you will accomplish is a state of constant worry and a feeling of missing out.

- Don't lie to yourself about what is important to you.
- Stop saying, "I have to." You don't have to do anything. Learn to say "I want to" instead.
- Focus on what is essential, and don't get distracted by vain desires and vices.
- Always focus on the task at hand and learn to live in the moment. You will accomplish more, and you will be more satisfied with your life.
- Treat people with respect and always fully focus on the person you are talking to.
- Stop obsessing over social media and consuming content in general.
- Spend your time producing rather than consuming.
- Learn to say no to things that distract you from your life's mission.
- Get comfortable with being uncomfortable and with making sacrifices.
- You can't have it all, but you can have all the things that are truly important to you.
- Get comfortable with letting go.
- Stop chasing money. Whatever your life's mission is, I can assure you that it's not "being rich." If you believe that being rich is your goal, then you are lying to yourself.

Questions and Next Steps

- How do you make decisions about your priorities? Do you have the any-benefit approach, saying yes to everything? Or do you follow the craftsman approach of being very deliberate about what you say yes to?
- What are the things you do at work that are just distractions? Are there things you can say no to? What do you need to focus on to be successful?
- Do you pay attention to every single conversation you have? Or do you get easily distracted by your phone? When talking to others, make it a point to stop whatever you are doing, put down your phone, and focus on the person. This will dramatically improve your ability to communicate, build better relationships, and get a reputation as someone who cares. All of this will have a positive benefit on your career.
- Consider doing a time audit. For the duration of one or two weeks, note what you are doing every fifteen minutes. You can use software to make this easier. Alternatively, you can finish each activity with a note about how long it took and what type of activity it was. If you spend half of that time distracted, make sure you list the time as "distraction." Once you have this visualized, it is easy to stop working on things that are not important to you and focus on what will enhance your success. I suggest running this exercise every couple of months, as distractions have a way of creeping in without us realizing it.

$$10$$

Own Everything

*"I own everything in my life. I speak up and ask for what
I want and need. I own my failures."*

You are in complete control of your life and your feelings. You may not be in control of your environment. You may not be in control of what others around you are doing, saying, or thinking. But you are in control of what *you* do, say, and think. You can choose to take this control, this power, in a positive direction and build a life you want. Or you can take this control and power in a negative or even destructive course and complain, whine, and blame the rest of the world for your misery.

If you like option number one, then know it won't be easy. Taking control of your life is a lot of hard work. It requires you to get out of your comfort zone—or rather expand your comfort zone—so it includes proactivity, assertiveness, and the willingness to speak up and stand your ground. This expansion will require you to practice accountability and own your failures. It will force you to stop waiting for others to do or decide things and to instead find your way to make things happen.

Taking ownership means that you are proactive in everything you do. You don't blame others for your misfortunes, and you own your mistakes. When something goes wrong, you learn from it and fix it. You make decisions, and then you are accountable for them. You proactively and assertively ask for what is yours. You understand that the world doesn't owe you anything, and if you want to have a successful career, you need to be the one to make it happen.

Once you learn to own everything in your life, you stop complaining and stop blaming others. You realize that only you decide how your life will turn out. This will help you build a more positive approach to life and your career. You will have more healthy relationships with others at work and at home. You will know that it is you and only you who makes your life great. You will learn to celebrate the small wins along the way, you will learn to enjoy the hard work, and you will feel that your life has meaning. You will be on the path toward a successful career.

Ownership Mindset

Personal or individual leadership is at the heart of every successful team. It is not only a question for management—everyone needs to show individual leadership and ownership. As Jocko Willink and Leif Babin wrote in *Extreme Ownership*, leaders must own everything in their world. There is no one else to blame.[83]

Having ownership means that you take initiative, trigger activity, and then own the results. Accountability then means that you are taking responsibility for the outcome of the activity. I'm using the term "ownership" as I find it more comprehensive. Ownership starts with getting rid of your ego. Ego is the most likely culprit in blaming others and not taking ownership of your work, mistakes, and life. Getting to a place where you stop equating how your environment reacts to your actions with who you are is the most important thing to learn.

Have you received negative feedback? Don't take it personally. Just listen, think about whether there is some lesson you can learn from it, and implement if it makes sense. Don't worry that negative feedback makes you a bad person. Have you failed in your project? Do a retrospective, consider what went fine and what went wrong, and learn from it. Failure of the project doesn't mean you are a failure yourself. Getting to this mindset may not be an easy thing to do, especially for people who tend to overthink everything, like most introverts. It requires a certain level of confidence in your skills and abilities that takes time to build.

You need to own your whole world, and that means you are to be blamed for everything that goes wrong. Only by adopting the mindset that you are the one who messed up and can fix things can you be truly successful. Just make sure you don't forget the "fix" part. Never just blame yourself, as that would lead you to a dark place. Every single time you admit a mistake, follow up with "I can fix it." This is incredibly powerful. It can sometimes be scary and humiliating, but it is always an empowering mindset.

Consider this example: You spent a lot of time working on a proposal for a new initiative. When you presented it to your boss, she said, "No." Guess what? That is your fault! You shouldn't blame your boss for not understanding your brilliant idea. You probably didn't provide the right level of detail. Your arguments were not good enough. You didn't understand your boss's priorities, or you came up with something that wasn't aligned with the company mission. Whatever the problem was, it wasn't your boss. You could have done something different to get the approval. Try better next time. It may sound counterintuitive, but stop blaming your team, your boss, and other people in your life when you're not able to get things done. This is the first step to personal leadership.

This may feel like putting the weight of the world on your shoulders. It can be stressful. But it can also be empowering, depending on how you look at it. It is you who takes ownership and sets the goals. No one is pressuring you. As I mentioned before, most of the stress in the workplace comes from being in the wrong role or having unrealistic expectations. Taking ownership gets easier the more you learn to utilize your strengths of prudence, preparation, focus, and perseverance. It gets less stressful when you know in your heart that you have done everything you could. You did your best. If it wasn't enough, that's fine. You can't win every time. But you can still feel good about the job.

Learn to Step Up

"It's not my job" is the single most irritating and career-limiting answer you can give to your boss and your coworkers. You might be correct—whatever you're talking about may not be your job—but that doesn't mean that you can't do it. That goes directly against the ownership principle. Let us consider a rather trivial example. You have a meeting with ten people. After the meeting, everyone leaves, and there is an empty cup on the table. Now, what happens? One person sees the cup and decides to ignore it. It is not their job, so why should they take it to the kitchen? The second person sees the cup and grabs it to put it into the dishwasher without a word. It is like a reflex to them. They are not even thinking about who should do what. Which of these two characters would you prefer to work with?

"It's not my job" is a common excuse that hides all sorts of fears. So what are you saying when using this excuse? What are the things you say to yourself that hold you back?

I Don't Care: If you are at work just to do as little as possible to earn your paycheck, you will never get a chance for career progression. You will most likely just be a mediocre performer who will be miserable and eventually leave. You should get out now for your own good and the good of the team.

I Don't Have the Authority: There are very few situations where this matters. This is a valid excuse only when legal aspects are involved, like when you don't have the authority to sign a contract. However, even then, you could still prepare the contract or review it.

I Could Make Mistakes: You are right. You probably will, and that is fine. How else do you expect to learn? Don't let the fear of doing something for the first time get in the way of your personal development.

It Is a Considerable Effort: Most things worth doing are difficult. Of course, there is always an opportunity cost, so you need to consider your priorities carefully. But often, the potential benefit of learning, building goodwill, or just doing the right thing is worth it. Just split it into smaller, manageable pieces and get started.

I Got Burned in the Past: Understandable, but that doesn't mean you should give up. Analyze what exactly caused you to get your hand slapped and develop strategies to mitigate it in the future. Sitting in the corner doing nothing is not a good strategy.

I Don't Know How to Solve the Problem: Great, so go out and learn. You can say this about anything that you do for the first time, so don't let this fear hold you back.

I Don't Have the Skills: How else do you want to grow other than by learning new skills? Very often, no one has the right skills, but someone brave takes the job anyway and learns. This is the person who grows and gets ahead. Or, if you genuinely don't have the right competence, then reach out to others to help you out.

I'm Not Good at This Kind of Thing: This is an excellent example of a self-fulfilling prophecy. You need to reframe this negative, self-defeating monologue in your head to something more constructive. Try this instead: "If I put all my best into the effort, I will succeed, or I will at least learn."

I'm Too Important, and This Job Is Too Menial: This is just an arrogant attitude that will shape who you become and what culture you create and will ultimately lead other people to stop respecting you. "There is no job too small for me to do" is a much healthier attitude that will serve you well in life and that will make you a better human being.

Remember that you don't need permission to do an excellent job! Whatever your role in the organization, it is an unsaid expectation that you work to the best of your abilities and use your best judgment to make the organization successful. Let me list a couple of strategies used by people who don't have the "It's not my job" sentence in their vocabulary. These attitudes lead to the exact opposite: instead of avoiding tasks outside of their jobs, they embrace them and expand their skills and sphere of influence.

Constantly Seek to Improve Things: By finding ways to make your life, the life of your boss, and the lives of others around you easier, you not only solve problems but also learn about how the organization works.

Volunteer to Help Others: Very similar to the previous item. By volunteering to help others, you learn about their jobs, expand your understanding of the organization, and grow your skills.

Always Ask Questions: You obviously shouldn't ask the same question repeatedly, but by questioning things that are being taken for granted, you not only help yourself get to a better understanding, but you may unearth gems in the form of potential improvements. Times are changing, and the process that was set up five years ago might not fill the needs of today.

Don't Complain: If you constantly complain, not only will you be seen as someone who whines all the time and doesn't help, but you will create internal self-talk that will make you feel miserable with your own life.

Be Prepared: This is a no-brainer for introverts. Learn to spend the time upfront to ensure that you understand the big picture, know what options you have, and have your arguments well backed up with data and solid reasoning.

Understand That Ideas Are Not Enough: You can have tons of great ideas, but no one will ever care about them as much as you do. If you want to see them implemented, you need to be the person who has the energy to drive them through.

Don't Shy Away from Difficult Tasks: Volunteering for tough assignments is a great way to develop new skills, grow as a person, and even grow your reputation. People will give you all the support they can if they see that you took on a job they were scared of.

Learn to Enjoy Even the Boring Bits: When you find some positive in things that other people hate, you can gain significant influence—especially when things need to get done for the good of the group, and no one is too keen on doing them.

Utilizing this proactive attitude, you can expect the ultimate reward. You will strengthen your character, learn new skills, build resilience, and have a positive can-do attitude. This will then reflect positively on your self-image, how others see you, and the career opportunities open to you. To be completely clear, I'm not advocating that you should say yes to every small, unimportant thing someone throws in your direction. As we saw in Chapter 9, you need to prioritize. It is important to say no often, but make sure you are strategic about *when* you say it and smart about *how* you say it.

Decision-Making

The ownership mindset means that you take action. And that means that at some point, you have to make some decisions. What sort of decisions are easy to make? What decisions are difficult? How do you define a really tough choice?

Each of us has a certain capacity to make a decision. We make decisions all day long. Most of them are small, trivial things like, "What should I have for breakfast?" or "Should I wear blue or white today?" When making these decisions, we spend our decision-making power. This ultimately leads to something in psychology called "decision fatigue" that refers to a deteriorating quality of decisions or even the inability to decide after a long streak of decision-making.[84]

Let me give you an example from my life. It is a bit silly, but I have observed it pretty consistently in the way I act, and I have observed it in others, too. I love yogurt. I love trying new things. Logically, I love trying new brands of yogurt. I have discovered that when I go shopping for food in the evening after a whole day in the office, I usually spend a couple of minutes looking at the myriad of choices, deciding what yogurt to buy, and then buying the plain one—the same as the last time and the time before. I'm essentially not able to make decisions anymore, so I default to the safe choice. If I go shopping on a Saturday morning, I tend to buy one or two brands I haven't tried before, and the decision about which one to pick comes easily. To take ownership of my shopping experience, I would need to remove this external decision fatigue factor. If my goal were to keep trying new things, I should deliberately go shopping in the morning. If my goal were to save money and only buy what I truly need, I might, for example, write a list of things to buy and then go shopping in the evening and just mindlessly go around the shop and fill the cart with things I decided on at home when my mind was still fresh—preparation at its best.

Let Your Values Guide Your Decisions: What do you do when your mind is fresh, you can make a decision, but you are paralyzed by a worry of not making the right choice? In reality, very few decisions you are making are really tough choices, even when they may appear as such at first glance. What you do in such situations is to compare the options available to you. You check some metrics, try to list all the pros and cons, and then one of them usually comes as a winner. The actual criteria used will come from your overall goal and value system. If you base your decision on your values, it usually makes it very simple. It also makes it very difficult to regret decisions when you go with your values and what your heart is telling you is the right choice.

Understand What Type of Decision-Maker You Are: According to James Gardner March, an American sociologist and a professor at Stanford University, there are two ways we make decisions. Some of us use the logic of consequences and some the logic of appropriateness. When using the logic of consequence, we consider which action will produce the best results and go with that. When using the logic of appropriateness, we don't care about the results as such. We instead think about what someone like us would do in the situation. It is more about our identity than about the outcome.[85] This may explain why some people are more readily willing to take risks. If you use the logic of consequences, you can always find risks and possible negative consequences that will discourage you from taking the risk. It is much easier for someone who uses the logic of appropriateness to take risks, as they don't consider the potential negative consequences. They say that they are the type of person who always jumps first, and they go and jump.

Stop Overanalyzing: Introverts are great at finding meaning where there is none. Your boss tells you to clean up your desk, and you deduce that he is angry with you. A person you have a crush on smiles at you, and you conclude that they are in love with you. You get a gift from coworkers, and you assume that they want something. Don't overanalyze and give things hidden meanings. Sometimes a gift is just a gift.

Stop Gathering More Data: What do you do when all the options are comparable, even when you look at your value system? If all the options are more or less the same, then just stop comparing and pick one! It doesn't matter which one, as all are fine, and you are wasting your time trying to figure out which of the two or three acceptable decisions is the best. Stop getting more data. Just make a choice, any choice, flip a coin, and move on to spend your energy on other stuff. Having 80 percent of the data is more than enough. Even 60 percent is okay. More information often makes the decision harder and harder, as you have to analyze more stuff, compare more things, and get to the point of being boiled alive with data, unable to decide. Having more data will not make your decision easier. It will just require you to spend more decision-making energy.

Don't Worry about Making a Mistake: Introverts overthink because they want to make sure they make the right choices and learn from past mistakes. That is all well and good as long as it doesn't lead to paralysis. This is often driven by the fact that many introverts use the logic of consequences as the default decision-making paradigm. When you find yourself unable to move forward for fear of making a mistake, just consider what the worst thing that can happen is. The chances are that you are not talking about life-or-death situations. When considering the worst-case scenario and its likelihood, you can then look at the most likely scenario that is not as bad. Fear of making a mistake is unfounded in most cases, and it just holds you back.

Don't Worry About a Negative Reaction from Others: You may overanalyze things, as you want to be liked. We all do. It is part of human nature that we want to be loved, feel included, and be part of a tribe. But just consider all the people around you and think about what they have done that looked silly, was embarrassing, or damaged them in the eyes of others. And yet they are still here! They still have friends. Most of the stuff is forgotten or lives on in funny anecdotes. Life goes on. The same goes for you. Think about some of your awkward moments, and you'll realize that not only does no one remember them today, but chances are that no one even noticed when they happened. Yes, you probably fell off your bike a couple of times when you were a kid. Someone might have even laughed at you at the time, but it just didn't matter in the long run.

Set Routines to Limit Decision Needs: Lots of anxiety and overthinking comes from a need for constant decision-making. When you learn to establish routines and limit the number of decisions you have to make, you will also lower your stress, limit overthink, and generally make your decisions and life easier.

Decide When You Still Have Enough Energy to Do So: In the situations where decision fatigue kicks in, I have found that what works is to acknowledge this fact and just go with the intention to pick the first option you see. Basically, decide what you will do or choose even before you see the choices. One of the best ways to prevent decision fatigue is to not make decisions. This can be accomplished by setting up routines and rituals. They put parts of your day on autopilot, so you save the energy for decisions that matter.

Decide Now or Set a Date: Don't keep postponing decisions. Either decide now, even if you may feel you don't have enough information. Or, if you genuinely feel like it is not the right time, then set a time when you know for sure you will be able to make a decision. Till then, forget about the problem, so you don't overanalyze and overthink.

Accept That Not All Decisions Are Perfect: The vast majority of choices we make are far from perfect. And that is fine. Learn to accept that you will make decisions that may be suboptimal, and you will make decisions that turn out to be wrong. This is still vastly better than not making decisions at all because of overthinking and overanalyzing every minor problem. If you don't make a decision, someone else will make it for you. Way too often, people complain about their bosses or spouses making decisions for them, while in reality, the reason that happened was that their bosses or spouses just got frustrated with waiting for a decision and moved on with whatever they wanted to do.

Learning from Mistakes

When you are making decisions, the chances are that you make the wrong one now and then. We all make mistakes. Some are small, some are bigger, and some impact other people's lives. As you go through your life, you will make your share of mistakes. That's, well, life. Get comfortable with it! It is completely fine to make a mistake, as long as you learn from the experience. The thing that makes moving on more difficult for introverts is that we tend to overanalyze our errors. And if you are in a leadership role, it gets even worse, as your mistakes tend to be more visible and have a bigger impact. You need to own your own mistakes and deal with them promptly.

Admit It: The first step is to recognize and admit that there was a mistake made or, even better, that there is a mistake in the making. To be able to do that, you need to listen and frequently review what you are doing. Listening to the feedback also means creating an environment where the feedback you are getting is honest. If you are surrounded by yes-men, then no amount of feedback from them will help, as they are just saying what they believe you want to hear and not what they think.

Apologize: The most challenging step is to apologize. Apologize to yourself, to your colleague, or to your team. Apologize to whomever was directly impacted and also to those who were affected indirectly and have to live with the consequences. And really apologize. A statement like, "It was unfortunate that you were not invited to the party, but you know my boss wanted it, and I don't think she realized that you should be there," is not an apology. The genuine apology starts with "I." It is short and to the point and shouldn't involve blaming anyone else. "I'm sorry for not inviting you to the party yesterday. I apologize for forgetting. I have taken steps to ensure it doesn't happen again." A genuine apology gives you credibility and the trust of others that you will fix the mistake.

Fix It: The next obvious step is to fix the actual mistake. At least, as much as is possible. It doesn't make too much sense to overanalyze and try to figure out who to blame. The important part is to act and act fast. Don't make promises, don't try to talk the others into feeling happy, don't hide what needs to be done. Just get the work done. Swift action will make you believable and help others accept that you mean to address the issue. You don't need to fix everything immediately, but you need to make the right first step and show that you have a realistic plan for the rest.

Prevent It: The last and often forgotten step is to prevent similar mistakes from occurring again in the future. That is not for the benefit of others as much as it is for the benefit of yourself. You want to make sure that you don't need to firefight the same issue or mistake again. It is okay to make a mistake once, but you shouldn't keep making the same mistake again and again. It is very exhausting and very dumb. Don't focus just on one issue but try to cover a similar type of situation.

Introverts tend to blame themselves more than others. Because we live so much in our heads, we may feel bad even about things we couldn't possibly influence. I have talked about self-awareness in Chapter 8. When you are self-aware, you are realistic about what you could have done, and it helps you not to take the blame for things outside of your control.

Learning from your mistakes means that you own them, but don't try to own the mistakes of others. Take ownership of everything you have done or not done. However, there are situations where we tend to blame others, and rightly, while we had the power to do something to prevent the disaster. By being proactive and assertive, you can take ownership even of things that don't seem to relate to you directly. The advantage is that you take ownership of your own feelings down the road, as I will explain in the next section.

Stop Blaming Others

I firmly believe that pretty much anyone can achieve greatness when nurtured and nudged in the right direction. It is only up to your upbringing, environment, team, boss, and especially you to get over any potential disadvantage and become great at what you do. Many talented people never amounted to anything since they didn't have the drive, the grit, and the wherewithal to push and become truly great, and vice versa. The lack of talent can be remedied with the right kind of effort, so you become truly great.

Regardless of whether you want to become successful or you want to help someone else, the journey starts in the head of the person with ambition. Let's consider the concept introduced in *Leadership and Self-Deception* by The Arbinger Institute.[86] They call it "being in the box." The core of why so many people struggle to become truly great is that they live in a world of self-deception. This comes from a belief that the problem is out there and not within you. You are doing your best, but the world doesn't listen. The world fights back. The world acts stupid and doesn't know what's good for it. That is self-deception. Forget that. The problem is you.

Imagine this situation. You walk around the desk of your colleague, who is visibly struggling. This colleague, let's call him John, is making some calculations in a spreadsheet, and you know he is still new to the job. You are pretty good with spreadsheets. You know you could quickly solve it, but you are on your way to get a cup of coffee, so you ignore the struggle and pretend you don't see it. When you think about it, you may say that this is no big deal and that things like this happen all the time, and you are right. It is not your job to help others with their tasks. But then again, you are one team. You work toward the same goal. You could have just as easily stopped by and spent a minute of your time helping your struggling colleague. The benefits of doing that are immense. You could make John more efficient, you could help him learn something new, you could build a better relationship, and you could show real team spirit. You acted contrary to what you knew deep down was the right thing to do.

Once you choose the action or inaction, you start inventing justifications that prove you were right. You continue to walk to the coffee shop and get your coffee and, in your head, justify why you didn't help out. It is not your job, right? You can't do the work for everyone else, and what's more, you can't remember a time when that person would have helped you. How else can he learn, other than by getting through the struggle? You have so many other things on your plate. And you need the coffee. You can't waste your coffee break with this type of nonsense.

What happens when you come back from your coffee break? You realize that you need the results of John's work so you can proceed with your own task. He is still not finished. Why did the company hire such a stupid person who can't even make simple calculations in a spreadsheet program? You get angry with him, and you vocalize your dissatisfaction. He is slowing you down. You should probably complain to your boss. If you don't get things done around here, no one else will. By betraying yourself and finding the justifications for your actions, you shift the blame to others. And by shifting the blame to others, you invite defensiveness and counter-attack.

By vocalizing your distress to John, he, of course, gets defensive and sees you as a jerk who cares only about yourself and no one else. He believes that it is you who is the problem. You should have told him earlier that you would need the calculations so that he would have enough time. You are always complaining about others not working while you spend tons of time in the coffee shop. You always take credit for the work of others and are a backstabbing bastard who complains to the boss rather than working things out within the team.

So here you are. The work is not done. You have damaged the relationship with your colleague, and you have created a toxic atmosphere on the team.

One of the basic skills of successful people is to own everything in your world and have the ability to get stuff done. If you showed a bit of ownership mindset, you could stop all of this negativity at the very beginning and make the team perform better.

By blaming others, you are not helping them. You blame others to help yourself and to justify your unhelpful behavior. In the end, you don't help anyone. Regardless of circumstances, you need to learn to treat others with respect all the time. All this doesn't necessarily mean that you put the weight of the world on your shoulders and you become the scapegoat for the whole universe. On the contrary, when getting to a truly unbiased state of mind, you can assess situations without prejudice and with clarity. That helps you connect with others and hold both yourself and them accountable without getting into a blame game. Start with thinking about others as human beings with the same needs, desires, and fears as you have. Don't try to change others, but rather look at what you can do differently. Don't try to suck it up and suffer unacceptable behavior, as that just makes your internal dialogue more and more toxic. Don't try to communicate with others from a bad place. First, get into the let's-not-blame-others state of mind. That means an ownership mindset and proactive behavior.

Proactivity

Proactivity or proactive behavior usually refers to self-initiated behavior that is anticipatory and often change-oriented. It means that you are able to anticipate future needs and start acting on them right away, as opposed to waiting and reacting to them when they occur. It is about being in control of the situation rather than being controlled by it.

This makes sense. If you can prevent something bad from happening, it is, of course, preferable to waiting and then doing damage control after the fact. The most common situation where proactivity pays off is communication. Being able to defuse potentially heated conversations before they have a chance to escalate is the one most useful skill in working with people.

Choosing How to Act: One of the great things evolution granted to human beings is our ability to imagine. You can create an entire world in your mind. You can imagine potential futures and prepare for them. You can even imagine several different results, anticipate the most likely outcomes, and act preemptively to ensure the most favorable results. However, this only works when you want to, when you care. It means that you can focus on a particular problem and think it through before plunging heedlessly into action. On the other hand, you also need to be aware that even not taking action has consequences. Whether you choose to act or not, you should do it with an understanding that there will be consequences in either case.

Choosing How to Respond: Proactivity is not only about how we act but also how we choose to respond and feel about external stimuli. If you are a proactive person, you will never get angry with someone or depressed about something that was out of your control. You know that there are some things in this universe that you can't influence, and you made your peace with that fact. Instead of brooding about the fact that life is not fair, you accept it and learn to live with it. It doesn't bother you. When something terrible happens, you can shrug it off and focus your attention on other things. You focus on what you can influence and what is under your control. You don't react; instead, you choose how to respond. You also choose to feel good about the world around you, even if it doesn't comply with your wishes. If you are a proactive person, you are not a slave to your environment, but you live by your values. Values provide immunity to a changing environment and keep you sane and happy.

Introverts often struggle to be proactive. We have a hard time getting moving, but when we do, we persevere. The best remedy for a lack of proactivity is routine and creating an environment that makes it easier for you to be proactive. If you believe you don't have a choice but to make a decision or take action before it is too late, you will make it. Proactivity is not about being fast and always keeping moving. It is not about urgency. It is about a mindset that keeps you firmly grounded in difficult times. It is about having strong values. It is about having the ability to anticipate the future. Ultimately, it is about choosing how to respond to the world on your own terms. That means stopping using others as an excuse for your own inaction.

Stop Waiting for Others

"I'm waiting for . . ." is the one sentence that shows you don't have a sense of ownership and that you are not proactive. These words may sound reasonable at times, but they promote a culture of passivity and a feeling of "me against them," as well as leading to lost momentum, lost drive, and lost opportunities. If you use these words in your internal monologue, you create an excuse for not getting things done. Successful people don't wait for something or someone. They go and proactively move things forward. Just consider these statements and how you can turn them around to drive toward success.

- "I'm waiting for Bob to deliver his part." Well, go and help him to get his part done!
- "I'm waiting for approval from my boss's boss." Well, get the preliminary work done so you can move quickly once approved!
- "I'm waiting for more data to make a decision." Paralysis by analysis. Get the necessary minimum of data and just decide!
- "I'm waiting for the results of last year's employee survey before I do anything." So you really have no idea what the most likely outcome is? Unlikely!
- "I'm waiting for summer to start my exercise regimen." Oh, I guess because it is impossible to exercise in winter?

If you have a sense of ownership, you move things along regardless of whether it is your job or not and irrespective of whether you have the formal authority to do so. The top achievers have a bias for action. Instead of waiting for something to happen or forever debating what needs to be done, they just go and do it. That is the strategy you should follow if you want to be wildly successful.

Will you always make the right choice? Of course not. You will make your share of mistakes, get your share of beatings, but that is all fine because you also know that you won't be "waiting for" someone else to course correct you when needed. You move and move fast, and when you realize you are not moving in the right direction, you don't stop but just change where you are heading and continue at full speed. Live the life you want, and don't wait for life to happen to you!

Assertiveness

Proactivity works best when combined with assertiveness. Assertiveness is a crucial skill for anyone who wants to get their share in life, and it is one skill that introverts also struggle with. We tend to be too passive, and if we care strongly about something, we switch to unintentional aggressiveness. But there is a better way to communicate. Assertive communication is about being self-assured and confident without being aggressive.

Assertiveness is based on the premise that everyone has a right to express their opinions, needs, and wants and that you don't need permission to do so. To be able to hold your ground and behave assertively, you need to build up your self-esteem. Without confidence and a belief that your opinion is as important as the opinions of others, it is challenging to communicate assertively.

When you look at aggressive communication, you often hear people lying, threatening, passing judgment, deflecting questions, stonewalling, and generally disrespecting others. Passive communication then sits on the opposite side. You adopt a victim mentality and allow others to treat you with disrespect. The more you allow this, the more likely it is that others will use that to their advantage, and their attacks will become more aggressive.

Assertive communication is demonstrated by being clear about where you stand on a given topic. Assertive people can ask for what they want and need in a manner that respects others. They don't get easily dismissed and will defend their position and their views. Assertiveness is the middle ground you take when confronted with negativity or aggression without becoming passive or aggressive yourself. You focus on the issue rather than on the person. You try to appeal to a common interest of both parties and thus remove unnecessary aggression.

If you feel that you are not assertive enough, you can use some tricks and techniques to help you out. Of course, it is always a question of what technique to use in a particular situation. In *When I Say No, I Feel Guilty*, Manuel Smith talks about some of them.[87]

The Broken Record Technique is the simplest one when you are under pressure, though it can be incredibly difficult to stick with. It is simply repeating your position or request every time you meet resistance or attempted misdirection. You can sometimes see this at work when journalists question a hostile politician who doesn't want to answer their questions. They will ask a question. The politician starts talking about something else. The journalist doesn't get distracted but asks the same question again. The politician again tries to talk about something else. So the journalist asks the same question one more time without acknowledging the change of topic. With this technique, you don't get passive, accepting the question won't get answered, and you don't get aggressive by starting to argue with the politician that he should answer your question. You hold your ground and respectfully repeat the same question. Obviously, there are limitations. There is a limit to the number of repetitions you can make before giving up. Especially if there is an external audience at some point, they will get annoyed with you more than with the evading party. This could also lead to you losing face, as it would be clear that you have no power at all over the other person.

Agreeing in Principle is a technique based on the idea that even if you disagree with the other person, you can find at least one thing you can agree on to defuse aggressive communication. You may say something along the lines of, "I agree with you in principle," and then focus on a particular detail that is an issue for you that you want the other party to change.

Negative Assertion is one technique that is useful when you need to provide feedback or demand your rights in situations where the other party also has some negative feedback or demands of their own. It is also helpful when people try to wiggle out of their responsibility by blaming others for not cooperating. You might come to your teammate who promised to get something done and respectfully ask whether the task has been done as promised. The person in question starts blaming the IT department for not doing their part, so it was impossible to finish what was promised. Instead of getting distracted and starting to talk about the IT department, you acknowledge that the IT department may not have done what they were supposed to, but it still doesn't change your original request and the fact that your teammate didn't deliver on their promise.

Negative Inquiry is a technique best used when you feel the other party is coming at you too aggressively and has high-level and unspecified negative feedback or is asserting things that may not be true or are at least misleading. Instead of jumping up and arguing back that they are lying, you request that they provide more details and be more specific about what exactly the issue is. Insisting on the details either shows that the person doesn't have a clue and disarms their ability to bully you, or shows that they indeed have a valid point, and that you then showed a willingness to listen and take the feedback seriously.

"I" Statements are a way to express your needs without passing negative judgment on others. You don't talk about what the other person should change, but instead focus on yourself and what you need. I found "I" statements particularly effective when providing feedback to people higher up in the chain of command. You probably don't want it to appear that you are whining and complaining about your boss's incompetence or pointing all their flaws out to them. Don't talk about what they need to change in their behavior, but talk about what you need that you are not getting. For example, you might feel that your boss is micromanaging you. Instead of going to them and aggressively demanding, "Stop micromanaging me!" you can just say something along the lines of, "I realized that I could be more effective if I have time to process things on my own. It will help me if I could have more freedom to do things my way, and I could deliver better results." In communicating this way, you talk about yourself and don't blame the other person. You make it easy for them to give you what you need without them losing face.

Declaration of Needs: Don't apologize for your needs. If you understand what your legal rights are and accept that you have the same human rights as others around you, then there is no reason why you need to crawl and apologize for invoking these rights. Just unapologetically declare what you need and stick with it. There is no need to search for excuses and multiple reasons. Of course, state your needs in a manner that doesn't feel aggressive or arrogant.

As with anything else, assertiveness also shouldn't be abused. If you try to act tough and be assertive all the time, it will eventually backfire, and it will negatively impact your ability to influence the world around you. If you decide to assert yourself in every small, unimportant situation, you won't win popularity points, and if you say no on principle to every request and never help anyone, even if you could say yes and it would cost you nothing, then you are not assertive, you are just a lazy jerk.

Learn to Say No

With assertiveness also comes the ability to say no. Saying yes to every single request coming your way may be easier for introverts, as it doesn't require you to get out of your comfort zone and say no. Still, it can quickly become a problem for your career. Helping others is a career enhancer, but doing so in excess while ignoring your own tasks is a career-killer.

Sometimes people trespass on your turf or have high demands on you to help them out without acknowledging that you have responsibilities of your own. In these situations, instead of agreeing to help and then being annoyed about it and blaming the other person, just remind them that you also have your own work to do. A firm and polite no without a need for a five-minute-long monologue apologizing for why you can't help is the best you can do in these situations. It merely states that your needs are just as important as the needs of others. Pushing back on extra work that doesn't benefit you or those around you also means you free up some of your time to spend on tasks important to you. And yet it can be tough to say no to your colleagues and especially to your boss. So what can you do to get better at pushing back and saying no when you want to say it?

Show Your Value: It is so much easier to push back without creating a negative image for yourself if everyone already knows that you can do a good job. So if you are new to the team or to the organization, then focusing on doing a good job, being hard-working, having the right attitude, and delivering results is the first step that will build a solid foundation for your ability to push back, as it builds credibility and respect.

Differentiate Between a Perspective and a Person: When you disagree with another person and voice that disagreement, there is always a danger that you will activate their defenses. People may feel you are not only challenging their point of view and their view of reality but that you are also attacking them directly. If you can voice that you don't have an issue with the person and only disagree with that one particular point of view, it will make the disagreement less threatening and make it easier for you to push back and for the other person to stay factual and not skip into an emotional fight-or-flight response. Saying things like, "You don't know what you are talking about," or "You are always against my ideas" makes things personal, so avoid it. Removing emotions and sticking with the facts will make disagreeing with others much more manageable.

Be Prepared: Unless you are surprised by a request, it is always good to prepare some data and arguments to support your point of view ahead of time. This helps in situations when you are pushing against something familiar to the other person and want to propose something new. For most people, new equals dangerous. If you can point out that others have tried your way, that it is less risky than it may look, it will be easier for you to push back. This is especially important in business-related matters where data is often king when making decisions. If others see that you are pushing back with legitimate concerns and care about the business, it will be easier for them to back off.

Listen and Then Talk: Use your listening skills to build rapport and connect with the person who is pushing on you. If they feel you are listening, if they feel they are being understood, they are more likely to listen to your arguments. You can enhance this by not stating your position but by asking questions that will force the other person to think the situation through, be more specific in their needs, and possibly come up with alternative solutions.

Understand the Big Picture: It is always good to have a holistic view of any situation in order to pick the proper response. A significant portion of that view is understanding the culture and background of the person you want to push back on and the organizational culture of the company you are working in. In some cultures, it is not only acceptable to push back, but it might even be required. If you don't push back, it may feel like you don't care, you don't have your own opinions, or you are not leadership material. In other cultures, pushing back may be taken in the exact opposite way. You may be seen as not being a team player or as someone who cares only about themselves or is unwilling to help others, or as someone who may be working behind people's backs and doesn't respect the chain of command. If you choose the wrong approach for pushing back, you create friction.

Ask Questions: Before you even start pushing back, make sure you understand what you are saying no to or what you are disagreeing with. When listening to the responses, try to understand your position and what exactly triggered your disagreement. Sometimes you may have issues only with a specific subset of the activity, or there might be some conflict with your core values, goals, and beliefs. Verifying whether you understand what is being asked from you helps in two ways. First, you understand what you are pushing back against and can put how you interpret the request into your words. By paraphrasing what you heard, you give the other person a chance to hear back what they are asking you to do and tone it down if the request sounds unreasonable. Second, the other person will feel that you are interested in what they are saying. They will feel respected even if you refuse them.

Offer Alternatives: Saying no is easier when you help the other party see different options and alternative solutions. Saying that you disagree is rather unhelpful. Even something like, "No, I'm busy" doesn't explain anything. So what? It brings no value and makes you look bad. If you can disagree by not only saying why you think something is a bad idea but also suggesting alternatives, it makes you more constructive and more in control, and will make it easier for both parties to have a conversation that will lead to mutually beneficial results.

Avoid Saying "But": If you listen to the other person's perspective but then you say something along the lines of, "Yes, but I think . . ." that automatically shows you didn't listen, you disagree, and you just want to be nice and get your way. It is much more powerful to react by saying, "Yes, and I would add/ask/change." This response doesn't invalidate the other person's point of view. It just adds a layer of your own thoughts and helps to keep the conversation on the topic. This strategy, of course, doesn't fit any situation, but you would be surprised how often it works.

Use the Right Words: There is enormous power in using the right words. If possible, use "we" rather than "you." That way, you create a feeling of collaboration and the sense that you are trying to help. For example, instead of "You may consider asking Jim to help you," you might say, "We should consider asking Jim for help." The outcome will be the same, as the requestor will go to Jim, but the overall feeling from the conversation will be much more positive for both you and the person you're speaking to.

Pick Your Battles: It is difficult, and not even healthy, to push back on everything that doesn't 100 percent meet your approval. There are some sacrifices worth making. Some battles are better not to fight to build social credit with others. If you are known as a generally helpful person, people accept your no more easily without damaging the relationship.

Pick the Low-Hanging Fruit: Always be willing to help with stuff that doesn't cause any significant effort for you but that may be helpful to others. I love using the example from my life when building new offices. Even though I was the boss, I would often step in for the office administrator and sit at reception when they were sick or had to take care of other tasks. Of course, I wouldn't do their whole job, but I would help with urgent matters. I would meet and greet candidates coming for interviews and take mail. Minimal effort, a bit of inconvenience, but not much of a distraction. I could still do my job almost at 100 percent, and I helped someone else. As a side effect, I led by example and showed that we all worked as a team and needed to step in for one another when needed.

Keep Your Boundaries: Never agree to anything that would violate your core values in a significant way. Never agree to anything unethical or illegal. If you are being asked something that fits these criteria, be direct and honest about it. When saying no for these reasons, be clear about what exactly makes you uncomfortable about the request and if there is a way to change it in such a way that it won't violate your integrity. It is possible that you just misunderstood the context and things are not as bad as you believe. It is also possible that things indeed are that bad. If the person keeps pressuring you, you just need to walk away rather than ending up in jail or tarnishing your reputation by doing something unethical.

Be Consistent and Persistent: If you push back consistently, and you are persistent in the way you explain your no to people, you are training them. Eventually, they will understand what your priorities are, and they will consider them. They will learn what you can help with and what would create distractions and maybe even derail some other initiatives. Just make sure you don't shut off the external world completely. You still want to be seen as a team player who is easy to work with and cares about others. You just demand the same care in return.

Take It in Stride: Even if you push back on a request from someone else, don't make a big deal out of it. There is no need to boast about the fact you said no to your boss. Just keep doing a good job and keep talking to the person you refused as if nothing happened. It is business as usual. You can still go for lunch together and have a laugh. It is not about you or the other person winning or losing. It is merely about a decision that needed to be made. You have made it, and that is the end of it. Being professional about it will help both of you to feel good about it.

If you feel the other person feels hurt, don't try to change your decision and help them. That would be succumbing to emotional blackmail. The one thing you can do is to naturally volunteer for something else, if it makes sense to do so, to show that there is nothing personal in your decision. You are more than happy to work with that person and help out when it makes sense.

Pushing back may sound scary for introverts, but it is a critically important skill and one you can learn. You deserve to have your life prioritized the way you want, not according to what someone else decides for you. By learning to push back the right way, you will build up your confidence, feel less stressed, find more time for what is essential, and be seen by others as a confident and competent human being.

Learn to Speak Up

Assertiveness is not only about learning to push back but also about learning to speak up when the time is right. One of the communication challenges we all face is knowing when to talk and when to listen. Some people are more biased toward talking too much and not listening, and many introverts tend to do the opposite, staying quiet even when they should speak up. This is especially the case for those with anxious introversion, as described in Chapter 1, who feel awkward when talking to people they don't know well, or those with restrained introversion, who need more time to think things through before speaking up. So why is it so difficult for introverts to speak up? There are many reasons, but the most common ones are these.

You Just Don't Care: This one is straightforward. If you don't care about the topic, it is entirely acceptable to say nothing. There are way too many others, usually those who feel insecure or threatened, who always need to contribute even though the topic is irrelevant to them or they have nothing meaningful to say. It doesn't matter that everyone is giving their two cents to the conversation—there is no need to jump in just because everyone else is doing it. If you genuinely believe the topic is not important or you don't care what decision will be made, then stay quiet and, if being directly asked, just say so. "I'm fine with whatever you decide since I don't have strong feelings about the topic." You can play to your strengths as an introvert to create some calmness in case of a heated conversation about something that is just not important. Someone needs to be the adult in the room.

You Don't Want to Be Wrong or Feel Stupid: This one is much more serious. Because of your inner drive to make sure that whatever you say is 100 percent correct, you may sometimes miss opportunities to contribute and move the conversation forward. If you believe something needs to be said or think that you might have pertinent information that others don't, then it is your responsibility to speak. Even if you are not sure that what you say is entirely correct, "I may misremember, but didn't we agree on this or that already last year when working on the previous version of the product?" Someone will most likely chip in and say that you are right, and the conversation will move forward.

You Don't Want to Say Something Meaningless and, in Your Eyes, Obvious: This is the most common reason why introverts don't speak up. "Well, there was no need to say that there won't be any bonuses since we already said that the company is doing badly, so it is common sense." It might be common sense, but it is in no way obvious. Making assumptions about a situation or a person is the easiest way to create misunderstandings and conflicts. And I'm sure that you, being an introvert, want to avoid conflict at any cost. Even things obvious to you should be said out loud, so they are obvious to everyone.

You Are Overwhelmed by Others and Don't Have Time to Prepare a Proper Response: It happens pretty often that introverts will stay quiet in team meetings, but afterward, they will catch up with their bosses in one-on-one sessions and share their thoughts on the topic. It took me some time to get rid of this habit, and I spent lots of time coaching various introverts on my team to do the same. If there is a meeting where a specific topic is discussed and a decision made, that is the time to speak up. It may not be comfortable, but that's business. You can use some strategies to make speaking up easier for you, but you must not avoid it.

You Don't Want to Stand Out and Be Put in the Spotlight: This is often a problem not just for introverts but for most employees. You want to say something, but you believe that everyone else has the same question, so you are hoping that someone else will do it so you don't have to. In the end, no one gathers the courage to ask, and the meeting ends with everyone being dissatisfied, except the boss, who believes that everything is fine and that there are no questions. There are strategies that the boss could try to use to get the questions out there, but if they don't implement these strategies, it is your responsibility to stand up and ask.

What are the strategies you can use to be more comfortable speaking up?

Speak Up Early: Speak up early in the meeting to establish your presence. The longer you wait, the more difficult it will be for you to pitch in. To be able to do this, tap into your superpower of preparation. When you know what the agenda is, you can write down a couple of bullet points on the topics to summarize your thinking. When the time comes and everyone is asked for an opinion, be the first one to speak. Even when what you say is something that would most likely be said by someone else, you can establish your presence by speaking first. It is much easier to step in later in the conversation if you already showed the others that you are there.

Help the Meeting Organizer: Agree with the meeting organizer on introvert-friendly rules. If you work in a high-trust organization where everyone's opinion is genuinely cherished, then agreeing on some rules that give everyone an opportunity to talk is even better. It shouldn't be about putting people into the spotlight, but it should be about giving people the time to speak up if they have something to say. You would be doing a favor not only to yourself and other introverts, but to everyone, as you would be helping to make the meeting more inclusive in a broader sense.

Use Assertive Language—It Builds on Itself: If you start with more assertive statements, that helps you keep going. Phrases like "in my humble opinion" or "correct me if I'm wrong" are all great ways to present your thoughts in a non-threatening manner and are good ways to present something you are not sure about. However, you shouldn't use them when talking about something you know is correct, when you want to persuade others, or when you want to move the team forward. These statements are too soft, and that can be translated as, "I don't want to make a decision, so I will instead make a suggestion or ask a question and hope that someone else takes the lead and decides." So yes, these sentences show that you are humble, but they also indicate that you are indecisive or unwilling to lead. They do have a place in your vocabulary, but you should be very careful when using them.

Similar to saying no, speaking up requires introverts to get out of our comfort zone. It is not something we do naturally, and it requires focused effort. But it pays off, as it dramatically enhances your ability to influence those around you, provides you with a voice, and, ultimately, helps you to have a successful career.

Summary and Key Takeaways

You need to own everything in your life. This means adopting an ownership mindset and taking responsibility for your own life and career. You need to learn to make decisions, get comfortable making mistakes, and be proactive. Don't wait for the world to come to you. Take the first step and go to meet the world instead. Regardless of how uncomfortable it may feel, learn to say no and speak up when you have something to say. This will help you to have a successful career, and it will help you to grow as a human being.

- You are in complete control of your life and your feelings. Ignore whatever is outside of your sphere of influence, and double down on things you can control. Own what you do, say, and think. Own your life.
- Never use the words, "It's not my job."
- Decision-making takes a lot of energy and leads to decision fatigue. Routinize your life and limit the number of decisions you need to make so you have enough energy for decisions that matter.
- "I'm waiting for" are words you need to remove from your vocabulary. They lead to passivity.
- If you want something, you need to ask for it.
- Owning your life also means owning your mistakes and failures. Accept that no one is perfect and mistakes are part of life.
- Understand that assertiveness has nothing to do with aggression. On the contrary, assertive communication is about clarifying where you stand, having willingness to listen, and finding mutually agreeable solutions to problems.
- You need to prioritize and say no to requests that are not important so you have time for those activities that matter.

Questions and Next Steps

- Do you have the ownership mindset? Think about situations when you blamed others for your misfortunes, then consider whether there was something you could have done. Could you have influenced your manager's decision before it was made? Could you have prepared better? Would things have been different if you had taken a proactive first step instead of waiting for others to move?
- Are you comfortable making mistakes? Do you learn from them without getting paralyzed? When was the last time you took a risk and tried something new? Did

you fail? What did you learn? Did you then use your strength of perseverance and improve in subsequent attempts?

- Are you proactive, or do you keep waiting for others? Next time you say to yourself or others, "I'm waiting for . . ." stop right there and consider what you can do instead. Stop waiting and take a proactive first step toward a solution. Getting into this habit will have a tremendous positive impact on your career.

11

Act with Integrity

"I'm dependable and trustworthy.
I say what I mean. I do what I say. I always do my best."

Integrity is the one trait that distinguishes the best from the rest. It is most often described as being honest with yourself and others and having strong moral principles. It shows when your actions, your words, and your values are aligned. This internal consistency drives who you are, regardless of whether you work with others on important projects or whether you just decide to change one of your habits. It is the ability to hold yourself accountable for your decisions and actions. When you act with integrity, you act with consistency, and you make it easy for others to understand who you are and what you stand for. You act according to your values and beliefs, and others identify these with you.

Integrity is not something you are born with. It is a personal choice. It is something you can learn, something you can decide to do. The decision to act with integrity is life-changing. It increases your ability to lead yourself and others. Integrity helps you to be credible and trustworthy. If you have integrity, you are dependable and always do what you say you will do. This can have a hugely positive effect on your career. Your teammates and bosses will value you more if they know they can depend on you.

Integrity is also challenging to master since it requires many sacrifices, especially at the beginning, when you are fighting some of your bad habits that go against the notion of acting with integrity, but it is worth the effort. Your strengths of loyalty, humility, introspection, perseverance, and prudence will help you on your journey to act with integrity.

Trustworthiness and Credibility

Everything starts with trust, and trust can't be built without trustworthiness. If you, your boss, or your team don't trust each other, it leads to a rather lousy collaboration and ultimately lower performance. And trust starts with each individual's trustworthiness.

How do you know whether someone is trustworthy, or even if *you* are trustworthy? To follow the thoughts of Stephen R. Covey, you need to consider a person's character and competence.[88] The character will tell you whether your core values are in line with the needs of the job. For example, would you trust a brilliant accountant to keep your books if you knew he regularly embezzles money? No. Go back to Chapter 3 and consider what your core values are. Would you describe yourself as a generally trustworthy person? Do you have some values, habits, or behaviors that make it difficult for others to trust you?

Competence then informs you whether you are equipped to do the job from the technical side. You probably wouldn't give an accounting job to the most honest man in the world if you knew he couldn't read, write, and count, would you? This is one of the reasons we spend quite a bit of time in Chapter 5 and Chapter 6 talking about doing what you are good at and the various ways you can build your skills.

You can break this down into additional components. Character is a combination of integrity and intent. It is about how ethical you are and whether you will always do what is right. Competence is then a question of capabilities and actual results. It is not enough to have the knowledge, the capability. You also need to have the willingness and drive to spend the effort to bring things to fruition.

Consider this example: Imagine that I tell you that the company I'm CEO of has this mission statement: "The company was founded to revolutionize space technology, with the ultimate goal of enabling people to live on other planets." Would you join me in this endeavor and help me to achieve that vision? The chances are that you would not. Why should you? I have no credibility with you. I haven't shown you that I'm able to achieve that goal. I didn't build enough trust with you, and so you will not join me. You would think that I'm either crazy or a fraud.

What if I told you that the name of the company in question is SpaceX and that the leader to follow is not me but Elon Musk? And, to quote from SpaceX's official website, it is the only private company ever to return a spacecraft from low-Earth orbit, which it first accomplished in December 2010. The company made history again in May 2012, when its Dragon spacecraft attached to the International Space Station, exchanged cargo payloads, and returned safely to Earth—a technically challenging feat previously accomplished only by governments. And, in May 2020, it became the first commercial company to successfully send people to space. What if I told you that Elon Musk is also CEO of Tesla, Inc., building cool electric cars? You would probably say, "Yep, I would follow that guy because he has already shown he can do it." He has built enough credibility with you even though you have never met him.

John C. Maxwell coined the term "The Law of the Buy-in," claiming that people buy in to a leader and only then buy in to their vision and strategy.[89] But how do you build that trust and credibility when you don't have massive rockets and electric cars to show off? You get back to basics and focus on your core values and how you interact with the world around you. Just follow these steps.

Know What Your Core Values Are: We have already talked about this. It is a rather critical piece in the whole puzzle. How can you expect others to follow you and trust you if even you don't know what you stand for? So step number one is to identify what your core values are. What is important to you? Who are you? How do you want to act? How do you want to be perceived? What do you stand for?

Be Clear with Others on What You Stand For: The key is to be transparent and consistent. If you repeatedly show certain behavior, people will associate it with you. They will understand what you stand for and what is important to you. The worst thing you can do as a manager is to be erratic and unpredictable. No one can trust or follow such a leader since it is unclear where to follow and why.

Fight for What You Believe Is Right: What is the point of having clear values and principles when you ignore them at the first sign of trouble? If you genuinely believe in something, then you show it by being willing to put your skin in the game. It is surprisingly easy to stick with your principles if people around you know what those principles are.

Be Willing to Admit When You Are Wrong: This may be a bit counterintuitive. Why would anyone follow a leader who is wrong? Well, no one will follow you if you are wrong all the time, but that is rarely the case. Unwillingness to admit a mistake even though everyone around you sees that mistake was made is the easiest way to lose credibility with a team. On the other hand, being bold enough to get in front of your team and be very open about the mistake you made, what you learned from it, and how you can fix it can boost the trust the team has in you. We are all just humans, and we make mistakes.

Have Your Words and Actions Aligned: This one is obvious. You need to walk your talk, lead by example, and . . . fill in your favorite leadership cliché. It is fine to be a great orator, but ultimately the genuine trust and credibility are only built by being the first one to charge. Not by talking but by doing.

Always Listen Before You Speak: Listen attentively and truly. Don't try to think about your response while listening. Listen until you genuinely understand. Don't make assumptions, and don't try to guess what is best for others. Don't interrupt. Through attentive listening, you show that you genuinely care.

Tell the Truth As You Understand It: Don't tell half-truths or leave false impressions. Use simple language and make it clear where you stand. Don't try to manipulate others or distort the facts. Learn to get to the point quickly so you can be easily understood. Giving too much context can often muddle your message.

Create Transparency: To build transparency, communicate as simply as you can and provide data points that are easily verified. If you have data you used for your decision, point to that data. If there are things you don't know, be clear about the gaps. Don't hide any information to keep power, and don't pursue any hidden agendas.

Show Loyalty to Your Team, Your Company, and Yourself: Acknowledge the contributions of others and give them credit as much as possible. Never gossip and always speak about others as if they were present. When speaking on behalf of others, make sure you genuinely represent them and don't push only your agenda. Never disclose information given to you in confidence.

Be Courageous and Always Address the Tough Stuff Head-On: If something needs to be said for the good of the team, then say it. Address the elephant in the room. Never shy away from having tough conversations, and have them in a respectful manner.

Be Clear on Your Expectations: You can't hold others accountable if you are not clear on what you expect them to do. Never assume that everyone understands what the expectations are. Be clear on what you want to verify that others understand it correctly.

Be Clear with Others on What You Are Going to Do and Then Do It: Never make a promise you can't keep. Don't say yes automatically to everything without considering whether you truly have the desire, capability, or time to follow through on the commitment. It is better to say no and later change your mind than to say yes and not deliver.

Deliver Results: Leaders are leaders because they get things done. Establish a strong track record of getting results, as that is important for building credibility and, ultimately, trust. Don't overpromise and underdeliver. Hold yourself accountable, and don't make excuses when you fail to deliver what you promised. Again, don't make promises you can't keep.

Lead by Example and Hold Yourself Accountable: Only when people see that you hold *yourself* accountable will they be comfortable with letting you hold *them* accountable. Take responsibility for the team's results and don't blame others if the team doesn't deliver. It is your fault.

Trust Others: Trust starts with you. If you don't trust others, you can hardly expect others to trust you. For some people, being trusting comes naturally; some are more cautious, while some just don't trust anyone at all. The fact is that, if you don't trust those around you, your life will become pretty stressful and miserable, and it will be incredibly difficult for you to achieve lasting success. Extend trust unconditionally to those who earn it, and extend it conditionally to those who haven't had the opportunity yet. When extending trust, understand the character and the competence of the individual in question and what you trust them to do. There is a risk with extending trust, and it is okay.

These are some of the fundamental behaviors that can guide you on your journey to find how credible and trustworthy you are. They can also give you a feel for what areas you need to work on. I suggest you make a checklist of these steps, and, every evening for a week, sit down, go through the checklist, and ask yourself, "What have I done today where I exhibited this behavior?" After a week, you may start seeing some trends and figure out what behavior prevents you from building trustworthiness and credibility. Then, the next week, make a conscious effort to improve that particular behavior.

Stop Gossiping

What is one of the biggest killers of trust in the workplace that can derail your career? Gossip. What is one of the most unproductive ways employees spend their time (aside from social networks, I mean)? Talking about others. Gossip is an excellent social building strategy that has survived for eons. A group of people gets together and complains about what others did or didn't do. It may not necessarily have ill intent—it is just a way human beings are. We like to bond with others, and one way to do it is to show that our little group has a common enemy.

Unfortunately, in work settings, this leads to a lot of wasted time, bad blood, and the development of habits that will hold you back. It leads to a lack of respect, lack of trust, and even hostility. Just consider the last time you were gossiping about someone else with a group of friends. And now imagine that they do the same about you when you are not around. Ouch. Gossiping is the ultimate trustworthiness killer.

The definition of gossip for our purposes is two or more people talking about someone who is not present. More often than not, this talk is about negative aspects of the missing person's personality or the perceived evil deeds they have done. That is where most of the value was in the past: to get your frustration in the open in the hopes of feeling better and warning others.

According to a study by Matthew Feinberg, Robb Willer, Jennifer Stellar, and Dacher Keltner of the University of Toronto and the University of California, gossip can be beneficial to society as a whole.[90] There is evidence that it helps to maintain social order. It can be seen as a preventive measure, as people tend to comply with social norms more if there is a danger that their reputations will be tarnished by gossip. It can even make people who gossip feel better. As they get their grief off their chests, it makes them less frustrated. So-called "prosocial gossip" can warn others about untrustworthy individuals who may take advantage of them. Most people are even willing to take a financial hit to be able to gossip in an effort to warn others about people who may try to deceive them. Sounds good.

Bianca Beersma and Gerben A. Van Kleef of the University of Amsterdam ran three studies to discover motives leading people to gossip.[91] They focused on students as the tested group and came to three main conclusions. First, the most common reason for gossip is information sharing. It has no malicious intent, just pure informal exchange of information. Second, gossip acts as protection against those who broke social norms of a group. Third, when people ascribe gossip as protection against social norms violation, they consider gossip socially acceptable. Whether to gossip or not depends on the topic and context. If your heart is in the right place and you talk about those who are selfish and try to hurt the group's interest, you are doing the group a favor by ostracizing these individuals. Sounds even better!

All is not just roses though. The human brain tends to misremember. We tend to forget the context in which information was received, and thus we can equate gossip with objective truth. Often, we don't have a way to verify what we've heard or don't care enough to do so. We can then be manipulated by gossip by malicious individuals into acting against our best interests or against the interests of others.

Gossip may have its usefulness, but more often than not, it is destructive. Every time you get into a conversation about others, you should consider these three questions: Does what is being said help me? Does what is being said help the person who is saying it? Does what is being said help the person we are talking about? If the answers are no, no, and no, then change the topic. At best, all that is being said has neutral value. At worst, it removes value. If nothing positive comes from the interaction, then you probably shouldn't have it in the first place.

If you don't get dragged into gossiping, not only will you have more time for productive work, but you will also be seen as more professional and trustworthy. Yes, you may not be part of the small clique that spends their day around the water cooler talking about others, but that is fine. Chances are that those are not the most successful individuals anyway, so why emulate them?

Those who can truly help your career may frown upon you gossiping. They may see you as less trustworthy if you gossip. They may see you as unable to keep secrets and therefore won't share confidential information with you. This can have an obvious negative impact on your ability to get things done and may result in a lack of career opportunities.

Follow your introvert instincts and exchange small talk and gossip for meaningful conversation. If you have nothing nice to say, then say nothing. It is far better to stay quiet than to engage in destructive gossip. Learn to use informal relationships and water-cooler talk to gather information that might benefit your job and your career and share information to genuinely help others. Just be careful about the context and what words you use. You shouldn't say anything that you don't want to be recorded for posterity.

Also, never participate in destructive gossip and negative comments about other people. Make it a point to intervene when you hear other people making unfounded hurtful statements about others and stop the talk. Once again, every time you want to talk about others behind their backs, ask yourself a simple question. *Is the conversation I'm participating in for the benefit of the person we are talking about?* If not, then stop. If there is hostile intent or you wouldn't have the same conversation with the person in question, you are gossiping, and you are hurting the person, the group you are talking with, and even yourself.

Commitment and Dependability

Acting with integrity means not only being trustworthy, but also being dependable. It requires you to make commitments and then deliver on what you committed to. There are few things more important for a manager than having a subordinate who is dependable. Only when you are dependable will you get things delegated to you, and you will get empowered. If you are not dependable, your manager will have no choice but to micromanage you. Not good for your career!

Let's say you decided to improve your health by running regularly. You commit to yourself that every morning before breakfast, you will go for a short run. You do it once, twice, and then, on the third day, you wake up and it is raining. What do you do? You go for a run. If not, if you make an excuse, you just made your first step to failing miserably. If you compromise once, you will easily compromise again and again.

Why do people quit before they achieve their goals? In most situations, they don't care enough about the goal, so they give themselves permission to fail. The reasoning goes along the lines of, "Well, at least I tried," or "I did my best, so I can quit now." If you start with a mindset that you will try and see, it is easy to give up. If you start with an attitude that failure is not an option, you are more likely to persevere until the end.

To help with the commitment, you may want to make a public promise. The fear of embarrassment of not living up to that promise may provide an additional push, so you keep going. Presenting your views and goals to others makes you more likely to stick with them. Just make sure you don't overdo it. As with everything, if you spend too much time talking about how you plan to climb a mountain, you may get back respect and accolades as if you had already reached the peak, so you may decide that that is all the endorphins you need and not even start the climb. Before you state your goal publicly, make sure it is the right goal, a goal you genuinely care about, and ideally try to have already taken the first step toward accomplishing it.

It makes sense that breaking your word is not something positive. When you commit to something and don't deliver, you are hurting your credibility. This shows that you either don't have the capability or the character to do what you said you would do.

The same goes for promising to show up and then changing your mind. This is something quite a few introverts struggle with. We tend to "sort of promise" to show up at a social event, only to find some excuse just before it starts for why we can't attend. Internally, we are very comfortable justifying our choice not to attend, but from the outside, it doesn't look good—especially if that becomes a pattern. Others will soon realize that we don't mean it when we say we will show up to something. So what else don't we mean?

You may decide to use the legal strategy and claim that you never actually promised. You never said, "I will show up," you probably used the words, "I will do my best" or "I may come." But even those words can still be seen as a promise. They are unintentional promises that introverts make all the time. You don't want to disappoint someone with straight refusal, so you indicate that you will try, even though you really don't want to. You already know that it is unlikely for you to come, but you are unwilling to be transparent about it. Guess what? Saying, "I won't come" will disappoint the person less than saying you will come and then not showing up.

Sometimes you have the best intentions at heart, and you genuinely want to do what you say or come to the social event when you are invited. You are just full of energy. You like the people who are participating. It will be fun. However, when the time comes, your energy is drained, the weather is terrible, and it is just so much more appealing to stay at home. So you come up with an excuse. Once again, you broke your word. You hurt those who expected you, you hurt your credibility, and you hurt the relationship. People will give you only so many chances before they give up on you and stop inviting you to join them.

For many introverts, it is enough to know that other people care about us and want us to be around. That's all we need to feel like we belong. But what happens when the invitations stop coming? What if you turn up to the office on Monday and everyone talks about a party they had on Saturday you knew nothing about? Suddenly, you don't belong anymore. You are not part of the group.

Breaking your word, either intentionally or unintentionally, is a big no-no. It can quickly become a habit, and it will have a negative long-term effect on your credibility, reputation, and, ultimately, self-confidence. Learn to carefully consider what you promise and then keep your promises, whatever the costs. In most situations, you will realize that the price wasn't that high, and you will feel much better about yourself, while having better relationships with those around you.

Candor

Say what you mean and mean what you say. Being candid with yourself and with others is a skill that very few people truly master. It takes courage, it takes ownership, and it takes a particular skill to do it properly.

If people know that you will candidly speak up for the good of the team, they will see you as more trustworthy, dependable, and incorruptible. You will be seen as having a leadership potential that will reflect positively on your career opportunities. Just make sure your candid remarks are followed by action; otherwise, you may come across as whiny.

Kim Scott, in *Radical Candor*, introduced a framework of the same name. When people believe you care about them, they will accept direct, candid feedback from you and will be more willing to act on it. They will also be more likely to provide similar candid feedback to you and even to each other. They will ultimately feel valued as human beings, which will help their motivation and performance.[92]

Scott talks about what happens when you don't care or you don't challenge. When you provide feedback directly to someone without caring about them, your guidance feels obnoxious and aggressive. It may work sometimes, but ultimately this makes you a jerk, and it won't work for long. The worst example is when you don't care about others and don't challenge them directly. This usually happens when you want to be liked, and you don't care whether the job gets done or the other person gets better. You can always blame them behind their back, right? This approach is manipulative and insincere and shows that you care only about your own well-being and nothing else.

When you care about the person but are afraid or unwilling to provide direct feedback, you do them a disservice. You are so worried about the short-term discomfort the feedback would bring that you instead keep quiet and exchange it for long-term suffering. You can see this with parents who love their children so much that they are unwilling to discipline them when they do something wrong. Consequently, the kids don't even know they are doing something they shouldn't be and thus never get better. This is a case most frequently seen even in well-functioning teams. It is also one that is very close to the introvert's heart. Don't rock the boat. In the name of keeping a good atmosphere and social harmony, we don't say what needs to be said. However, this is somewhat irresponsible. Being responsible means that you do the right thing, even though it may make you unpopular and make people angry. In fact, if no one is ever angry with you, chances are that you don't challenge them enough.

To adapt an anecdote about training dogs from Kim Scott's work, what do you do when you want your dog to obey? Do you endlessly explain that it is in their best interests to sit on your command and tell them how to do it? No, you provide a simple command that is not open to interpretation: "Sit!" As Kim says, the command "is not mean; it is clear."

On the flip side, you need to make sure you don't use honesty to excuse toxic behavior. There are those who, in the name of "speaking the truth," bring up all sorts of things that can destroy relationships and productivity in a team. Just because something is true doesn't mean you have to say it. Always ask yourself whether what you want to say helps that particular individual, yourself, or the team. And if the answer is negative in all three cases, then just don't say it.

Doing What Is Right

Integrity requires that your actions are aligned with your words. It is not enough to say what needs to be said. You have to follow up and do what needs to get done and what is right.

How often do you decide to do something just because "you can"? When you think about it, you may realize that it is way too often. Did you just jump in the car and drive half a mile to buy a bottle of water when you could have walked? Did you just come home and turn on the TV without really thinking about it and then not even watch it? Did you just send an inflammatory email on a hot topic instead of picking up the phone and calling the person in question? Did you just buy something without really needing it because it looked nice and you had some money and free time?

Very few of us behave responsibly and think through our actions all the time. That applies even to us thoughtful, overthink-everything introverts. Thinking logically about every action we take would be taxing on our internal resources, and we would not enjoy life at all. But when it comes to business, we should pay a bit more attention, as the resources we are using are not just external ones like the company's money, other people's time, and others. We need to also consider our internal resources, like attention and willpower.

Time: This one resource is very easy to waste on things we don't need or want. Did you just spend three hours sitting in front of a TV watching a movie you didn't enjoy because the TV was on and it was easy not to go and do something else? You could go out with friends, spend time with family, exercise, read, work, learn to paint, or take a walk and relax. And instead of these, you decided to sit and mindlessly stare at something you forgot about the next day. Why? Because you could.

Money: Just imagine a typical situation in a corporate environment. Your boss came to you and told you that you have five hundred dollars to spend to celebrate some team success. What do you do? Will you think in terms of "I have five hundred USD, let's spend it," or in terms of "I want to celebrate our success in the most meaningful way, and I have five hundred USD in case I need it"? The first approach is wasteful of company resources and may not even bring about the effect you want to achieve. You might say, "Let's all go to a fancy restaurant and order some expensive wine," while most of the team would prefer just to hang out in their favorite pub over a couple of beers. You just spent five hundred dollars in a rather inefficient way, and why? Only because you could. The responsible approach would have been to think first about what type of celebration was right for your team and then just figure out how the five hundred bucks fit in. And if you only ended up needing two hundred? So what? You had your fun, and by acting like a responsible adult, you even saved some money for others.

Attention: There are so many distractions in modern society. Social media, old-school media, and an overload of information coming from all sides. But just because the information is available doesn't necessarily mean you need to consume it. Herbert Simon, a winner of the Nobel Prize for Economics, once said, "What information consumes is rather obvious. It consumes the attention of its recipients. Hence a wealth of information creates a poverty of attention."[93]

Just sit down and spend a couple of minutes replaying your actions from the last week and try to understand the decisions that led to them. Did you do what you did because they were the right things to do or just because you could?

Show Courage

Not only don't we do the right things because we don't think, we don't do the right things because we are scared and lazy. These are all the situations when you know deep down in your heart that what you are doing is wrong and that you should do the complete opposite. And yet, you keep moving ahead.

Doing Something Illegal: If someone asks you to do something illegal, chances are you will push back. You will say no. If they keep pushing, you may even escalate your response and tell them. You may even go to the police, or at least to the human resources department or your boss. You will do everything in your power not to get involved. I hope that most of us would also try to stop the activity. We feel that preventing a crime is such a no-brainer that most of us would do something. We would do the right thing.

Doing Something Unethical and Immoral: This is where things get tricky. By doing something unethical and immoral, you are not breaking the law, you are just breaking some societal norms. If you are asked to do something unethical, and there is a big enough reward, you may succumb to the pressure and do it. For example, if the whole team is already doing it, you can justify it as acceptable. Doing this unethical thing is sort of a norm within the group, so you reluctantly join in. Do it frequently enough, and you won't even realize that you are doing anything wrong. You become part of the problem. Only those with a strong moral compass, with a clear set of values, are not willing to compromise and will stand their ground. If something is wrong, it is wrong regardless of how many people are doing it. Mustering your courage and being firm in the face of unethical behavior shows true character and personal leadership. It requires a strong-willed person who is willing to stand their ground and keep explaining not only why they will not join in the activity, but that it is wrong to do it in the first place.

Doing Something Disrespectful and Hurtful: This is something that pretty much everyone is guilty of. Very few of us are willing to do something about it. Just consider this example. You are sitting in a meeting with a couple of colleagues, and your boss yells at and belittles one of them. What do you do? What the boss is doing is not illegal. It is not unethical. It is just plain wrong. It is disrespectful to the individual he is yelling at and hurtful to the team. And yet, how many people in the meeting will raise their hands and come to the rescue of the person being shouted at? How many people will gather the courage to tell the boss that this behavior is completely unacceptable? Doing so feels scary. Doing so is also very far out of our comfort zone. But it is still the right thing to do. You may think that it is a sucker's choice and that if you sit quietly and do nothing, you silently agree with the practice, while if you stand up and voice your concern, it may end your career. Well, there is always this danger. However, unless the boss is a total psychopath, chances are you can communicate your concerns to the boss in such a way that it doesn't get you fired. It may even enhance your status.

Having the reputation as someone who will always do what is right and say what needs to be said leads to future opportunities. People want to work with those who will stand for truth and what is right. Most managers appreciate having people on their team willing to give them candid feedback and keep them honest. No one wants to be seen as a fool who is being mocked and bad-mouthed behind their back.

Summary and Key Takeaways

Acting with integrity is an excellent reputation-enhancer. When you are trustworthy, credible, willing to commit, and then dependably follow up on your commitments, you become someone who will be seen as a leader and a moral authority. Others will be more willing to help you out and provide opportunities that will help you to have a successful career. For introverts, the most challenging part is getting the courage to voice our candid opinions in a way that is accepted by those we are addressing.

- Integrity shows when your actions, your words, and your values and principles are aligned. Integrity is not something you are born with. It is a personal choice.
- Trust starts with trustworthiness. Trustworthiness is a combination of character and competence.
- Gossiping and bad-mouthing others is the easiest way to lose the trust of those around you.
- Commitment and dependability show in times of crisis when you encounter adversity.
- Once you make a promise, keep it at any cost.
- Being candid with yourself and others is an important skill few people master. It requires you to say what needs to be said in a way that others will accept and act on.
- Do things not because you can, but because they are the right things to do.

Questions and Next Steps

- Try this exercise for a week. Make a checklist of steps mentioned in the trustworthiness and credibility section, and every evening sit down, go through the checklist, and ask yourself, "What have I done today where I exhibited this behavior?" After a week, you may start seeing some trends and figure out what behavior prevents you from building trustworthiness and credibility. Then, the next week, make a conscious effort to improve that particular behavior.
- Don't gossip. Every time you have the urge to talk about others behind their backs, ask yourself this question: Is the conversation I'm participating in for the benefit of the person we are talking about? If not, then stop.
- Another exercise that requires you to observe your behavior during the week: Sit down and spend a couple of minutes replaying your actions from the day

and trying to understand the decisions that led to them. Did you do what you did because it was the right thing to do or just because you could? If you find that you do most things simply because you can, consider whether they are beneficial to you, your team, or your career, or whether they are just a waste of resources.

12

Keep Learning

"I want to learn. I'm curious about life.
I listen to others. I keep getting better every single day."

Many kids who have to go to school every single day sit in their classrooms and dream about the holidays or about getting out of school, being like grown-ups, and starting to work and make money, never needing to learn anything again. Unfortunately, life is not that simple. In fact, when you get out of school, real learning starts. We learn every single day, and if we want to be successful in our professional careers and keep up with the brave new world we live in, we need to dedicate conscious effort to learning new things.

Over the years I've been managing teams, I have very often heard that "HR should provide some training." When I ask what the developmental needs of the particular individual making that comment are, the response is often, "I don't know, just tell HR to give me a list of training options, and I will pick some." The implication here is that people don't really know what they need. They just want something, anything.

Those who don't take the time to think about their real needs will then sit through some classes that will be irrelevant, boring, and bring them nothing except the feeling that the company gave them training. This is the most common waste of money many companies fall into. Human resources departments are here to provide tools and guidance. They are not supreme beings who will miraculously push knowledge into your head.

So if not the human resources department, then I guess it should be the manager's role to provide training, right? Wrong. Your manager, who works with you daily, understands what skills you have today, what is required for your job, and what skills you may need in the future. Your manager is in a unique position to help you identify any skill gaps that you need to bridge and that you may not see yourself. Your manager is here to provide you with opportunities so you can learn on the job. Your manager can provide regular feedback and course corrections and can work with the HR group to provide the tools or training you need. However, even the manager can do very little when you are not willing to learn or when you disagree with the direction they want you to head.

It is your responsibility to take ownership of your own personal and professional development. You can't blame HR or your manager if you are not growing and not learning anything new. It is your responsibility to make an effort, seek new opportunities to learn, and go above and beyond your current duties. Learn on the job, learn from colleagues, learn from external mentors, and learn from books or articles in magazines and on the web. Your manager and the human resources department are there to support you, but you are the owner of your own future.

And if you don't know what to learn? Well, go back to Chapter 5 and run through the skill inventory matrix exercise and find out what skills you need to get to your Quiet Success Sweet Spot. Follow some of the tips in Chapter 6 to find the best way to get that particular skill or knowledge. Most importantly, don't get satisfied with basic knowledge. If the skill is important for getting into or staying in your Sweet Spot, then you may consider giving it enough focused effort that you reach mastery.

Growth Mindset

We all know someone who was a brilliant kid with a high IQ but ultimately didn't achieve much success in school and life. These kids were always praised for being the smartest in their class. Everything was easy for them, and so they didn't build the necessary discipline and mindset to achieve the same success when the challenges increased and things stopped being so easy. We would often say that they wasted their talent.

Carol S. Dweck is an American psychologist who coined the terms "fixed mindset" and "growth mindset." According to her theory, everyone can be placed on a continuum indicating where they believe their abilities come from. Those with a fixed mindset believe in talents one either is or is not born with. Abilities are innate, and there is not much you can do if you are not talented in a given field. You are born with a certain level of intelligence, talent, and ability, and that decides the limits of what you can achieve in life. Those with a growth mindset, on the other hand, believe that anyone can learn any skill and acquire any ability, regardless of their innate talents. All it takes is focus and effort. This is not necessarily a belief that everyone can be the next Mozart or Einstein, but that everyone can certainly be more than what they are today.

These worldviews determine how people react to adversity. Those who have a fixed mindset tend to give up more quickly and blame their genes for their failures. Those with a growth mindset tend to keep working hard and persevere, even when encountering setbacks. They believe they have the capability to learn, grow, and overcome the obstacles that life throws at them.

Research suggests that even though actual cognitive ability is, to a large extent, fixed, mindset can impact the ability to learn. Incremental theorists, those with a growth mindset, demonstrated more significant gains in knowledge than entity theorists, those with a fixed mindset.[94] This is one of those situations where a bit of self-delusion can help a person in achieving more. When you believe you have the capacity to learn, or you even delude yourself that you can become the best at a particular activity, you will be more motivated and give it more effort than someone who is more grounded. It is often those who see the world not as it is but as they want it to be who succeed.

It is not necessarily the belief itself but rather what follows because of that belief that makes the difference. If you have a growth mindset, you are more likely to try to learn something new and persevere. Your actual IQ might be the same as that of someone with a fixed mindset, but you will have the edge in terms of the effort you put in. You will be more likely to believe that you have your life in your hands and under control. A feeling of control is a powerful motivator and a source of success and happiness.

People with fixed mindsets are usually afraid to try new things where they could fail because they worry about how they will be judged. In their minds, their success or failure is a direct reflection of whether they are good or bad as a person. This is pure self-esteem preservation. It also means that people with this mindset tend to hide their failures and shy away from feedback. That then has a negative impact on their ability to grow. When facing setbacks and adversity, instead of increasing effort, they give up. This makes sense. Why would you increase effort if you believe that it is your innate ability that matters, not your effort? Based on Dweck's research, people with fixed mindsets are also more prone to cheating to retain a positive image in the eyes of others.

For people with growth mindsets, it is all about effort. They are less concerned with their innate abilities and more with what they can do to become better. They are more likely to listen to feedback, and when they fail, they learn from their mistakes and try again. If things go wrong, these people are more likely to escalate their efforts and keep going in the belief that they can overcome adversity with enough effort.

Curiously enough, this all starts in childhood and the type of praise children get. The wrong kind of praise can reinforce the fixed mentality, while the right kind of praise can create a growth mindset. Dweck studied this phenomenon extensively and concluded that reinforcing the feeling that a child has succeeded because they are special can have adverse effects. It's better to reward effort.[95] When it comes to praise, focusing on effort is much more meaningful than focusing on innate talents. Saying to others that they achieved something "because they are talented" doesn't bring any useful encouragement for the future. And worse, it can lead to less effort next time, as, "Why should I work hard when I'm talented?" Praising effort—"You worked hard and gave it your best, and that is why you succeeded"—ends up having the opposite effect. It will lead to more effort in the future, as, "if I work even harder next time, my success can be even bigger."

Since there is some reluctance in the scientific community to accept this concept, it is worth pointing out that some psychologists question the power of mindset as defined by Dweck. Her research is difficult to replicate, and there is limited evidence that growth mindset has a substantial impact on ability to learn as compared to fixed mindset.[96]

Whether that is true or not is irrelevant. Very few techniques have a meaningful impact in isolation. Raw brainpower, or intelligence, still matters, and someone more intelligent has a higher ceiling of what they can achieve than someone with lower intelligence. But that is not the point. The point is that with a growth mindset, you believe that you can achieve more than you do today, and you are more likely to try.

Attentiveness

The great news is that most introverts are willing to learn. Since we don't have the need to constantly talk, we do the other natural thing: we listen. However, there is always the danger that even though we listen, we don't hear what is being said. So how can you hone this particular strength and get it to the next level?

Take Listening Seriously: Don't take it for granted. Just because you were born with two ears and you like to listen rather than talk doesn't mean there is nothing to learn and nothing to improve. Most introverts are naturally inclined to listen more than talk, but that doesn't automatically make them excellent and attentive listeners. It is not only about listening but about actually hearing the message the way it was intended. So even though listening is most likely one of your strengths, it still pays off to take listening as a specific skill that we can steadily improve.

Stay Focused: Take it one conversation at a time. Especially if the content of the discussion is of no significant interest to you, you may have a tendency to think about the next meeting or about your plans for the evening, or to just daydream and let your mind wander.

Don't Multitask: Checking a mobile phone or trying to answer an email while listening to others are the most common culprits behind poor listening in a corporate setting. At home, it might be the TV or, again, the phone that divides your attention across several tasks. The human brain is incapable of multitasking. If someone claims they are good at it, the chances are that they have a blind spot, and they are most likely particularly bad at it. As I wrote in Chapter 2, don't delude yourself into believing that by multitasking, you get more done. You won't. And what's worse, multitasking will remove one of your strengths: being a good listener.

Remove Distractions: As with anything that requires focus, removing distractions from your environment goes a long way toward ensuring you stay focused. Close down your laptop, position your chair to face the person who is speaking, sit with your back to the window, or do whatever makes it easier for you to truly focus on the conversation. By doing these things, you also communicate good intentions to the person you are talking to. If they see that your attention is on them, they will feel that they are important to you and that you care. Ultimately, both sides will not only have a better understanding of what was said but will also have a good feeling from the interaction.

Don't Try to Have a Parallel Dialogue in Your Head: The most prominent problem people face when listening is trying to move the conversation forward in their minds by thinking about an answer rather than listening, by completing sentences in their heads, or by judging the content or the speaker. This is especially true when there is an imbalance in expertise or in the information both parties have. If you know much more than the other person does about the topic, you may lose patience with them if they don't say the right things. I always considered myself to be a good listener until I realized that for topics I care about or at times when I want to have conversations done as quickly as possible, I tend to finish the other person's sentences. Finishing someone else's sentences is an excellent indicator that you are not really listening and that you are not trying to understand—just the opposite. You are trying to push your perspective on the other person.

Ask Open-Ended Questions: The right question asked at the right time is a potent tool in the introvert's toolbox. It can stimulate deep thinking and move the conversation deep into what needs to be said. It also shows that you are actively listening and not pretending. You don't need to say much during the conversation, but when you do speak, you can move the discussion along and play a critical role. The ability to ask the right question is then especially useful when coaching or using a coaching approach to lead people.

Use Silence: I can't emphasize enough the power of silence. As introverts, it comes naturally to us to give everyone the space they need to present their thoughts. The way to do this is not only by asking questions but by not jumping in to fill any empty space during the conversation. The same applies even when you have a presentation to a bigger group of people. Using a dramatic pause, a moment of silence, brings everyone's attention to the point, emphasizes that what you are saying has some special meaning, and gives everyone a chance to think about it.

Use Your Other Senses: We have more than one sense. During a conversation with others, you shouldn't rely just on your ears but be fully immersed in the scene. The tone of voice, the pauses, the body language, the facial muscle movements, the way the speaker behaves, what he focuses on, all these things are part of the message. If the content is not aligned with all the other aspects, that is a red flag, and you need to figure out what exactly is being communicated. This is especially important when working across cultures. The most common example is when you ask someone to do a task and they answer yes. In some cultures, this means that they will do as asked. In other cultures, it merely means that they acknowledge the request but don't necessarily agree that it will be done. By taking into account the other aspects of the scene, you will be alerted that maybe the message you received is not the one that was intended.

Watch the Body Language: Watching body language is not only observing the body language of the other person in a conversation, but it is also about your own body language as a listener. By saying, "I'm listening" while continuing to focus on your mobile phone, you are sending clear signals that the speaker or the content is actually not the most important thing for you at the moment. The same goes for eye contact. It may feel challenging to have a decent amount of eye contact with other people when talking to them, but you can do it just fine with a bit of practice. Scientists claim that ideally, you want to have eye contact 60 to 70 percent of the time to have the best effect. Most of us tend to look at others when we listen and break the connection when we talk, as looking into the distance or at the floor helps us collect our thoughts. That is just fine.

*Connect Emotionally: A*ttentive listening not only has the immediate benefit of actually letting you hear what was said but also leads to better long-term relationships. By giving people your undivided attention, you show that you care. We all want to be treated with respect. We all want to feel that someone cares about what we want to say. We all want to matter. We all want to belong. You can offer all this just through the simple act of attentive listening.

Paraphrase to Make Sure You Verify You Understood Correctly: During a conversation, you are getting not only the actual content of the message but also the emotions, feelings, moods, worldviews, and other information not relevant for the actual conversation. This is dangerous, as it can influence how you hear the real message, and you may misunderstand its original intent. The same applies when the content of the message doesn't align with the speaker's body language. In these situations, you need to speak up to make sure you correctly understand what is being said. The best way to do this is to paraphrase what you understood. Summarize the key points in your own words to allow the speaker to either confirm that you understood correctly or provide corrections. Paraphrasing is better in these situations than asking questions as it has a bigger chance of removing any cultural aspects. It is also non-threatening. You are not trying to challenge the speaker by asking questions that may imply you disagree. You are just being respectful and genuinely want to make sure you understood correctly.

The lesson learned is that you should always listen and look for clues, and you should never try to interpret what they mean. If you see some behavior you don't understand and believe it means something, ask for clarification. Describe what you see and ask whether your interpretation is correct. Obviously, before you can start listening, you need to be interested in what the person wants to share, and that leads us to curiosity.

Curiosity

Thomas L. Friedman writes about the importance of curiosity in today's world. Friedman introduced the new concept of CQ (Curiosity Quotient). He proposes that CQ should stand side-by-side with EQ (Emotional Quotient). CQ and EQ are in many ways superior to the good old IQ (Intelligence Quotient).[97]

Anyone who has spent any time around small kids remembers the wonder they experience all the time. Kids are infinitely curious and wonder about everything. How does this work, smell, feel, taste? Why is the world the way it is? What happens if I press this or pull that? Children keep asking because they don't know, and they are not afraid of the answers. They don't even care if there is an answer. As we grow up, this changes. We often lose open curiosity. We don't ask questions to which we don't want to know answers. We don't accept that, for some questions, there are no answers. We expect that there always has to be an answer. It is the goal of our life to find it. Instead of living our life, we are solving it.

Curiosity As a Way of Life: Some of us are fine with getting just a general idea of how things work, some of us don't care at all about life around us, and some of us have a natural curiosity about everything. You may be content with never learning to drive and always asking someone else to drive you places. You may be curious enough to learn to drive, but the working of the combustion engine is still a mystery to you. And you might be someone who wants to be a great driver, so you study every single detail about the engine, the transmission, the brakes, and the inner workings of a modern car. Learn to find the right balance of being curious enough to master something and being curious enough just to have a sense of wonder in your life.

Curiosity As a Path to Mastery: There is very little you can do to increase your IQ, but there are certainly ways to improve your EQ and CQ. You can learn to empathize with others, and you can learn to be curious about things around you. To be good at something, you don't necessarily need a big IQ, even though that usually gives you an advantage, but you need to spend a significant amount of time and effort to build the necessary skill, and that means passion. It also implies curiosity to understand every detail and inner working of the world.

Curiosity As a Leadership Trait: For a leader to be really good at leading others, you need to know more than that people have two eyes, two ears, and one mouth. You need to be a student of human nature and a student of language. You need to observe their behavior. You need to aspire to understand that behavior and how to influence it and use it for the good of everyone. The curiosity about how and why people behave, combined with the passion for learning and helping them to grow, are the things that will make you great at working with others. Your curiosity will help you to be better at what you do. But your ability to spark an interest and make your team more curious will increase their chances of success in life. And as they learn, grow, and spread their curiosity around, it will create an exciting environment to work in, an environment that will positively reflect on the success of your team and your company.

Curiosity As a Distraction: If you belong to the curious bunch, there is one danger though. In today's hyper-connected world, there is tons of information at your fingertips. If you are curious about everything, you may get overwhelmed and be constantly distracted. So, in my mind, having a high curiosity quotient also means having an ability to focus your curiosity on the things that matter. It is incredibly satisfying to know how long an average bee lives. Still, unless you are a beekeeper, that information is somewhat irrelevant. The line between being curious in order to learn and improve and being curious just for the sake of accumulating unnecessary background noise can sometimes be rather thin. It takes some self-discipline to filter out the things that are way too irrelevant and will just cause a loss of concentration and derail your train to success.

In *Hidden Brilliance,* Katie Rasoul proposes a practice she calls Curiosity Hour.[98] To keep your mind fresh, get the creative juices flowing, and learn something new, she suggests keeping a list of things that pique your interest and regularly have an hour on your calendar dedicated to researching these topics. I use a similar practice, and usually, my research leads me down the Google rabbit hole, and I find some new exciting views on the world.

Curiosity can be a considerable career enhancer. It will directly impact your career, as increasing the breadth of your knowledge will open new opportunities for you. In fact, curiosity was what got me into management. This was early in my career when I was still a software developer. When talking to my boss, he mentioned that he was going to meet a potential partner to negotiate a deal. I asked him a couple of questions about how he planned to approach it. After giving me a lesson in negotiations, he finished with, "Why don't you come with me?" That was the first and last time we went to that partner together, as, at the meeting, he introduced me and told the partner that I would be running it from our side from now on. But curiosity and attentiveness are not enough. You need to put in some effort to get the actual competence.

Competence

You may have the best intentions in your heart, but you won't be successful if you don't know what you are doing. It is not only about integrity and hard work. It is also about knowledge and competence in your chosen field.

In Chapter 6, I talked extensively about various ways to learn and gain competence, so I won't be rehashing those here. Instead, let's quickly consider what areas to tackle when you want to succeed in your selected job at a specific company. Where should you spend your time and effort? What are the things to learn? In the majority of jobs, it boils down to these six skills. This applies to both managerial and individual contributor roles.

Company Basics: You need to understand the company culture, its values, and what it stands for to be able to work with others without friction. If you don't know the company's overall objectives and how the company operates, you will struggle. Not only will you not be able to get things done, but you will be frustrated and unhappy. The unwillingness to adapt to the company culture is most often one of the reasons why employees feel frustrated and disengaged. They want to do things one way, and the company culture and processes don't allow that.

Technical or Functional: You need to have the necessary technical skills related to the function you selected. Without the technical or functional skills, you are unable to contribute. If you are an accountant, you need to know bookkeeping. If you are a software developer, you need to be able to write good source code. If you are a project manager, you need to understand the necessary project management methodologies. Having functional knowledge is an essential must-have for any job.

Management: This is a technical skill focused on getting things done and possibly getting them done through other people. For example, a project management background is pretty handy for most jobs, as it teaches you how to organize your time, plan, track, and stick with the goal. People management starts with self-management and continues through working with peers toward managing other people. It is not only the people in the actual managerial roles who benefit from the basics of management.

Communication: We all need to communicate. In fact, communication is a significant part of almost any job. And it is the most often ignored, so invest your time in improving your communication skills, or even your language skills when in an international environment. Without excellent communication skills, everything gets much harder. Only when you know how to ask for what you need, when you know how to present your results, and when you know how to build alliances can you be truly successful.

Leadership: This skill is the most difficult to learn and will take time to master. It is a lifelong journey. Leading people, influencing others, and inspiring teams is more art than science and thus needs to be continuously improved and adapted and cannot be learned in any training course. The only way to learn it is through continuous everyday practice. It is also the most powerful skill set, as it can help you multiply your impact on the world enormously. Similar to management, it is not only for those who are formally put in charge. Personal leadership is a must for anyone who wants to be in control of their career.

Interviewing: One could argue that this is a critical skill meant mainly for managers. I believe it is a great skill for anyone who wants to be successful in a big way. Anything truly impactful is rarely done by one person. It is most often a team of people that tackles big problems and projects. Who you select for your team will shape the culture that will be created and will have a massive impact on your ability to get things done.

Some of these areas are easy to cover when talking to your boss or HR. Learning some of them will require a mentor, some a good book, and some just the right mindset and lots of patience, perseverance, and on-the-job training. Just remember that whatever help you get is always just a beginning. If you participate in training focused on improving presentation and public speaking skills, it will give you a theoretical basis, and it will also give you a chance to practice in a safe environment. But if you want the skill to stick, training is just the first step, then you need to regularly get in front of people and talk. That is the only way you will develop the skill and ensure the training wasn't just a waste of your time and money. To become truly great at what you do, you need to strive to get a bit better every single day.

Getting Better Every Day

If you want to learn a new skill, you need to give it the time and effort it deserves. The more frequently you can practice, the better. The most obvious recurrence is daily. If you can carve out time to practice whatever skill or craft you are trying to master daily, you will see much better progress than if you do it irregularly or infrequently—common sense. Consistency and perseverance are critical to any skill-building.

Doing anything daily also builds habits and routines. There is no need to overthink or decide whether today is the right day or whether it would be better to do it next week. You need to do it every single day! That's who you are! And if you don't have anything significant you are trying to work on right now, keep learning at least small things, just to keep the habit and become a better and better person every single day. Before you get to bed in the evening, ask yourself questions like, What did I learn today? Did I make a conscious effort? Have I stretched my limits? Did I get feedback? Am I a better human being today than I was yesterday?

If you find yourself giving positive answers, excellent. Have a good sleep. You did well today. If you realize that you haven't done anything today to become better, be very deliberate in planning your activities for tomorrow and make sure you include the learning piece. It is the small changes and minor improvements that you make every single day that can have a substantial cumulative impact. Evolution is always easier and less disruptive than revolution.

Imagine you decided to get into better shape. You can have two options. You can pay a big fee and join a local gym. Put two hours of workouts on your calendar every day starting tomorrow and work out tirelessly. The chances are that after three visits, you will start coming up with excuses for not going. The chances are that you won't keep it up for too long. Or you can decide that, every morning when you get out of bed, you will do one pushup more than you did the day before. You will start tomorrow with one pushup. It takes two seconds. In a month, you will be doing thirty pushups every morning. In a year, you will be at 365. You will be in pretty good shape! And all it took was a bit of consistency and perseverance.

You can do the same with learning any new skill at work. What about learning a new language that would open up new career opportunities? If you make it a point to learn five new words a day, in a year, you will know more than 1,800 words. That is a solid basis for a basic everyday conversation in most languages. What about reading a couple of pages a day from material preparing yourself for an exam to get a certificate in accounting or project management?

For any learning to have a long-lasting effect, it needs to have a certain level of difficulty. If you make your learning experience too easy, you are doing yourself a disservice. You won't learn. What you want is a learning experience that is challenging, even frustrating. It may drive you crazy in the short term, but you will remember more and apply it better in the long term. Cheating or getting hints and excessive guidance from the teacher may help your short-term performance, and you may feel better, but it will hurt you in the long run. Unfortunately, this is a massive pitfall for teachers. Those who are not particularly good at their jobs focus on short-term performance, and, therefore, on making their students feel good. They will be rated highly. Those who genuinely teach you something will appear rather lousy in the short term. Because of the frustrating learning experience, you won't appreciate that they are teaching you more.

So-called "desirable difficulties" make for a more effective learning experience. Keep this in mind when you are frustrated with a difficult problem and want to give up.[99] Coming up with answers on your own rather than being told might take you longer but will also imprint better in your memory.[100] In fact, this is true even if you arrive at the wrong answer. As research by Janet Metcalfe and colleagues indicates, errors committed with high confidence are more likely to be corrected than low-confidence errors when learning the correct answers.[101]

Learning something new that will significantly improve your chances for a successful career can be intimidating. It will most likely require a huge amount of time and won't happen overnight. It will get significantly less intimidating when you split it into smaller chunks of learning. Don't expect to become a master of a new topic by using shortcuts. It rarely works. Build the knowledge step by step. Use your strengths of preparation, focus, and perseverance to get a little bit better every single day.

Summary and Key Takeaways

David J. Epstein retells the story of Frances Hesselbein, a former CEO of the Girl Scouts of the USA. She participated in a training event and heard another trainee complain that she was getting nothing out of the training. A woman next to her said, "You have to carry a big basket to bring something home," meaning that if you keep your mind wide open, you will take something away from every experience.[102]

Having a growth mindset and being attentive and curious about everything in your professional life will help you build the necessary competence to succeed. And with focus, consistency, and perseverance, you will get better at something every single day for the rest of your life.

- It is your responsibility to take ownership of your personal and professional development.
- Adopt a growth mindset, a belief that abilities come from learning and practice, rather than from being innate. This will help you to focus on things you want to improve, try harder, and persevere.
- Listening might be your strength, but that doesn't mean you can't improve it.
- Curiosity is a way of life, a path to mastery, and a welcome leadership trait.
- Don't dismiss the importance of competence for a successful career.
- Take your personal and professional development step by step, and get a little bit better every day.
- For any learning to have an effect, make it desirably difficult.

Questions and Next Steps

- Do you have a growth mindset? Answer these questions to find out. Do you believe you can become better at anything as long as you give it some effort? Do you believe that you have the capacity to learn, grow, and overcome anything that life throws at you? Did you answer yes to both? Good. Or do you have a more fixed mindset and believe that no effort on your part can change what nature made you? If you have a fixed mindset, I challenge you to give it a try and, for at least a month, every single day, try to improve the one thing you are bad at and believe you can never improve. I bet that whatever the activity, as long as you give it focused effort over a decent period of time, you will get better.
- Try this simple exercise to build your curiosity. Every time you hear a word or expression you don't really understand, open an encyclopedia or check the

internet and find out what exactly it means. Not only will you learn something new, but you will build a habit of curiosity that will help your career in the long run.

- To create a habit to become a better and better person every single day, try this exercise. Before you get to bed in the evening, ask yourself these questions: What did I learn today? Did I make a conscious effort to learn? Have I stretched my limits? Did I get feedback? Am I a better human being today than I was yesterday?

13

Show Up

"I'm always prepared. I manage my energy.
I'm disciplined. I show up even if I'm uncomfortable."

If you want to have a successful career, you need to go out and do stuff. You need to show up. And you need to show up regularly, even when you are not comfortable. The daily discipline of showing up and putting effort into whatever you have committed to doing is the key. Only through consistent, targeted effort can you achieve great results.

Showing up means that you put in an appearance. You participate. You take action. You get involved when you promised you would. It requires discipline and resilience. For introverts, it also includes preparation and routine.

Many introverts, myself included, struggle with this principle. We are so comfortable in the virtual imaginary worlds of our minds that we have a hard time getting out to the real world and among real people. I'm an avid reader, and it is so much more comfortable to read about things than to go out and actually do them.

It starts with being prepared and having the energy and courage to show up. For many introverts, the beginning is the biggest problem. We tend to have a decent ability to persevere once we get moving. But the get-moving part is holding us back.

To help you keep moving and keep you from expending your energy on things that are not important, figure out how to routinize your life. It may not sound particularly appealing, but by creating various routines, you are also creating habits. And good habits will be indispensable for persevering, reaching your goals, and having a successful career.

Being comfortable with being uncomfortable is the key. By learning to delay gratification and purposefully getting into challenging situations, you build the resilience to keep going and show up day in and day out.

Challenge and Discomfort

Have you ever looked back at your life and career accomplishments? Did you find periods of quick progress and then periods of stagnation? If not, think about it now. We all have our ups and downs. We have times when things seem to be working great for us and times when we just can't get a break. Interestingly enough, it is the times when we struggle that give us the push necessary for the periods of growth.

You can start by asking some of these questions to determine whether you truly dare to be uncomfortable or whether you are set in your comfort zone, unwilling to step out. Do I rely on what I have always done, or do I try new approaches to old problems? Do I raise my hand and volunteer for new challenges, or do I just react to those pushed on me? Do I care about my pride and ego enough to worry about being ridiculed for doing something unexpected? Do I wait for others to speak up to formulate and express my thoughts, or am I the one who always expresses their opinion, even if it's not a popular one? Do I ask for what I want or just sit back and wait for others to figure it out and give it to me?

To show up and grow, you need to be able to embrace discomfort and challenges. Do you remember when you learned to ride a bike or drive a car? Do you remember the first time you tried any new activity? It felt awkward. You were unsure of what you were doing, nervous, uncomfortable. However, the results were worth the discomfort. You learned a new skill, and you grew! So how do you embrace being uncomfortable? Do something every day that takes you out of your comfort zone.

Start Before You Think You Are Ready: When you keep waiting to "be ready," chances are it will take ages, and you will either never be ready or you will start too late.

Share Your Thoughts on a Topic even When You Don't Feel Like the Biggest Expert: This will force you to step out of your comfort zone and take a stand.

Learn to Give Feedback and Own It: Giving honest feedback is often a rather uncomfortable thing to do unless you realize that you are doing the other person a service. Your ego or needs should play no role in the feedback you give. That is the reason why I'm not a big fan of anonymous feedback. If I'm asked to provide feedback in anonymous surveys, I always do my best to be as honest as possible, and I sign the feedback so the recipient can put it into context and come for clarification. I'm ready to stand by my words.

Normalize the Discomfort: Be very upfront about the drawbacks of honest communication with those around you. Empathize with others and acknowledge that things can be uncomfortable at times. It is by design so everyone can learn and grow. These little pieces of discomfort benefit everyone and will stop being awkward.

Keep Looking Out for Discomfort and Step In: Seek discomfort in others and help them through it. It doesn't mean taking all the uncomfortable tasks on your shoulders, but it means being there to help so the level of discomfort in others is not paralyzing but is bearable enough so they can cope with it and grow from the experience.

Understand Why You Are Doing It: You probably don't want to be uncomfortable all the time in all aspects of your life, so instead, be strategic about it. Understand what skill you are trying to grow and focus on it while having other areas with enough comfort that you can recharge.

Celebrate Small Wins: It may be challenging to keep going when doing something uncomfortable, so aside from having a reason, you should also learn to keep a positive mindset and celebrate small wins.

I'm a big believer in setting up routines to limit distractions and decision fatigue. So how does that work with the need to get out of your comfort zone and do something new? Very nicely. I'm advocating routine in the mundane daily tasks where you don't need or want to grow. This gives you the energy and mental power to dare to be more uncomfortable in the areas of your life where you want to make a meaningful change and grow.

In *The Introvert Power Advantage*, Samantha Claire talks about the need to get out of one's comfort zone but not overdo it. You need to stay in what she calls your sanity zone.[103] If you get so far out of your comfort zone that you freeze or panic, that is not going to end up well. Recognizing what is out of your comfort zone but is still manageable, still in your sanity zone, is important. You recognize your sanity zone by being a bit uncomfortable, maybe experiencing slight anxiety and a bit of stress, but it is a good type of stress. You are excited to try something that will challenge you, but you don't experience toxic stress and don't have the numbing feeling that you will fail. You are nervous only as much as it forces you to perform at your best. Anything more, and you would get paralyzed and fail.

I would also warn you not to confuse doing more work and having challenging work. If your goal is to feel genuine satisfaction, keep growing, and have a successful career, more work won't get you there. There is always more and more work to come. If it is the same old same old, then it won't move you forward, it will just keep you busy. Being busy is not equivalent to achievement. It is the challenging work that will stretch you and get you closer to where you want to be.

Preparation

If you are an introverted person, you probably already figured out how to deal with stressful situations where you were required to interact with others. This uses one of your strengths, preparation, as we discussed in Chapter 2. For as long as I can remember, I had this life motto: "Fortune favors the well-prepared." Living by it enabled me to achieve many things that I thought I wasn't capable of achieving. Preparation allows me to show up even when I'm uncomfortable, as it is a good way to mitigate any outsized anxiety I may feel. I know I'm prepared and will do my best.

Always try to see what is coming and be prepared for it. If you want to perform at your highest level consistently, that means consistent preparation. If you are good at your job, you can occasionally get away with improvisation, but you can't do it all the time, as you could end up being inconsistent in the way you communicate, in the priorities you set, and in the way others perceive you. Being prepared means that you know what is going on, you have your facts straight, have an opinion, and are consistent and reliable.

For example, imagine a simple meeting at work. If you have your agenda ironed out before the meeting and you have a couple of talking points for each of the topics, you will be able to focus on the crucial issues. You will deliver your message in an organized and impactful manner. And you will be seen as a strong leader who knows what you are doing. With proper preparation, you will *appear* confident, and with enough repetition, you will *become* confident.

As the old saying goes, "If you don't have a plan B, you don't have a plan at all." When it comes to critical or important things in life, you should never rely on one option, one person, or one idea. As you would do with your money, diversify your portfolio to remove or at least limit risks and negative consequences. Most introverts are not big risk-takers in terms of life security. You will always have a preferred option for what to do or how to do it, but there might be other options close enough, so you should never close your mind to them. This applies especially to situations when you don't have things under control, when there are external forces that may impact your efforts. And yes, you should put all your energy and focus on achieving the primary objective. A plan B just gives you a way out if all your efforts fail so you can easily cut your losses and start in a new direction without much fuss.

I love the concept of 6P, believed to originate from the British army at the time of WWII: "Perfect Prior Preparation Prevents Poor Performance." There are different versions, from 5P to 12P, but the 6P is easy to remember and goes nicely with my life motto. To make sure this concept delivers on what it seems to promise, I would add one more P: Perseverance. It may not fit in neatly with the rest, but it is a crucial component. When you decide to do something, then do it and do it consistently. Don't give up until you achieve the goal you set out to achieve. Consistent performance requires discipline and routine.

Discipline and Routine

Discipline is the key to success. And discipline starts with you. Even though it demands control and a level of asceticism, it results in lots of opportunities and freedom. Just consider the discipline of waking up early and not sleeping for twelve hours a day. This gives you a lot of free time that you can use however you want. Or consider the discipline of continuous education and what that gives you in terms of increased potential, efficiency, and, ultimately, time savings. Discipline leads to freedom. It may be a bit counterintuitive, but by making the sacrifice today and sticking with the discipline to learn and achieve, you are creating more options for yourself in the future. You are creating freedom.

For example, when I realized early in my life that I would be spending most of my waking hours in front of a computer screen writing stuff, be it software programming, preparation of presentations, emails, or blogs, I had the discipline to carve out a substantial portion of my time for a couple of months to learn typing. Since then, I have been able to type with all ten fingers without looking at the keyboard. This has made me significantly more efficient and effective ever since. I have the freedom to choose how I want to write. I can write notes in meetings and still pay enough attention to what's being discussed that I can participate—a big advantage for my career. I can write faster than others, and that makes me more productive. Again, an advantage for my career. Someone who didn't have the discipline to learn touch-type doesn't have that freedom, and they have to painstakingly write using two fingers. Similarly, even though I like playing guitar, I never had the discipline to practice regularly and to get to mastery. As a consequence, I don't have the freedom to play the songs I like beautifully. Discipline is incredibly empowering.

Discipline is best built through routine. A good routine will build habits. Habits are good, as they help you to persevere. But habits can also be dangerous when they distract you from your goals. Identifying what distracting habits you have is as important as building new ones. The way to get rid of bad habits is to find the triggers that cause them and then replace your reaction to the trigger with a new habit.

Let's say you get home, and your first steps lead you to the kitchen to grab a beer. But you know that getting that beer will lead to more beers, and you want to get healthier, and you planned to go for a run. Do two things. First, remove the beer from the fridge and your house. You want the environment to work for you, not against you. Second, when you get the trigger of getting home, have an apple waiting for you on the table so that you grab it automatically and don't think about beer and unhealthy snacks at all.

In order for the discipline and routine to show up , consider the good old example of regular physical exercise. You have a goal to become healthy. You have committed to exercising five days a week, so you need to show up. To do that, you build a daily routine of preparing your sporting gear the night before, you get to bed early and at the same time every day to create a consistent sleeping pattern—therefore making it easier to get up in the morning—and you get a trainer as an additional motivator to show up at the gym on time. It will still feel uncomfortable, but preparation, discipline, and routine will help you to show up.

Create Daily Self-Discipline

I used to tell myself this excuse: "I just don't have the willpower to do this, so I might as well just give up." In fact, I still claim that I have exceptionally low willpower. That is why I don't rely on my willpower. I simplify my life and decisions, and I rely on processes and a routine to get things done.

I love to sleep. I hate to get up in the morning, especially in winter. It's so cold and dark. Yet I get up at 5:00 a.m. every single day. I don't need to make that decision every morning. I don't need to rely on my weak willpower. I just get up. That's what I do. That's who I am, even on the weekends. That's my routine I can depend on. Of course, I also know that I need some sleep, so part of the discipline is to get to bed at a reasonable time so my body gets the rest it needs.

Daily self-discipline and willpower are not things you are born with. Self-disciplined people are not genetic freaks. They understand that there are ways to do things without relying on willpower. Years ago, I had a conversation with the head of an engineering team in the USA who was asked to work with teams in Europe. He had a pretty distributed team already, but all were located in the same time zone. He really resisted the idea of working with people who would be removed by eight hours. There would be a limited overlap every day. He reasoned that, with the way the team worked, they would need constant communication to be effective. As it turned out, he was right. The problem was that there were no daily processes, no rules, nothing that would allow for the type of work that wouldn't rely on instant communication. It worked great for the original small team, but it just wouldn't scale for any sort of serious project.

"Process" is not a dirty word. In *The Motivation Myth*, Jeff Haden says, "Dream big. Set a huge goal. Commit to your huge goal. Create a process that ensures you can reach your goal. Then forget about your huge goal and work your process instead."[104] Don't get distracted daily by dreaming about your final goal. It is too big, too far, and not motivating for the day-to-day grind. Focus on doing the right thing instead. And do it consistently. Process and discipline are your friends.

Routine removes choice. And that is a good thing. Having a choice is the archenemy of achieving your objectives. You are wasting your decision-making energy, your willpower, on making decisions you shouldn't be making. There are many non-negotiables in your life. You have to take care of your kids. You have to earn money to do so. You have to eat and sleep. You don't have to go for a run or eat healthily. Unless those things become a routine! Then they are part of your non-negotiables. Once you set up a process and make it a habit, you remove the choice. You don't have an option to do the task. You just do it.

Don't Expect Motivation from Outside

"But what about motivation?" you ask. For centuries and even millennia, the human race achieved incredible feats. We left our humble beginnings behind and became the top species on the planet. We invented, built, and destroyed. How much did our predecessors think and talk about motivation? Motivation is not required to achieve great things. And yet, discussion about motivation has become more and more prominent in the last decades. Why? Because as a civilization, we are becoming weak and comfortable. We don't do things merely because they need to get done. We don't do things to survive. We don't do things to contribute. We are much more self-centered. We do things only if we are motivated to do them. And we expect people around us to somehow motivate us into doing them. Unfortunately, that is not how motivation works. Motivation is not the trigger to get going.

Success breeds motivation. If you tend to blame your humble roots, parents, teachers, or unsupportive environment for your life's misfortunes, you can stop right there. Very rarely are these the real causes for why you are unable to achieve your goals. In reality, they could be advantages for you. Motivation is based on having success. And when you start at the bottom, there is an endless opportunity to have small victories on your way up. As Jeff Haden writes, there is only one recipe for getting motivation: success! Even a small success can fuel your motivation for more achievements in the future. It is a virtuous cycle.

So how do you start? You grit it out. Don't wait to find motivation. Don't wait for someone else to motivate you. Just start doing things and get the first small successes.

The often-overlooked fact is that you actually have these small successes already, and you may not even realize it. Let's say you want to learn a foreign language. You can set a goal that you want to be able to converse in that language at a native level in ten years. However, with this goal, you won't find the motivation. It is an excellent long-term mission, but it doesn't help you with sitting down every single day and learning some new words. The way to go is to break it down into small tasks with clear success criteria that you can celebrate. In your goal to learn the language, you set a task for yourself to learn to count to a hundred in that language this week. Then, on Sunday afternoon, you sit in your chair and count aloud to a hundred. Success! You just showed knowledge you didn't have a week ago. You have a small win. It is motivating. You've gotten better. You are having fun, as you can now respond to others when they ask you something in that new language that requires a number as a response. Have that bit of fun. And while you are at it, you might as well learn twenty different colors the next week. You just got the motivation to take the next step. Motivation is not required to start an activity, but it is useful to keep you on track and help you finish.

Discipline and routine not only help with motivation, but they are also important for building resilience. And resilience is important for showing up, even when faced with adversity.

Resilience

Modern society is weak. We get annoyed with rain and don't want to step into it without an umbrella, as if it could dissolve us. We get annoyed when we don't get regular meals, even though we never get hungry. We are scared of spending a night in a tent, as doing so would be uncomfortable. We get depressed when we don't get promoted fast enough. We get angry when our plane is late. We are weak, and we have a very low tolerance for things going wrong. How can someone like that cope with real challenges? How can someone like that live a satisfactory life and have a successful career?

Think a bit about your behavior. How do you react when you face even a little adversity, and what things are you unwilling or unable to endure? Chances are that, just like the rest of us, you are weak! You complain a lot. You feel like a victim of life's circumstances. You won't take any risks. You don't seek discomfort. You are just somehow comfortable where you are, even though you are, at the same time, not particularly happy to be there. You might be stuck at the job you hate, but you don't have the courage and resilience to do something about it. It feels easier to complain than to get uncomfortable and take a step into the unknown.

As Joe De Sena writes in *The Spartan Way*, humans need challenges to thrive, grow, and accomplish significant feats.[105] The ancient Spartans built one of the first democracies and one of the greatest militaries on a foundation of a rigorous training program and a strict moral code designed to develop endurance. There are things to be learned from them if you want to become stronger, enjoy life to the fullest, and have a good career. The only way to get your career under control and get stronger is to face challenges and even seek them out. You can't hide from the inescapable adversity that life brings. You can't keep looking for shortcuts because they are more comfortable. You need to summon your courage and face life head-on.

Psychological resilience is defined as a positive adaptation or the ability to deal with a crisis, stress, or adverse conditions and bounce back quickly. Resilient people develop capabilities to remain calm during crises and to overcome them without lasting negative consequences.

Learn to Be Enthusiastic: Apathy is energy-draining. It is not caring. It is an indifferent and passive approach to life. Enthusiasm is a proactive way to deal with life's challenges. It keeps you energized and optimistic. And both are easy to spread. If you are around positive and enthusiastic people, you will feel yourself get more energy. If you are around downers who show apathy and negativity, you may want to kill yourself within a day. Keep the company of people who will provide fuel so you can drive to your goals. How do you learn positivity and enthusiasm? Learn to say yes to new things and new challenges. Learn to smile a lot, even without a strong reason, as just the act of moving your facial muscles to smile will have the side effect of making you feel better. Learn to focus on the bright side of life. We get more of the things we focus on. That's how our brains work. If you focus on good things, that will cause you to see them all around you. It will create a virtuous cycle of being more positive and optimistic and seeing more of the good around you. Life will feel good.

Stop Lying to Yourself: In 1957, Leon Festinger of Stanford University came up with a theory of cognitive dissonance.[106] He claimed that we often interpret what we believe we know and what we do to fit with what we think about ourselves and the world around us. This is a way our brains make us comfortable and protect us from getting too depressed. It is the rationalization we use every day to commit minor sins, even though we know we are doing something we shouldn't. "But why shouldn't I do it when everyone does it?" "One cigarette a day won't kill me." "I want to be healthy, and I just read an article that a glass of beer provides lots of vitamins, so it is healthy to drink beer, and I will ignore any research that says that alcohol is not healthy."

Start with Building Self-Control: Do you want to get physically stronger? You need to go to the gym and exercise your muscles regularly. Do you want to get more self-control and discipline? You have to exercise it periodically by resisting temptation and by following through on your commitments. Just through the act of getting out of bed and into the rain for your daily run, you make it more likely that you will do the same tomorrow and the day after. By delaying the gratification of a cushiony bed and getting uncomfortable, you eventually achieve your goal of being healthy and able to run long distances, which will bring much more satisfaction, as that is something you want. As a side effect, you got more resilient and more likely to achieve other things in your life as well. You built your self-control and discipline muscles. The ability to delay gratification is a potent tool. It leads to more patience, more perseverance, more willingness to do what others don't, and a substantial competitive advantage in life.

To Get Genuinely Resilient, Suffer on Purpose: Get out of your comfort zone and suffer a bit now and then. Changing your frame of reference is a powerful way to get more grounded and satisfied with your life. Even though life itself doesn't change at all, it is all in your head. Be grateful.

Go Beyond Your Limits to Experience Pain and Grow: In *Endure*, Alex Hutchinson talks about the limits of human performance. He describes endurance as "the struggle to continue against a mounting desire to stop." This definition captures two aspects of reaching your limits: the physical and the psychological.[107] How do you condition yourself to endure more than you think is possible? At the point of perceived limits, you can try the techniques Hutchinson describes with 5Rs: Recognize, Refuse, Relax, Reframe, and Resume. Recognize you reached your limit, Refuse to accept it, Relax your mind and body, Reframe how you feel and what you think, and Resume the activity. Keep going beyond what you felt was possible for you to do. By pushing yourself beyond your psychological boundaries, you will move these boundaries for the future. You will also train your physical side to get stronger and endure more the next time. As Jesse Itzler quotes in *Living with a SEAL*, "I don't stop when I'm tired. I stop when I'm done."[108]

Many other things impact our satisfaction with life and career. Shedding the weakness brought up by modern society and getting stronger and more resilient is just one step, but it is an important one. Resilient people don't complain about their life circumstances, but they go and change them. Resilient people don't panic easily and are not derailed by suffering. They endure, embrace the pain, and grow stronger. Modern psychologists may disagree and say that people who emerge from catastrophic events are not strong because of them, but they were strong to start with. I would still finish with a quote by German philosopher

Friedrich Nietzsche, "That which does not kill us makes us stronger." Don't shy away from difficult challenges and a bit of suffering. Go out and have your daily run in the heavy rain.

Delayed Gratification

Showing up and doing something uncomfortable means delaying the gratification of doing something pleasant. Do you want to have a good career? Well, instead of playing a video game, you need to get out of your house and show up at work. The pleasure of playing the game needs to wait.

The ability to delay gratification is the willingness to sacrifice pleasure for future opportunities and growth. If you are constantly getting distracted by short-term enjoyment, you won't achieve anything significant. Being able to say no to social networks, TV, unhealthy food, or anything that provides you with short-term happiness but tramples all over your long-term goal will help you get your priorities straight. People who can delay gratification are more likely to persevere and more likely to overcome fear and obstacles. They are grittier.

Delaying gratification is about separating your actual needs from your wants. You want a new fancy car, but do you really need it? You want to go to an expensive restaurant, but again, do you need to go? There are very few things in life you really need. Most of what you want are optional things and activities that you want because of the society around you. You hear your friends boasting about what they just bought, and you want those things too. You want to belong to the group, and you feel you need to conform. You want your luxuries.

Just a thought: What about belonging to a group that will be more aligned with your true needs? Then the wants and needs are the same, and they are all forcing you in the same direction to achieve your goals.

But living a life of constant sacrifice without any rewards is no fun either. Fulfilling your goals may take many years. You don't want to wait that long for the satisfaction, but you also don't want to rely on getting your enjoyment from distractions. Learn to find happiness and joy in the daily discipline, in the small wins along the way, in the actual journey. Every time you get a bit better, a bit closer to your goal, is an excellent time to feel good about your achievements.

Finding and enjoying the small daily wins that are getting you closer to your goal is a potent motivator. Let's say you want to live a healthier life and exercise more. You decide to go to the gym every morning to work out. Just the fact that you are keeping a streak and showing up every day is a small win to celebrate. You have said you will do it, and indeed you are doing what you said. Win. You have a particularly good workout today. Win. You resist the temptation to get a doughnut for breakfast and instead eat something healthier. Win. You help an old person cross a busy street. Win.

There are so many things, both inside and outside of work, every single day, that you can feel good about. It is just about opening your mind to the possibilities, being in the moment, and observing the life around you. The inability to delay gratification and unwillingness to make sacrifices can derail your efforts to achieve what truly matters to you.

Be Willing to Sacrifice

Showing up also means being willing to make sacrifices. Risk-aversion and unwillingness to sacrifice are the most common reasons people don't act on their dreams. This is especially true for introverts, as we often rely too much on our strength of prudence. You dream of a better life, starting a company, moving to a remote island, but that's it. You don't turn your dreams into actions. Why? Because it is difficult to get out of the status quo and get moving. It is scary to get out of your comfort zone and do something new. And it would require sacrifices you are not willing to make.

So I ask again, why are you not willing to make the necessary changes and sacrifices? You hear the answer in almost every interview with a winning team after a match in any collective sports. "The opponent was good, and it was a great game. Why did we win? I guess we just wanted it more." The winning team feels they were willing to make sacrifices and give it everything they've got, and that is why they won.

When you think about your dream, are you willing to give it all you've got? Probably not. Chances are, the dream is not yours. You saw some pictures of someone living on a remote tropical island, so you started dreaming about how great it must be. You started comparing your life with the lives of others. So you are saying that your dream is to live on a tropical island, but in reality, deep down, it's not. You want to be close to your family. You love your job and couldn't live without it, and you like the temperate climate of your hometown. Your unwillingness to sacrifice in this situation stems from your priorities. In reality, you don't sacrifice and change your life because your so-called dream is not what you want. Whether it is conscious or unconscious, you have different priorities.

The second reason people are unwilling to sacrifice is rooted in the belief that you deserve more than others do. Your sense of entitlement leads you to a very indulgent life when you consume as much as you can simply because it is your right and you can. You buy a big house or an expensive car, go to expensive restaurants or splurge on lavish vacations. You buy stuff and consume instead of creating stuff and producing. This especially permeates the so-called developed countries or consumer societies. We are so entitled to what we have that we rarely think about whether we should consume so much or whether we even deserve it. We are entitled, and we are miserable.

Once you get used to the big house and expensive car, it is tough to give it up. And any meaningful change in your life will most likely require that you adjust the way you live and how you approach the world around you. Comfort and entitlement lead to general weakness and low resilience. The more you rely on others, the technology, and the status quo, the more resistant you are to any change. You become reliant and weak. Your resilience in the face of change and disruption gets lower and lower. You freak out even when it rains outside or when the shop runs out of your favorite coffee. These things can completely destroy your day.

This is also the reason why it is so difficult to completely change careers later in life. You have already built a certain level of success in a particular field, and even if you don't enjoy it anymore, the thought of sacrificing it all and starting from scratch somewhere else is preventing you from taking the next step and embarking on a new career.

How can someone like this ever hope to achieve any meaningful change and success if they get disturbed by rain? The total lack of resilience, both mental and physical, is something that is going to hold you back big time.

The way out is simple, but not necessarily easy. Get your priorities straight, and just start doing whatever it takes. Understand what you want and build your whole life around that. Adopt the "that's what I do" mindset. You may hate rain, but if you said to yourself that you would run every day for half an hour, then whatever the weather, you go out and run because you tell yourself, "That's what I do." This will eventually become, "That's who I am." And who you are is a more resilient person, willing to get really uncomfortable to achieve your goals.

Learn to enjoy suffering. The only way you can truly enjoy success and be proud of your accomplishments is to deal with adversity. If everything goes too easily and things are handed to you on a silver platter, you won't enjoy them as much as when you have to work hard for them and suffer. It is an entirely different feeling when you can say that you have run every single day of the last year, even in rain, storm, or snow. You will get a true sense of accomplishment. You were willing to make the sacrifices needed to reach your goal. You can be proud of what you achieved.

Summary and Key Takeaways

Nothing substantial can be achieved without showing up and doing the actual work. If you want to grow and have a successful career, you need to get comfortable being uncomfortable. I'm not advocating for paralyzing stress, but slight anxiety is a sign that you are doing something new, something you couldn't do yesterday, and therefore growing. This will help you use your strength of preparation and rely on discipline and routine. It will help you to build resilience in the face of adversity, and that will, in turn, help you to show up even when things get tough. It is at these times when you learn the most and can earn the biggest accolades, which will move your career forward. To show up, learn to delay gratification and be willing to sacrifice things that are no longer important for your future career.

- Embrace discomfort to accelerate your growth.
- Use your introvert's superpower of preparation to summon the courage to get out of your comfort zone.
- Discipline demands control and sacrifice, but it leads to opportunities and freedom.
- Routine will help you overcome discomfort and will lead to healthy habits.
- Don't rely on willpower. Create an environment and daily discipline that will nudge you to do the right thing, regardless of whether you have the willpower or not.
- Don't expect motivation from the outside. Successes, even small ones, breed motivation.
- Delay gratification by separating your needs from your wants.
- Get your priorities straight and sacrifice the unimportant for the critical.

Questions and Next Steps

- Ask these questions to determine whether you embrace discomfort and dare to do things that will help you grow and become successful. Do I rely on what I have always done, or do I try new approaches to old problems? Do I raise my hand and volunteer for new challenges, or do I react to those pushed on me? Do I care about my pride and ego enough to worry about being ridiculed for doing something unexpected? Do I wait for others to speak up to formulate and express my thoughts, or am I the one who always expresses their opinion, even if it's not a popular one? Do I ask for what I want or just sit back and wait for others to figure it out and give it to me? If the answers are mostly negative, make a focused effort to become a bit uncomfortable every single day. You will normalize the discomfort, and it will help you grow.

- What is the most important goal you have at work? What is the most important thing you need to learn to move your career forward? Sit down and write a routine that will help you get there. Don't rely on your willpower. Consider what steps you need to take and how you can make them as automatic as possible. Consider what you need to change in your environment to help you keep the routine. Consider what triggers can destroy your routine and try to find a way to eliminate them.

Work Hard

"I deliver results. I'm passionate about what I do.
I don't give up easily. I do my best every single day."

If you rely only on your talent, chances are you won't get too far. Even the most talented person can't utilize their talent to the full extent without the right attitude and focus. Over the years, I have worked with many gifted people who, from childhood, sailed through their lives with ease because of their inborn talent and IQ. They were smart, they were talented, they were satisfied with what they had, and they became lazy. Nothing wrong with that if they were also happy with their lives. But often, they were not. They had the raw potential and didn't realize that they could be so much more with a bit of effort and the right attitude.

Effort is the way great people distinguish themselves from merely good ones. When someone puts more focused effort into improving themselves or building something, more often than not the results are way above their initial expectations. It is the internal drive and sometimes even single-minded dedication that distinguishes the best from the rest. No distractions, no workarounds, just pure hard work on the right things can help even the underdog win over others who are more talented but complacent.

You can't have a successful career if you can't get things done. Working hard and smart will help you to be productive. Having grit and passion will put you on the right track and keep you motivated. This eventually turns into mastery when you are in the right place in the Employee Emotional Life Cycle at the company and in your Quiet Success Sweet Spot. When you do what you love and you are good at it, it is easier to achieve flow, a state where you lose yourself in work and achieve supreme efficiency and effectiveness while enjoying every minute. Nothing worthwhile is ever truly easy. Stop taking shortcuts and learn that hard work is essential for both career success and life satisfaction.

Working Smarter and Harder

I hate the ever-present motto of "work smarter, not harder." Sure, work smarter, why not? Finding more effective and efficient ways to get things done is always helpful. But don't stop working harder. It is only up to you to figure out whether it is worth it, but if you are not willing to put in the effort, don't complain about your perceived misfortunes.

Remember my exercise example in Chapter 6? I find the exercise example illustrative of several principles of the Quiet Success Concept. Let's say you decide to improve your physical and mental health by running. You go for a run a couple of times a week. It is hard. You don't like it much from the beginning, but after a couple of weeks, you see that you are improving. You can run longer distances, and you feel better after the run. Now the motivation kicks in. You are starting to like it. You are getting better, and you are increasing the effort to reap even more benefits. You start talking about it with other people. You join some mass runs. Running is becoming your lifestyle. You are a runner now. It is not what you do, it is who you are. The way you are talking about running has changed from "I have to go for a run" through "I want to go for a run" to "I'm a runner, that's what I do." No shortcuts. No excuses.

Becoming someone new and something more feels great precisely because of the effort and the pain you experienced to get there. You earned it. The same applies to your job. If you work hard, you build expertise. Others see you as a go-to person for a particular topic or task. Then you get promoted to the role you are doing already, you feel satisfied, and you have the confidence that you can do the job well. If you use a shortcut and get promoted to the role because you are your boss's favorite pet, you may feel the rush of joy that comes with a bigger paycheck, but it will quickly evaporate. You didn't need to work for it. There was no pain. Others are resentful of you. You feel like a fraud. You didn't earn it. You don't enjoy it. It is just an endless pit of stress and misery. You don't feel like you achieved anything, and you either grow a thick skin or leave.

As Adam Grant mentions in *Originals*, people throughout history who are currently praised for their originality and who had a lasting impact had only a couple of masterpieces or ideas that are remembered today. They produced a huge amount of work, and most of it has been forgotten. Even Albert Einstein wrote several hundred publications and is now remembered mostly for his general and special theory of relativity.[109]

The Pareto rule of 80/20 or its equivalents can be applied in numerous human endeavors. 80 percent of results are achieved by 20 percent of efforts. As Jordan B. Peterson points out, consider classical music. You will discover that a vast majority of modern orchestras play music written by a small number of composers, like

Bach, Beethoven, Mozart, or Tchaikovsky. And even with them, the orchestras play only a tiny portion of what these giants of classical music composed.[110] Brilliance requires an extraordinary amount of effort, and the vast majority of what you do will never be considered a big success. But without the effort, you will never produce that one thing that would make a difference.

Look at some of the successful companies of the twenty-first century that seemed to pop up overnight to great success. A great example might be a small company called Rovio, which became an overnight sensation with its mobile phone game Angry Birds. Did you know that it was their fifty-second game? Before they developed this hit, they built fifty-one games that few people ever heard of. The lesson learned is that if you want to be seen as successful and leave a dent in history, you have to produce a lot of work. The notion that there is an inverse relationship between quality and quantity is false. If we talk about creativity and idea generation, the more there is, the better. Quantity eventually leads to quality.

Get Things Done

There is no point in being great at anything if you can't turn it into tangible results. Getting things done is the essential measure of your ability to succeed. To get things done, you need knowledge and skills in your given field. And you need the will, the drive, to go through ups and downs and not quit until the finish line.

Knowledge is what you get by listening to your teacher or by observing what others do. Having knowledge is the first step in achieving anything. You need to know what to do. But that is far from enough to be successful. As an engineering leader, I interviewed countless software developers who were able to answer any theoretical question brilliantly. They knew their particular domains inside and out. And I still didn't hire them. Why? Because their knowledge was very academic, and when asked to produce a piece of code, they struggled to turn the knowledge into a product. They lacked the skill.

Skill is the second step. Once you know what to do, you need to put in the effort and turn it into a skill. That is not something you can learn just by observing others. You need to practice. Knowledge and practice will create skill. Skill will transfer what to do into how to do it. Curiously enough, even skill is not enough to be successful. Once you build the ability, you are still not done. You have to expend even more effort to produce results that matter.

The last step is to keep going and follow through until you reach your desired results. Too often, people give up too early, get distracted, lose focus, or lose interest, and things don't get done. What's the point of all the effort you put into an activity if you don't reach the goal? You may say to yourself that at least you tried, but the hard truth is that you didn't try enough. And because of that, no one benefits from your efforts. Your effort was meaningless. Following through and getting things done is the ultimate satisfaction generator. If you achieve what you said you would achieve because of the hard work you put into it, you will feel great. You will feel that what you do matters, that your life has a meaning.

If you keep failing to reach your goals, you will become more and more dissatisfied with your life. You may even start blaming others, talking about the lack of vision by the company, or doing work that has no meaning. The reality is that the only reason your work doesn't have meaning is that you didn't finish what you started.

Luckily for you, introverts can rely on their strength of perseverance. We tend to stick with things longer and don't give up too quickly. Even with that in mind, it is still important to keep following through on any commitments (Chapter 11: Act With Integrity) and following up with others to make sure things get done even when others get involved (Chapter 10: Own Everything).

Learn to Follow Through and Follow Up

Successful people follow through on everything they commit to. They finish what they start. They don't give up easily. Once they commit, they persevere and do whatever it takes to complete the task they've committed to. It is not only a question of getting things done, but it is also a question of personal pride. That's what they do. That's who they are.

They also follow up regularly on what is essential. They follow up on feedback. They make sure to reach out regularly to check on the progress others are making that may impact them. They keep returning to the basics and make sure things are progressing as planned. "Follow up, follow up, follow up" is a mantra of a good project manager, and the same is true for the successful person who wants to reach their goals.

Not following through is the most common reason people don't achieve their goals. You have the best intentions at heart, you are full of enthusiasm, and you jump right into the action and start working toward what you want. But things take time. It becomes rather tiresome. The excitement evaporates. What sounded like a cool new initiative becomes a boring routine. You still want to achieve the goal, but there are also other things coming up. And they look more exciting. So you slow down the original initiative to make room for some of the new stuff. You work very hard. But you stopped working on the item you set out to accomplish in the first place. As time progresses, you even start questioning whether you wanted to finish it in the first place. You spend less and less effort on it, and, finally, you stop. By not following through with your actions to reach the goal, you are robbing yourself of the satisfaction of finishing things up. You work hard, but you don't have a good feeling that what you do makes sense. You never really finish anything worth being proud of. You don't have the focus, grit, and willingness to finish what you started. And you pay the price by being unhappy.

The twin sibling of not following through is not following up. It manifests with a lack of focus on details and the desire to move on to the next thing once the previous task is done. You finish your task and feel that that means things are done. But are they? Let's say you work in the IT department at the helpdesk. Your role is to help other people in the company with their IT-related problems. One of the employees comes to you with a simple request. They forgot their computer password and ask you to reset it. So you click a couple of buttons and tell the person that the problem is solved and their password is set to a default one. Job well done. Or is it? In fact, you don't know. You may have reset the password, but the real problem was that the person wasn't able to log in to their computer. Can they now? You haven't checked. You haven't followed up. In reality, your work is only done when the person with the problem verifies that the problem is solved. Just think about how often you end up on the receiving end of people not following up to make sure that your problems are solved. You need to bring the problems up to them again, and you get frustrated by the lack of care. Make sure you don't fall into this category. Do follow up.

Introverts tend to be good at perseverance and focus, but we may struggle with asking for help. But for us to be truly successful, we need to learn to follow through on long-term commitments and follow up regularly on things we consider important.

Stop Taking Shortcuts

If you want to accomplish something significant, something that very few people achieve, you need to behave differently than those people. If you're going to run a marathon, build a successful business, or rise to the top of your organization, you need to give your goal the priority, the focus, and the effort it deserves. You need to be willing to make sacrifices that others are not willing to make. If your priority is to rise quickly in the ranks of your organization, you can't expect to have the same lifestyle as others. You need to outwork the others, and that will cost you effort. Working hard and making sacrifices are parts of success. The good news is that it doesn't need to feel that way. It doesn't need to feel that you are making sacrifices. The hard work doesn't need to feel like hard work. You can find some pleasure in it.

Finding shortcuts and workarounds to hard work can sometimes work for simple tasks, but it won't work when you need to acquire skills that are difficult to master. It also has a somewhat adverse effect. Since you are not getting the skills and experience, you are not increasing your confidence in your abilities. You will just feel lucky that you found a workaround this time and hope for the same in the future, instead of working hard to get the skill and, with it, the competence and confidence that you can repeat the same the next time without a problem if the need arises in the future.

I have to repeat this: "Work smarter, not harder" is such a cliché. And it is wrong. Yes, you should try to find ways to work smarter, but there is no way around working hard. And this brings us to grit and passion.

Grit and Passion

Many successful people are not particularly talented. It is often those who struggle but keep going who reach success. Gifted children often learn that they don't need to try particularly hard to do well in school, so they never build the habit of working hard and not giving up. They rely on their talent. However, once the talent runs out, they may often face the reality of not being good enough and not having the perseverance to get better. With the right support, kids who struggle are more likely to become more resistant and more willing to put in the effort to get better. They learn that nothing in life is free and that they have to work hard to be successful. They develop grit. This is a trait that is very handy later on in life. When their talent runs out, they just double down and get over the bumps by working hard and persevering.

Most of us are biased toward talented people. Even though we may not admit it out loud, we subconsciously believe that people who are "naturals" at something are somehow superior to those who had to work hard to accomplish the same. We emphasize and focus on talent. That means we tend to forget all the other traits and aspects of becoming successful. Daniel F. Chambliss, who completed a study of competitive swimmers, postulates that exceptional performance is a confluence of many small skills and activities that have been drilled into habits.[111] You don't need to be exceptionally talented to perform at an exceptional level. You just need to do the right small things correctly, consistently, and with perseverance to produce excellence. Effort and not talent is what leads to excellence. In *Grit*, Angela Duckworth has this to say about talent: "Talent is how quickly your skills improve when you invest effort. Achievement is what happens when you take your acquired skills and use them."[112]

Success involves not only getting things done but getting them done even in the face of adversity. Your strength of perseverance will help you to get there, but you may give up when running into too many obstacles. That can be solved with grit. You can look at grit as perseverance on steroids. Duckworth defines grit as passion and perseverance for very long-term goals. She claims that grit consists of several ingredients: passion, practice, purpose, and hope. It is interest in an activity, willingness to practice consistently, seeing a purpose in the endeavor, and having hope and optimism that you can succeed. All these things can be learned and developed. You can become more gritty if you want to.

To develop a genuine interest in something, you need to dig into details. By doing that, you develop appreciation even for things that, at first glance, look boring and uninteresting. You practice, you see the purpose, and you become passionate about it. Real experts can get excited about the smallest of details of their jobs, something that an outsider would never give a second thought to.

Gritty people are overwhelmingly optimistic. Optimism gives hope. Or, the other way around, optimists are more likely to be gritty and to persevere than pessimists. Why? Even when faced with the same setbacks, optimists will look for ideas for how to explain the setbacks as temporary or rare events, as something that happened but won't last and can be worked around or overcome. Pessimists often see the setbacks as something permanent, something that will always be there to hold them back. They tend to overreact to failures. Optimists would take failures in stride, analyze them, learn from them, and move on with a firm belief that nothing can hold them back. It is having hope in a better future, hope in the goodness of other people, and hope in their ability to improve and do better next time that drives the success of gritty individuals.

Duckworth gives a great example of how we unlearn perseverance and grittiness as we grow. Consider toddlers who are trying to learn to walk. You will see them try and try again and make one failed attempt after another. They don't have the skill to stand up and walk yet, but they keep trying. And it doesn't look like they see it as torture. It is something they see other people do, something they want to do themselves, so they persevere. They don't care whether others are laughing at their failed attempts. This changes as the children get older and start feeling embarrassed when they fail at things. The less supportive the environment they grow up in, the more others around them point out all their faults, the less likely they are to keep trying. Failure is not an option, as it is too embarrassing. So they decide it is better not try at all.

When I was a kid, I was led to believe that hard work is important. First work, then play. This was something that I took with me throughout life. You may be smarter than me. You may be more talented than me. You may be better connected or have more resources. But I will outwork you. How hard I work is the one thing that is entirely under my control. That is the one thing that I know that, if I invest in it, I will get results. If I don't work hard enough and, as a result, don't achieve the desired results, I only have myself to blame. And if I do achieve the results after putting in the effort, I feel great satisfaction that I accomplished something hard, something that didn't come easily to me.

Don't Give Up Too Early or Too Late

Successful people don't quit easily. It is easy to justify stopping before we reach a successful outcome. You may say that you did your best, you reached your limits, you have done all you could. The reality is often different. Yes, you are tired. Yes, you encountered some problems. Yes, you are even better than you were yesterday. And yes, you just created a self-imposed limit to what you can achieve. The chances are that you have run into a mental barrier rather than a physical one. If you just grit it out, if you persevere, you can reach your goal. Too often, we succumb to our weak minds that are looking for comfort. Very rarely do we reach our absolute limits.

I love the quote by Henry Ford, "Whether you think you can or you think you can't . . . you're right." It summarizes what self-imposed limits are all about. If you accept defeat even before you start, then you will get defeated.

Perseverance is a significant competitive advantage. Being able to grit it out and overcome any obstacle is what leads to success. I mean, as long as you are on the right obstacle course. Unfortunately, as with anything else, you can take even perseverance and grit too far.

"Winners never quit" is a dangerous misunderstanding of how success works. Winners quit all the time. They don't quit because something is hard, they quit when they realize that they are doing something not worth their time. They quit when they recognize something simply won't work. They quit to give themselves the option to succeed at something different.

It is the losers who often don't quit, even when it is apparent that what they are doing doesn't work. They succumb to the sunk cost fallacy and will keep doing what they know won't lead to good outcomes. They stick with a job they hate. They find excuses why they can't leave because they already invested a lot of time in their current endeavor.

Life happens. It changes you. Not being willing to admit that your skills, interests, and opportunities evolved and may be very different from what you are doing today is a sign of someone too afraid of change. Whether you want it or not, change happens.

This is an important realization. It means that all the things you have learned about yourself in Chapter 3 and even your Quiet Success Sweet Spot (Chapter 5) will evolve over time. You need to regularly check whether you are still the person you were a year or two ago or whether your needs, desires, and skills changed you enough that you need to also adjust what you do.

Ask for Help

Working hard is important, but no one can become truly successful on their own. For many introverts, asking for help feels like a failure. It is often even terrifying. Yet this unwillingness or inability to ask for help is often what stands between us and success. The modern world is complex, and walking through life on your own will not lead to a satisfying and fulfilling life. No one can do it on their own. We all need help now and then, and help rarely arrives on its own. You have to ask. In *All You Have to Do Is Ask*, Wayne Baker notes that studies have shown 90 percent of help in a workplace is only provided after someone requests it. If you don't ask, others may not know that you need help.[113]

Baker identified several reasons why people don't ask for help. It starts with underestimating the willingness of others to help us. Baker points to an experiment run by psychologists at Columbia University. They asked participants to approach complete strangers and ask, "Can I use your cell phone to make a call?" No emergency, no further explanation. Just this simple question. On average, it took only two tries to get a stranger to lend them a phone.

Often, we worry that by asking, we are creating an obligation. Sometimes, the unsaid, "If you do this for me, I will do something for you in the future" is certainly there. However, not always. There are two typical approaches to requesting help: autonomy-oriented help-seeking, or asking to learn how to fix a problem, and dependency-oriented help-seeking, or asking a helper to correct the problem. Dependency-oriented help-seekers expect that the other party does the work. They are not motivated by the desire to learn and grow but by the need to get the job done and move on. On the other hand, autonomy-oriented help-seekers want to get the work done and learn how to do it to be better equipped in the future. Autonomous help-seeking doesn't have the social costs associated with it that the dependent approach might. If I ask you for help and you see that I'm engaged and trying to do my best to solve the problem, you will give your support freely and enthusiastically. If you know that I let you do all the work, that I'm not interested in seeing how it is done, and that I will ask for the same help again in the future, you start keeping a score and will expect something in return eventually.[114] Help-seeking may imply weakness when help seekers are low-status individuals; it may imply strength when they are high-status individuals. However, when low-status persons seek autonomy-oriented help they are not seen as chronically dependent and are instead seen more positively.[115] Asking for autonomy-oriented help is preferable anyway. It leads to more confidence and self-respect than just getting the help that will keep us dependent on someone else—at least, when this help comes from someone we see as having greater expertise or higher status.[116]

Often, when we meet new people or join a new team, we feel we haven't earned the right to ask for help. We feel like we need to prove ourselves and show we can contribute before we can bother others to help us. We know that everyone is busy, and we don't want to add to their workloads. We don't want to be seen as selfish. There certainly are times when asking for help would be insensitive, but those times happen less often than you may think. Most of the time, asking for help shows the other person that we value their expertise. Asking for their help validates them. Everyone wants to feel useful and validated.

Learn to ask for help. Things you need are often more available than you may think. People are more ready to offer help when asked. Whether it is physical help, mentorship, information, advice, funds, referrals, or just a compassionate ear to talk to, don't hesitate to ask.

Don't rely only on your inner circle of friends and family. Reach out to your weaker ties in your professional network and acquaintances you may not know that well. In the internet age, you have various public forums to ask questions, so use them. You even have marketplaces for people with specialized knowledge where you may need to pay a fee for the help. However, it can still be the right thing to do if it unblocks you or helps you solve your problem efficiently and with better quality than you would.

Asking for help starts a virtuous cycle of asking and giving. Once you ask others, people are more comfortable with asking in return. You achieve true collaboration when people freely ask and freely provide help to others. There is evidence that once someone does you a favor, they are more likely to do it again in the future. They already invested in you, they see you as someone worth their investment, and thus they are less reluctant to keep investing. By helping you, they like you more.[117] It's called the Ben Franklin effect, inspired by Benjamin Franklin's quote: "He that has once done you a kindness will be more ready to do you another than he whom you yourself have obliged."[118] This works even when someone rejects your request. If that happens, they are more likely to respond positively if you make a second request, as they feel bad about refusing the first one. When you get into the cycle of giving and asking, others will get invested in your success, and the world will conspire to help you succeed.

Mastery

We talked about mastery in Chapter 3 as a way to build a passion for a particular activity. Passion is motivating. And, as mentioned in the previous section, paired with perseverance, passion leads to grit, and that leads to getting things done. It all comes nicely together. But how do you achieve mastery?

In 1993, Swedish psychologist Anders Ericsson published a paper called "The Role of Deliberate Practice in the Acquisition of Expert Performance." Ericsson claims that you don't need inborn talent to master performance. It is not DNA that decides whether you will be a master pianist, chess player, or manager, or just a mediocre one. It is practice that makes masters. And not just any sort of practice. You won't become great at something just by doing the same things over and over for years and years, repeating the same mistakes.

This is often referred to as the 10,000-hour rule, indicating that it takes many hours of practice to reach mastery. We can question the actual number, but it is hard not to consider that the more effort you give something, the better you become at it, as long as you give it the right type of effort. Ericsson coined the term "deliberate practice" to describe what sort of practice you need to do to become truly great at any activity. Deliberate practice requires three things: total focus on what you are trying to improve, targeted feedback so you can correct what you are doing wrong, and an ever-increasing challenge.

Let's say you decide to learn to play the guitar. You can certainly buy a book or a CD, find some courses on the internet, and sit down every Saturday for an hour to practice. You are going to learn a bit, but you will plateau fast. You will get frustrated with the lack of progress. You get distracted and just abandon the activity. Or you can take it seriously and get a guitar teacher to meet with you three times a week. The role of the teacher is to show you how to do things properly, to observe you and provide real-time feedback on how to hold the guitar properly, how to position your fingers. The teacher will point out every time you are cutting corners and will be there as an accountability buddy to make sure you practice as promised. Every week you will get a more difficult piece to play. The rate of improvement will be significantly bigger than if you just tried to play on your own.

Deliberate practice is both about quantity as well as quality. You can't become an expert without hard work. The time and effort you put into the activity are crucial. You can't avoid it. What is worse, deliberate practice is, by definition, not particularly enjoyable. It is not motivational. Just think about it. Even if you are reasonably good at something, you will be constantly asked to expand your comfort zone and pushed into something you can't do yet. Not just that, but there will be someone who keeps pointing out the things that you do wrong and how you can improve. Not much fun at all! That is why so few people become really great, master-level great, at anything. It is not that there are so few people born with these talents. It is that very few people are willing to stick with the hardship of deliberate practice. When we get to a decent level, most of us decide that we are good enough and stop trying. We are comfortable staying at a mediocre level. We no longer have the drive to go further, unless there is a compelling reason ingrained deep down in our subconscious that tells us we have to. That is why many people don't practice a healthy lifestyle until a major health issue resets their priorities. On a logical level, we know what a healthy lifestyle looks like. We understand the benefits. We understand the adverse effects of an unhealthy diet and a sedentary lifestyle. It is not a lack of knowledge or understanding that prevents us from changing our lifestyle. It is the expected effort, sacrifice, and "no fun" aspect that holds us back.

Ericsson says this about motivation to practice: "Engagement in deliberate practice is not inherently motivating. Performers consider it instrumental in achieving further improvements in performance (the motivational constraint). The lack of inherent reward or enjoyment in practice as distinct from the enjoyment of the result (improvement) is consistent with the fact that individuals in a domain rarely initiate practice spontaneously."[119]

Deliberate practice is a potent tool for acquiring new skills. It requires the right mindset, perseverance, listening to feedback, and internal drive to become good at the activity. Luckily for you, many introverts have the right attitude, and introverts' strengths like focus, perseverance, and attentiveness give you a decent edge. The good news is also that you can learn pretty much anything. You can become great at any skill you need to advance your career. It is a question of how long you will persevere that will determine the limits of greatness you can achieve. Keep in mind that we are not talking about hours or weeks. We are talking at a minimum about months, but most likely about years, to become truly great at anything. So think hard before you commit to improving a skill. It may be a lifetime journey.

Just don't get locked into a single-minded approach to building your expertise. Single-mindedness may help you to become good at your job, but it may cost you your career. Understand the requirements and the skills, and work hard to master them. Mastery is good, but it also has a dark side. Mastery of your current job is what may keep you in it for longer than is healthy. Being an expert in something makes you indispensable for that particular role. You get typecast. This is not a path toward promotion. Go back to the Employee Emotional Life Cycle in Chapter 4 and consider whether you are getting into the coasting stage, where you are so good at your job that you are being held in place because the company believes they can't afford to let you do anything else.

Of course, give it your best and do your job well, but don't let the quest for mastery consume you completely. Expertise is expected, but it is not enough. Put aside enough time to build the relationships and skills required to get to the next level.

Flow

Pursuit of mastery has the obvious benefit of helping you acquire a skill to get things done, but it also has a secondary benefit: giving you the ability to enjoy what you are doing. You can't really say you have a successful career unless you find some satisfaction in your actual work. In his book *Flow*, Mihaly Csikszentmihalyi talks about the psychology of happiness.[120] He suggests that one of the first things you need to do on the road toward overcoming anxieties and stresses and living a fulfilling and successful life and is to get independent from the social environment. Stop responding exclusively in terms of rewards and punishments. This means you need to find rewards inside yourself. Develop the ability to find enjoyment and meaning in life, regardless of external circumstances. Understand and learn to manage your desires. Seeking pleasure is nature's way of preserving the species. Nature doesn't care about your personal advantage. In reality, succumbing to your desires often goes against the best interests of an individual. Introverts are naturally good at this. Because of the amount of time we spend in our heads, we are pretty good at finding satisfaction with life and work within ourselves.

There are limits to our consciousness, though. We are unable to truly parallelize thoughts that use the same areas of the brain. The brain works in a serial manner. You need to finish one thought before you can start another. That's where flow comes in. Flow is when you focus on one task and remove all distractions. While in the flow, you can't feel sad or happy. These feelings can pop up only after you get out of the flow and your brain starts task-switching again. As Csikszentmihalyi writes, the human brain can process about 126 bits of information per second. Understanding what another person is saying takes about 40 bits of information per second. These numbers are only approximations, but this means you can, in theory, listen to three people and try to process what they're saying. Still, this would totally overwhelm you, and you wouldn't even be able to follow their gestures or facial expressions. You couldn't have the inside monologue to analyze the information you are receiving. Because of this limit in information processing power, we get overwhelmed easily.

Evolution tried to help us with this with a bit of automation. You can learn to automate some things, thus lowering the amount of information you need to process consciously. Remember when you were learning to drive? It took all your attention to know where you were heading, how fast, what the road rules were, and how to shift gears, so you were not even able to follow all the signposts. After years of practice, you can now do all these things seamlessly. You even have room for some bad habits like having a conversation on the phone or checking your messages!

Truly intense focus on a task or being in the flow can effectively isolate our attention from any distractions. Christopher Chabris and Daniel Simons ran a famous experiment dubbed "the invisible gorilla."[121] It showed that intense focus makes us virtually blind to things we don't expect to see. Chabris and Simons created a short film of six players passing basketballs. The study participants were then asked to count the number of times the basketball was passed to the players with white shirts, ignoring the players with black shirts. The task required a significant amount of concentration and was completely absorbing. In the middle of the game, a person wearing a gorilla costume crossed through the middle of the group. This person was in full view for nine seconds. After the experiment, the researchers asked the participants a series of questions, one of them being, "Did you observe anything unusual that didn't belong in the game?" About half of the participants didn't notice anything unusual. They didn't see the gorilla! This effect, called inattentional blindness, is more pronounced the more concentration the primary task requires. What this experiment illustrates is how easy it is to be blind to the obvious—and also how easy it is to be blind to our blindness.[122]

Flow, or optimal experience, happens when the information we are receiving and processing aligns with our immediate goal and the psychic energy starts to flow effortlessly. When you are in the flow, you create order in your consciousness. Your attention is so focused that you ignore everything else around you. You live in the moment, and even the most tedious work can feel purposeful and enjoyable, though you don't feel the enjoyment until after you finish and realize what was happening. Then you have a flood of satisfaction from both the achievement and the process that led to it. This is what happens when you are in your Quiet Success Sweet Spot. It is easier for you to get so consumed by what you are doing that the time flies by and you get an incredible amount of work done. At this stage, success comes easily.

Csikszentmihalyi describes several elements of enjoyment. When researching the topic, he found out that, regardless of the activity, regardless of the person's cultural and social background, enjoyment is always described the same way. People who just enjoy a specific activity describe it with at least one, but usually more, of the following. An enjoyable experience is when we have a chance to finish the task. We must be able to focus on the task. There are clear goals we need to accomplish. There is immediate feedback. When performing the task, we get our awareness disconnected from the worries of everyday life. We have a sense of control over the results. We are so drawn into the activity that we lose concern for the self. The sense of time gets altered, and it feels the time flies or slows down depending on the activity.

Optimal experience is not about the destination but the journey. It is an end in itself. Csikszentmihalyi calls it "autotelic experience." This comes from the Greek words *auto*, meaning "self," and *telic*, meaning "goal." It is an activity that is not done for some future benefit, but that is a reward in itself. Playing a game of chess to beat your opponent is not autotelic. Playing it because you enjoy the game is.

Painting a picture so you can sell it is not an autotelic experience. Painting just for the sheer joy of seeing the canvas fill up with life is autotelic. The result in both cases is the same, but the experience one has during the activity is different.

Most of our activities fall somewhere in the middle. Often, we may start with an end in mind and, over time, as we are gaining mastery of the activity, it becomes more autotelic. Consider something as mundane as running. I know, I talk about it a lot. When you decide to take on running, you have some clear benefits in mind. You expect to lose some weight, get in shape, or win a marathon. The beginnings are often painful, and you keep your mind distracted as you find the process of running boring. You are just looking forward to getting it over with. As your physique gets better, you start enjoying it. At some point, you don't go for a run to get in shape. You do it because you are looking forward to the activity itself. You enjoy the feeling of running through the fields, the light breeze, being in nature, clearing your mind. You enjoy the feeling that you can do it.

"The autotelic experience," "the flow," and "the optimal experience" are all descriptions of the same phenomenon that can get your career to the next level. The more you can get these experiences into your job, the more satisfaction you will derive from your time on this planet. Flow is an intrinsically rewarding experience. It happens in the moment. It doesn't require any future benefits.

Csikszentmihalyi proposes that flow happens in a channel that is where challenge and skill match. This means that, as you are getting better at an activity and your skill increases, you need a more significant challenge to keep in the flow. If the challenge is not big enough, it gets boring. On the other hand, if the challenge is too great and your skill is not adequate, you experience anxiety instead of flow.

Sports are a natural way to accomplish that. Let me go back again to running. There is a way how to measure progress. It can force your attention to focus on what you are doing. You need to develop the necessary skills to be able to run for any significant amount of time. You can keep increasing the challenge to keep up with your newly acquired skill by increasing the distance or speed.

To get the optimal experience, you need to design your environment in a way that allows you to focus on what you are doing without disruptions. Remember Chapter 9? You need to structure the activity to be able to receive real-time feedback. And you need to ensure that the challenge matches the skills you have just right. Then you have a chance to get into the altered state of consciousness when the time stops, and you experience a pure enjoyment of what you are doing. It is not easy to create the optimal experience, but most people are capable of doing it. It is only people with severe psychological conditions, like schizophrenia, who can't alter their consciousness and get into flow. Concentration is a big part of the optimal experience. Some of us are better at concentrating than others. Most of us, however, can get better at it if we chose so.

Flow at Work and Home

To end this chapter, let me give you some food for thought. Where do you experience more flow, at work or at home? If you are like most people, you work toward a better work-life balance. You feel that you spend way too much time at work and too little at home. Work is seen as a necessary evil to give you the means to enjoy your leisure activities. Yet, according to Csikszentmihalyi's research, when it comes to enjoying the experience, the reality is very different from what we believe. In one study, he and his team collected over 4,800 responses to answer a simple question of whether people have more instances of flow at work or leisure activities. On average, people self-reported forty-four flow activities a week. The more time a person spends in flow, the better the flow experience became. Surprisingly, participants reported being in flow 54 percent of the time when at work, when discounting all their time being idle and participating in water-cooler gossip. When it came to leisure activities, participants reported being in flow only 18 percent of the time. Here, 52 percent of responses fell into the apathy experience.[123]

Answers to whether they wished to be doing something else indicated that people still didn't want to be at work and preferred to be at home. This is pretty incredible, as it means that we derive more satisfaction from our time at work than our time at home. Yet we try to spend as little time at work as possible and as much time as possible participating in leisure activities. The explanation to this lies in us believing cultural propaganda. When at work, we don't believe our own senses telling us that when a challenge matches our skills, we enjoy the work we are doing. Instead, we focus on the cultural stereotype that work is supposed to be hard and tedious, a necessary evil. It infringes on our freedom and, therefore, should be avoided as much as possible.

And why the abysmal results of the flow in leisure activities? The answer is in consuming rather than creating. You won't get into flow by being passive and just consuming work done by other people. You need to be actively engaged and use your skills to overcome a challenge. Many people equate leisure with passivity. Instead of playing soccer, we sit in front of a TV and watch others do so. Instead of playing the piano, we visit a theater and listen to others producing music. Instead of learning to paint, we go to an art gallery to admire the work of others. Passive entertainment doesn't lead anywhere. It may provide a short-term distraction to mask the emptiness of our lives, but it doesn't lead to a fulfilling and satisfying existence.

Mastery and flow work in tandem. The progressive difficulty is an essential part of flow. The challenge needs to increase as your skills increase. That is why computer games are so addictive. With each new level, they get harder and harder. But that is acceptable because the longer you play, the more your skill at the game increases as well. You are constantly driven to improve and to show that you can beat the next level. Being immersed in a computer game is an excellent example of how flow works. If the game is too easy, you get bored. If the game is too difficult, you get frustrated. In both cases, you drop it and do something else. Only when the game has progressive difficulty and allows you to improve while facing a progressively bigger challenge do you get hooked.

Unfortunately, this is not something that we try to promote in the workplace. Most companies shoot for efficiency. Efficiency means simplicity. We try to simplify the work as much as possible so the automaton can do it. We remove any challenge from work and then wonder why employees get demotivated. Only by setting goals that are just a bit beyond our current abilities, by having stretch goals that require us to be at the top of our game, by staying challenged and growing, can we experience flow at work. And flow leads to higher engagement and more satisfaction with work.

Summary and Key Takeaways

If you want to have a successful career, you need to bite the bullet and work hard. There are no shortcuts that work long term. Get into the habit of getting things done. Don't give up too quickly, but don't stick with an activity too long if it doesn't lead anywhere, either. Adopt deliberate practice to build mastery in your field. This is how gritty people differ from others. Keep continuously improving your skills and never be satisfied. That way, you will never reach a plateau. Gritty people have the perseverance and passion for what they do, and they experience more flow. Flow is more comfortable to achieve if you are good at what you do. Deliberate practice is for preparation, and flow is for actual performance. Even if the practice is not fun, persevere with the knowledge that the actual performance will be more fun when you get better. You will enjoy what you do more, others will recognize it, and it will lead more directly to a successful career.

- Forget the "work smarter, not harder" motto. Go for "work smarter *and* harder" instead.
- Talented people may have an advantage early in life. Still, in the end, it is effort and perseverance that lead to success.
- Become gritty by being passionate about what you do, optimistic about the outcome, and persevering to achieve long-term goals.
- Don't give up too early, and don't give up too late.
- Asking for help starts a virtuous cycle of asking and giving, and it can kickstart your success.
- To achieve any meaningful success and satisfaction with your life, you need to get good at what you do.
- Deliberate practice is powerful for building skills in domains where success is well understood and clear and measurable steps for improvement are defined.
- Flow, or optimal experience, happens when what we do is aligned with our immediate goals and our psychic energy flows effortlessly.
- When we are in the flow is when we produce our best work and have the most satisfaction from our achievements.
- Deliberate practice is for preparation, and flow is for actual performance.

Questions and Next Steps

- Do you subscribe to the notion of working smarter and not harder? Why do you believe this is better than working smarter *and* harder? Do you believe that true success can be achieved without hard work? Look at your own definition of success and consider how working hard can make you more successful.
- What is the one thing you are trying to master that would significantly impact your career? Now consider how deliberate practice can help you to achieve mastery. You need three things to pursue deliberate practice: total focus on what you are trying to improve, targeted feedback so you can correct what you are doing wrong, and an ever-increasing challenge, so you keep pushing to the next level.
- Can you remember when the last time was that you were in flow? When time just flew by, and you got a tremendous amount of work accomplished? What were you doing? How did you feel afterward? What can you do to get more flow into your life?

● 15

Respect Others

*"I'm humble. I care about others and treat them with respect.
I'm positive. I know that life is not only about me."*

Life is not about you. All the major religions and philosophies would tell you that life is bigger than you. It is about how you interact with others and what you do that matters, and about how your actions impact those around you. Does your life add to the good of humanity? When you are on your death bed and look back at your life, would you be able to say that you left the world in a better place than when you were born? Were your efforts, words, and thoughts positive and for the betterment of humankind?

Being seen as good is vital to most of us. It helps us feel good about ourselves and think that we are successful. Being humble and having the emotional intelligence to listen to and understand those around you is very important. It allows you to be likable and to build a positive attitude toward life. Having a positive attitude toward life allows you to see those around you as good people and helps you be kind. It will enable you to be respectful and see others as fellow human beings with the same rights, wishes, dreams, and needs as you have.

If you treat others with disrespect, you put your own needs above the needs of others, and you are deaf to your surroundings, you won't achieve any lasting success. Everything you achieve will be tainted by the suffering of those you used to get what you want. You will become a jerk and a negative or even destructive person. No one will want to work with you. People will shy away from helping you and will cheer on your failures. That is not the way to a successful career.

Emotional Intelligence

We live in a world where a high IQ is not enough. Being successful is not only about pure brainpower but also about the ability to work and communicate well with others. That is where emotional intelligence and empathy come in. EQ, emotional quotient or emotional intelligence, is an incredibly powerful set of skills for anyone who wants to succeed. Emotional intelligence is also something you can learn. It won't be easy, but unlike IQ, which is inborn and doesn't significantly change during your life, emotional intelligence can be improved considerably, given enough time and effort. Being emotionally intelligent helps you work better with others, build better relationships, and deal with various social situations. Success at work is often a combination of your raw brainpower, your competence at the job, and the emotional intelligence that allows you to work well with those around you.

If you want to learn a new technical skill, it is a relatively simple matter of focus and study. Within a couple of days, you can master simple technical concepts. The moment you involve emotions, which is something you will do when improving emotional intelligence, you tap other parts of the brain. For the habit to take root, you need much practice and repetition. New neural pathways need to be created, and it takes time. Don't listen to people who say that emotions have no place in business. They do. Emotions are key to relationships, and that applies to the workplace too. It is a question of how you use the emotions that makes all the difference.

Emotional intelligence is, in its essence, an ability to manage ourselves and the relationships we have with others. You can look at emotional intelligence and slice it in several different ways.[124] The most popular are the five areas introduced by Daniel Goleman and the one I use below for its nice symmetry, introduced by Travis Bradberry and Jean Greaves. Each of the four areas or capabilities is made up of several traits that can be developed.[125]

Self-Awareness: Being able to understand yourself is an important stepping stone to having strong emotional intelligence. If you don't understand who you are and what makes you tick, it makes the other aspects much more difficult to achieve. We talked about this in Chapter 8. Self-awareness is about knowing your strengths and weaknesses, understanding your emotions and what drives you. It is about knowing what your core values are and seeing the impact your actions have on others. Self-aware people can listen to feedback that removes any blind spots they might have. You can split this aspect into three areas: emotional self-awareness, which focuses on understanding your emotions and their impact on others; accurate self-assessment, which means understanding your strengths and weaknesses; and self-confidence, which is a strong sense of who you are and what you can do.

Self-Management or Self-Regulation: Once you know who you are, you can focus on more constructively managing your potentially dangerous emotions, which may lead to friction and disruption. Self-management is about making the most of the internal resources you have. It is made up of six areas. Self-control helps you make sure that your emotions don't run wild. Trustworthiness and transparency focus on having your actions aligned with your core values and acting with integrity. Tenacity and optimism help you persist in getting work done regardless of obstacles and setbacks. Adaptability deals with being able to handle changes in your environment and circumstances. Initiative enables you to identify and act on opportunities presented to you. And finally, achievement orientation pushes you to constantly strive to meet your own standards and keep getting better. You probably recognized that I addressed these within the various Quiet Success Principles.

Social Awareness: The previous two areas deal with you as a person. The other two focus on the way you interact with others. It is about your ability to work with others and manage your relationships with the world in such a way that you can move people in the direction you desire. There are three aspects of social awareness. The first, empathy, is about tuning in to and considering the feelings and emotions of other people when making decisions. It is not only about your understanding but also about others feeling that you have an interest in their needs and concerns. The second, organizational awareness, is about being able to read the room. It is about understanding the interpersonal dynamics in the team, the power relationships, and the emotional eddies flowing through the team. The third, service orientation, is the ability to recognize, understand, and meet the needs of your partners and customers. Since empathy and attentiveness are introverts' strengths, as an introvert you are well-positioned to become more socially aware if you give it some effort.

Relationship Management: This capability, or trait, is the twin of self-management. Once you build social awareness, you also need to actively manage the environment, social interactions, and relationships around you. It is about being able to get the desired responses from other people around you. You can split this skill into six areas. Visionary leadership focuses on inspiring others, whether they're individuals or groups, and guiding them in the desired direction. Change catalyst helps you to be the one who actively initiates and manages changes. Influence deals with your ability to effectively move others in the direction you believe the group needs to go regardless of reporting structures or formal relationships. Developing others focuses on your ability to understand the strengths and needs of others and actively help them improve their abilities. And finally, teamwork and collaboration deal with creating a real team spirit and synergy to move the group toward a collective goal.

This is not a book on emotional intelligence, as it is such a broad topic. My goal in this section was to give you a glimpse into the complexity of emotional intelligence and the understanding that it can be significantly improved if you want to. In the following sections, I will talk about likability, positive attitude, humility, and respect, as they can all make you better at building solid relationships and therefore more likely to succeed at work.

Likability

"Tomas, this was a great conversation. You are a very likable person." This is how the CTO of one company ended an interview with me. I thanked him, felt good, but also felt confused. I had never really thought about what being likable actually means, not to mention whether I fit the category. Since that one conversation, I started to pay attention and realized there are many likable people around me—and some not so likable. We all enjoy being around likable human beings. What's more, likable people create their own fortunes by being who they are. We are all more likely to help those we like, so being likable can play a huge role in being successful.

Luckily for introverts, likability has nothing to do with how much you talk. You can be very quiet and still be likable. In fact, your strengths of humility, loyalty, attentiveness, empathy, calmness, and thoughtfulness all help you to be likable.

So if talking is not the way to likability, what is? Start with the basics. Smile, listen, be interested in, and care about the other person. And think of yourself as likable without being ego-driven. To be likable, you need to get your ego out of the way. Researchers from the University of Waterloo show that when we think others will like us, we act more naturally and create a self-fulfilling prophecy. And I'm not talking about some crazy positive self-talk, just a bit of confidence coming from the fact that you know you are doing all the right things to be likable, and therefore you are.[126]

If you want to hear the thoughts of another titan, consider what Dale Carnegie says about the topic. In his book *How to Win Friends and Influence People*, Carnegie talks about six principles to make people like you: "Become genuinely interested in other people. Smile. Remember that a person's name is to that person the sweetest and most important sound in any language. Be a good listener. Encourage others to talk about themselves. Talk in terms of the other person's interests. Make the other person feel important—and do it sincerely."[127]

Smile and Use Positive Language: Using positive language is a no-brainer. Just consider how these statements make you feel. "I need to sit through this boring meeting listening to those fools," compared to, "I want to meet with those great people and listen to what ideas they have about the topic." Whether I utter the first or the second sentence will significantly affect how you feel about me. Would you want to spend your day with someone full of negativity who creates a toxic environment? Or would you like to be around someone whose positive outlook on life will spread like wildfire and who will always find ways to make you feel better? And the same goes, of course, for body language and especially facial expressions. If you meet someone who is smiling all the time and laughing wholeheartedly, you will see them more favorably than someone who frowns all day long.

Use People's Names and Thank Them: As Carnegie would say, a person's name is the sweetest sound in the world to that person. Using people's names during conversation is an excellent way to make them feel special. Other words fit this category as well. What about "thank you"? People who show a genuine appreciation of something we have done for them are more likely to get our help in the future.

Genuinely Care: Caring about others and helping them is a great way to feel good about ourselves and build a positive image in the eyes of the person you care about. It feels good when we know there is someone out there who has our best interests at heart. Likable people make it a point to care about others and make it visible that they do care. Offering help to others and being clear that it is your pleasure to help makes you someone people want to be around. They know that, if they have the need, you will be there for them. You can start with something as simple as ending your conversations with words like these: "It was great talking to you today. Is there anything more I can do for you?" You would be surprised how powerful these words are and what a positive impact they will have on your relationships. And what's more, they will make you feel better too.

Give Well-Meant Compliments: We all like it when someone compliments us. We may not know how to react, but being praised still feels good. Not only will people feel good about what you said, but they will also associate you with that positive feeling. You made them feel good. Similarly, as mentioned in Chapter 8, be graceful when receiving compliments. A heartfelt thank-you will make the person who praises you feel great about themselves too.

Ask Questions and Don't Talk About Yourself: Talking too much about yourself in the hope of sounding interesting is not usually something introverts do. It is somewhat narcissistic behavior, and it is the exact opposite of what you need to do to be likable. Instead, show interest in others and ask questions. And then, of course, listen for answers. Even introverts like to talk about themselves now and then, as it provides the brain with a pleasurable experience. By giving others a chance to talk about themselves, you are providing that opportunity, and you are, in retrospect, seen as a great person to speak with, even though you may not say much.

In *All You Have to Do Is Ask*, Wayne Baker suggests using the FORD guidelines for conversations designed to build rapport. "FORD" is an acronym for Family, Occupation, Recreation, and Dreams. These guidelines force you to talk about things other than work and problems you are facing. They allow the other person to get to know you as a human being. A conversation following FORD guidelines should flow like a natural conversation, and you don't need to hit all areas at once. It is all in the service of getting to know each other and creating psychological safety where people are not afraid to voice their thoughts and ask for help.[128]

Don't Be Afraid to Be Vulnerable: At least a little bit. This is not something that introverts do naturally. Like turtles, we like being hidden in our shells, protected from potential attacks and ridicule. But showing a little bit of vulnerability can go a long way toward being likable and building stronger relationships. You will be seen as more human when you show that you have some weaknesses and are not infallible. Likable people remove their egos and are humble. A bit of self-deprecating humor goes a long way. Of course, everything needs to be in moderation. You don't want to spend the whole day talking about all your problems, issues, and weaknesses.

As you can see, some of the areas described are pretty close to an introvert's heart. We don't need to talk about ourselves all day long, and we tend to be good listeners. If you can build a bit of a positive attitude and some confidence, you are pretty much there.

Likability will make you someone people will want to collaborate with and will increase your chances of a successful career. At the same time, it will make you more confident when dealing with others and allow you to be kind and respectful, even when you want to provide feedback or have a tough conversation.

Positive Attitude

Having an optimistic view of life and a positive attitude toward others is a potent motivator that keeps you going. It allows us to see the best in other people, respect them, be kind to them, and trust them. I'm not saying you should lie to yourself or try to act as if you are happy when you are not. I'm saying that only you can decide how to feel about life, regardless of the circumstances. Often you can't influence what happens to you, but you can certainly choose how to feel about it. That is why two people can have completely different reactions to the same event. One may freak out and start worrying, while the other might laugh and take it as a minor inconvenience to overcome.

Learn to Laugh: Don't be afraid to laugh. Too often, people feel that in a professional setting, they need to be deadly serious to be taken seriously by others, especially in leadership roles. If the leader stays serious all the time, the chances are that the team will also be afraid to laugh. And what sort of environment do you build where people are discouraged from laughing? A heartfelt laugh is a great way to remove tension, dissolve stressful situations, and give some life and enthusiasm to otherwise serious business. A good laugh spreads like a virus and helps build an environment where people can have fun even when asked to focus hard on performing their tasks.

Enjoy the Small Wins: Things may not always go as planned. You may work on a long-term project or tasks that won't see the light of the day for months or years. How do you stay motivated and on track? By breaking your tasks down into smaller pieces and celebrating small wins. Every day there is something that went well and can give you the energy to continue in your endeavor. Did you help an older woman cross a street during your trip to work? Did you have a great conversation with a customer? Did you get a pat on the back from your boss? Did you receive a kudos email from your team member? Did you just code a great algorithm? All these are small wins, small successes that are happening all the time, and we tend to overlook them and focus on the bigger things that go wrong. I love the commencement address at the University of Texas in Austin 2014 by Admiral William H. McRaven. He talks about a couple of life lessons and starts the speech by asking the audience to make their bed every day. This simple task may sound ridiculous, but it has significant symbolism and power. By making your bed first thing in the morning, you accomplish your first task of the day and can feel a sense of a first small win. And then the tasks pile up, and you have a successful day.[129]

So if you want to get the most out of your life and to have a successful career, learn to deal with stress by making sure you laugh often, trust others, enjoy small wins, and find positives in every situation. If you can then laugh about yourself, you remove some of the stress you put on yourself. You don't need to be perfect. You can make mistakes and then just shrug them off with a laugh. This obviously requires humility.

Humility

It's not about you. Introverts tend to be naturally humble—in fact, I showed in Chapter 2 that humility is one of our strengths—but it is good to remind ourselves why it is important to stay that way, even when our successes pile up. Humility is the quality of having a modest opinion about one's importance. It doesn't mean you believe you don't matter. You do matter. You are important, and your life has a purpose. It is just that none of these things are particularly important in the grand scheme of the universe. Humility is widely seen as a virtue. It is the opposite of narcissism, pride, or hubris. It includes both self-awareness and openness to other people's perspectives. How does humility manifests in the workplace?

Avoiding the Spotlight: This should give you no problem. Introverts don't seek the spotlight in the first place and don't have the excessive need to be visible. If there is an opportunity to shine some light on the accomplishments of others rather than yourself, then do so. However, learn to accept praise when deserved. You won't be able to get the success you want if no one knows what you do. You may not want to bask in the light of praise, but it is crucial to make your achievements visible. It is acceptable to be behind the scenes as long as everyone understands your contributions and that you are there.

Healthy Self-Confidence: Humility doesn't equal a lack of confidence. You may know the feeling where you are just totally unprepared for an activity or you worry that you will be found out as a phony, so you show a false humility and offer someone else the opportunity to do the highly visible job. You didn't do this because you were humble; you did this because you had no confidence in your abilities. Don't try to mask the lack of skill with humility. People will realize you are insincere. Moreover, it will be difficult to fix the lack of ability if you are not willing to accept there is something to be fixed.

Giving Credit to Others: Truly successful and confident people have no problem giving credit to others. I'm not even talking about sharing credit, but about wholly giving it to others without the need to keep a portion to yourself. Just the fact that you are the one who is giving credit to others creates an image of yourself as someone who has something to give. It means you are the person behind it, and you care enough about others to make sure they also get visibility. It is a win-win approach. You make the other person visible, and because you are the one who speaks, you make yourself visible too. You both are seen as successful people others will want to work with. Once again, don't surrender your own visibility. Fully giving credit only works when everyone knows about your skills and mastery of the topic. Then it is a win-win situation. On the other hand, giving credit you deserve to someone else and then quietly sitting in the corner and saying nothing if no one even knows you got the job done will lead to you losing.

Not Having the Need to Win at the Expense of Others: Humility comes from having the abundance mentality mindset. You understand that winning at the expense of someone else is not a real win. This especially applies when the people you won over are your colleagues or family members you need to work or live with long term. In these situations, your short-term win may turn into a long-term loss. Relationships are more important than the satisfaction of defeating the person. By having an abundance mentality, you understand that a real win only happens when everyone wins. You make it a point to constantly seek solutions to problems that will benefit more people than just yourself.

Celebrating Wins of Others: Being genuinely happy for the success of others is the best way to build strong relationships, and it increases the number of opportunities where you can feel good, even in sports. You may feel deflated when you lose a game of tennis or golf, and you could choose to hide somewhere sulking. Or you may decide to feel great, congratulate the person who bested you, and cheerfully comment on their skills and the great game. You have lost the game, but you can humbly admit the other person was better, and you can choose to feel good.

Accepting That You Don't Know Everything and That It's Okay: Humble people have one extremely helpful quality that makes them more likely to keep going and succeed even after initial failure. If you are willing to admit that you don't know everything, that everyone, including you, can make mistakes, you are on the path to learning from these mistakes and doing better next time. Those who can't admit that they are not infallible have a harder time improving. How can they improve something that, in their minds, doesn't need improving? It wasn't their fault that they failed. They didn't learn the lesson, and chances are that they may fail again next time.

Humility is a powerful weapon that will help you build rock-solid relationships. It will help you turn people around you into your fans and helpers. Because they know that you don't elevate yourself above them, they are more likely to go out of their way to help you. If you credit their work, they will make the same effort and appreciate what you do. This leads us to respect.

Respect

Respect has two primary meanings, and both are important for success. The first one is admiration for someone because of their abilities, skills, or achievements. You respect a person who you see as better than you in some way. You want to be like them, or you at least understand that they have a skill you lack, and you are willing to admit it. The second, a more all-encompassing view of respect, is to consider the feelings, wishes, needs, and rights of others. You respect everyone around you by showing civility and common courtesy, by being polite and considerate. You accept that everyone has the same rights as you.

"But we have freedom of speech, and I can say whatever I want. No one has the right to censor me," I hear you say, and you would be right. You can say whatever you want to whomever you want, but just because you can do something doesn't mean you have to. Even if you believe someone is an idiot, there is no legal or moral obligation for you to say that. Not to mention that saying it will make you be seen as a jerk, and in many situations, it won't be a career-enhancing strategy. One of the major reasons why people are disrespectful is that they don't consider the impact of what they are saying. Luckily, introverts tend to think a bit about what we are about to say, so the chances of us misspeaking are relatively low.

However, that doesn't prevent us from being disrespectful when we don't know we are being disrespectful. You may have a good idea about what is and what is not disrespectful in your country, culture, or age group. You may not realize that something you consider completely acceptable behavior may be seen as unacceptable by someone with a different cultural and educational background. You need to do your best to understand the perspective of the person you are speaking to so you can adequately consider their feelings, wishes, and needs. You can't project your own. Once you consider a different perspective, you also need to consider your own biases. Do you feel the other person is your equal? Do you know yourself and your view of people who are different from you? Are you able to put all this aside and treat others with respect? Or would you approach them with the condescension, mistrust, and even supreme arrogance of someone who believes they are better than them? You respect others when you are able to accept their wishes, even when you disagree with them. This is the ultimate test. You would prefer to do things differently, but you respect others' right to do things the way they want things done. You treat them like adults.

Behaving in a civilized, respectful manner is civilization-specific. The rule of thumb is that you should behave the way the particular society expects. Every group of people has certain social norms. If you violate these norms, your behavior will be seen as disrespectful or even outright unacceptable.

Successful people understand this. There are certainly exceptions when a radical revolutionary breaks all the norms of the society and still reaches success, but it rarely happens. Luckily, introverts' strengths are in being able to make others feel respected. This strategy works every single time. Making an effort to respect those around you will pay dividends whether you talk with your spouse, the company CEO, or the janitor. Make it a point to treat everyone as equals and with respect. Step by step, you will build an image of someone worthy of other people's care. If people see that you care, they will care back, and this will positively reflect on your career.

Don't Ignore Others and Don't Let Others Ignore You

I met Josh several years ago. He was a young, ambitious manager who went to a time management training and read some books about creating priorities. In this type of training, you usually learn that you can't be a slave to urgencies imposed by other people, as that prevents you from achieving your own goals. Josh decided that it was not essential to keep answering email requests if they were not aligned with his personal goals. Unfortunately, this happened within a company culture that pretty much revolved around email—email was their primary communication tool. Interpreting the advice of his trainers, Josh decided not to answer emails from people he didn't feel were important enough or about topics that were not on his priority list. The results? He had more time to finish his tasks. His performance should have skyrocketed. And it sort of did on these particular tasks, but it plummeted on his ability to get things done in general. Why? He alienated many people he needed for future projects. He made many hard-working people feel invisible, diminished, and ignored. These people created a story about Josh, believing he was an arrogant jerk, lazy, self-important, someone who thought he was above others. His reputation tanked within a couple of months to a level where no one wanted to work with him. Yet the only thing he did was ignore communication attempts from others, and if he decided to respond, it was in a way that indicated others were a nuisance to him.

There is one thing worse than rejection: being ignored. Being ignored makes you feel invisible, unimportant, and weak, as if you don't exist and don't matter. It is something that happens to introverts all the time. Because of our quiet nature and tendency to shy away from the spotlight, we may be regularly overlooked. If we sit in the corner long enough, people may forget about us entirely. Being ignored can slow you down or derail your career quite a bit.

Acknowledging others is the very minimum, though it is not enough to make sure others respect you. If you want to make sure that people interacting with you will value your opinions, you should exhibit the behavior you would expect from them. Lead by example.

You usually experience the "I won't answer to the person who is not at my level in the hierarchy" attitude with super busy top executives. It makes sense. They do run big teams, the demands on their time and attention are high, and they need to prioritize to get things done. It also makes sense for you to be careful about what you expect from them. You should be realistic about whether your problem is something you need to involve them in. But if you have done your homework and you genuinely do need the cooperation of people levels above you to achieve your business goals, then you should reach out to them. And being ignored in this situation is not acceptable. There is a relatively simple fix, though it is not necessarily easy to implement. It requires a certain level of courage on your part.

What do you do if you send an email asking for help, approval, or permission to do something, and all you get back is silence? Send it again. People may be busy, may have overlooked your first email, may have felt that there was more time and no urgency. Give them a second chance. Be very civilized about it. There is no need to even indicate that you sent the email once before, so the person in question can save face. If they didn't see it the first time, then they will respond without any problem. If they remember that you already sent it, they will feel guilty on their own without you reminding them, and they will respond quickly. If even the second attempt fails, and even if your phone calls are not returned, then you need to provoke a "no" answer. If that's the case, send a concise email along the lines of, "It seems you are busy with more important matters, so let me get this done. I consider this initiative approved and am moving forward. Please let me know if you want to proceed differently." You either get silence again, which at that point is fine since you can claim the silence was the approval. Or you trigger a "No, let's talk about this." In both cases, you broke through the fence to the other person. It may feel that you are mislabeling the reality, but you need to get a response in situations like this, and emotions will help. You may feel that that approach is not particularly professional. Maybe not. But what is truly unprofessional and rude is others ignoring you. In fact, knowingly ignoring others can be seen as a form of bullying, and there are other forms of bullying that can come up in the workplace too.

Stop Giving in to Bullies

Bullying is often associated with kids and schools. Bullying is defined as the use of force or threat to abuse, intimidate, and dominate others. However, since kids become adults, it should be no surprise that bullies also exist in the workplace. In fact, since one of the defining moments that distinguish bullying from conflict is the perception of an imbalance of social or physical power, you can find it pretty much everywhere. The bullies themselves are able to rationalize their behavior by building an image of themselves as being superior. The victims can be selected for various reasons, be it race, religion, gender, social class, personality, appearance, reputation, size, or ability.

Workplace bullying means that an employee is regularly mistreated by others, but this is rarely physical. It is more likely that a bully will use verbal and psychological abuse, humiliation, and inappropriate humor. The problem with this type of bullying is that it is often sort of supported by the rules and policies of the organization, and in a majority of the cases, the bully is in a position of authority over the one who is bullied. Bullying can have many different forms:

Physical Bullying: is unusual in the workplace, especially in white-collar jobs, but it can happen. It involves hitting, pushing, pinching, or any aggressive contact with another person. It can also include taking or damaging the property of the victim.

Verbal Bullying: is much more common in the office. It is present in the form of insults, making derogatory, sexual, or bigoted comments, unwanted harsh teasing, mimicking, using verbal threats, or abusive language.

Relational Bullying: is also more common in the workplace. It revolves around trying to exclude someone from the team, the peer group. Usually it is done through verbal bullying toward the individual, spreading rumors, and intimidating others not to engage with the individual being bullied.

There are even more subtle forms of bullying in the workplace that may not be considered bullying by people who perpetrate them—things like constant criticism, blocking promotions for reasons other than performance, overbearing micromanagement and supervision, or picking on others with inappropriate jokes.

As there are different types of bullying, there are also different types of bullies:

Violent Bullies: want to hurt other people physically or emotionally, often don't know how to handle their own emotions, and get angry quickly. Have you ever seen a manager who would get angry and start yelling at a subordinate? That is a violent bully who abuses their power to make others feel small. Regardless of what the subordinate has done, there is never ever a reason to scream at them, belittle them, or make them feel like trash.

Time-Sucking Bullies: who don't respect the time of others may not even realize what they are doing. They care only about their needs and wants and ignore that others have work to do. They just want to talk, or they demand your attention as their problems always have priority. They might just rush into your office and demand that you help them with their problem immediately. If you don't quickly jump on it and help them, they get abusive. They will use you as a scapegoat for their problems. It may happen that they ignored something they were supposed to do, left it until the last minute, and now they are making their lack of planning your problem.

Won't-Shut-Up Bullies: don't respect the opinions of others, interrupt you in the middle of a sentence, talk over you, and act as you don't exist. These are the people who always need to be the smartest person in the room, who are so confident in their abilities that they don't feel like listening to others. Often these are brilliant people who are even really valuable to the organization—and they know it. Management is often tolerant of these bullies, as they are perceived as key to the company's success. It usually takes a courageous senior leader or a human resources person to stop the abuses of this individual. In most cases, this is done by managing them out of the organization.

Why do I talk about this? I sincerely hope you are not a perpetrator, but you can become a victim or be a bystander. By being able to stand up to bullies, you show courage, you show that you care, and you show leadership. You create an image of someone fair, who fights for what is right, and who can't be ignored. You will build respect. So how do you deal with an office bully?

Assertive Communication: Practicing assertive communication will make you, to some extent, bully-proof. It starts with a mindset. You need to shed your victim persona and get some confidence. Learn to walk with your head up and with a smile on your lips, be positive, and look like you are in control. Often just looking weak and helpless attracts a bully. Don't give them that opportunity. There are different ways to deal with bullying, but there is one that never works: ignoring it. The sooner you address the bullying behavior, the easier it is to deal with it. The longer you wait, the more difficult it becomes.

Never Give In: Bullies expect you to cower. They expect that when you get challenged, you will feel weak, afraid, and uncomfortable. That is what makes them feel powerful and superior. In many situations, you can prevent being bullied by simply not playing that game, by ignoring the content of the verbal challenge and responding with something like, "Hi, Ralph, just on my way to the meeting. Have a good day." Responses like this, paired with walking past the bully confidently, may tell the bully that you are not the right target. If they see that you are not scared, they don't have the feeling of having power over you, and so they stop.

Don't Fight Back Using the Same Weapons: Trying to fight back using the same means just escalates the situation, and this means that the bully wins since it is their battlefield. Sometimes this can work, as you may surprise the bully with a violent action on your own, but most likely it won't, as it just isn't you.

Allow the Person to Vent: Especially in the corporate environment, and when the bully is also your boss, you fighting back or trying to deflect the rage toward someone else wouldn't work. Let them say what is on their mind and just sit and listen until they calm down a bit. Then restate what they said in your own words: "Chris, if I understand you correctly, you are angry because I did . . ." This may provoke an answer like, "You are damn right that I'm angry," but at least the rant is over, and there is a chance for resolution.

Offer a Way Forward: If you followed the advice from Chapter 8, you are calm, you are in control of your emotions, and you are the one who is acting like an adult. This forces the bully the reassess the situation. You are not weak and cowardly, as they thought, so they need to find a way out to save face. You can achieve that not by dwelling on what happened but by showing the path forward. Don't apologize, don't act subservient, but don't try to dominate either. Be professional and focus on what can be done so this doesn't happen again. Starting with something along the lines of, "I suggest we resolve this by . . ." can do the trick.

Stand Your Ground and Repeat: Repeat this process. Most bullies are looking for easy prey. They have no desire for the actual battle, especially if there is a danger that they may find their match. This process either helps or doesn't. If yes, you may not be bullied ever again by this person, as you showed that you are not afraid and there is no fun in bullying you. If it doesn't work, then escalate to your manager or human resources department. You may even bring it up during the conversation with the bully as a way to resolve the problem. "Since you don't seem to agree to any of my suggestions, I will bring the problem up to my manager to resolve."

Get Help from Others: Sometimes, all it takes is some bystanders or figures of authority to intervene calmly. If the bully sees that others are doing nothing, it encourages them to continue. However, if, in the early stages, someone with enough clout in the organization—like a manager or a well-respected employee—tells the bully that their behavior is not acceptable and it won't be tolerated in the organization, chances are it will stop.

It is essential to point out that office bullies often wield a lot of power, either formal or informal, and they can sabotage your work and your career. However, that still doesn't mean you should let them. Ultimately, either they stop, or your attempts to deal with them, including escalation, will fail. If you fail, if your manager and human resources team don't do anything even if you escalate, you should just leave. You don't want to work for a company that tolerates such behavior anyway.

Summary and Key Takeaways

Respecting others is a prerequisite to building strong relationships and being seen as someone great to work with. Increasing your emotional intelligence, adopting a positive attitude, and being humble will make you more likable. Treating others with respect and not ignoring those around you shows that you care. Speaking up, not letting others ignore you, and not giving in to bullies will show your strength, your leadership potential, and that you are confident and not afraid to do the right thing. All these things will work for you when building an image of a just and competent person and will open the doors for a long-term successful career.

- Life is not about you. Always ask yourself whether your thoughts, words, and actions lead to the betterment of humankind. Are you making the world a better place or a worse one?
- Emotional intelligence is your ability to manage yourself and your relationships with others.
- Don't try to be popular. Focus on likability instead.
- A positive attitude toward life is a powerful motivator and will help you to be more respectful.
- Learn to laugh and enjoy the small wins life brings.
- Respect those around you. Everyone has the same rights as you do.
- Don't ignore others and don't let others ignore you.
- Don't give in to bullies.

Questions and Next Steps

- How high is your emotional intelligence? Are you self-aware, meaning you understand your strengths, weaknesses, emotions, and what drives you? Do you exhibit strong self-management and self-control? Are you socially aware, meaning you exhibit empathy, are able to read the room and understand interpersonal dynamics within the team? How good are you at managing relationships and social interaction? Go back to the section about emotional intelligence and consider if you could improve your interactions with those around you.
- Try this exercise to judge your likability. For a week, stop yourself after every interaction you have with other people and answer these questions: Did I smile and use positive language? Did I genuinely care about the person and the interaction? Did I use their name and thank them for their efforts? Did I give them compliments if at all possible? Did I talk mostly about myself or let

them talk? Try to do better next time. Likability and emotional intelligence are things you can learn, and they greatly enhance your interactions with coworkers and, ultimately, your career success.

- Are you willing to stand up to bullies? Look back at the last week or two and consider whether there was a situation where you could have been considered a victim or bystander of bullying. If yes, what could you have done differently? As a good introvert, analyze and prepare. Next time you are in the same situation, try to use what you prepared. It may feel awkward and might be clumsy, but it is better than just giving in.

16

Build Alliances

"I need others, and I'm willing to admit it.
I believe that people mean well. I extend trust and play nice with others."

No one can do it alone. Even introverts need others to be successful. You need others if you want to feel like you belong. You need others so you can see the results of your work have meaning. You need others to help out with your work now and then. You need others to provide the expertise you lack. You need others to give you candid feedback, so you can remove your blind spots. You need others for emotional support. You just need others.

You may not need hundreds of friends, but you need a couple of really good ones. You may not need to know all your colleagues, but you should build good working relationships with some of them. Forging deep relationships and extending trust to people can be very liberating, and it will increase your chances for a successful career. It is infinitely easier to communicate with those you trust and who trust you. It is infinitely easier to influence others around you if you build strong relationships. If those around you see you as someone trustworthy, they will listen, and they will act on your suggestions. You will have an influence. And you do need influence and alliances if you want to make a dent in the world! The most natural way to overcome obstacles is to team up with others to build alliances or coalitions of like-minded people who will help you push your ideas and implement them. This means seeing others as equals, as people who mean well. It means you need to understand that people are different, that there are cultural and personal differences between them. It means you need to stop making assumptions.

Being open-minded and willing to extend trust, not judging people around you, and always listening with the intent to understand will make a difference.

323

Sprinkle in a willingness to show a bit of vulnerability, and you will make it easier for people to relate to you. Things will become much more manageable. You will stop the paranoia that everyone is trying to hurt you. You will stop the belief that people care only about themselves. You will be surprised by the response you get when you show others that you trust them and take them seriously. People will reciprocate and go out of their way to help you.

Alliances and Influence

Imagine a company without fancy titles. Would you follow the same people who are in managerial roles today? Sadly, in many situations, managers rely too much on their titles and thus don't do what needs to be done. They don't lead people; they try to manage them. They are not seen and accepted as natural leaders. They are not leaders at all. Individual contributors on the team then feel helpless, as it is not their place to make a decision. So they instead complain. Real personal leadership shows when you are asked to get something done by utilizing a team that you have no direct reporting line to and when there is no apparent incentive for this team to work with you. Real influence shows when you can guide decisions that are not yours to make. Luckily for introverts, we are often very good at working behind the scenes. Since we don't require the spotlight and often don't seek positional power, we can cultivate the natural power of quiet leaders. Consider again the strengths highlighted in Chapter 2. You are attentive and can listen. You are thoughtful. You exhibit empathy. You are humble, you prepare well, and you can persevere. You are calm, loyal, and independent. In short, you have many traits that make great leaders and influencers, whether that is influencing your boss or your coworkers, having a direct team, or managing a project with a virtual and distributed team. Consider the following points that will help you build alliances and get work done.

It Is Your Team: Cultivate this very simple mindset when working with others. Consider them as part of your team, regardless of whether they report to you or not. They might be your peers or even superiors. You should always see them as people who deserve your attention and believe that you are here to help them succeed. As a byproduct, things get done and you achieve your goal.

Show Them Vision: When marshaling your resources, you need to provide a vision, a goal, a target, something that needs to be achieved and that people on your virtual team should march toward. You may also want to show them what is in it for them. Show them how they may grow and achieve their personal goals when working with you on a particular initiative, even when you are not the boss.

Fight for Them: They are your team, and that means that you fight for them. You are the spokesperson, the guardian, and the person who needs to shield them from anything that may derail their effort. You may even need to step up and have a discussion with their boss if you feel they are not getting what they should from that boss.

Give Them Credit: Forget about sharing credit. Sharing credit doesn't really work, as "sharing" by definition means that you still keep part of the credit and that almost always translates to you being seen as the one who did the job. Don't share, but give all the credit to the team. You are not particularly important. You are just the coordinator, the enabler. It is the team that did the work, and they deserve the credit. When they don't report to you, make sure their managers know about the great job they did. And don't stop there. Remember, even if they don't report to you, they are your team. You are responsible for ensuring they get the recognition they deserve and that it helps them in their career objectives.

Mentor Them: Yes, they may work with you for only a short period, but that doesn't mean you should treat them as expendable resources. Again, they are your team, and you are responsible for giving them the opportunity to learn and grow. You must provide feedback and mentorship. Why? Well, as the saying goes, you always meet twice. If you provide real leadership and mentoring, if you help them to achieve their goals, they will see you as a leader and will want to work with you in the future.

Build Relationships: This brings up building relationships. You want to make sure you create rapport and have a good working relationship with the team. You may need their help in future projects or initiatives. When you build a deep connection with people and they understand that they matter to you and that you care, it is much easier for them to provide the help you will need to get the job done.

Build Alliances by Helping Others

Researchers Robert Kelley and Janet Caplan tried to understand what makes a star employee. At Bell Laboratories, the management identified 10 to 15 percent of employees as stars. However, it wasn't easy to discern what makes a star employee better than the average one. There was almost no meaningful difference between the best and the average employees based on a range of standard tests, like IQ or personality inventories. What made a real difference was not innate abilities but rather strategies the top performers used to do their jobs. Everyone Bell Labs hires is intelligent and technically competent. What makes the difference are nine strategies: taking the initiative, networking, self-management, teamwork effectiveness, leadership, followership, perspective, show-and-tell, and organizational savvy. And these things are learnable.[130]

Star performers build informal networks before they need them. They help others, and when the time comes that they need help themselves, they get that help much faster than an average employee without a strong informal professional network would get.

Regardless of your position in the company, you should always do your best to help others. Make it a point to know people not just from your department but also from other groups. Make it a point to greet everyone in the company, be positive, smile, and be willing to help others out, even when there is no immediate reward. Give credit to others and do your best to promote the excellent job they've done. Why? This is the way to build alliances. This is how to truly understand the business, expand your horizons, and get your name out there. Next time there is a discussion about who should lead a cross-departmental project, guess who will be on top of everyone's mind?

An excellent strategy for building alliances is by mediating contacts between others just by introducing two people you know to each other. Another approach is showing you care about their success and that you are happy for them. A third one is to talk positively about someone in front of others, as it creates an image of you as someone who does this as part of who they are, and people will feel you will do the same when talking about them.

In his book *The Introvert's Edge*, Matthew Pollard talks about not being a networker but rather a connector. I speak from my own experience, as I love when I can help someone, either directly or at least indirectly, by getting them in touch with someone who can offer help I can't.[131]

Connecting two people who may be helpful to each other is a great way to become useful in their eyes. And people tend to return the favor. It happens to me often that a friend, colleague, or acquaintance reaches out and wants to introduce me to someone. I enjoy these situations. Not only do I not need to go to big networking events to expand my network, but I can meet new people in a more comfortable one-on-one setting with a specific mission or topic of discussion in mind.

Partner with Your Boss

Your biggest ally is your boss. Your manager has the formal power, but that doesn't mean that there needs to be some subservient relationship between the two of you. The most productive relationship with your boss is one where you are partners.

You often hear that you need to learn to manage your boss. What does that mean? The common logic is that the manager manages the team. The less common view, but just as important, is that employees also need to manage their managers. Why? We are not slaves. We are all human beings with the same fundamental rights.

Your manager may have positional power over you, but that doesn't mean you just follow orders. If you want to have a successful and fulfilling career, you need to feel responsible for your own future, and you need to feel in control. Part of that responsibility is to build relationships with relevant people in your organization. One of these individuals is your boss. Your boss can have a substantial positive impact on your career, your growth as a person, and your ability to get things done.

Managing up has a negative connotation. It is often confused with sucking up to your boss. However, these two terms couldn't be more different. Sucking up means that you are the "yes-man." You are doing everything in your power to please the boss, to appear in the best light, and to earn some plus points. You hope that by being a favorite "pet" you will gain some privileges not available to others who don't suck up. This means that you don't shy away from throwing others under the bus if it helps to improve your image. This is unhealthy behavior. It may work in the short term to advance your career, but it will definitely destroy your reputation, kill your long-term prospects, make the team dysfunctional, and ultimately make you entirely dependent on the good graces of your boss instead of on your skills and effort.

In contrast, managing up is an ability to talk to your boss as an equal. Your boss is your partner in getting the work done and in fulfilling the company's mission. Managing up is about setting boundaries and rules for how you and your manager work together. It is about agreement on how you stay in dialogue, how you set priorities, how you keep each other informed, and how you hold each other accountable. It is about understanding the needs of the other person and helping them to achieve their goals.

Setting Boundaries: The first thing to do is to sit with your manager and talk about how you will work together. You want to understand how your boss works and what their general expectations are in terms of updates, reports, escalations. You should clarify the level of detail they want to be involved in. You should talk about whether they want to be informed when you need to speak to their management or other departments. You should agree on the "no surprises" rule. Nothing is more embarrassing for your boss than to be confronted by their manager about something you have done and they have no clue about. You should also talk about how you work and whether it is compatible with your manager's expectations. Especially in today's hectic environment, you should clarify what level of availability and responsiveness is expected. The boundaries of conversation also need to tackle the topic of feedback. How do you give each other feedback? This may be tough to do at the very first meeting, but it is important to indicate that you appreciate any feedback your manager is willing to give you and that you are also available to provide feedback when asked. For any two people to work well together, they need to get to know each other a bit. If you don't understand what your boss's worldview is, what is important to them, what pushes their buttons, and what they won't tolerate, it is very difficult to work with them effectively. Understanding who your boss is and what their values are can make your life significantly easier, and you will make fewer missteps.

Setting communication rules: Agreeing on how your manager expects to communicate with you is probably the most important conversation to have. Each of us is used to different communication channels, may have different ways of how we receive and process information, and may be used to a different method of communication from the previous job or even from other colleagues. It is important to agree with your manager on what communication channel is preferred for what information. For example, you may agree that regular updates are best over emails to be read at your manager's leisure, but any escalations or concerns should be communicated face-to-face or over the phone. This agreement is essential when you have a remote boss and is hyper-important when your boss sits in a different time zone. You can be flexible and adjust to the needs of your boss with one big exception. Never agree to not communicate! You need to build a solid relationship, which will not happen when you or your boss avoid interactions. It might be very seductive, especially for introverts, to limit the interactions, but it will hurt you in the long run. If your introversion gets in the way of building tons of different relationships, that is fine, but you need to cultivate a couple of them, and the relationship with your boss is the most important one on the professional side of your life.

If your manager says that there is no reason to talk regularly, insist on it anyway. You can appeal to the ego by asking for help, acknowledging you can learn from him or her, or just state plainly that it would help you grow, and you feel a regular contact will help build a good relationship between the two of you. If you talk with your boss only when there are problems, your relationship will have a significantly negative undertone. You need to take complete responsibility for making the relationship work. Your boss may have ten other reports, but you have only one boss, so the priorities are obvious. I personally tend to over-communicate with my superiors, so the conversation I would have with any new boss is along these lines: "I'm used to copying my boss on all emails that might be eventually brought to their attention. I don't necessarily expect you to read them, but I want to make sure you have them available if your manager or someone from other departments asks. If I need your help, I will specifically indicate that in the subject of the email. Does this work for you?" As you see, I'm not asking, "How do you want me to communicate?" since it would put me in a passive role as the one who needs to adjust. By proactively describing how the communication could look, you ensure your voice is heard and your needs are met. The boss can always say no. In my case, sometimes, the answer was "Works for me!" Sometimes the answer was, "No need, just include me when you need help." Regardless of the answer, it helped manage the expectations.

Setting Goals, Priorities, and Checkpoints: Having set goals, understood priorities, and agreed-upon checkpoints is critical for a healthy, surprise-free working relationship. You may hear from the human resources department that it is the manager's responsibility to set the goals for their team. Yes, that is most likely in their job description, but at the same time, it is in your best interests to make sure it happens. Let's imagine your boss won't set the goals for you at the beginning of the year or quarter or whatever period is being used to manage performance at your company. When the end of that period comes and your boss is required to evaluate your performance, there is no real data to judge against, and you have no opportunity to influence what the feedback on your performance will be. The boss can say that you were doing okay, but it could be better—nothing specific, nothing actionable, and a big surprise for you. The conversation would be very different if you agreed on the goals at the beginning and then had a regular conversation about how things were going and tracked progress. In the end, there would be no surprises, you could prove how well you did, and the boss would evaluate your performance based on data and not just gut feelings. The great thing is that this is entirely under your control. Even if your boss doesn't set the goals for you, nothing prevents you from doing it yourself. Just come up with the plans and share them with your boss for comments. And don't end there. Bring them up regularly in the conversation to show the progress you are making and ask for feedback. At the end of the period, you can summarize all your achievements and share them with your boss. Not only will you make their job easier, which will be appreciated, but you will also have everything under your control.

Asking for Help: One of the critical things your boss can do for you is to remove obstacles. This means that you need to have an explicit agreement with your boss about what level of issues they can help you with. This can be a very general statement, such as, "When you run into something you can't figure out, let me know, and I will help you." It can also be something much more specific, like, "Once you are ready to present the proposal to the CEO, let me know so we can review it together and I can help you by pushing it through." The key is to have a clearly stated agreement with your manager that it is okay to ask for help and doing so won't be held against you.

Offering Help: To paraphrase JFK, "Don't ask what your manager can do for you, ask what you can do for them." Why? Good relationships are all about trust. How do you build trust? There are a couple of ways to do it, but the basic one is to make sure that others see that you have their well-being on top of your mind. If you accomplish that, chances are that they will reciprocate. When your boss sees that you are willing to help solve their problems, it dramatically increases their trust in you. They will trust your skills and your loyalty and ultimately will find you indispensable. Common sense says that when you are indispensable, you are in a much better negotiation position to get what you want. When you can quickly show the value you provide, it directly impacts your ability to get the next exciting project, the next promotion, the next compensation increase, or the freedom to work the way you want. You don't need to do much. Just asking whether there is anything you can help with will do the trick. A better approach may be to get clues from what was discussed or what you already know your manager is working on and ask if you can help with that specific problem. In the long term, the best approach is to ask about their priorities since then you might be able to proactively solve the problems. Every now and then, I would ask my boss about his top priorities for the next couple of months and then see if I could bring some value, solve his problems for him, or contribute to the solution. The beautiful side effect of this practice is that you get opportunities to do parts of your manager's job, allowing you to learn new skills and expand your own job. In simple terms, this will enable you to grow. You don't need to wait for anyone to give you these opportunities. It is you who is enabling this growth for yourself! The next time you have a conversation with your manager, don't talk only about your needs. Before you end the conversation, just ask a simple question: "Is there anything I can help you with?"

Not Crossing the Line: Your boss can help you significantly with your career and your personal growth. They can cause havoc in both. You should draw a line in the sand that you won't cross. You want to be loyal to your boss, but at the same time, you need to be loyal to yourself. Sometimes your boss may not be the right person to provide you coaching or mentoring, and you may get help from someone else. This is especially true if both of you have the same weaknesses and blind spots. It is often a misplaced loyalty and fear of walking away that leads people to follow their bosses even when asked to do something unethical or even criminal.

That is the time when you need to be loyal to your company over your boss. A little bit less obvious is when you are being led in a direction that clashes with your core values. You may not necessarily be asked to do something illegal but still be asked to do something that is in such a dramatic clash with your values that you know you wouldn't be able to look into a mirror ever again. That is when you need to be loyal to yourself and let your boss know that you can't do that thing with a clear conscience. If your boss understands, good. If not, just walk away. You may lose your job, but you won't compromise your integrity. This may create a short-term setback, but in the long run, being able and willing to stand for what is right will pay dividends in the form of strong character and a reputation as someone who does the right thing and is worth following.

Playing Nice with Others

Having a great working relationship with your direct manager will make your life easier. It will increase your chances of a successful career. But what about your colleagues? As we have discussed in Chapter 4, your manager and your team are both important to contributing to feelings of a successful career. If they are present, you feel you belong. If you don't have good relationships with those around you, your satisfaction with your career will be significantly lower. And do you still remember the Quiet Success Sweet Spot we discussed in Chapter 5? Working with the right people, people you like, is an integral part of getting to your Sweet Spot.

Being a team player is often the mantra repeated in most organizations. We are a team. We work together. We succeed and fail as a team. We collaborate. We regularly communicate and solve problems together. It makes sense that people working together can achieve more than a single individual can But there are obvious drawbacks. We introverts are at our best when working alone. We get into the flow when we have the time to focus and do some deep thinking. That is often rather difficult to do in a group setting. So how do you combine the needs of the organization and your own needs to get the best of both worlds and work at your best?

It starts with a definition of what being a good team player means. In its purest form, a good team player is someone who works well with others as a member of a team, who is willing to help, and whose goals are aligned with those of the team. When you dig into more details, you can come up with a list of characteristics that may look like this. A good team player:

Listens Actively: Arguably, the most important trait for collaborating and communicating with others is the ability to listen. By understanding the opinions, needs, and wants of others, you can better find your place in the team and figure out how to work with the rest.

Does More Than Is Required: A willingness to go above and beyond your tasks is important when working with others. It means picking up tasks that no one owns and doing whatever it takes to get the job done.

Is Open-Minded: The ability to see the world through the eyes of others and being open to different opinions and views is important for finding common ground. If you always push your way and never bother to consider that the opinions of others might have some merit, you won't be a good team player.

Treats Others with Respect: It goes without saying that treating others as fellow human beings is at the core of successful teams and at the heart of any relationship. If your ego leads and you are not willing to consider others as equals, you won't build the type of relationships that will lead to a well-functioning team.

Is Flexible and Adapts Quickly: Things are changing all the time, and we need to change with them to keep up. There might be new people joining the team, new tasks, your role may change, you might be asked to drop what you are doing and help someone else. Things can get tough and stressful. Adapting to any given situation and circumstances without any fuzz will make you an invaluable team member.

Is Reliable: Others need to feel they can rely on you. If you say you will do something, you do it. If you can't manage to do what you promised, ask for help or at least admit that you overestimated what is possible and apologize. The moment you start blaming others for your lack of results, you create friction and cracks in the team. Always start with yourself and own up.

Is Committed to the Common Goal: It is always about the team and the team's mission. Your ambitions need to be set aside. If everyone on the team focused on their personal goals without regard for the reason why the team exists, there wouldn't be a team, just a random group of people where each is working on their own. What makes a team a team is that everyone is willing to make small sacrifices to reach a common goal.

Communicates Constructively: You don't need to talk all the time, but you also can't be quiet all the time. What needs to be said must be said. And it needs to be said in a way that is heard by others. This is usually just fine for introverts, as long as they are part of an already well-established team. If you know your coworkers and build solid relationships with them, you are probably pretty comfortable sharing your thoughts. It might be a bit more difficult when the team is being formed.

Shares Willingly: Sharing information, thoughts, suggestions, and, generally, any resources you might have with others is important for tapping the hidden creativity of the team. By sharing bits of information others may not know, you can give them ideas for how to do their jobs better. They may say something in return that helps you realize something you hadn't before and puts things in context. As the cliché goes, sharing is caring. By sharing, you are creating an environment of transparency and trust.

Participates Actively: One of the challenges introverts face is the need to be proactive and not just sit in the corner doing their own thing while seeing others chat away. Active participation doesn't necessarily mean you need to be part of every conversation, but you need to create the feeling with others that you are there and that you care and contribute. There are some strategies for how to get that done, and I talk about them below.

Offers to Help: Offering to help others is one of the key principles of a team. It is not only that each of us does our thing, it is also about each of us working together to get better and faster results. By helping others, you are increasing the team's capability while building relationships and strengthening the team's spirit.

Asks for Help: Introverts often struggle with this one. You may be either so convinced that you will figure things out that you don't ask for help when it would save you lots of time, or so convinced that others will find you incompetent and will laugh at you that you don't ask even when you know you are lost forever. For introverts, asking for help usually takes a lot of time. However, within a well-functioning team, it is vital to ask for help when needed. Otherwise, you may end up slowing down everyone who needs the output of your work, and they might even need to pick up some of the other tasks you couldn't do because you got stuck. There is nothing wrong with asking for help.

As you can see from the list, introverts make great team players. We may prefer to work on our own, but when asked, we can be critical to the success of any team. All you have to do is combine your needs with the needs of the team. This is a simple thing to do, though it is not without effort.

Volunteer as Much As You Can: By volunteering for stuff you are good at, you not only show you care for the team's well-being, but you also preemptively select tasks that align with your introversion and thus prevent your boss from assigning you work you would hate.

Write Meeting Notes: I love writing meeting notes. In fact, I'm known for writing notes from meetings before the meetings even start. Sound weird? Writing meeting notes helps you to collect your thoughts on the topics to be discussed. It helps you collect necessary data, and it helps you to easily follow what is being discussed. You can just tweak the prepared notes based on what is being said at the meeting, and it doesn't distract you. You can still pay attention to what others are saying. This plays to your strengths in preparation and listening, making you an important player in the meeting. It gives you reasons to speak up and reflect on what others are saying, increasing your visibility—the team benefits, and you benefit.

Find the Time to Work Alone: Get to work early or leave late to carve out alone time to focus. I personally like to work early in the morning before the rest of the team shows up to get some critical things done before the interruptions start. I also like being the first to arrive, as it allows me to welcome and have more meaningful conversations with the next person who shows up. This is opposed to situations when you arrive last, there are already twenty people in the office, and you just say hello or have some meaningless chitchat.

Agree on No Interruption Time: Especially in teams with a higher number of introverts, one strategy I saw successfully employed is to agree that specific times of day are no-interruption times. Let's say every day between 9:00 and 11:00 a.m., you don't talk, but everyone focuses on individual work.

Skip the Irrelevant: If you feel genuinely drained, learn to recognize small opportunities to skip the craziness and have some time alone. Fight the FOMO, or fear of missing out. You don't need to sit in on every single meeting and be involved in every single conversation. Some things are safe to skip without negative consequences for you or for the team.

Employ a Sense of Humor: Using a sense of humor, assuming you have one, is a great way to cement your place in the team. Just be careful about sarcasm and irony. Neither of those belongs in professional communication and both can make you appear unprofessional, childish, annoying, and defensive. Using bits of humor helps the team get through tough and stressful situations. It does the same to you personally. Again, a win-win approach.

Being a good team player and building alliances means you not only need to be trustworthy, as we discussed in Chapter 11, but you also need to trust others.

Extending Trust

Trust can't be given; it must be earned—or so we are being told. The idea behind this paradigm is that it is stupid to trust someone who is not worthy. And the worthiness shows through being trustworthy, which needs to be proven. This makes sense. It also is a rather pessimistic view of the world. If you approach every new relationship, every new person you meet, with suspicion and paranoia, you are putting up unnecessary walls. You make it more difficult to connect with others. You make it impossible to help others if you don't trust them. You see others as people with the potential to can cause you harm, and you don't build deep relationships. You treat others as children. They need to be watched over; they can't be allowed to make decisions; they need to be reminded of what is right and wrong.

But what other choice do you have? Flip the whole thing upside down. Extend trust first. Learn to live with the paradigm that people are, at their core, trustworthy. This is an incredibly liberating view of life. Suddenly, you don't need to build walls around yourself. You don't need to babysit and micromanage everyone around you. You can enjoy life for a change. When you start with trust, you treat others like adults. You give them the opportunity to prove that they are trustworthy after you already extended your trust. This leads to healthier relationships. It leads to you being more respectful. It leads to others trusting you more readily. If others see that you are trusting them, they will reciprocate. Most people will go out of their way to make sure that your trust is not misguided. They will put in the effort to earn your trust after the fact.

Will you occasionally get burned? Probably yes. That's life. If someone turns untrustworthy, you need to act accordingly. When dealing with broken trust in the workplace, be professional and firm. There is no point in acting like a five-year-old and creating drama. Be clear about what was promised, what was delivered, and what the consequences are for on the business and the relationship. Be clear that you are still colleagues who have to work together. You understand that mistakes happen and set the expectation that promises need to be kept to rebuild the trust and strengthen the relationship.

As the saying goes, "Fool me once, shame on you; fool me twice, shame on me." Treat others the way they need to be treated. If someone truly is untrustworthy and they prove that, you need to make sure they can't harm you. Once the trust is broken, you don't give it back easily. Now it truly needs to be earned. You need to let the person who broke your trust know what they need to do to earn it back. Extending trust to the person who broke it repeatedly is a bad policy, and it won't lead to success. If people see there are no consequences of their actions, there is little motivation for them to change.

Adopting the paradigm that others mean well, extending trust first, and being willing to take an occasional hit will remove many walls from your life and give you a bigger chance of a successful, positive, and rewarding life.

To extend trust first, you are putting yourself in a vulnerable position. You don't know the other person yet, but someone needs to take the first step to get the relationship started. Why couldn't it be you, even with your introverted reluctance?

Vulnerability

Vulnerability is a curious beast. It feels counterintuitive that showing weakness may lead to anything positive, but the surprising truth is that it does. Studies have shown that being willing to show vulnerability helps in numerous ways. It indicates that you can be trusted because you are ready to disclose something about yourself that others can potentially exploit. It can boost your ability to learn, as when you admit to yourself and others that you don't know something, there is a bigger chance you will learn it. Being willing to admit mistakes is the fastest path to fixing them and leads to forgiveness. All these things require you to show vulnerability.

So why are we afraid to talk about our shortcomings and mistakes? Showing vulnerability takes a lot of courage. The team around Anna Bruk researched the issue and came up with a name for it, the "beautiful mess effect."[132] Bruk and colleagues postulated that there is a difference in perception of how we think about our own vulnerability and how we see it in others. They explain the difference by using the construal level theory. This is a psychological concept that describes a relationship between our psychological distance from an object and whether we think about it in abstract or concrete terms. The more distant the object, the more abstract our thoughts about it will be.

This makes sense. Because we have detailed knowledge of ourselves, our motivations, and our thoughts, we think about how we behave in a precise, concrete way. When looking at others, we don't have that level of intimate knowledge, so we think about them in more abstract terms. When it comes to vulnerability, the effect is that we see our vulnerability in a somewhat negative light, so we are afraid to show it. We see ourselves as weak, and we are worried that others will exploit our weaknesses. We are uncomfortable with sharing it. When looking at the vulnerability of others, we see it in more abstract terms and much more positively. We think about others as more trustworthy, more courageous, more approachable.

Showing vulnerability takes a lot of courage, especially for introverts. It means you allow yourself to feel the good, the bad, and the ugly, and you are willing to show the world how you feel and who you truly are. It is tough to do this within a small circle of colleagues, but it gets even more difficult when showing it to the whole world. It takes courage, effort, and understanding that it can lead to you growing as a person and ultimately that it can bring you interesting career opportunities if done correctly. For me, starting a blog was pretty difficult. Yes, the blog was written and not spoken, so that helped, but I would still disclose things about my life and, more importantly, about what was going on in my head. And once you put something on the internet, it gets indexed by search engines, backed up, and stays there forever. Your thoughts are there for all the world to see. With time, I got comfortable with this type of vulnerability. My introverted nature helped, as I think very carefully before writing something that could haunt me down the road.

Vulnerability is about showing up when you are unsure about the outcome of your actions or when you have no control over the outcome at all. Those who don't show vulnerability are indeed protected from the outside world better than those who allow themselves to be vulnerable. If you erect a barrier around you, if you live in a protective bubble, you are safe. You are also less likely to enjoy life to its full potential. You don't have the opportunity to fully express and live your feelings. You shy away from intimacy, from being hurt. All these things are part of life, and you deny it to yourself.

Being hidden behind a wall takes a lot of effort and a constant guard on what you say and how you act. You can't enjoy the moment. You first need to make sure that you don't become vulnerable, dial down your response, build a protective bubble, and only then show your response. Exhausting.

What can you do to show a bit of vulnerability?

Authenticity: Being your authentic self is a powerful feeling. It also means you become more vulnerable. You live your life and behave in line with your code and values, and you don't try to build a facade that is expected by others. That, of course, exposes you to potential frowns and ridicule. It makes you vulnerable. And it is great since you just don't care. If you commit to being yourself, then what others think about you doesn't matter too much. You might be more vulnerable, but you also become more satisfied with your life.

Emotions: Emotions are a great way to show your humanity and your vulnerability. And they are healthy to express, as long as they are not extreme. If you don't know where to start and lack the courage to cry in front of others, consider some positive emotions. A genuine laugh is always a good way to show you have feelings. Of course, it doesn't show much of vulnerability. That comes later on, when you show more intimate emotions in times of tragedy. Showing strong emotions makes you more relatable. If you ever worked with someone who never shows how they feel, you know how disconcerting that is. It feels like working with a robot. Such a person also has trouble empathizing and creating a rapport with real human beings.

Limitations: Acknowledging your flaws, lack of skills, and knowledge gaps is a sign of strength, not a weakness. People are not fools, and they will quickly discover what the extent of your knowledge is. If you try to mask that you don't know something, they will know it anyway, and all you do is lose respect. They will ridicule your efforts behind your back. If you admit that you don't have a particular knowledge or skill and you show any interest in learning, you gain the respect of others. They will see that you are willing to listen, they will see you care, they will see that you acknowledge that they have something you can learn from them. You make others feel useful, needed, and valued. Asking others for help is a basic show of vulnerability. We all do this all the time. You can't go through life alone. You need others to help you. You *want* others to help you. It feels good. It may show that you are not a superhero who can do everything on your own, but people understand that no one is. And even if you can do everything on your own, it is more fun to invite others to join.

Mistakes: Admitting your mistakes and accepting blame when you mess things up is a must for healthy relationships. Once again, people around you realize when you do something wrong, and denying it won't win you many friends. All it does is lose you respect. Admitting a mistake not only humanizes you but is also the first step on a journey to fix it. By clearly stating what error you made, you can learn from it.

Not all vulnerabilities are created equal. There are some vulnerabilities you don't need to announce to the world. If you are in a leadership role, one vulnerability can be somewhat dangerous to show: showing indecisiveness and doubt in your skills or the direction you are leading the team. If people around you see that you doubt whether you are leading your team in the right direction, it is unlikely they will follow enthusiastically. A brief moment of indecisiveness at the beginning is fine, but it needs to quickly turn into an absolute conviction that what you are doing is right. Constantly doubting and second-guessing your own decisions is not a winning strategy. Learning to pick a direction, commit, and then stick to it is a crucial trait for any leader.

The same goes for unnecessary disclosure of personal details that should remain private. Exposing details from your private life on the internet or in a group of people is not a show of vulnerability, it is a show of a hidden agenda or possibly stupidity. Why would you do such a thing? What are you trying to achieve? Did you lose all your senses? You are not being vulnerable; you are just being plain stupid or cleverly shrewd. In any case, it won't help you feel better, be more authentic, or win you the respect of others.

Vulnerability can be a strength and advantage, but it can also lead to bad outcomes. As we discussed in Chapter 2, any strength becomes a weakness when overused. It also depends on the context. For someone from an underrepresented group to show vulnerability can be tricky, as it can enhance any biases or prejudices the rest of the group has. Vulnerability works the best when paired with credibility and competence that is already recognized by others. If everyone knows that you are good at something, they are less likely to use your vulnerability against you.

For example, in *How Women Rise*, Sally Helgesen and Marshall Goldsmith talk about habits that hold women back and keep them from achieving their goals.[133] Oversharing is one such habit. It is rooted in the idea of connecting with others through shared experiences. Women are often expected to show more emotions than men, yet when they show emotions, it is seen as too much. They are expected to be vulnerable, yet when they show vulnerability, it is seen as negative. For introverts, showing emotions feels like an on/off switch. We are either guarded, not showing much, or, if we trust the other person, we are willing to flood them and overshare. Emotions are part of who you are, and expressing them, even at work, is important for authenticity. Just be aware that others, especially men, may not know how to deal with them. Don't overwhelm others around you with too much emotion, too many words, or too much disclosure. Authenticity is a good thing, but too much of a good thing can become a problem. The best way to show vulnerability to connect better with others is in areas that are no big deal or by using self-deprecating humor, if that is who you are. This is something I do quite a bit. I have a rather peculiar sense of humor, and I like making fun of myself, but only when I know that the person I am talking to knows about my other strengths. That way, I mitigate any potential adverse effects of showing vulnerability and can enjoy the benefit of building a stronger relationship.

Introverts can show vulnerability if surrounded by people we know and if we are in a safe environment. That is when we are at the top of our game, when we feel secure to fully open up to the world and realize our potential.

Summary and Key Takeaways

Introverts tend to be independent and self-reliant, but we still need others to have successful careers. Building strong alliances and influencing those around you, even without having positional power, can dramatically accelerate your career. The place to start is with your direct manager. Your direct manager has a huge impact on your career, and building a strong working relationship can help you both. Next comes your closest coworkers, who may significantly boost your productivity with their help and your enjoyment of the work with their camaraderie. Learn to play nice with others, extend trust, and don't be afraid to be vulnerable when appropriate to strengthen and cultivate relationships.

- No one can do it alone. Even introverts need others to be successful and to feel they belong.
- Build alliances by helping others and by connecting them with each other.
- Having influence is not about positional authority. You don't need to be a manager or the loudest person in the room to wield significant influence.
- Redefine your relationship with your boss and learn to see it as a partnership.
- Introverts make great team players. Use your strengths to set team rules and contribute.
- Extend trust first and learn to trust others implicitly.
- When the trust is broken, don't let others take advantage of you the second time.
- Being willing to show vulnerability can boost your ability to learn and to lead.
- Not all vulnerabilities are created equal. Learn to distinguish between showing a vulnerability that will help others understand you and expressing an unnecessary disclosure of personal details that should remain private.

Questions and Next Steps

- What is your relationship with your boss? Do you work for them or with them? Working *with* your boss is a healthier approach than working *for* them. Go again through the section about partnering with your boss and consider what you can do to make your relationship more of a partnership than just a pure boss-subordinate relationship. Your boss can make or break your career, so being true partners can have a huge positive impact on your success.
- How do you approach new people? Is it with distrust or an open mind? If you are generally distrustful, try this the next time you meet someone for the first

time. Approach them with a smiling face and open mind. Try to act like their friend from the first moment you meet them and see what happens. Most people will react positively to a heartfelt positive approach. It will make the interaction less awkward and will set the relationship up for success.

17

Pay It Forward

*"I add value by helping others. I'm fair, inclusive, and flexible.
I keep giving without expecting returns."*

Most people derive genuine satisfaction from an unlikely source. It is not worldly possessions that make most people truly happy and satisfied with their lives. Getting a third car and a second house you don't need may feel good for a bit, but ultimately you will start asking yourself what the point is. No, most people who are truly satisfied with their careers, who feel they matter and their lives have meaning, find that meaning in helping others. It is the success of the person you mentored, the smile on the face of the child you fed, or the gratitude of the people who use the technology you developed that give you meaning.

True success comes to those who see the world as an endless opportunity. Those who have an abundance mentality see that life and career are not zero-sum games. For you to win doesn't mean that someone else must lose. If you believe that everyone can win, you will have a much more positive impact on the lives of others, and you will feel better. Giving without expectations of return can not only help you build a positive image, but it will also help you to be seen as someone other people will want to help. Being fair and inclusive, understanding your biases and hidden privileges, knowing that things get done differently in different cultures, and being adaptable enough can help you build an image as someone worth following. People will be more likely to want to work with you and to create a synergy where everyone succeeds. You have a positive impact on the lives of others—you matter.

Abundance Mentality

It is not about what happens to you but how you decide to respond and feel about it. It is the attitude that matters. In economic theory, a zero-sum game represents a situation where each participant's loss or gain is precisely balanced by the losses and gains of other participants. The total sum of all gains and losses is precisely zero. If one person wins, another one needs to lose. This leads to a scarcity mentality. There are limited options, limited resources, and only one can get to the top. Scarcity mentality leads to a competition where the goal is to win and destroy the opposition.

Career is not a zero-sum game. If one person wins, that doesn't mean that someone else needs to lose. If only one side wins, that creates a dent in the relationship. In the long run, no one wins if the relationships keep breaking. Ideally, you want everyone to succeed. If you can have that attitude and allow everyone to win, life flourishes, and everyone can have a successful career. For this to work, you need to have an abundance mentality. You need to believe that there is enough for everyone.

You can discover whether you have an abundance or scarcity mentality by considering the following questions.

Do you have an extreme need to be right? If yes, then you have a scarcity mentality. You feel that unless you have the last word, unless you give your two cents to every conversation, and unless you are the smartest person in the room, someone else may win. Therefore you may lose. To build up your abundance mentality muscle, use your strength of attentiveness and let other people speak (and you listen), try to allow others to be right, and try to step a bit into the background. Help others, and you may discover that you are still winning.

Do you need to always be the first one on the bus, to always have the best seat? The number of seats on a bus is limited, so if you wait too long to get on, you could indeed be left without a good seat. And yet, this approach still shows the attitude of someone with a scarcity mentality. You automatically assume that someone else may get a better seat, and that is not acceptable. By adopting the attitude that, regardless of where you sit, you will still get to the next destination, you may even offer a better seat to someone else to build a better relationship and feel good about it.

Do you believe you deserve more than others? If you feel that you are much better than the person next to you, that you deserve more money, a better title, a bigger house, and a faster car, and you are grumpy and envious if that doesn't happen, you have a scarcity mentality. You believe that because the other person has a better car, it somehow diminishes your achievements. It doesn't. Forget about others and focus on your own needs. You may discover that your salary, title, house, and car are just fine and nothing to complain about. If someone else has more stuff, good for them, but you can still feel happy about your fortunes.

Do you take credit for the work of others and marginalize their contributions? This goes back to the excessive need to win. You might be so blinded by scarcity mentality that you can't admit that someone else may have done something right. You may not want to acknowledge that you succeeded only because of the labor and sacrifices of others. You worry that, if discovered, you might lose, so you claim all the credit and diminish the contributions of others. If you can learn to praise others, to promote the work they did, to give credit to the people around you, then once again you will discover that it will elevate your status in the eyes of others and not diminish it. You won't lose only because you help others to win.

There is a second aspect of the attitude toward life. It is not only about the abundance of material possessions in the world, but also about whether you believe you are controlling your destiny. Do you believe that you make your own choices or that choices are made for you?

Do you blame others for your failures? Blaming others builds an internal self-image of victimization. It is not you who made a mistake; it is someone else, and you are the unfortunate victim. We talked about this in Chapter 8 and Chapter 10. Life is sometimes not fair, so get over it. Always ask first what you could have done differently before blaming others. Don't blame your boss for not agreeing to your proposal. Chances are you didn't present it convincingly or didn't gather the right data. Don't blame your team for not understanding your direction and for doing something different from what you expected. Chances are you were not clear on priorities or on what needed to be done. Don't blame others. Own your world.

Do you blame others for you being stuck? If you believe that it is your boss who is destroying your career by not promoting you, you are putting yourself in the role of victim. Take action into your own hands. It is not the world's responsibility to be there for you. If you want the next promotion, work hard for it, ask for it, or go to the company that gives you what you need. Don't blame your boss and be miserable. Are you always waiting for someone or something so you can get on with your work? Set clear priorities, escalate when you are blocked, and make sure people understand the natural consequences of their inaction. Don't blame the world for you not moving forward. Own your destiny.

Do you envy others their fortune? Do you believe that it is not fair that others have stuff you think you deserve? Maybe yes, maybe no. The important thing is that it just doesn't matter! Forget others. Focus on what you can do to get what you want. Focus on yourself. Being envious of your neighbor's new car won't help you to get a car on your own. If anything, it will slow you down. Stop paying attention to what others have and instead focus on what you need and work hard to get it.

Do you daydream about happiness while being miserable? Daydreaming is something that many introverts tend to do. It is the idea of living our lives inside our heads. It feels great when done occasionally and when we have positive thoughts, but it can derail your career when you do it all the time. If you spend hours daydreaming about how great it would be to have a big house or travel the world, you are wasting time that could otherwise be used to take action to get what you want. If you truly want something, then act as if you mean it. Be willing to make sacrifices to get what you want. If you are not willing to sacrifice, that means you don't want whatever it is bad enough. If you genuinely want to get in shape, get to the gym instead of sitting on the couch eating chips and watching sports on TV. You are watching people who wanted it badly enough, and they spent hours every day exercising and practicing. They made the sacrifices, and so can you.

Do you complain about small things in life? If you find something to complain about, anything and everything you see and experience, you have a problem. If you find a problem with everything in your life, you can hardly feel happy. Stop looking for problems. If you look for problems, of course you will find them. We talked about resilience in Chapter 13. Start looking at the bright side of life. If you pay attention, you will find many positives in everything around you. If you learn to enjoy the small things in life, you will be happier, and it will give you the energy to move forward. The more you focus on the small positive things in your life, the more you will see them. The more you see them, the more you will enjoy life. The more you enjoy life, the more positive things you will see around you. It is a positive feedback loop.

Life and career are not zero-sum games. Believe you own your future. Be more positive and confident about everything you do. Don't make excuses. If something doesn't work the first time, try again or change your approach. It is only you who is in charge. It is all about your attitude. Abundance mentality is learnable. You can choose to work hard to feel like you are in control of your destiny. You can choose to learn to feel good about life and be happy. It is all your choice. And it is also a choice to become a giver.

Giving

In *Give and Take*, Adam Grant talks about three types of people: takers, matchers, and givers.[134] Takers believe in "winner takes all" world order. Either you win or you lose. According to takers, the world is a very competitive place. Takers are self-focused. Givers, on the other hand, believe that there is enough in the world for everyone to thrive. They are other-focused. Often, they put the good of others above their own good. Takers will help you, but it will be a strategic help, and they need to get more from it than you do. For givers, the mental model is different. They are willing to help even if the costs of help are higher than the benefits they get. The important thing is that the other person benefits.

Many of us are somewhere in between. We are matchers. We operate on the principle that "I will help you, and I expect you to help me in the future." Things should be in balance. We say things like, "I owe you one," and we fully expect you will collect the debt. We are worried that the world is not fair and don't want to lose, so we protect ourselves by using the principle of reciprocity. The great news is that these styles are not genetically coded. They can be changed if only we want to change them. Each of us develops throughout our life a primary style, though we can use the other styles when we feel it is required. You may be a giver, but if you see that I'm taking from you all the time, don't appreciate what you do for me, and even abuse your kindness, you may switch your style toward me to that of a matcher. You will keep giving only when you see that I reciprocate.

Successful takers are often also good fakers. They act as takers toward their subordinates, but they can fake being givers when dealing with more powerful people. They can charm their way into good graces with those above them. The more powerful takers get, the less they care about those below or around them. That, of course, leads to a lost reputation and even animosity from others. Most of us are matchers, so when I mistreat you, you will reciprocate the same way if you can. If you can't punish me directly, you do it indirectly. How? Gossip is a rather efficient way to do it. You will trash my reputation because you feel I deserve it as punishment for my mistreatment of you.

The style you exhibit will impact your relationships with others and your career opportunities. While it might be tempting to be a taker and try to achieve success on the backs of others, it rarely leads to a long, successful career. You are burning bridges as you work toward success. You may get to the top of the organization, but to get there you have potentially built a toxic culture, destroyed your reputation, and possibly killed any chances of more success in the future.

As Grant describes, there is one style that is vastly superior to others when you want to achieve lasting success, as long as it is done correctly: be a giver. Givers can enhance everyone's success, but they need to do it in a way that doesn't harm them personally. Too often, givers sacrifice their own good for the good of others. They help you succeed while failing themselves. There is no need for that. Successful givers have the same ambitions as takers, but their way of going about it is different. The way givers succeed is based on the network effect. The success spreads all around them. When takers succeed, others envy them and want to put them down. When givers succeed, others are happy for them and keep supporting them even more. This also works in the other direction, as givers help those around them achieve their goals. Unlike takers, who often excel in independent roles, givers outperform them in positions where collaboration and interdependency are required. They pay it forward without the expectation of future benefits to themselves. They build communities and ecosystems.

Sociologist Fred Goldner came up with the term "pronoia," the opposite of paranoia. Paranoia is the state where you feel others are plotting against you. Pronoia is the belief that other people are praying for your well-being and saying nice things about you behind your back.[135] This belief is often correct when it comes to givers. Their reputation feeds on itself, and people around them go out of their way to help these givers to succeed. Even though takers desire a high status in society, it is often givers who get it. Because of their willingness to volunteer, help, and share their knowledge and skills, they demonstrate value and are respected for it.

Givers are the best collaborators since they will make decisions in the group's interest rather than on their own. The more giving the group, the better the performance the team has. You put the group's goals and the mission first. You show the same care and concern for others as you do for yourself. This encompasses such behavior as selflessness and generosity. You can see this type of behavior in many situations when the group realizes that it is just them, and they need to rely on each other. When I traveled through Africa, I was often amazed by the helpfulness of the people in remote areas. It makes sense. These people understand that if they don't help others, the others may not survive. They also know that it could just as easily be them who need help. They pay it forward. When everyone does it, you have a great culture of giving and collaboration, where people can rely on each other.

There is a pitfall, though. Givers have a bigger chance than takers do of becoming pushovers. Because they care about others, they may forget about themselves. But successful givers are not only other-oriented, they are also quite self-interested. They are as ambitious as takers. They know that selfless giving is unhealthy. You can't keep doing it, as that means you focus on others to your own detriment. As Adam Grant mentions, successful givers are not selfish or selfless, they are "otherish." They care about others, but they also take care of their own needs and interests.

People often act as takers because they believe that everyone does that. If you show them that taking is not the norm, they are more likely to adjust and become givers. This is because, deep down, most of us are matchers, and we will match the behavior of others. Leading by example has a powerful effect when you want to influence others to become givers. Things like paying it forward work precisely because of this effect. To turn people into givers, don't work on their attitude but on their behavior. Nudge them into giving, ideally into giving without a distinct advantage to them. If they do it consistently for some time, the cognitive dissonance will force them to change something. It won't be easy to stop giving without looking bad and feeling like a hypocrite, so it is easier for them to start thinking about themselves as givers. It is now part of who they are, part of their identity.

Since most introverts are naturally humble, loyal, and empathetic, we have a head start on becoming givers. What is needed is to see others around us as human beings with the same needs, desires, and rights as us, and for that, we need to understand our assumptions, biases, and prejudices.

Biases

In her book *The Person You Mean to Be*, Dolly Chugh asks a simple question. Would a truly good person behave the way we do? And she immediately answers: No! Even if we convinced ourselves that we mean well, deep down, we are full of biases and misconceptions that force even the best of us to act in ways that, in retrospect and with a different perspective, are not always good. The "you" that you aspire to be is often somewhat different and better than the "you" that actually exists.[136] To become the best possible "you," learn to recognize and deal with cognitive biases.

Fundamental Attribution Error: There are many cognitive biases that significantly impact how we see ourselves and others.[137] Fundamental attribution error is the bias that makes you find a good excuse when you do something aggressive or generally not acceptable, while if someone else does the same thing, you scoff at them. They must be jerks. You understand why *you* act a certain way, so it is easy for you to come up with a reasonable explanation. However, you are not a mind reader and don't see what's going on in the heads of others, so you forget that they can also have reasonable explanations.

Let's say you are late to board your flight. You cut a line in front of the security check at the airport. In your mind, this is a perfectly reasonable behavior, as otherwise the plane would leave without you. Now, imagine another day when you have plenty of time, and you are waiting in a queue for the security check.

Suddenly, someone rushes in and cuts in front of you. You get angry. *What a jerk*, you think. *I've been waiting here for half an hour already, and he just skips all the people and gets in front.* What's going on in your head is the fundamental attribution error in real life. The same situation, and your brain cooks up two very different perspectives.

Confirmation Bias: Our brains are not impartial data-collecting devices. We choose subconsciously to hear and see mostly information that supports our already existing point of view. And if what the eyes see and the ears hear doesn't support it, we tend to forget or at least interpret that information in ways that are aligned with our view of the world. We are far from impartial, whether we realize it or not. Research indicates that we are more likely to ignore any adverse effects and negative information we may receive about something when we care about it. For example, I consider myself somewhat ecology-conscious. I also love to travel. So I tend to ignore the impact any travel, and especially air travel, has on our planet. I tend to skip over information related to the negative effects of tourism. My brain prevents me from knowing something that would make me feel bad about what I'm doing.

Bystander Effect: The bystander effect is easiest described when you consider a situation of a stranger collapsing on the street with a glaring need for medical help. If you are the only person around, you will likely try to help to the best of your abilities. However, if there are many other people on the street, everyone assumes that someone else will help, and ultimately no one helps. You can see the same effect in many other situations, even in corporate life. You may be in a meeting where everyone knows that something unpopular needs to be said, or a figure of power needs to be challenged, and no one does it.

As you can see, our relationship with our brain is somewhat complicated. Our mind is our best frenemy. It is capable of lying to us if it will make us feel better. We all need affirmation from those around us that we are good people. That is often one of the reasons why we would rather conform than be seen as different. If we are conformists, functional and productive members of society, the chances are that we get that affirmation more easily than if we act like rebels.

Our reaction to what psychologists call "self-threat" says a lot about who we truly are deep down. If someone describes us in a way that doesn't match our self-image, we react. We often lash out aggressively, starting to argue that they are wrong or, more passive-aggressively, thinking that they don't know what they are talking about. Just consider this. I believe that I'm a good person who is always fair. If you disagree with my decision on how to split a box of chocolate among the team members based on their merit, you are not only explicitly challenging my decision on who from the team brings more value, but you are also implicitly challenging the idea that I am a good and fair person. I may easily take this personally. Instead of having a logic-driven conversation about the merits of people on the team, I jump into an emotionally charged conversation about why you are attacking my fairness and why you are saying I'm a terrible person. Self-threat triggers my self-preservation mode.

Psychologists Karl Aquino and Americus Reed talk about moral identity.[138] From their research, it is clear that most of us want to feel that we are good. That doesn't necessarily mean that we want to *be* good; we just want to feel that way. As Dolly Chugh says, our behavior is driven not by our moral values but by our identity. We want to see ourselves as good people. That goal can be accomplished either by being a good person and acting that way or convincing our minds that we are good people while doing things that are in exact contradiction. That is why so many people are willing to do terrible things in the name of their god or their cause. Even though the deeds are evil, these individuals convince themselves that what they're doing is for the good of the world.

Think of Christmastime. For many people in the Western world, not only actual Christians, Christmas is a time when the environment pushes us to be good. Love is in the air. So we suddenly go to church or make donations to charity. Why? Is it because we want to help others? Or is it because we want to feel good about ourselves? The chances are that the second is true. We want to feel that we are good people who are helping others. That feeling is important. However, if we were really outstanding citizens who wished to help others, we would do it regularly during the year. It would be our habit, and we would make sacrifices to make it happen. But most of us don't do so.

Hidden Privilege

I consider myself to be pretty successful. As I got more and more successful, I was more and more dedicated to a meritocratic view of the world. I was more and more convinced that it was only my hard work and dedication that had brought me success. If someone else was not as successful, they probably hadn't tried hard enough. The more success and power we get, the more likely we are to dismiss the role our privilege plays and the headwinds others may have.

The first step in becoming truly good and making the world a better place is recognizing how privileged you are. This applies to most of those who are reading this book. Just the fact that you've picked up this book assumes you speak English, have access to the internet, have some disposable income, and most likely have your basic needs covered. You are privileged, at least in some ways. This applies doubly if you are part of the majority in the society you live in, and a little less if you are in some way underrepresented, whether on the basis of race, gender, religion, or anything else that makes you different and likely not to be accepted as part of the majority.

For example, I live in central Europe, and I'm a successful white, educated middle-aged man. You can't get more privileged than that. I have no moral right to complain about anything in my life, and there is a lot I can do to help others who are not as privileged as I am. Ask yourself, don't you, by any chance, belong to the same or a similar group? If yes, what are you doing with that privilege? Are you grateful for what you've got, or do you spend your days whining about how life is unfair? How do you behave at work when working with those from underrepresented groups? Are you inclusive and supportive?

Helping others is not necessarily about money or worldly possessions. It is about how you treat others, how inclusive you are, how you fight biases, and what opportunities you give to others. Dolly Chugh talks about willful awareness. Take the extra step to consider the impact your words and actions may have on others. Try to understand those who are not as privileged as you are. With this better understanding of the world and yourself, you are more likely to do the right thing. This will pay back in creating a healthier workplace and surrounding you with people who will enjoy working with you. Remember that good working relationships are important for getting to and staying in your Quiet Success Sweet Spot, as discussed in Chapter 5.

As Chugh says, "If you are not part of the problem, you can't be part of the solution."[139] It is the people from the biased majority who need to take action, not those in the minority who struggle. The people who show bias need to get self-aware and drive education and action to change things. They have the most significant power to do so. Most of us have problems accepting that we belong to the privileged group. People often prefer to feel like the victims, removing some of their responsibility for their own lives. It is not their fault that they feel miserable. The one way to remove that belief is to realize that other groups truly are the victims. Change the frame of reference, and you will get a bit more accepting that maybe you are not doing as poorly and that, in fact, you are lucky. Way too often, we claim that we support equality and meritocracy, while in reality, we ignore all the hidden forces that push the privileged group up and put minority groups down. Before you use the words "meritocracy" or "equality" again, consider whether your definition of these words is inclusive or whether it ultimately applies only to people from the privileged group.

Speaking of equality, there is a crucial difference between equity and equality. Equity and equality are two ways you can achieve fairness, but equity is much more powerful, as it removes biases and privileges from the equation. Equity is giving everyone what they need to be successful, while equality is treating everyone the same way. Equality is truly fair only when everyone starts from the same starting position and requires the same help. If you are big into equality, you should reconsider. Go for equity instead.

Cultural Awareness

Whole books have been written about working across cultures, so I'm not going to write a comprehensive guide on the subject but rather open the door for you to realize what a significant impact cultural differences have on the workplace and how things are not as simple as they may appear in Western literature when it comes to success.

Even when it comes to introversion, you will discover that different cultures treat it in different ways. If you are an introverted kid in the US or Canada, you may be at a disadvantage among your peers. If you are an introverted kid in China, you may find that, on the contrary, you are pretty popular for your listening skills and quiet manners. This then, of course, reflects in the way you behave and lead people in different cultures and in how much advantage you as an introvert can have.

Stop making assumptions. Assumptions usually don't work even within your own culture, and they definitely won't work with a significantly different culture. A couple of years ago, I had an interesting conversation that illustrates this point. The team working on a product was distributed across two locations in the USA and the Czech Republic. Both teams had great people, everyone tried their best, and still, the collaboration didn't go particularly smoothly. It started with a different perspective on what "decision" actually means and how decisions are made. Everyone understood that the team needed to move fast, but each part of the team had a different way to do it. The team in the USA would briefly discuss the problem, make a decision, and move forward. If they later found that the approach didn't work, they would change the decision and keep going. The team in the Czech Republic would spend significantly more time discussing all the details, talk about risks, try to get more data, and eventually arrive at a decision everyone was comfortable with. But that decision was a "Decision." Once it was made, the team could move fast without second-guessing and get the job done.

Each approach has its pros and cons. There is no right way to make decisions. But it creates a lot of friction if each team keeps doing it their own way. Then one team feels the other team takes too much time to make a decision, while the other team feels the first one is making chaotic rush decisions and then changing them later on. All that is needed is for both teams to get together, acknowledge different ways of making decisions in their respective cultures, and agree on the way decisions will be made. People can be incredibly flexible, but they need to understand the rules and expectations.

A word of caution. Be careful and do not use cultural stereotypes indiscriminately. Understanding another culture is a way to open your mind and be more willing to accept other forms of working. You shouldn't automatically label people though, because even within the same culture, each of us is different. It is not only the culture we were brought up in that forms who we are. It is also our basic personal characteristics, education, and life experiences that play a significant role.

The fact that people from different cultures are different is sort of obvious. What may be less obvious is that even the actual language you use can impact your perspectives and decisions. A study done by psychologists at the University of Chicago found that people using a foreign language take a less emotional approach to moral dilemmas. This applies even in situations where they are asked to sacrifice one life for others to survive.[140]

Adaptability

All this talk about biases, privileges, and cultures leads us to adaptability, as the world is more complicated than one might like. You can define adaptability as the ability to deal with uncertainty. David H. Jonassen and Barbara L. Grabowski talk about tolerance to ambiguity as an individual's willingness to accommodate or adapt to encounters with ambiguity.[141] Whatever you call this trait, it is not something introverts usually possess. We have a higher sensitivity to our environment, so unexpected changes are not welcomed. Extroverts have a higher tolerance for inconsistency and typically are better able to deal with uncertainty and change. And the world keeps changing. Being able to adapt to what the environment throws at you is essential for success. If you can adjust quickly, you spend less time in unproductive limbo. You spend less time brooding or being stressed out. You realize that what you were doing up to this point won't work anymore, and you pivot. Luckily, there are workarounds. Many introverts have strengths that compensate and can help deal with ambiguity and with adaptation to the ever-changing environment.

Trusting Your Own Opinion: Don't panic; instead, think things through. It is the thoughtfulness and ability to analyze a situation that can help you get on the right path. Most changes are not as bad as they may appear. Taking a step back and looking at them with a logical mind can help you remove anxiety. With a positive outlook on life, you will quickly discover that proverbial silver lining on every cloud of change. If the real culprit is the uncertainty and lack of clarity on what's coming, then you need to consider possible responses and proactively step up to resolve the ambiguity. You need to happen to life, rather than letting life happen to you.

Ability to Solve Problems on Your Own: Introverts may not be the first to get moving, but once we do, we tend to solve problems our own way, on our terms. That is excellent news in times of uncertainty as well. You don't necessarily need others to clarify things for you, as you can find your place even under these conditions. It may be a bit uncomfortable, but that is fine.

Having Lower Sensitivity to External Rewards: Introverts don't seek external rewards to keep going. We are more likely to find intrinsic motivation, and that helps in times of uncertainty. If you can tap into your inner strength, you don't spiral into a self-defeating state of mind when things don't go as planned. Many introverts can persevere when apparent solutions don't exist, and we don't give up that easily. If we encounter pushback, we don't stop. We reassess our options and keep going.

Adaptability is something you can learn. You may hate change. You may hate uncertainty. But once you accept that they are part of life, you have the skills to adapt. All it requires is to be willing to be uncomfortable and tap into your strengths as an introvert. Growth requires change, and change requires getting out of your comfort zone. Nothing in the universe can grow without changing. To have a long, successful career, you need to learn and grow. You need to evolve, get better, and become someone new.

Summary and Key Takeaways

You would think that work is a simple transaction. I give you some money, and you get some work done. This works fine just for survival. But if you want to have a truly successful career, work needs to become more than just a transaction. You need to work for more than just money. You need to work to help others and to make the world a better place. You do this by paying it forward. Adopt an abundance mentality and the attitude that there are enough opportunities for everyone to have a great career. Keep giving without expecting anything in return. Understand your biases and hidden privileges that may influence the way you treat others. Make no assumptions about people from other cultures, and keep an open mind and adapt to the needs of the business and the needs of every single person you interact with. Don't make your career one big transaction, but rather learn to enjoy the feeling that you are here to not only be successful yourself but make others successful too. Pay it forward.

- Your success is tied to the success of others. Learn to derive satisfaction from life by helping those around you.
- Life and career are not zero-sum games. If one person wins, that doesn't mean someone else needs to lose.
- There are three types of people: takers, matchers, and givers. Be a giver.
- There is a significant difference between equality and equity. Equality is treating everyone the same way, while equity is giving everyone what they need to be successful.
- Understand your biases and that you are not as good as you believe yourself to be.
- If you are in the majority, realize that you are privileged, even if it doesn't feel that way.
- Stop making assumptions about other people and other cultures.
- Don't succumb to cultural stereotypes. We are all people, and each of us is unique regardless of what culture we come from.
- Use your strengths as an introvert to compensate for your weaknesses when it comes to dealing with uncertainty.

Questions and Next Steps

- Do you have an abundance or scarcity mentality? Think about the interactions and decisions you made over the last week. Did you always go for the win-win? Or were your actions driven by the fear that someone may beat you or the desire to beat them? Did you always have the last word? Did you take credit for other people's work? Did you marginalize their contributions? Did you blame others for your misfortunes? Did you constantly complain about everything? If you realize that you have a scarcity mentality, make it a point to stop yourself every time you make a decision and consider what drives you. Then do your best to make a decision that will allow wins for everyone impacted.
- Do you believe that you are a genuinely good person? Consider some of the following statements and see whether your belief survives: How many of your friends are from other cultures, races, and educational backgrounds, and how many are similar to you? Are you attached to gender stereotypes? Do you laugh at jokes about other races, cultures, or genders? Do you judge others who are different from you? Do you find excuses to believe that it is the fault of less fortunate people that they are less fortunate? Chances are that, if you are honest with yourself, your answers to some of these questions might not make you particularly happy. Consider them in your daily interactions and try to do better in the future.
- Are you a giver, taker, or matcher? For the next week, pay attention to how you interact with others. Does your presence enhance the success of everyone around you? Do you help others succeed? Do you cheer others on and feel good when they succeed? Do you make decisions for the good of the team and not only for your own good? If you are a taker or matcher, what do you need to change in your interactions with others to be a giver? Take it step by step and try to give more than you are getting. Learn to pay it forward, and it will help you feel good about yourself and your career in the long run.

Conclusion

Half of the population of this planet are introverts. Many introverts have a considerable influence, are immensely successful, lead global companies, and impact the lives of millions of people. Yet, when we look for our heroes, we often don't see those introverts, and if we see them, we don't realize that they are introverts. It is the nature of introverts to stay out of the spotlight, but that doesn't mean we don't matter.

I hope that this book gave you the tools and the motivation to work on becoming the best you can be. Find your strengths and use them to build your career success. Don't try to emulate extroverts, don't succumb to cultural expectations, and find your own way.

The concepts I gave you are generalizations. They will work for most people, but they need to be tweaked and adapted for your particular circumstances. If you feel that something wouldn't work for you, that is fine. Don't use it. However, be careful not to dismiss things just because they look hard to implement. Nothing worthwhile is ever easy. If you want to change your life for the better, expect that it is going to be hard work.

I started this book with a claim coming from the world of coaching that everyone has the resources they need to succeed at the things they care about. At its core, finding the right job and being satisfied with your job is easy, even though a large percentage of people struggle to find their meaning. It is all in your head. Only you can decide whether you want to take a proactive approach to your life and career and become successful. It is my hope that, after reading this book, you learned enough to set out on an exciting journey to grow, become better, and get to your Quiet Success Sweet Spot.

To remind you of the steps you need to take, start with understanding who you are and taking the quiz in Chapter 1. Consider what your strengths are, as we discussed in Chapter 2. Then consider your core values, what you care about, and what your passions are, and run through some of the exercises from Chapter 3.

In Chapter 4, I introduced you to the various types of careers and to the Successful Career Wheel framework summarizing the critical aspects any successful career needs to have. Think about it and find out what your definition of a successful career is. Don't let others push you into a career path that won't work for you. Then move to the Quiet Success Sweet Spot concept as introduced in Chapter 5 and analyze what options are available to you. What are the activities you love? What are you good at? What do others need that they are willing to pay for? What people do you enjoy working with? Use this concept to figure out what work will lead to your life satisfaction and a fulfilling career. You will discover, not surprisingly, that not all jobs are created equal. However, it is not the job title that differentiates them; instead, it is your approach that makes the difference.

Once you understand your Quiet Success Sweet Spot, move on to the ideas described in Chapter 6 and plot a path to get there. I showed you what approach to take depending on where you are in relation to your Sweet Spot. Depending on what you need, focus on training and practicing, marketing and networking, reframing your view of the world, and coaching to build the right habits and attitudes. If you come to the conclusion that you need to change your job, read through the parts about interviewing and negotiating one more time to use your introversion to your advantage during the recruitment process.

In parallel to all this, consider adopting the Quiet Success Principles as a way of living. The principles, habits, and attitudes described in Chapter 7 onwards will make it easier for you to not only get to your sweet spot but to stay there. These principles will enable you to enjoy a long and successful career in any field you choose, and you will be rewarded with years of fulfillment at work and a feeling of meaningful existence.

To have a comprehensive view of how all the things I described in this book fit together, consider Figure 10, describing the Quiet Success Concept. It combines the concepts of the Quiet Success Sweet Spot, Successful Career Wheel, and the Quiet Success Principles into a cohesive big picture overview. Your Sweet Spot will be at the crossroad of doing what you are good at, what you love, what someone else needs, and working with people you like. If you get there, your career will provide you with a feeling that you learn, you matter, you survive, and you belong.

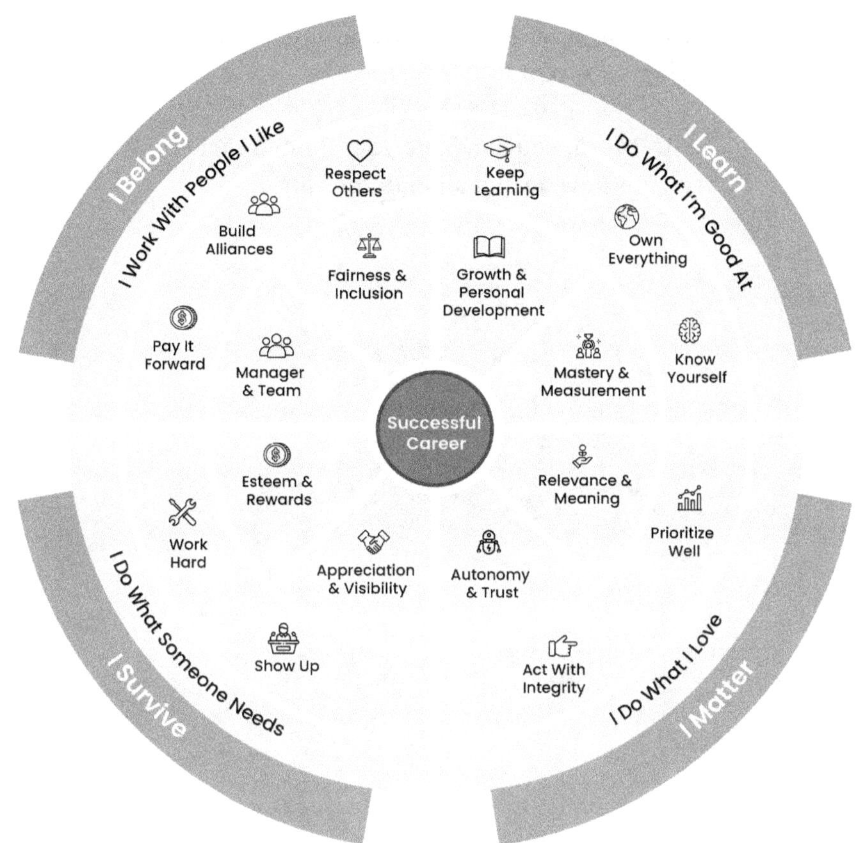

Figure 10: Quiet Success Concept

As you can see, there is a clear relationship between the concepts. Let's look at the picture and analyze it. When you "do what you are good at," as described by the Quiet Success Sweet Spot, you will get better. You "learn," as discussed in Successful Career Wheel, and the "growth and personal development" and "mastery and measurements" aspects of a good career are fulfilled. The Quiet Success Principles supporting this are "know yourself," "keep learning," and "own everything." When you "do what you love," you understand the "relevance and meaning" of your job and have "autonomy and trust"—you feel that you "matter." Principles supporting this are "prioritize well" and "act with integrity." When you "do what someone needs," you are "appreciated and visible," you get "esteem and rewards," and you have what you need to "survive" and feel good. "Work hard" and "show up" are principles supporting this aspect of a successful career. And finally, when you "work with people you like," in an environment that is "fair and inclusive," and you like your "manager and team," you get the feeling you "belong." This is supported by principles of respecting others, building alliances, and paying it forward.

With these, you can have your Quiet Success.
Now go and change the world.

Thank you for buying and reading *Quiet Success*. If
this book helps you in your career or life or helps you
figure out who you are, please let me know. I would
love to hear from you, fellow introverts, who found
their way to successful and happy lives.

If this book inspired you, I would ask you
to pass it on to others who may benefit.

Yours Tomas Kucera

Website: www.kuceratomas.com
Twitter: @GeekyLeader

List of Images

Acknowledgments

Over my years in management, I have been influenced by countless others. I worked with some great leaders, I led some great teams, and I studied the works of the best. This book has grown over time, influenced by the works of researchers, business gurus, sociologists, psychologists, and writers who helped me to shape my thoughts about work, career, leadership, and life.

I want to thank Susan Cain, Dale Carnegie, Dolly Chugh, Samantha Claire, Stephen R. Covey, Robert B. Dilts, Angela Duckworth, Carol S. Dweck, Daniel Gilbert, Ashley Goodall, K. Anders Ericsson, Viktor E. Frankl, Francesca Gino, Adam M. Grant, Daniel Goleman, Marshall Goldsmith, Jeff Haden, Jesse Itzler, Andy Johnson, Daniel Kahneman, Jennifer B. Kahnweiler, Patrick M. Lencioni, Sylvia Loehken, John C. Maxwell, William H. McRaven, Merve Emre, Erin Meyer, Jacob Morgan, Cal Newport, Joan Pastor, Daniel H. Pink, Matthew Pollard, Phil Rosenzweig, Kim Scott, Joe De Sena, Chris Voss, Jocko Willink, and countless others for the work they have done. Without them, this book would never have happened, and I would be a very different person.

I would also like to thank Friedrich Brezina, my first boss, who showed me what good management and leadership look like and who gave me opportunities to learn and grow. I want to thank all the mentors and senior leaders I learned from: Doug Hibberd, David Owens, Jen Alessandra, Melissa Garza, Nick Hamblin, and many others. I also want to thank Jan Tegze, an author in his own right, for his relentless nagging that forced me to finish the book.

A big thanks also to Bethany Davis for editing this book, Jenna Love for proofreading, Abu Hanif for designing the graphics, and Vanessa Mendozzi for the typesetting and the cover. Without you all, this book would never have seen the light of day.

Finally, I want to thank my parents, Josef and Marie, for the upbringing and dedication. Without their hard work and patience, I wouldn't have the means, the education, and the attitude that helped me to be where I am. And I can't forget about my sister, Jitka, and little niece, Gabriela, for being inspirations and a source of many anecdotes.

About the Author

Born in the Czech Republic, Tomas started his career as a software developer (an obvious job for a technically oriented introvert) after getting his master's degree from the Czech Technical University. But it didn't last. He got his MBA from Nottingham Trent University and trained as a professional coach at Erickson College. Within a couple of years, he was fully immersed in management and dedicated his life to leadership, coaching, and helping others succeed. Tomas is an introvert who hates the spotlight and big stages, likes to work alone, and yet is passionate about working with other people. Tomas has built, led, coached, and mentored teams in the Czech Republic, Austria, Germany, Romania, Croatia, Poland, Belarus, Ukraine, the Philippines, India, and the USA. His passion for meeting people from other cultures and helping them grow and succeed has never left him. Tomas has lived in several countries and loves to travel in his free time, with Africa, Asia, and South America being his favorite destinations. Aside from travel, he likes to write and runs the *Geeky Leader* blog. Tomas is an introverted engineering and operations leader and coach, passionate about setting up offices, building teams, developing people, solving challenging problems, and sharing the experience with others.

Notes

1. **Kucera, Tomas.** The Geeky Leader. [Online] [Cited: 05 01, 2021.] https://thegeekyleader.com/.

2. **Merriam-Webster.** Merriam-Webster Dictionary. [Online] Merriam-Webster, Incorporated. [Cited: 11 21, 2020.] https://www.merriam-webster.com.

3. **Cain, Susan.** *Quiet: The Power of Introverts in a World That Can't Stop Talking.* s.l. : Broadway Books, 2013. p. 368. ISBN-13: 978-0307352156.

4. **Psychology Today.** Understanding Shyness. *Psychology Today.* [Online] https://www.psychologytoday.com/intl/basics/shyness.

5. **Aron, Elaine N.** *The Highly Sensitive Person.* s.l. : Broadway Books, 1997. p. 251. ISBN-13: 978-0553062182.

6. *Four Meanings of Introversion: Social, Thinking, Anxious, and Inhibited Introversion.* **Jennifer O. Grimes, Jonathan M. Cheek, Julie K. Norem.** San Antonio, TX : s.n., 2011. Presented at the Society for Personality and Social Psychology.

7. **Loehken, Sylvia.** *Quiet Impact: How to be a successful Introvert.* s.l. : Hodder Audio, 2014. p. 224. ISBN-13: 978-1444792850.

8. **Encyclopædia Britannica, Inc.** Acetylcholine. *Encyclopædia Britannica.* [Online] Encyclopædia Britannica, Inc. [Cited: 09 12, 2020.] https://www.britannica.com/science/acetylcholine.

9. *Individual differences in extraversion and dopamine genetics predict neural reward responses.* **Michael X.Cohen, Jennifer Young, Jong-Min Baek, Christopher Kessler, Charan Ranganath.** 3, 2005, Cognitive Brain Research, Vol. 25.

10. *Relationship between Personality and Gray Matter Volume in Healthy Young Adults: A Voxel-Based Morphometric Study.* **Lu F, Huo Y, Li M, Chen H, Liu F, Wang Y, et al.** 2014, PLoS ONE 9(2).

11. *Differences in regional brain volume related to the extraversion-introversion dimension-A voxel based morphometry study.* **Lea Forsman, Örjan de Manzano, Anke Ninija Karabanov, Fredrik Ullén, Guy Madison.** 2012, Neuroscience Research, Vol. 72.

12. *Individual Differences in Amygdala-Medial Prefrontal Anatomy Link Negative Affect, Impaired Social Functioning, and Polygenic Depression Risk.* **Randy L. Buckner, Avram J. Holmes, Phil H. Lee, Marisa O. Hollinshead, Leah Bakst, Joshua L. Roffman, Jordan W. Smoller.** 50, 2012, Journal of Neuroscience, Vol. 32.

13. **Isabel Briggs Myers, Mary H. McCaulley, Naomi L. Quenk, Allen L. Hammer.** *MBTI Manual: A Guide to the Development and Use of the Myers-Briggs Type Indicator. 3rd.* Palo Alto : Consulting Psychologists Press, 1998. p. 420. ISBN-13: 978-0891061304.

14. *Reversing the Extraverted Leadership Advantage: The Role of Employee Proactivity.* **Adam M. Grant, Francesca Gino, David A. Hofmann.** 3, 2011, Academy of Management Journal, Vol. 54.

15. *Rethinking the Extraverted Sales Ideal.* **Grant, Adam M.** 6, 2013, Psychological Science, Vol. 24.

16. **Ryan M. Niemiec, Robert E. McGrath.** *The Power of Character Strengths: Appreciate and Ignite Your Positive Personality.* s.l. : VIA Institute on Character, 2019. ISBN-13: 978-0578434292.

17. **Michelle L McQuaid, Erin Lawn.** *Your Strengths Blueprint: How to be Engaged, Energized, and Happy at Work.* s.l. : Michelle McQuaid Pty Ltd, 2014. ISBN-13: 978-0987271419.

18. **MacKinnon, Donald Wallace.** *The Personality Correlates of Creativity: A Study of American Architects.* 1961. p. 77.

19. **MacKinnon, Donald W.** Creativity: a multi-faceted phenomenon. [book auth.] J. D. Roslansky. *Creativity: A Discussion at the Nobel Conference.* Amsterdam : s.n., 1970.

20. **Goleman, Daniel.** Three Kinds Of Empathy. [Online] 2007. www.danielgoleman. info/three-kinds-of-empathy-cognitive-emotional-compassionate/.

21. **Sara D. Hodges, Michael W. Myers.** Empathy. [book auth.] Kathleen D. Vohs Roy F. Baumeister. *Encyclopedia of Social Psychology.* s.l. : SAGE Publications, Inc., 2007, p. 1248.

22. *Executive control of cognitive processes in task switching.* **Rubinstein, J. S., Meyer, D. E., Evans, J. E.** 4, 2001, Journal of Experimental Psychology: Human Perception and Performance, Vol. 27.

23. **Wallis, Claudia.** genM: The Multitasking Generation. time.com. [Online] *Time Inc.* [Cited: 03 24, 2019.] http://content.time.com/time/magazine/ article/0,9171,1174696-6,00.html.

24. *Cognitive control in media multitaskers.* **Eyal Ophir, Clifford Nass, Anthony D. Wagner.** 37, s.l. : Stanford University, 2009, PNAS, Vol. 106.

25. **Daphne M. Davis, Jeffrey A. Hayes.** What are the benefits of mindfulness. *American Psychological Association.* [Online] [Cited: 01 20, 2020.] https://www. apa.org/monitor/2012/07-08/ce-corner.

26. *Energy's role in the extraversion (dis)advantage: How energy ties and task conflict help clarify the relationship between extraversion and proactive performance.* **Kristin L. Cullen-Lester, Hannes Leroy, Alexandra Gerbasi, Lisa Nishii.** 7, 2016, Journal of Organizational Behavior, Vol. 37.

27. **Collins.** Loyalty. *collinsdictionary.com.* [Online] https://www.collinsdictionary.com/dictionary/english/loyalty.

28. **Lencioni, Patrick M.** *The Ideal Team Player.* s.l. : Jossey-Bass, 2016. ISBN-13: 978-1119209591.

29. *Reversing the Extraverted Leadership Advantage: The Role of Employee Proactivity.* **Adam M. Grant, Francesca Gino, David A. Hofmann.** 3, 2011, Academy of Management Journal, Vol. 54.

30. **Marcus Buckingham, Ashley Goodall.** *Nine Lies About Work: A Freethinking Leader's Guide to the Real World.* s.l. : Harvard Business Review Press, 2019. ISBN-13: 978-1633696303.

31. **Whyte, William H.** *The Organization Man.* s.l. : University of Pennsylvania Press, 2002. ISBN-13: 978-0812218190.

32. **Newport, Cal.** *So Good They Can't Ignore You.* s.l. : Piatkus , 2016. ISBN-13: 978-0349415864.

33. **Pink, Daniel H.** *Drive: The Surprising Truth About What Motivates Us.* s.l. : Canongate Books, 2018. p. 256.

34. **Dilts, Robert B.** *A Brief History of Logical Levels.* www.nlpu.com/. [Online] NLPU International, 2014. http://www.nlpu.com/Articles/LevelsSummary.htm.

35. **Michael Puett, Christine Gross-Loh.** *The Path: What Chinese Philosophers Can Teach Us About the Good Life.* s.l. : Simon & Schuster, 2017. ISBN-13: 978-1476777849.

36. *Psychological Conditions of Personal Engagement and Disengagement at Work.* **Kahn, William A.** 4, 1990, The Academy of Management Journal, Vol. 33.

37. **Llewellyn, Robert N.** The Four Career Concepts. *shrm.org.* [Online] SHRM, 2002. [Cited: 03 02, 2018.] The Four Career Concepts .

38. **Pink, Daniel H.** *Drive: The Surprising Truth About What Motivates Us.* s.l. : Canongate Books, 2018. p. 256.

39. **Lencioni, Patrick M.** *The Truth About Employee Engagement: A Fable About Addressing the Three Root Causes of Job Misery.* s.l. : John Wiley & Sons, 2016. p. 272. ISBN-13: 978-1119237983.

40. **Pink, Daniel H.** *Drive: The Surprising Truth About What Motivates Us.* s.l. : Canongate Books, 2018. p. 256.

41. *Happiness, income satiation and turning points around the world.* **Andrew T. Jebb, Louis Tay, Ed Diener, Shigehiro Oishi.** s.l. : Springer Nature Publishing AG, 2018, Nature Human Behaviour.

42. **Luscombe, Belinda.** Do We Need $75,000 a Year to Be Happy? [Online] *Time Inc.,* 2010. http://content.time.com/time/magazine/article/0,9171,2019628,00.html.

43. **Merriam-Webster. Fair. Merriam-Webster.** [Online] Merriam-Webster, Incorporated. [Cited: 07 21, 2019.] https://www.merriam-webster.com/dictionary/fair.

44. **Morgan, Jacob.** *The Employee Experience Advantage: How to Win the War for Talent by Giving Employees the Workspaces they Want, the Tools they Need, and a Culture They Can Celebrate.* s.l. : John Wiley & Sons, 2017. p. 304. ISBN-13: 978-1119321620.

45. **Wikipedia.** Johari window. *Wikipedia.* [Online] Wikimedia Foundation, Inc. https://en.wikipedia.org/wiki/Johari_window.

46. *Are we all less risky and more skillful than our fellow drivers?* **Svenson, Ola.** 47, s.l.: North-Holland Publishing Company, 1981, Acta Psychologica.

47. **Sandberg, Sheryl.** *Lean In.* s.l. : WH Allen, 2015. ISBN-13: 978-0753541647.

48. **Pink, Daniel H.** *Drive: The Surprising Truth About What Motivates Us.* s.l. : Canongate Books, 2018. p. 256.

49. **Marcus Buckingham, Ashley Goodall.** *Nine Lies About Work: A Freethinking Leader's Guide to the Real World.* s.l. : Harvard Business Review Press, 2019. ISBN-13: 978-1633696303.

50. **Harter, Jim.** Dismal Employee Engagement Is a Sign of Global Mismanagement. *www.gallup.com.* [Online] Gallup. https://www.gallup.com/workplace/231668/dismal-employee-engagement-sign-global-mismanagement.aspx.

51. **Michael M. Lombardo PhD, Robert W. Eichinger.** *Career Architect Development Planner.* s.l. : Lominger International; 4th edition, 2004. ISBN-13: 978-1933578019.

52. **Homer.** *The Odyssey.* s.l. : Penguin Classics, 2003. ISBN-13: 978-0140449112.

53. *Who gets a mentor? A longitudinal assessment of the rising star hypothesis.* **Romila Singh, Belle Rose Ragins, Phyllis Tharenou.** 1, 2009, Journal of Vocational Behavior, Vol. 74.

54. **Merriam-Webster.** Eminence. *Merriam-Webster Dictionary.* [Online] Merriam-Webster, Incorporated. [Cited: 11 23, 2020.] https://www.merriam-webster.com/dictionary/eminence.

55. **Carnegie, Dale.** *How To Stop Worrying And Start Living.* s.l. : Cedar, 1993. p. 304. ISBN-13: 978-0749307233.

56. **International Coaching Federation.** *2020 ICF Global Coaching Study.* s.l. : International Coaching Federation, 2020.

57. **Pollard, Matthew.** *The Introvert's Edge: How The Quiet And Shy Can Outsell Anyone.* s.l. : AMACOM, 2018. p. 242. ISBN-13: 978-0814438879.

58. **Pollard, Matthew.** *Introverts Edge to Networking: A Step-by-Step Process to Creating Authentic Connections.* s.l. : AMACOM, 2021. ISBN-13: 978-1400224913.

59. **Sally Helgesen, Marshall Goldsmith.** *How Women Rise: Break the 12 Habits Holding You Back.* s.l. : Random House Business, 2019. ISBN-13: 978-1847942258.

60. **Casineanu, Gabriela.** *Introverts Leverage Your Strengths For An Effective Job Search.* s.l. : Thoughts Designer, 2017. p. 336. ISBN-13: 978-0995967700.

61. **Bandura, Albert.** *Self-Efficacy: The Exercise of Control.* s.l. : Worth Publishers, 1997. ISBN-13: 978-0716728504.

62. **Lipkin, Nicole.** *What Keeps Leaders Up at Night: Recognizing and Resolving Your Most Troubling Management Issues.* s.l. : AMACOM, 2013. ISBN-13: 978-0814432112.

63. **Sally Helgesen, Marshall Goldsmith.** *How Women Rise: Break the 12 Habits Holding You Back.* s.l. : Random House Business, 2019. ISBN-13: 978-1847942258.

64. **Rosenzweig, Phil.** *Left Brain, Right Stuff: How Leaders Make Winning Decisions.* s.l.: PublicAffairs, 2014. p. 336. ISBN-13: 978-1610393072.

65. **Rosenzweig, Phil.** *The Halo Effect: . . . and the Eight Other Business Delusions That Deceive Managers.* s.l. : Free Press, 2014. p. 288. ISBN-13: 978-1476784038.

66. *Are we all less risky and more skillful than our fellow drivers?* **Svenson, Ola.** 47, s.l.: North-Holland Publishing Company, 1981, Acta Psychologica.

67. *Psychosocial working conditions and the utilization of health care services.* **Sunday Azagba, Mesbah F. Sharaf.** s.l. : BioMed Central Ltd., 2011, BMC Public Health.

68. *Psychological aspects of workload.* **T.F. Meijman, G. Mulder.** 1998, Handbook of work and organizational psychology, Vol. 2.

69. *Work, recovery activities, and individual well-being: a diary study.* **Sonnentag, S.** 3, 2001, Occupational Health Psychology, Vol. 6.

70. *When can employees have a family life? The effects of daily workload and affect on work-family conflict and social behaviors at home.* **R. Ilies, K.M. Schwind, D.T. Wagner, M.D. Johnson, D.S. DeRue, D.R. Ilgen.** 5, 2007, Applied Psychology, Vol. 92.

71. *Explaining the Variable Effects of Social Support on Work-Based Stressor-Strain Relations: The Role of Perceived Pattern of Support Exchange.* **Inbal Nahum-Shani, Peter A. Bamberger.** 1, 2011, Organizational Behavior and Human Decision Processes, Vol. 114.

72. **Carnegie, Dale.** *How To Stop Worrying And Start Living.* s.l. : Cedar, 1993. p. 304. ISBN-13: 978-0749307233.

73. **Cain, Susan.** *Quiet Power: Growing Up as an Introvert in a World That Can't Stop Talking.* s.l. : Penguin Life, 2017. ISBN-13: 978-0241977910.

74. **Cain, Susan.** The power of introverts. *TED.* [Online] TED Conferences, LLC., 2012. [Cited: 05 02, 2017.] https://www.ted.com/talks/susan_cain_the_power_of_introverts.

75. **Goldsmith, Marshall.** *What Got You Here Won't Get You There: How successful people become even more successful.* s.l. : Profile Books, 2008. p. 256. ISBN-13: 978-1846681370.

76. **Newport, Cal.** *Deep Work: Rules for Focused Success in a Distracted World.* s.l. : Piatkus, 2016. ISBN-13: 978-0349411903.

77. *Executive control of cognitive processes in task switching.* **Rubinstein, J. S., Meyer, D. E., Evans, J. E.** 4, 2001, Journal of Experimental Psychology: Human Perception and Performance, Vol. 27.

78. *A Wandering Mind Is an Unhappy Mind.* **Matthew A. Killingsworth, Daniel T. Gilbert.** s.l. : Science, 2010, Vol. 330.

79. **Gloria Mark, Jennifer Robison.** *Too Many Interruptions at Work?* Gallup. [Online] Gallup, Inc. [Cited: 12 30, 2019.] https://news.gallup.com/businessjournal/23146/too-many-interruptions-work.aspx.

80. *Cognitive control in media multitaskers.* **Eyal Ophir, Clifford Nass, Anthony D. Wagner.** 37, s.l. : Stanford University, 2009, PNAS, Vol. 106.

81. **Newport, Cal.** *Deep Work: Rules for Focused Success in a Distracted World.* s.l. : Piatkus, 2016. ISBN-13: 978-0349411903.

82. **Johnson, Spencer.** *Who Moved My Cheese: An Amazing Way to Deal with Change in Your Work and in Your Life.* s.l. : Vermilion, 1999. ISBN-13: 978-0091816971.

83. **Jocko Willink, Leif Babin.** *Extreme Ownership: How U.S. Navy Seals Lead And Win.* s.l. : St Martin's Press, 2017. p. 352. ISBN-13: 978-1250183866.

84. **Wikipedia.** Decision fatigue. *Wikipedia.* [Online] Wikimedia Foundation, Inc. [Cited: 02 12, 2019.] https://en.wikipedia.org/wiki/Decision_fatigue.

85. **March, James G.** *Primer on Decision Making: How Decisions Happen.* s.l. : Free Press, 2009. ISBN-13: 978-1439157336.

86. **The Arbinger Institute.** *Leadership And Self-Deception: Getting Out of the Box.* s.l.: ReadHowYouWant, 2012. ISBN-13: 978-1459626188.

87. **Smith, Manuel J.** *When I Say No, I Feel Guilty: How to Cope, Using the Skills of Systematic Assertive Therapy.* s.l. : Bantam USA, 1975. ISBN-13: 978-0553263909.

88. **Covey, Stephen M. R.** *The Speed of Trust: The One Thing that Changes Everything.* s.l. : Simon & Schuster UK, 2008. ISBN-13: 978-1847392718.

89. **Maxwell, John C.** 21 *Irrefutable Laws of Leadership.* s.l. : Thomas Nelson, 2007. ISBN-13: 978-0785289357.

90. *The virtues of gossip: Reputational information sharing as prosocial behavior.* **Feinberg, M., Willer, R., Stellar, J., Keltner, D.** 5, 2012, Journal of Personality and Social Psychology, Vol. 102.

91. *Why People Gossip: An Empirical Analysis of Social Motives, Antecedents, and Consequences.* **B. Beersma, G. A. Van Kleef.** 11, 2012, Journal of Applied Social Psychology, Vol. 42.

92. **Scott, Kim.** *Radical Candor: How to Get What You Want by Saying What You Mean.* s.l. : Pan, 2018. ISBN-13: 978-1509845385.

93. **Ratcliffe, Susan.** *Oxford Essential Quotations.* s.l. : Oxford University Press, 2017. eISBN: 9780191843730.

94. *Why do beliefs about intelligence influence learning success? A social cognitive neuroscience model.* **Jennifer A. Mangels, Brady Butterfield, Justin Lamb, Catherine Good, Carol S. Dweck.** 2, 2006, Social Cognitive and Affective Neuroscience, Vol. 1.

95. *The Perils and Promises of Praise.* **Dweck, Carol S.** 2, 2009, Educational leadership: journal of the Department of Supervision and Curriculum Development, Vol. 65.

96. **Chivers, Tom.** A Mindset "Revolution" Sweeping Britain's Classrooms May Be Based On Shaky Science. *BuzzFeed News.* [Online] 2017. [Cited: 03 25, 2020.] https://www.buzzfeed.com/tomchivers/what-is-your-mindset.

97. **Friedman, Thomas L.** It's P.Q. and C.Q. as Much as I.Q. *The New York Times.* [Online] The New York Times Company, 01 29, 2013. http://www.nytimes.com/2013/01/30/opinion/friedman-its-pq-and-cq-as-much-as-iq.html.

98. **Rasoul, Katie.** *Hidden Brilliance: A High-Achieving Introvert's Guide to Self-Discovery, Leadership and Playing Big.* s.l. : Team Awesome, 2018. ISBN-13: 978-0999806906.

99. *Learning Concepts and Categories Is Spacing the "Enemy of Induction"?* **Nate Kornell, Robert A. Bjork.** 6, 2008, Psychological Science, Vol. 19.

100. *The Generation Effect: Activating Broad Neural Circuits During Memory Encoding.* **Zachary A. Rosner, Jeremy A. Elman, Arthur P. Shimamura.** 7, 2013, Cortex, Vol. 49.

101. *The hypercorrection effect in younger and older adults.* **Teal S. Eich, Yaakov Stern, Janet Metcalfe.** 5, 2012, Aging, Neuropsychology, and Cognition, Vol. 20.

102. **Epstein, David.** *Range: How Generalists Triumph in a Specialized World.* s.l. : Macmillan, 2019. ISBN-13: 978-1509843497.

103. **Claire, Samantha.** *The Introvert Power Advantage.* s.l. : CreateSpace Independent Publishing Platform, 2018. ISBN-13: 978-1717217318.

104. **Haden, Jeff.** *The Motivation Myth: How High Achievers Really Set Themselves Up to Win.* s.l. : Portfolio Penguin, 2018. ISBN-13: 978-0399563768.

105. **Sena, Joe De.** *The Spartan Way.* s.l. : St. Martin's Griffin, 2018. ISBN-13: 978-1250153210.

106. **Wikipedia.** Leon Festinger. *Wikipedia.* [Online] Wikimedia Foundation, Inc. [Cited: 04 05, 2019.] https://en.wikipedia.org/wiki/Leon_Festinger.

107. **Hutchinson, Alex.** *Endure: Mind, Body and the Curiously Elastic Limits of Human Performance.* s.l. : HarperCollins, 2018. ISBN-13: 978-0008285098.

108. **Itzler, Jesse.** *Living with a SEAL: 31 Days Training with the Toughest Man on the Planet.* s.l. : Center Street, 2016. ISBN-13: 978-1455534685.

109. **Grant, Adam.** *Originals: How Non-Conformists Move the World.* s.l. : Penguin Books, 2017. ISBN-13: 978-0143128854.

110. **Peterson, Jordan B.** *12 Rules for Life: An Antidote to Chaos.* s.l. : Penguin, 2019. ISBN-13: 978-0141988511.

111. *The Mundanity of Excellence: An Ethnographic Report on Stratification and Olympic Swimmers.* **Chambliss, Daniel F.** 1, s.l.: American Sociological Association, 1989, Sociological Theory, Vol. 7.

112. **Duckworth, Angela.** *Grit: Why passion and resilience are the secrets to success.* s.l.: Vermilion, 2017. ISBN-13: 978-1785040207.

113. **Baker, Wayne.** *All You Have to Do Is Ask.* s.l. : Bantam Dell Publishing Group, Div of Random House, Inc, 2020. ISBN-13: 978-0593236970.

114. *"I" Seek Autonomy, "We" Rely on Each Other: Self-Construal and Regulatory Focus as Determinants of Autonomy- and Dependency-Oriented Help-Seeking Behavior.* **Svetlana Komissarouk, Arie Nadler.** 6, 2014, Personality And Social Psychology Bulletin, Vol. 40.

115. *Helping them stay where they are: Status effects on dependency/autonomy-oriented helping.* **Arie Nadler, Lily Chernyak-Hai.** 1, 2014, Journal of Personality and Social Psychology, Vol. 106.

116. *To teach or to tell? Consequences of receiving help from experts and peers.* **Katherina Alvarez, Esther van Leeuwen.** 3, 2011, European Journal of Social Psychology, Vol. 41.

117. *Liking a Person as a Function of Doing Him a Favour.* **Jon Jecker, David Landy.** 4, 1969, Human Relations, Vol. 22.

118. **Independence Hall Association.** Ben Franklin. ushistory.org. [Online] Independence Hall Association. [Cited: 04 23, 2021.] https://www.ushistory.org/franklin/autobiography/page48.htm.

119. *The Role of Deliberate Practice in the Acquisition of Expert Performance.* **K. Anders Ericsson, Ralf Th. Krampe, Clemens Tesch-Romer.** 3, s.l. : American Psychological Association, Inc., 1993, Psychological Review, Vol. 100.

120. **Csikszentmihalyi, Mihaly.** *Flow: The Psychology of Happiness: The Classic Work on How to Achieve Happiness.* s.l. : Rider, 2002. ISBN-13: 978-0712657594.

121. *Gorillas in Our Midst: Sustained Inattentional Blindness for Dynamic Events.* Daniel **J. Simons, Christopher F. Chabris.** 9, 1999, Perception, Vol. 28.

122. **Christopher F. Chabris, Daniel J. Simons.** gorilla experiment. *theinvisiblegorilla.com.* [Online] [Cited: 03 13, 2021.] http://www.theinvisiblegorilla.com/gorilla_experiment.html.

123. **Csikszentmihalyi, Mihaly.** *Flow: The Psychology of Happiness: The Classic Work on How to Achieve Happiness.* s.l. : Rider, 2002. ISBN-13: 978-0712657594.

124. **Wikipedia.** Emotional intelligence. *Wikipedia.* [Online] Wikimedia Foundation, Inc. [Cited: 02 20, 209.] https://en.wikipedia.org/wiki/Emotional_intelligence.

125. **Travis Bradberry, Jean Greaves.** *Emotional Intelligence 2.0.* s.l. : TalentSmart, 2009. ISBN-13: 978-0974320625.

126. *Deconstructing the "Reign of Error": Interpersonal Warmth Explains the Self-Fulfilling Prophecy of Anticipated Acceptance.* **Danu Anthony Stinson, Jessica J. Cameron, Joanne V. Wood, Danielle Gaucher, John G. Holmes.** 9, 2009, Personality and Social Psychology Bulletin, Vol. 35.

127. **Carnegie, Dale.** *How to Win Friends and Influence People.* s.l. : Vermilion, 2006. ISBN-13: 978-0091906818.

128. **Baker, Wayne.** *All You Have to Do Is Ask.* s.l. : Bantam Dell Publishing Group, Div of Random House, Inc, 2020. ISBN-13: 978-0593236970.

129. **McRaven, Admiral William H.** University of Texas at Austin 2014 Commencement Address. *Youtube.* [Online] [Cited: 04 18, 2019.] https://www.youtube.com/watch?v=pxBQLFLei70.

130. *How Bell Labs creates star performers.* **Robert Kelley, Janet Caplan.** 4, s.l. : Harvard Business Review, 1993, Harvard Business Review, Vol. 71.

131. **Pollard, Matthew.** *The Introvert's Edge: How The Quiet And Shy Can Outsell Anyone.* s.l. : AMACOM, 2018. p. 242. ISBN-13: 978-0814438879.

132. *Beautiful mess effect: Self–other differences in evaluation of showing vulnerability.* **Anna Bruk, Sabine G. Scholl, Herbert Bless.** 2, 2018, Journal of Personality and Social Psychology, Vol. 115.

133. **Sally Helgesen, Marshall Goldsmith.** *How Women Rise: Break the 12 Habits Holding You Back.* s.l. : Random House Business, 2019. ISBN-13: 978-1847942258.

134. **Grant, Adam.** *Give and Take: Why Helping Others Drives Our Success.* s.l. : W&N, 2014. p. 384. ISBN-13: 978-1780224725.

135. *Pronoia. Goldner, Fred H.* 1, 1982, Social Problems, Vol. 30.

136. **Chugh, Dolly.** *The Person You Mean to Be: How Good People Fight Bias.* s.l. : HarperBusiness, 2018. ISBN-13: 978-0062692146.

137. **Wikipedia.** List of cognitive biases. *Wikipedia.* [Online] Wikimedia Foundation, Inc. [Cited: 01 23, 2019.] https://en.wikipedia.org/wiki/List_of_cognitive_biases.

138. *The self-importance of moral identity.* **Karl Aquino, Americus Reed.** 6, s.l. : Journal of Personality and Social Psychology, 2002, Journal of Personality and Social Psychology, Vol. 83.

139. **Chugh, Dolly.** *The Person You Mean to Be: How Good People Fight Bias.* s.l. : HarperBusiness, 2018. ISBN-13: 978-0062692146.

140. *Your Morals Depend on Language.* **Albert Costa, Alice Foucart, Sayuri Hayakawa, Melina Aparici, Jose Apesteguia, Joy Heafner, Boaz Keysar.** 4, 2014, PLoS ONE, Vol. 9.

141. **David H. Jonassen, Barbara L. Grabowski.** *Handbook of Individual Differences, Learning, and Instruction.* s.l. : Routledge, 1993. ISBN-13: 978-0805814132.